People
in
Quandaries

Wendell Johnson

PEOPLE
IN
QUANDARIES

The Semantics of Personal Adjustment

Harper & Brothers
Publishers

New York and London

To

EDNA *and* NICKY *and* KATY LOU

Contents ~~~~~~~~~~~~~~~~~~~~~~~~~~~~

INTRODUCTION

PART V. APPLICATIONS

Introduction ~~~~~~~~~~~~~~~~~~~~~~~~~~~~~

THIS IS A BOOK ABOUT THE PROBLEMS WE HAVE IN trying to live with ourselves and with each other. These problems, together with ways of dealing with them, are discussed from the point of view of general semantics. This point of view emphasizes those aspects of scientific method that are useful in daily living.

With regard to personal problems, it is to be appreciated that as we grow up we tend to become accustomed to our own behavior and to the people and the world about us. We develop a strong inclination to take for granted whatever is familiar or customary. Our notions of what is "normal" are therefore determined largely by the behavior, beliefs, attitudes, and social conditions which we come to accept as "right" or "natural." This means that we may be clearly below par, as judged by very reasonable standards, and yet feel that we have no "personal problems." Many people become so thoroughly accustomed to the frictions, frustrations, and general floundering of their day-to-day existence that nothing short of murder or stark insanity strikes them as peculiar. They are so utterly adjusted to maladjustment that it does not even occur to them that human life might be, except by sheer luck, different from what they know it to be. The particular peepholes that define their outlook on the world become too small for them to see its large and exciting horizons.

We all have personal problems, of course. Our awareness of them and the importance we attach to them depend on the amount of tension, misery, and confusion we have learned to tolerate. Generally speaking, if we examine carefully what we call our big problems we find that they are made up for the most part of little things, which accumulate all but unnoticed until we find ourselves practically overwhelmed. The most effective way, therefore, to apply what is in this book is to sharpen our awareness of the little things and apply it to them. In other words, the seemingly insignificant, moment-to-moment applications of adjustment principles make the greatest difference in the long run. The semantic exercises described at the end of the book are designed, in part, to illustrate various possibilities of such moment-to-moment applications, and a careful reading of the book as a whole will suggest many more.

Aside from the problems that center around intimately personal concerns and relationships, we have also the problems that arise as we engage in a profession or business or in running a household; in learning a trade, a skill, a game, or in teaching something to others. General semantics can be put to use in many ways by doctors, lawyers, teachers and students, editors and writers, radio program directors, motion-picture executives, government officials, personnel managers, housewives, merchants, etc., through the long catalogue of human occupations. Likewise, in the general business of being a citizen, of evaluating social, economic, and political issues, of contributing constructively to the life of the community and of society in a broad sense, the possibilities of using general semantics are varied and ever present. These possibilities are indicated in various ways throughout the book.

While *People in Quandaries* is necessarily addressed to a varied reading public—to anyone sensitive to opportunities for personal growth and the enrichment of our general culture—certain parts of it are of special interest to particular groups. For example, students in the new and rapidly growing field of communication, and teachers of communication skills, will find in Chapter XVIII a stage-by-stage analysis of the process of communication which is designed to clarify the functions and the disorders involved in the various aspects of speaking, writing, reading, and listening. Additional material of special interest to such readers is to be found in Chapters XI and XII, which deal with the language of maladjustment. Major and minor types of personality maladjustment have been described from a semantic point of view in Chapters XIII and XIV, while methods of personality reeducation have been dealt with particularly in Chapters X and XVI; and although these chapters are designed to be of interest and value to the general reader, they are doubtless of professional interest to workers and students in the fields of psychiatry and clinical and abnormal psychology. The indicated chapters, however, are not to be lifted from the context supplied by the book in its entirety; any one part of the book is to be interpreted in relationship to the whole.

There are a growing number of college and university courses in general semantics and an increasing number of adult study groups, many of which are affiliated with the Society for General Semantics, and I trust that the students and teachers in these courses and study groups will find this book stimulating and useful. In attempting to make it so, I have been particularly mindful of the fact that general semantics simply cannot be presented effectively in a dry or tiresome fashion, and I have done my best, therefore, to make this book not only sound and practical, but also as interesting and readable as possible.

Although footnotes have been almost entirely avoided, source materials have been indicated in many instances at appropriate places in the text. Others are included in the bibliography. One particular source, *Science and Sanity*, by Alfred Korzybski, has been drawn upon so heavily, and so many liberties have been taken with it, that a word of explanation is in order.

Science and Sanity, first published in 1933, is the original source book of general semantics. Each reader who applies the principles set forth in this book necessarily does so according to the interpretations he is prepared to make of them. He applies the principles to the particular problems with which he happens to be concerned, and he does this in ways that are determined largely by his prior training and experience. My own presentation of general semantics has been developed in the course of my attempts to use it, since 1936, in dealing clinically with stuttering and with the more common personality maladjustments of university students. Since 1939 I have taught a course in general semantics each year at the State University of Iowa, and over the past five years or so I have conducted research dealing with certain semantic problems. During this period, and for many years previously, I have taught, done research, and worked clinically in speech pathology and psychology. My particular formulations of general semantics are to be understood in relation to this background. In this book I have not hesitated to modify Korzybski's original formulations, to add, delete, and in general improvise and make adaptations in ways that have seemed useful. I have retained, however, those features which I should regard as most essential in general semantics as presented by Korzybski, and I have taken the liberty, though with his approval, of using a number of his terms and many of his statements without specific documentation. I have had the benefit of his reactions to the manuscript. In any case, he is not to be held accountable for my own ineptitudes, and he is to be given due credit for such value as there may be in the uses I have made of his principles.

Several persons, including a considerable number of my students, have read and evaluated the manuscript in whole or in part, and I am grateful for their many helpful suggestions. Major Irving J. Lee, Army Air Forces, on leave from Northwestern University, went over the complete manuscript; at his suggestion, Chapters V and VI were considerably expanded, Chapter XVI was added, and a few other minor changes were made. To Major Lee I am very grateful indeed. Lieutenant John R. Knott, USNR, on leave from the State University of Iowa, read Chapter XIII with unusual care, and his notations and comments were used to advantage. Professor S. I. Hayakawa, of the Illinois Institute of Technology, read Chapter I and suggested a number of changes which were incorporated in the final draft. The statements concerning progressive relaxation in Chapter X were read by Dr. Edmund Jacobson, Director of the Chicago Laboratory for Clinical Physiology, who originally developed the techniques described, and his suggestions were used in preparing the final draft. Nevertheless, I am alone responsible for any possible misinterpretations of Dr. Jacobson's methods. Professor Bryng Bryngelson, of the University of Minnesota, reviewed the account of his group therapy methods that is included in Chapter XVI, but again, of course, responsibility for adequacy of statement must fall upon the writer.

Miss Lousene Rousseau, of Harper & Brothers, contributed with stimulating interest and astuteness to the editorial processing of the book, and gave of her time to an extent which, I am sure, extended well beyond "the call of duty." I am grateful also to Miss Carolyn Wood who compiled certain materials from library sources. Miss Mary Dean Fowler, Mrs. Lorna Stobbart Nance, and Miss Elizabeth Erdice, all of whom have been students in my course in general semantics, did the major part of the work involved in preparing the manuscript for publication, and in doing so they suggested a very considerable number of improvements in style and organization. Miss Erdice also assisted with proofreading and she and Miss Fowler prepared the index. The assistance of Edna Bockwoldt Johnson, my wife, not only in reading and evaluating the manuscript but in other respects as well, has been altogether too considerable to be acknowledged adequately.

Every author of a book of this sort is indebted to various teachers, students, and friends in ways which he can neither fully know nor clearly indicate. There are many, I am sure, who will see some reflection of their personal influence in these pages. Certainly Professors Carl E. Seashore, George D. Stoddard, Edward C. Mabie, and Lee Edward Travis will recognize more fully than I might ever hope to appreciate the pervasive effects of their teaching and kindness. To the late Professor John A. McGeoch I owe a special word of gratitude. Had it not been for his constant encouragement at the time this book was being planned, and his kindly insistence that time be set aside for it, the actual writing would have been delayed indefinitely. Further acknowledgments could be attempted only with the almost certain risk of inadvertent omission of many names which should, in the interests of full accuracy, be included. I can only express my warm appreciation to all who know that I am referring to them.

To the publishers and individuals listed below I am grateful for permission to quote from the indicated publications:

ALEXANDER, JEROME. [Editor.] *Colloid Chemistry,* Volume V. New York: Reinhold Publishing Corporation, 1944, pp. 2–3.

EINSTEIN, A., and INFELD, L. *The Evolution of Physics.* New York: Simon and Schuster, Inc., 1938, p. 33.

KEYSER, CASSIUS J. "Mathematics and the Science of Semantics," *Scripta Mathematica,* 1934, 2, 247–260.

KORZYBSKI, ALFRED. *Science and Sanity: An Introduction to Non-Aristotelian Systems and General Semantics.* Lancaster, Pa.: The Science Press, 1st ed., 1933, 2nd ed., 1941, pp. 14–15, 2nd ed.

The New Yorker, March 20, 1943, p. 51; February 10, 1945, p. 15.

THOMAS, W. I., and THOMAS, DOROTHY SWAIN. *The Child in America.* New York: Alfred A. Knopf, 1928, p. 572.

Chapter I was published, substantially as it stands in this book, as an article entitled "People in Quandaries" in the Autumn, 1943, issue of *Etc.: A Review of General Semantics,* published by the Society for General Semantics and edited by Professor S. I. Hayakawa, of the Illinois Institute of Technology. Parts of another article, "You Can't Write Writing," from the Summer, 1943, issue of *Etc.,* appear in somewhat modfied form in Chapter III. A brief passage in Chapter IX is reproduced from a book review published in the May 21, 1944, issue of the *Chicago Sun Book Week,* by permission of the *Sun's* literary editor, Mr. A. C. Spectorsky. Chapter XVI was originally published through the National Association of Teachers of Speech as two articles in the *Quarterly Journal of Speech,* then edited by Professor Norwood Brigance of Wabash University, and was later reprinted in *Etc.* Except for minor additions, the material in the Appendix appeared in Volume 56, No. 2, of *Psychological Monographs,* 1944, published by the American Psychological Association and edited by Professor John F. Dashiell, University of North Carolina.

To the publishers and editors concerned I am most grateful for permission to reproduce these materials in the present book.

Iowa City   **W. J.**
September 1, 1945

PART I

People in Quandaries

VERBAL COCOONS

HAVE SPENT MUCH OF THE PAST TEN YEARS IN OTHER people's quandaries, being company to misery, holding the damp, trembling hand of frustration. It has seemed necessary to conclude that these quandaries, these personal maladjustments, are not strictly private affairs. They not only appear to involve individual frailties and confusions, but also, and more impressively, they signify a set of conditions peculiar to our general culture. Such maladjustments intimate, as it were, that civilization is more or less allergic to itself.

Beneath their fascinating individualities one may discern a provocative similarity among unhappy and inefficient people. The mosaic of misery is not altogether haphazard. In the contemplation of this fact one acquires a sense of the pervasive social forces influencing human behavior. George D. Stoddard has said that one can only be what one could have become—and it is to be soberly considered that what one could have become is determined not alone by the physical structure with which one is born, but also, and profoundly, by the structure of the society into which one is born. As a matter of fact, one can scarcely understand individual personalities except as one understands the social framework within which and by which their main characteristics are determined. Since this is so, it also follows that the individual reflects that social framework; and thus an analysis of individual personalities, particularly the extreme types that we call maladjusted, enables us to gain a

3

peculiarly keen insight into those social and cultural forces that shape the lives of all of us as individuals.

FRUSTRATED AND DISTRAUGHT IDEALISTS

It is neither an index to human nature nor an accident of chance that most, if not all, so-called maladjusted persons in our society may be viewed as frustrated and distraught idealists. Distraught because they are frustrated, and frustrated because they are idealists, they are a living testimony of the price we pay for the traditions we cherish, and for the aspirations which those traditions encourage, together with the restrictions which they tend to enforce. It is not that this idealism is always immediately apparent—on the contrary, it is rather likely, as a rule, to elude the superficial observer. It is our unstudied tendency, indeed, to assume that what maladjusted persons need most is something that we call a sense of direction, of purpose, of noble aspiration. In this we are not altogether mistaken—but a partial understanding serves usually as an effective barrier to more penetrating wisdom.

The ideals of the maladjusted are high in three chief respects. In the first place, they are high in the sense that they are vague. Being vague, they are difficult to recognize; being difficult to recognize, they appear to be elusive. It is the consequent misfortune of the individual whose ideals are vaguely defined that he has no sure way of determining whether or not he has attained them. He maintains, therefore, the disquieting belief that he has failed, and he becomes increasingly convinced that his ideals are difficult to reach. Ideals that are difficult to achieve, though it may be primarily because one remains uncertain of whether or not one has achieved them, have the practical effect of high ideals.

As we contrive to go from A to B, from what we may refer to generally as "failure" to something else which we may value as "success," the crucial point in our journey is that one which we agree to recognize as the point of transition—the point at which we leave A and enter B. Unless such a point *can* be recognized, we are denied the experience of believing that we have reached our destination, that we have achieved "success." And until we *can* believe that we have achieved "success," we continue to assume that we have not achieved it—we continue to experience "failure." Under such circumstances we feel frustrated and, eventually, distraught.

When B is vaguely defined, A is correspondingly obscure—when "success" cannot with certainty be claimed, "failure" cannot with confidence be disavowed. There can be no transition point on the road from A to B; no matter what may be the appearance of the country through which the road passes, there is nothing about it to indicate that it lies within the cherished land of B. A gentleman of my acquaintance, whose ideal is "wealth," has acquired two million dollars—and stomach ulcers. A lady whom I have known for many years has pursued the will-o'-the-wisp of "charm" with such unrelenting intensity that she has achieved almost innumerable symbols of decorum, and memories of Cairo, Vienna, London, and Vera Cruz—and headaches of medically obscure origin. To such persons in pursuit of "success," their definite accomplishments are like a display of etchings which they readily concede to be beautiful but cannot ever thoroughly enjoy because they are haunted by the question, "But are they Art?"

In a word, these individuals recognize their specific achievements, are sometimes temporarily buoyed up by them, and may even recount them with an air of unmitigated boasting. But they do not find them satisfying. As a matter of fact, they frequently *appear* to state their goals in quite definite terms, but the uneasy fervor with which they continue to grope beyond these goals as they annex them, one by one, suggests something of the Hitlerian delirium, so well distilled in that ironical refrain, "I have no more territorial claims in Europe!" Unable to recognize any one of these specific goals achieved, any one definite accomplishment, as the point of transition from A to B, from "failure" to "success," the individual comes at last to the unhappy and exasperating state in which he evaluates each new achievement as further evidence of "failure." In spite of all the prizes he captures, "success" eludes him!

It eludes him for the remarkably obvious, but persistently unnoticed, reason that it is merely a verbal mirage. What he seeks to escape is an *absolute* failure, what he anxiously pursues is an *abso-*

lute success—and they do not exist outside his aching head. What he does in fact achieve is a series of *relative* success*es;* and these are all that he, these are all that anyone, can ever achieve. But in the midst of *relative* abundance, *absolutistic* idealists suffer the agonies of famine. They suffer because they do not know, because it has never occurred to them, because in our culture they are not clearly informed that *success* is a word that may signify many, many things but no one thing. It is the *one* thing that they seek; it is the *one* thing that eludes them. Not gaining the *one* thing, not gaining "success," they are not comforted, they are rather dismayed, by the many things—they are dismayed by their very success*es.*

EITHER-OR

Another respect in which the ideals of the maladjusted are high is that they are highly valued. The intensity with which they are wished for generates the despair with which they are foregone. And the intensity with which they are wished for is generated by the dread with which the foregoing of them is contemplated. If not to succeed absolutely is to fail utterly, then to succeed absolutely becomes utterly important. It is simply that "success" becomes indispensable, as "failure" becomes catastrophic. "Success" becomes indispensable when it appears to be the only alternative to "failure" —and *absolute* success is, by definition, by virtue of a semantic trick, the only alternative to *absolute* failure.

In order to give to these remarks a more lively significance, it is necessary to place them in a proper context by indicating the basic pattern of thought to which they refer. If we are to appreciate the tremendous human importance of this basic pattern, we must go for a moment to the man who, for the most part, established it as *the* pattern upon which our traditional culture has been based. That man lived 2300 years ago in Greece. His name was Aristotle. So influential were his works that our civilization has come to be referred to as Aristotelian. There is not one among us who has not been deeply affected by his teachings. What each one of us could have become has been determined in no small measure by the fact that Aristotle lived and wrote twenty-three centuries ago. Many of us may not be particularly conscious of all this; undoubtedly many of us have scarcely heard of Aristotle and know little or nothing about him. Nevertheless, insofar as we are not scientific, we are essentially Aristotelian in our outlook, in our fundamental attitude, or set, or orientation to life. This is to say simply that we share the orientation that has been for so long a time characteristic of our culture; each new generation absorbs it from the last, and quite unconsciously transmits it to the next.

We need not be academic or complicated in what we must say briefly about Aristotle. What he did was to observe the behavior, and especially the language, of the people of his day and of his world. He was a remarkably astute observer. Then he formulated in words, words that have proved to be all but indelible, the as-if-ness, so to speak, of the behavior and the language of his people. What he said, in effect, was this: "They act as if, they talk as if, all that they feel and believe and live by might be reduced to three fundamental premises or rules. First, they seem always to talk and to act as if a thing is what it is. It is possible to put it in this general form: A is A. That is to say, man is man, truth is truth, etc. This we may call the premise or the *law of identity*.

"In the second place, they speak and they behave as if they assumed that anything must either be a particular thing or it must not be that particular thing. We may give this notion the general form: Anything is either A or non-A. That is, anything is either a man or it is not a man, anything is either true or it is not true, etc. We may call this the premise or *law of the excluded middle*. It represents the fact, as I observe it, that men are oriented in an either-orish, or two-valued way.

"Thirdly, they talk and they conduct themselves generally as if they took it for granted that something cannot both be a particular thing and also not be that particular thing. This we may state in the general form: Something cannot be both A and non-A. That is, something cannot be both a man and not a man, something cannot be true and not true, etc. We may refer to this as the premise or *law of non-contradiction.*

"These, then, the laws of identity, of the excluded middle, and of non-contradiction—these appear to be the basic laws of thought for these people. It will be noticed that each implies the others: If A is A, then everything must be either A or non-A, and, of course, nothing can be both A and non-A. It may be said that the law of identity is basic to the other two; but at least, if it is accepted— and it appears to be—the other two laws are necessary also, are required by the law of identity. These three laws, then, taken to- gether, constitute the basic mold in which men shape their feelings and their thoughts and all their living reactions."

In large measure they still do. These laws are, in the final analy- sis, what we speak of when we speak of *common* sense. That is to say, they are, and they have long been, commonly accepted. Most of us, however, are as unconscious of Aristotle's laws, as such, as he formulated them and as they have been expounded by teachers of logic ever since, as were the ancient men whose actual conduct and language the laws were intended to describe. But once stated, they sound as "right" to us as doubtless they did to the ancient Greeks. What Aristotle did was to give men words with which to make acquaintance with themselves. What he did, that is, was to make men more precisely conscious of themselves, conscious of the rules of their own behavior. Being more conscious of the basic pat- tern of their conduct, they could behave more deliberately, more consistently in accordance with the basic pattern. They could *plan* what they might say and do, for they had been given a "blueprint," a "map," of language and of thought and of action. And the plans which they proceeded to work out, on the basis of Aristotle's laws, gradually became civilization as we know it.

The value of Aristotle's generalizations is to be measured, there- fore, in terms of the benefits which that civilization has yielded, just as the viciousness of his generalizations is to be gauged by reference to the misery which that civilization has entailed. Latest reports from our own country, the United States, indicate that the number of persons admitted each year to hospitals for the insane tends to equal the number entering colleges and universities. (In fact, some of them go from the universities to the hospitals!)

Against this background, we shall resume presently our discussion of the idealism of maladjusted people. Before we do that, however, it is appropriate that we take due pains not to leave the impression that Aristotle is to be regarded as having been a malicious or stupid person. Beyond question he was neither. His contribution to human progress was stupendous. The difference between an Aristotelian and a more primitive society is vast indeed. As a matter of fact, insofar as the consequences of Aristotle's generalizations have been unfortunate, they have been due chiefly to the shortcomings not of Aristotle himself, but of his followers. After all, when Aristotle formulated his laws he made it possible for men to become not only more highly conscious, but also more effectively critical, of their behavior and their language. But men made the tragic error of mistaking the laws of Aristotle for laws of *nature*, to be consciously employed but not revised. They accepted them as Truth in an absolute, that-is-that, A-is-A, sense. Consequently, if they were Truth, modifications or contraries of them were non-Truth. Thus, they were perpetuated, and they were used wittingly and unwittingly to build a system of doctrine and an elaborate social structure. This system and this social structure we shall call Aristotelian—without implying, however, that criticisms of them and suggestions for their revision are to be construed necessarily as criticisms of Aristotle. Indeed, the genius of Aristotle was such that one may well assume that he himself would have succeeded in improving upon his original notions. If he were living today he would surely be numbered among the great non-Aristotelians.

Against the backdrop of this brief sketch of the Aristotelian system, we are able to gain a more revealing view of what Karen Horney has called "the neurotic personality of our time." Maladjusted individuals appear to take an A-is-A attitude toward "success," or "wealth," or "happiness," or whatever other ideal they pursue. Automatically, therefore, they operate in terms of a two-valued (excluded middle) orientation in terms of which anything must be either "success" or "failure," "wealth" or "poverty," "happiness" or "misery." And the pattern is rounded out with their further assumption that nothing can be both "success" and "failure," nothing can be both "wealth" and "poverty," etc. (non-contradiction). Locked within this two-valued structure of orientation, they weave about themselves a web of wonderful confusion.

Just as the premise that "truth is truth" leads eventually to Pilate's jest, and thence to cynicism—since no man can answer for all men, nor for himself in absolute terms, "What *is* truth?"—so the premise that "success is success" leads ever nowhere but to worry and frustration. Moreover, the assumption that there is something that is "success" requires the further assumption that all other things are "failure," and so the bedeviled individual reduces himself to only two alternatives, the one to be cherished as the other is to be abhorred. In this sense, and by these means, he comes to place a very high value upon his ideal. And when one strives long enough for a highly valued ideal that appears also to be persistently unattainable, one feels not only thwarted but also, at last, demoralized.

UNREALISTIC ASPIRATIONS

It has already been said that in some instances maladjusted persons appear to set for themselves goals that are not vague but that are quite specifically defined—although such goals turn out usually to be transitory. It is by means of a consideration of these specific goals that we discover the third respect in which the ideals of the maladjusted are high. They are high in the sense that the odds against their being achieved are very great.

It has been reported, for example, that approximately two out of every three students enrolled in a large midwestern university expressed themselves as wanting to become doctors, lawyers, university professors, or to achieve some other comparable status. The crucial fact is that only about one out of sixteen university students *can* achieve such an ideal in our society. People who turn away from listening to *Information Please* with a reinforced conviction of their own stupidity; young girls striving to look like reigning movie queens; people driving bigger cars than they can pay for; young brides frantically wondering whether to give up their husbands or their Hollywood-engendered definition of *husband*—all these, and the millions they resemble, live the high idealism that leads usually as far, at least, as what Dr. P. S. Graven has called "unsanity."

This tendency of maladjusted persons to set unrealistically high standards for themselves appears as a necessary consequence of their Aristotelian orientation. Since their notions of "success" and "failure" are ultimately of an absolute character and are consequently vague and two-valued, they tend to assume that they have "failed" until they have *unquestionably* "succeeded." As a result, they feel driven to aim high, to be "tops," to break records, to do something "bigger and better." In this they are continually encouraged by many of the more obvious features of their semantic environment. It is this urge to aim high, to out-snob the snobs, that is appealed to—and stimulated by—advertisers generally, and by Hollywood producers, popular magazine writers, etc. All of which means that this reaching for the moon is not a unique characteristic of the maladjusted individual; it represents, rather, a characteristic of our society, and the maladjusted person simply reflects it. And it is one of the influences of his semantic environment that contributes definitely to his difficulties.

IN BRIEF

Quandaries, then, are rather like verbal cocoons in which individuals elaborately encase themselves, and from which, under circumstances common in our time, they do not tend to hatch. The peculiar structure of these cocoons appears to be determined in great measure by the structure of the society in which they are formed—and the structure of this society has been and continues to be determined significantly by the structure of the language which we so unconsciously acquire and so unreflectively employ. Simply by using that language and by living in terms of the basic orientation which it represents and fosters, we tend to cultivate the idealism and so to suffer the frustration and demoralization which are so conspicuous in the lives of people in quandaries.

Nothing Fails Like Failure

Because such people are idealists, they subject themselves more or less continually to the experience of "failure," and from this fact they acquire another of their outstanding features—a tendency to develop what we have learned to call inferiority feelings or inferiority complexes. There is an old saying that nothing fails like failure. Nothing does, indeed. The tears which it produces water the soil from which it grows ever more luxuriantly.

Various investigations made by psychologists have served to demonstrate beyond reasonable dispute that feelings of inferiority are the rule rather than the exception among people generally. As a matter of fact, so common is the tendency of individuals to regard themselves as under par that the renowned Viennese psychologist, the late Dr. Alfred Adler, constructed an elaborate theory of human behavior, and sought to explain the greater share of our personal adjustment difficulties, on the basis of such negative self-evaluation. He made the term *inferiority complex* a part of our common vocabulary; the fact that it has been so generally adopted indicates that it does express a feeling with which most people are familiar.

In definitely maladjusted persons this common mode of self-evaluation is merely exaggerated. In this, as in practically all other respects, people whom we call maladjusted, or neurotic, or abnormal are not unique. They are not a different *kind* of people; they simply present more extreme forms of what is, after all, quite ordinary behavior. "Everyone's queer but thee and me"—and we wouldn't know about ourselves, of course. In a sense, there are no "crazy" people—there are only "crazy" ways of behaving. And we all behave in those ways more or less.

The sense of failure or of inferiority is more readily observed in maladjusted individuals, because in them it is more elaborately developed than it is in ordinary folk. When clearly observed, it is seen to be quite vague or generalized, very persistent, and bound up with anxiety or fear, discouragement, and other "emotional" reactions. Unless persons with inferiority complexes have progressed to the grave stage of sheer despondency and stuporous lassitude, they tend to be on the defensive, to exhibit a high degree of "insultability," to resent criticism, and to be generally touchy. They appear to be, and if you examine them you find that they are, quite tense. Frequently they react to something they see, and especially to something they read or that is said to them, in a sudden, undelayed manner and in an exaggerated way. They tend, that is, to react too quickly and too much. In conversing with them one senses that they might be easily offended or "hurt," and so it is somewhat difficult to feel at ease in their company. They do not make good companions—least of all for themselves.

Now, what these people have not learned is the simple fact that there is no failure in nature. Failure is a matter of evaluation. Failure is the felt difference between what you expect and what you get. It is the difference between what you assume you have to do, what you demand of yourself, and what you actually do. It is what you feel when your expectations exceed your realizations. If your ideals or goals are too high, in the sense that they are too vague, or too highly valued, or unrealistic, then you are likely to experience a sense of failure. Eventually you are likely to suffer from an inferiority complex, a low opinion of yourself. You are likely to be more or less overwhelmed by what you will call "the general impenetrability of things."

To this unhappy development, however, you do not remain indifferent. At least until you become quite thoroughly demoralized, you fight back. You feel anger, more or less, toward the persons and even toward the social rules and material circumstances which, as you suppose, are responsible for thwarting you. This tends to become very complicated; you even develop food dislikes, aversions to colors, to names, to places, or to other things associated somehow with your frustrations. You tend to behave accordingly. If aggressiveness is permitted—and in some forms and under certain conditions it is definitely encouraged in our culture—you are likely to attack openly or indirectly the persons who seem to be blocking your progress. You will try to weaken their influence by talking about them, by opposing them in elections, by trying to block their plans, and in various other ways. By any means permitted, you will carry out your own variety of "bloodless purge." Of course, now and then whole nations go on a rampage of war and vengeance, of systematic human destruction. Occasionally, too, individuals resort to outright murder, but they are in the minority. The important point is that you end up devoting more and more of your available energy to these sidetracking activities of hatred and aggression. You have less and less energy, therefore, to expend in efficient and productive work. Besides, you increase the number and the vigor of your enemies. "Success," therefore, recedes further and further from your grasp. You cannot forever escape the growing realization that you are waging a losing fight, and a kind of desperate weariness creeps over you as the clouds of failure more deeply darken your horizons.

The sense of failure, thus generated and nurtured, tends sooner or later to blend into a state of boredom, a generalized loss of interest in possible opportunities for achievement. Finally, you find yourself in a state of depression. This happens because in our society you are not permitted, as a rule, to be simply bored. The influences of your semantic environment, acting through the urgings, pleadings, scoldings, threats, encouragements, and taunts of your family, friends, and associates, and the incessant stimulation from press, radio, movies, and whatnot—these influences keep prodding you. They will not let you rest. They will not allow you the easy solution of sheer boredom. Because of this persistent goading you may continue to sally forth from time to time to storm the bastions of "success," but absolute success continues, as always, to elude you. As your sense of failure deepens, you settle more and more into despondency. You are then not only bored, but also sorry about it. You are forced to evaluate your "failure"—to feel inferior because you feel inferior.

IFD

In all this is to be seen the basic design of our common maladjustment. We may call it the *IFD* disease: from idealism to frustration to demoralization. Probably no one of us entirely escapes it. It is of epidemic proportions. Certainly anyone occupied professionally with personal problems of men and women—and of children—comes to recognize it as a sort of standard base upon which are erected all manner of specific difficulties and semantic ailments. In "the troubles I've seen" it has predominated conspicuously. In my experience, no other ailment is so common among university students, for example, as what I have termed the IFD disease. It is, moreover, a condition out of which there tend to develop the various types of severe "mental" and nervous disorders, the neuroses and psychoses that fill our "mental" hospitals with such a lush growth of delusion and incompetence.

THE IMPORTANCE OF BEING CLEAR

There remains to be considered one other symptom of what we regard as personality maladjustment. It is so obvious that it is generally overlooked, although it has been stated in various ways by various writers. However, a practicing psychiatrist, Dr. Coyne Campbell, speaking in 1941 before the Central States Speech Association meeting in Oklahoma City, expressed it so pointedly and so simply that it will serve our purpose well to recall his main statements. What Dr. Campbell said, in effect, was that the patients who were brought to him because they had been judged to be seriously maladjusted or even "insane," showed one chief symptom: *They were unable to tell him clearly what was the matter*. They simply could not put into words the difficulties with which they were beset. Surely no one who has made it his business to help people in trouble has failed to observe their relative inarticulateness. In the course of some conferences with a lady in distress, who laid claim to a pronounced feeling of personal worthlessness, I one day placed a mirror in front of her and asked her what she saw in it. For a full minute by the clock she stared at the mirror and said nothing at all. Then she said weakly, "I can't say anything."

Such a reaction is not to be taken for granted. It is something that must be understood. So, also, is the sort of reaction one frequently encounters in persons who talk at a great rate, with an impressive verbal output, but who never get outside their elaborate verbal circles. They are full of theories spun from almost pure sound. One suspects that their seeming compulsion to talk on and on is due mainly to the fact that they themselves realize vaguely that, after each outburst, they have not yet said anything, and so they try again to put into words the feelings from which they suffer. Essentially they are no more articulate than are the individuals who scarcely speak at all.

Dr. Campbell remarked further that when he had succeeded in training a patient to verbalize his difficulties clearly and to the point, it was usually possible to release him. The patient was usually able then to take care of himself. This will seem strange to anyone who has not thoroughly considered the role of language in personality adjustment. The wild and irrelevant and vague remarks of people in quandaries have been regarded generally as nothing more than the foam on the beer, so to speak. That they might be an integral part of the beer, that the language of distress might be part and parcel of the distress, this does not seem to be a commonly held notion. It has not even been emphasized clearly and definitely by the psychoanalysts, who have demonstrated so elaborately the curative value of talk and more talk. The tremendous amount of talking done by the patient on the psychoanalyst's couch is hardly to be regarded as unrelated to such changes in the patient's behavior as may come about during the long course of treatment.

Back of Dr. Campbell's apt statements lies the plain fact that before a problem can be attacked effectively it must be stated with reasonable clarity. And as soon as it has been so stated, some kind of solution to it becomes more or less apparent. In other words, people who are confused and maladjusted are likely to remain so until they learn to state their problems clearly enough to indicate what sort of steps might be taken in order to change their situation or their behavior to advantage. Certainly any scientific worker of experience knows that by far the most important step toward the solution of a laboratory problem lies in stating the problem in such a way as to suggest a fruitful attack on it. Once that is accomplished, any ordinary assistant can usually turn the cranks and read the dials. Competent research directors understand the uses and limitations of their apparatus, certainly, but their major contribution comes not in the answers they wring from nature with their own hands, so to speak, but in the incisive and crucial clarity of the questions they put to nature. Technicians can man the scientist's machines and obtain answers to his well-stated questions; what distinguishes the scientist is his ability to state problems, to frame questions, so that the technicians can make the machines yield facts that are significant.

Now, intimate personal problems are not greatly different in this respect from problems of the laboratory. Before they can be solved, they must be stated. Before helpful answers can be got, suitable questions must be asked. We all want answers. They can be very relaxing. What the maladjusted person cannot do—and what he must learn to do—is to specify the sort of answers he needs. This is a way of saying that he has a conspicuous lack of ability to ask questions in such a way as to obtain answers that would be relaxing, or satisfying, or adjustive. As soon as he develops such ability, he can, as Dr. Campbell has implied, take care of himself for all practical purposes.

There cannot be a precise answer to a vague question. The terminology of the question determines the terminology of the answer. Scarcely any other principle is more important in relation to a consideration of the befuddlement and conflict that make for personal inefficiency and unhappiness. The particular questions we ask ourselves determine the kinds of answers we get, and the answers we get make of our lives, in large measure, the sort of lives they are. Unschooled in the techniques of inquiry, we tend to flounder in a fog of obfuscation and error, individually and socially. If all that we have ever tried to mean by *mental hygiene* might be reduced to one word, that word would be *accuracy*. And the techniques of accuracy are, in the main, techniques of language. The verbal confusions of maladjusted people are not independent of the confusions in other aspects of their behavior. The relation is close; the one cannot be understood in isolation from the other.

OUR AGE OF QUESTIONING

In this view of maladjusted persons as frustrated and distraught idealists we may glimpse the broad outlines of problems that are common to us all in varying degrees. The IFD disease, as we have sketched it, is not so much an affliction of individuals as it is a reflection of strong semantic forces that play upon and through individuals. So long as these forces are prevalent, each one of us is in some measure susceptible to the misfortunes they engender. There is a contagion about semantic maladies. We are continually exposed to them, and we tend to "catch" them.

This raises the question as to how they are transmitted. What sort of "bacilli" infect our lives with confusion and frustration and despair? A clue to an answer is to be found in the relative inability of maladjusted people to verbalize their difficulties, to state their problems, to ask their questions clearly and in such a way that they might be answered readily and effectively. This clue points somehow to language. It indicates that in the structure of our common language there are disintegrative factors which affect adversely, in varying degrees, the living reactions of those who use the language. To a significant degree, the structure of our common language can be described in terms of the Aristotelian "laws" previously discussed. The problem has been treated elaborately by Alfred Korzybski in *Science and Sanity* and it has been concisely considered by Hayakawa in *Language in Action*.

A systematic consideration of these matters points to the double significance of our language structure. On the one hand, it plays a role in determining the structure of our culture, our society, our civilization. On the other hand, it serves as the chief medium or means whereby the individual acquires or *interiorizes* that culture structure. Thus, a study of language structure leads both to a deeper understanding of our civilization and its problems and to a keener insight into the basic designs of individual lives and personalities. It is as though mankind had spun an enormous web of words—and caught itself. Our problem is, in large degree, one of unraveling this net of symbolism in which our human destiny has become entangled.

It is to this problem and its many ramifications that general semantics is addressed, and it is with general semantics as applied to personal problems that this book is concerned. General semantics, however, is not to be adequately grasped or effectively applied except as it is viewed in a proper setting and in relation to the individual and social problems upon which it bears. Among the problems in relation to which its foundations and significance can be well appreciated are those of personal maladjustment which we have discussed in the preceding pages. The idealism that leads to frustration and the demoralization that rounds out the unhappy sequence become something more than merely unfortunate and mysterious when viewed in relation to the neurolinguistic rigidity and confusions which general semantics is designed to illuminate and counteract.

It is in relation to this fact, with its pervasive and intimately personal implications, that one may recognize the reasons for both the appeal and the significance of general semantics. In later chapters, therefore, we shall return to a more detailed consideration of personal problems of the type here discussed.

A fuller understanding is to be gained by considering, as we shall in the next three chapters, the relation of general semantics to certain basic and large-scale trends that have served to distinguish comparatively modern times, and which in our own day are particularly apparent. There is something about the time of the world in which we find ourselves that is conducive to restiveness and self-searching, though not necessarily—not at all necessarily— to weariness or cynicism. Whatever else we may say of our time, we must, if we do not deceive ourselves, recognize that this is an age of intensive and candid questioning. As we come to appreciate the degree to which an older generation did not know the answers, we come to understand more and more clearly the importance of knowing the questions—the importance of designing techniques of inquiry by means of which a greater wisdom might be distilled from

experience. It is in its deliberate and systematic concern with the
techniques of inquiry that one may most readily find the distinguishing features of general semantics and the degree of promise
which it holds for the emancipation of the future from the misfortunes of the past, in our own lives individually and in that
cooperative adventure that men call civilization.

PART II

Scientific Living

NEVER THE SAME RIVER

---

*H*ERACLITUS THE GREEK CAST A LONG SHADOW BEFORE
him. He contended that one cannot step in the same river twice.

The Greek was going beyond the assertion that no two things
are exactly alike to the assertion that no one thing is ever twice the
same, that reality is to be regarded as a process. And we might enlarge his contention by pointing out that one may not step in the
same river twice, not only because the river flows and changes, but
also because the one who steps into it changes too, and is never at
any two moments identical.

Heraclitus was over two thousand years ahead of his time. The
notion which he so aptly expressed has about it a distinctly modern
flavor. It is one which Einstein might heartily endorse. It is the
basic notion of science, and science as we know it is not as old as
Heraclitus—far from it.

What Heraclitus expressed in his delightful metaphor represents
also the basic notion of general semantics. Upon the foundation of
the process-character view of reality the whole structure of general
semantics has been erected. It is a general statement of the implications of that view, implications concerning the crucial character
of reality, concerning man's possibilities of knowing about it,
concerning man's resources for adjusting to it.

In this sense, science and general semantics are as old—and as
new—as Heraclitus. It is in our own day that the Greek would have
found his most congenial companions, for what he contended was

long disregarded. The culture in which he lived, and which has come down to us through the centuries, embodied and still embodies a strikingly different point of view. The orientation of science, of general semantics—of Heraclitus—is not traditional. It represents rather a major break with tradition in the broadest sense. For this reason it will be most instructive to contrast briefly and in high lights these two great tendencies, the one traditional and still quite dominant, the other new but very powerful indeed. Against the background provided by the conflict between these tendencies, the old and the new, we may gain a richer appreciation of general semantics and of the problems to which it is relevant.

DIFFERENT ALL THE TIME

No other fact so unrelentingly shapes and reshapes our lives as this: that reality, in the broadest sense, continually changes, like the river of Heraclitus—and in recent years the river of Heraclitus appears to have been rising. The currents are faster, the eddies more turbulent, and the stream is overflowing its banks more and more each day. What we once thought of as safe ground has been abandoned to the flood. The dikes of civilization are watched with anxious eyes.

But change, however all-pervading and rapid, need not be terrifying. It does not terrify the physicist, it fascinates him. And change in the lives of nations, groups, and individuals does not terrify the social scientist; it merely determines the lines of his investigation. Change is terrifying only to those who do not expect it, only to those who, in planning their lives, leave it out of account.

But in large measure, unfortunately, we have been and still are taught to leave it out of account. Change has been suspect and has been resisted throughout the history of the race. It has been customary for fathers to pass on to their sons the creeds and customs which their own fathers had passed on to them. Ancestors have been worshiped and the Old Man has been honored from time immemorial. Education has been chiefly a matter of compelling the child to conform to the ways of his elders. The student has been taught answers, not questions. At least, when questions have been taught, the answers have been given in the back of the book. In the main, knowledge has been given the student, but not a method for adding to it or revising it—except the method of authority, of going to the book, of asking the Old Man. The chief aim of education has been to make of the child another Old Man, to pour the new wines of possibility into the old bottles of tradition.

Nevertheless, one cannot step in the same river twice. Physicists, chemists, geologists and all others who scrutinize physical phenomena, anthropologists, sociologists, psychologists and all others who study men, report that what they find are processes, growth and decay, energy transformations, social changes, etc. *No event is ever exactly repeated.* The great scientific advances since Galileo, and particularly during the last fifty years, have made more and more obvious the process character of reality. Generalizations, those great symbolic nets in which men try to capture the eagles of time, have been wrecked, one after the other, by the creatures they were designed to snare. Aristotle and Euclid and Newton and the other Old Men of the school books have been challenged, to their loss, by modern mathematicians and scientists, by Einstein and Korzybski and Russell and the other new-day students of change and process.

If the momentous work of men such as these continues to gain influence, we may assume that in the schoolbooks of tomorrow there will be questions for which there will be no answers in the back pages. In the education of tomorrow, knowledge will be presented as tentative, as "subject to change without notice," and with it there will be taught a method for revising it and for adjusting easily to its revision. The student will be taught not only how to "make up his mind" but also how to change it easily and effectively. It will be the aim of education to make the child different from the Old Man out of recognition of the fact that he is different and that he must live in a world that is "different all the time."

For once we grasp clearly what has been "known" for centuries and what is, in fact, the central theme of modern science, that no two things are identical and that no one thing is ever twice the same, that everywhere is change, flux, process, we understand that we must live in a world of differences. We understand that what we see as a difference between the boy and the man represents a process that has been going on ever since the man was a boy. The effort of the man to remain a boy we recognize as maladjustment, just as we recognize as cultural maladjustment the effort of a society to function in 1946 as it did in 1900—or in 1945.

CHANGE AND DIFFERENCE

As we have said, this basic notion of process differences occupies a fundamental place in the system of general semantics, and it has extremely far-reaching implications, as we shall see. These implications suggest certain principles of adequate human behavior, principles that are different in many respects from those to which we are accustomed by virtue of our formal training and by virtue of the subtle and powerful influences of our traditions and of our general culture. Indeed, this notion of the process character of reality underlies and generates nothing less than a new kind of civilization.

For it has been the tradition of our race that similarities have been heeded and respected more than differences. Men have cherished sweeping generalizations: you can't change human nature; like father, like son; the law of "supply" and "demand"; you get just about what you pay for, etc. Exceptions to the rule have been disposed of by the deft maneuver of proclaiming that they "prove" it. There is no intention here to assert that generalizations are useless or "bad"; indeed, throughout this book we shall be concerned largely with the principles of adequate generalization. Our purpose is rather to focus attention upon the traditional tendency to adopt general rules, beliefs, creeds, theories, without thoroughly questioning their validity, and to retain them long after they have been shown to be meaningless, false, or at least questionable. On the whole, once we have adopted a belief, we give particular attention to cases that seem to support it, we distort other cases in order to make them seem to support it, and we ignore or belittle other cases.

We feel deeply that somehow it is a sign of weakness to "change our minds."

Now, a generalization is a statement that asserts that different things are somehow similar, or even identical, and so are to be reacted to or treated alike, or nearly so. Thus not only do we say that all patients who exhibit such and such symptoms are alike in that they have appendicitis, but we also go on to remove the appendixes of all of them. Certain religious sects not only hold that all babies are born "impure" or "in sin," etc., but also proceed to submerge them all in water, or sprinkle them with it, or in some fashion baptize them, all of them. In some countries not only are all persons with certain pedigrees classified together as Negroes, but they are also all deprived of various privileges and rights. The fact that not all appendicitis patients nor all babies nor all Negroes are alike, even though we say they are, is something that we do not seem able to take into account very easily. The similarities, however slight, impress us much more than do the differences, however great, once we have stressed the similarities by naming them and by generalizing *in terms of the name* we have given them.

It is not that we are unacquainted with this fact. On the contrary, we are thoroughly familiar with our tendency, as individuals and as organized groups, to orient ourselves on the basis of similarities, even supposed identities, to a much greater degree than on the basis of differences. That is, we are familiar with our tendency to treat the disease rather than the patient, to teach "the child" rather than Johnny, to speak of falling in love rather than fallings in loves. And we are well acquainted with the strong inclination most of us have to cling to our generalizations, to defend our beliefs, to resent criticism of them, and to distrust or laugh at outlanders who have different views and customs. We seem to dread inconsistency. Professor Edward L. Thorndike, eminent psychologist, once began an address before a national convention of an educational association with the remark that he was going to say something that he had heard *no one else* say to that association during the twenty-five years he had been attending its annual meetings. "I am going to say," Professor Thorndike announced, "that I have been wrong."

"AND THIS, TOO, SHALL PASS"

This tendency to disclaim error, to strive for consistency, to preserve and defend a generalization once adopted, is, of course, merely one aspect of the tendency to disregard differences. For it is precisely by taking due account of differences that one modifies, sometimes radically, one's established beliefs. We "change our minds," to some degree, exactly by giving thought to such observations as that a quite healthy appendix is sometimes removed from an "appendicitis" patient, or that some of the unemployed turn out to be extremely competent workers when provided with jobs, or that certain expensive blankets don't wear as well as other low-priced ones, etc. It is simply by ignoring these cases that are different or exceptional that we retain the views we held before we encountered them. Once we begin to look for differences instead of similarities, it is practically impossible to retain intact, or at all, our generalizations, beliefs, assumptions, etc. It is almost impossible, that is, not to get new ideas. For the habit of asking, "How do these things differ?" or "How might this be different?" is one of the basic techniques of originality or creativeness.

And it is just such a habit that is required for optimal adjustment to a reality of process, change, flux, with its consequent incessantly occurring differences. If you cannot step in the same river twice, it is folly to try. If love on Tuesday is not the same as love on Monday—and it never is the same—the consequences of expecting it to be the same range from mild disappointment to suicide. If one man's meat is another man's poison, the "cook" who generalizes too readily is a public menace. Insofar as Jones at age twenty-five retains the attitudes and behavior of Jones at age five, he is likely to be regarded as an ass, a poor sport, or a sufferer of some kind of "mental" disease. Infantilism, the failure to grow up, to change one's "mind," one's behavior, sufficiently with age, appears, indeed, to be in varying degrees an almost universal form of maladjustment in our civilization, in which similarities are respected more than differences and change is resisted accordingly. We resist the change from childishness to maturity, from one stage of social development to the next. We remain infantile, just as we remain culturally retarded. We pine for the golden age of the past, deplore the new generation, and fear for the "collapse of civilization." It is an old pattern, and it is not to be thoughtlessly taken for granted. It is not "human nature," it is only a cultural heritage.

In our society it is considered complimentary, indeed, in greeting a long-absent friend, to tell him that he "has not changed a bit," that he "looks just the same as ever." "A bird in the hand is worth two in the bush," "Don't rock the boat," and many other folk maxims reflect this basic conservatism and aversion to change. The doggedness with which some men will resist change has been strikingly exhibited in recent years by the "dust bowl" farmers who refused to be moved, at government expense, to more fertile lands. They illustrate rather literally what Hayakawa has referred to as the underlying furtiveness with which we move into our more stately mansions, disturbed by an uneasy feeling that we have lost our homes.

Abraham Lincoln played dramatically upon this basic and traditional distrust of change in an address which he delivered in 1859, two years before the outbreak of the American Civil War. Speaking at a time of ominous conflict and unrest, and in an effort, or so it would seem, to instill confidence and hope in the people—and, no doubt, in himself as well—he recounted the story of the Chinese emperor who commanded his wisest philosopher to prepare for him a statement that might be made appropriately on any occasion. The philosopher prepared for his emperor these words: "And this, too, shall pass away." But in citing this, Lincoln spoke of it not with full endorsement—"And yet, let us hope, it is not quite true." He viewed it, if one does not misjudge him, as a sentiment contrary to the basic feelings of "right-minded" men. It was a sentiment against which he spoke to the friends and countrymen who looked to him for wise guidance. And in so doing, Lincoln aligned himself with historic forces. For the story of man's eventful trek down through the ages has been in the main a story of man's doggedly resistant retreat before the relentless avalanche of continuous transformation. Man's astonishing capacity for struggling against the inevitable is one of his most inspiring, but tragic, qualities. But again it must be emphasized that in this struggle, in this shaking of fists in the face of change, men do not exhibit "human nature"; rather, they do the bidding of the Old Man, they behave as they have been taught, they merely carry on an old tradition.

THE DIFFERENCE SCIENCE MAKES

And of this old tradition itself, it can surely be said, in the words of the Chinese wise man, "This, too, shall pass away." It shall pass, perhaps, much sooner than we think. For the river of Heraclitus is rising and already fills the lowlands. It is rising ever faster as we watch it. Nor is this to be taken for granted. There is a reason, and for somewhat dramatic purposes we may look for this reason in the story of a lively little man who lived not very long ago in Italy. Because of him the world is much different now from what it used to be.

In Italy, in Pisa, on the fourteenth of February, in 1564, only 382 years ago, there was born, to a not very well-to-do nobleman of Florence, a son. His name was Galileo Galilei, but we usually speak of him simply as Galileo. We are told that at the age of seventeen he entered the University of Pisa as a student of medicine and of the philosophy of Aristotle. The Old Man of our culture, above all other Old Men, was Aristotle. It was he who built the dikes, so to speak, of our civilization. And it was Galileo who made the first gravely serious hole in those dikes. As we shall see, he made it with a cannon ball! And the venerable followers of Aristotle, including the Old Men of the church, punished him severely for it. But there it was, that hole he had drilled in the dikes of Aristotelian civilization; and punishment or no punishment, the hole grew, until now the dikes, although they had been well constructed indeed, and seem yet in many places to be sound as ever, are crumbling quite definitely—and the river of Heraclitus is on the rampage.

We shall come back to the cannon ball in a moment. As we have said, Galileo entered the University of Pisa as a young man of seventeen, and he was not long in creating most unusual distress by questioning the dogmatic statements of his instructors. From many points of view, it may be stated that that was the beginning of the decline of the Aristotelian, *prescientific* civilization. For with Galileo, in a generally true sense, something new came into the world, and the world has never been the same since, nor can one imagine how it might ever be the same again.

What was this strange new thing which Galileo gave to mankind? It was what we have come to call, so glibly, by the name *science*. It was a point of view, a general method, a rather intangible sort of thing, which most men even today do not yet understand. They feel its effects, certainly; they use its products, they live in new and strange semantic environments which it has created; but to most persons science is essentially a vague mystery, and to many it is still a word that arouses distrust. Galileo is still remembered as a heretic!

Science, the policy of subjecting The Word to the test of experience and of revising it accordingly, no matter how old The Word may be or who defends it, this certainly is new in the world. For it was scarcely more than three hundred years ago when Galileo climbed to the top of the leaning tower of Pisa and performed one of the first deliberately executed scientific experiments, in which he demonstrated that a heavy cannon ball drops no faster than a light one. He did, indeed, blast a hole in the dikes of civilization. He showed what could be done with cannon balls, what really could be done. He shook the world as it had never been shaken before. What he demonstrated was not so much a fact about falling weights, a fact against which Aristotle had contended, as a new problem-solving method based not on the authority of age and prestige, but rather on the authority of observation and experiment. He started the Old Man tottering on his throne. And although the Old Man has clung, these three centuries, to his perilous pedestal, he has never regained his former poise.

It is true that in most matters we still feel our deepest respect for the authority of age and precedence, the authority of venerated names and of robed and besymboled titles—but it has been hardly more than three hundred years since Galileo. In the history of the race, after all, three hundred years is but a small part of the morning. In those three short centuries the face of the earth has been in no small measure transformed, and the transformation gains rather than loses momentum. The Old Man is still dominant in our world, but it is a world that becomes increasingly strange to him and distrustful of him. It is the authority of science that is already shaping the future of civilization, in ways which even we in our time may understand and learn to cherish, and to which our children will probably adapt easily and no doubt with enthusiasm.

An old culture, a *prescientific civilization,* is passing, and wisdom does not lie so much in assuming a posture of regret as it does in keen participation in the exhilarating change to a *civilization of science.* Those prophets of despair who proclaim that all civilization is dying and that we are returning to the Dark Ages mistake the propelling force of destiny for the vigor of a death agony. It is not that we are going out by the same door wherein we entered. This is not, in the jargon of the movie-goer, where we came in. The show is changing, but history is not repeating itself.

There are differences between the old and the new tendencies, differences which have exciting implications. The fundamentally distinguishing feature of the culture now deteriorating lay in the fact that it was based upon a *static* notion of reality and involved, therefore, a resistance to change, an overvaluation of similarities, a profound respect for established generalizations, for convention and tradition, and for the authority of age and precedence—the authority of the Old Man. In all that, it was sharply different from the scientific culture now emerging, which is based upon a *process* notion of reality and involves, accordingly, a strong tendency toward change, a high valuation of differences, a critical attitude toward established generalizations, a conviction that traditions are to be outgrown, and a profound respect for the authority of systematic observation and evaluated experience—the authority of science *as method.*

What is particularly to be underlined in all this is the notion of the process character of reality, a notion that is peculiarly basic in the scientific view of the world and of man. The great laws of science, themselves held subject at all times to revision, are laws concerning the continuous processes of reality—what Max Born has so aptly called the "restless universe." The ultimate purpose of science is not merely to study these processes, certainly not to resist them, but rather to predict and thus to control them, in order that men may stay attuned to the great flux of nature by which they are surrounded and of which they themselves are part. A scientific way of life rests squarely on a clear recognition of all this, a constant awareness of change, flux, process; a frank rejection of the belief that reality is basically static, that there is nothing new under the sun, that history merely repeats itself.

As special laboratory techniques, as technology, science has enabled us to remake, in large measure, the material world in which we live. But this in itself, combined with a prescientific "philosophy," can well make for stark tragedy—as we in our time need hardly be reminded. It is science *as a general method of orientation,* a way of life, no less, that promises the means whereby we may learn to live, with grace and without rancor, in the world with which we have, by our own perilous ingenuity, surrounded ourselves.

THE BASIS OF GENERAL SEMANTICS

General semantics may be regarded as a systematic attempt to formulate the general method of science in such a way that it might be applied not only in a few restricted areas of human experience, but *generally* in daily life. It is concerned with science not as specialized laboratory techniques, not science as it depends upon highly refined precision apparatus, not science in the form of esoteric theories concerning the moons of Jupiter or the chemical composition of spot removers, not science as compilations of facts and statistics with regard to everything from wind velocities to petroleum—not science as technology—but science as a general method, as a basic orientation, as a generalized way of solving problems—and with due regard for the language of science; it is science in such a sense with which general semantics is concerned.

It belongs, thus, in the tradition of Galileo and Newton and

Maxwell, of Darwin and Pasteur and Pavlov, of Peirce and Russell and Einstein—of Heraclitus—the tradition of breaking traditions as a changing reality and a changing humanity require. What the men of science have learned to do with such unprecedented effectiveness in their technical laboratories, general semantics would prepare all men to do as well as they may from moment to moment in their daily lives, and from day to day in their handling of the social problems by which they are all affected.

Since general semantics has been distilled from science, it will be to our advantage to have a look at science—at those characteristics of it that are important in general semantics. Then we may examine more intelligently the basic principles and procedures of general semantics, and then, too, we may more effectively apply them.

Chapter ～～～～～～～～～～～ III

SCIENCE AND PERSONALITY

Our common difficulties in personal and social adjustment tell us something, as we have previously noted, not only about ourselves but also about the particular culture and the semantic environments in which we have these difficulties. In order to understand our troubles, it is necessary, therefore, to look about and make ourselves acquainted with the world of men and meanings in which we indulge in our groans and bristlings.

It has been the burden of the preceding chapter to indicate that our culture has been traditionally, and that it still is for the most part, *prescientific*. What men call science, however, has for the past three centuries, and increasingly in more recent times, exerted strong influences tending to change our customary outlooks and ways of living. As this *scientific* culture emerges, it comes into conflict with our traditional institutions, beliefs, and habits. Out of this conflict and out of certain features of our traditional modes of behavior, many of our personal and social problems arise. The attempt to maintain old views and customs would appear more hazardous than the effort to understand and to take advantage of the powerful forces moving us in new directions. Through an understanding of these forces, through an understanding of science as a basic orientation to life, we may hope to gain a greater sense of security and of achievement now and for the future. Toward this end, we shall consider for the next several pages, in simple but basic terms, the meanings and the ways of science.

Science, in the sense in which we are here using the term, involves, as we have stressed, the fundamental notion that reality is to be regarded as a process. Process implies change—in us and in the world about us. This change is continuous, although it is not always steady or gradual; it is sometimes so slow that we can hardly notice it, and at other times it is remarkably sudden and extensive.

We do not, as a rule, observe processes directly. Rather we infer them. For example, it is summer and apples are growing on a tree in the orchard. We notice one day that a particular apple has a different color and is larger than it was a week ago. We *observe* the differences. We *infer* the processes by which we explain the differences. We speak, in this case, of the processes of growth, and we say that the apple is *becoming* ripe. We do not actually see the growing and the ripening; we infer them from what we do see. What we see is a *series of differences* in the appearance of the apple from day to day or week to week.

Now, looking at the apple this week, we remark that it is different, but that nevertheless it is the "same" apple we saw last week. It is the same but it is different! Here, then, is a very curious problem. How can two things be the same and yet different?

Strangely enough, two things that are different may also be the same, and two things that are the same may also be different. Whether they will be the same or different—so far as we individually are concerned—depends on the way we are set to react to them.

We have already seen that our traditional set is such that we tend to notice and emphasize similarities and to overlook or minimize differences. We are set primarily to expect different things to be the same, and to expect any one thing to stay the same. Thus, we may speak of our set as representing a *static* orientation. It indicates that we do not assume that reality constantly changes. We talk as if, we act as if, we believed reality to have an unchanging character, a stability, a "once and for all" constancy, and that we ourselves, therefore, need not be particularly flexible or changeable.

THE SCIENTIFIC SET

Keeping this well in mind, let us examine more closely what we mean by science. The scientific set is quite different. It represents a *dynamic* or *process* orientation. With a scientific set, we tend to react to things that scem to be the same as though they were also different. Starting with the assumption that reality is not static, but that it is process-like, we are set to expect differences—because in a process reality no two things turn out to be the same and no one thing stays the same. Our expectations take shape accordingly, and we are set to pay attention, first of all, to differences.

This kind of set is to be seen clearly in the way in which a skilled physician goes about the task of making a diagnosis. He sees differences between symptoms, or between patients, that look as much alike as two milk bottles to an untrained eye. He determines, first of all, what diseases a patient does not have. He determines, that is, the important respects in which this patient differs from as many other patients as possible. Finally, he gives the patient's ailment a name, but it is the most specific and narrowly defined name he can find to use, and he uses it only after he has satisfied himself that *this* patient is not crucially different from other patients whose ailments have been given the same name. Nor does he stop there. Having named the disease—thus differentiating it from all other diseases—the skilled physician does not treat *this* case of it as though it were exactly the same as every other case. He notices the particular patient who has the disease, the conditions under which he has it; he notices the temperament, the interests, the habits of the patient, and of the nurse, if there is one, and of the friends and relatives who visit the patient; and he notices scores of other details that make *this* patient different from every other patient with the "same" disease. It is the genuinely scientific physician who says—and means it—that no two sick individuals are the same, and who treats the patient as well as the disease.

It is to be carefully noted that when such a physician does recognize a similarity between two patients or two symptoms, it is likely to be an important one. He will not recognize it as a similarity until he has satisfied himself that the differences involved in it—and there always are some—are not crucial. The point is that to a scientific physician, as to any other scientifically oriented person, *a similarity is comprised of differences that don't make any difference*. There is a saying that a difference, to be a difference, has to make a difference—and we should add that only if it doesn't, does it imply a similarity.

These considerations need to be carried one important step further. When a scientist says that two things are similar, he is saying, as we have indicated, that certain differences between them do not serve to make them different one from the other, for certain purposes. Two diamonds, for example, differing as to size and shape may be the same for purposes of making a particular cutting tool. But the scientist is also saying that the similarity is important precisely because it serves to differentiate the things that are similar from everything else—again, of course, for certain purposes. The fact that diamonds resemble each other in certain respects, such as their cutting properties, is significant because these are the very respects in which diamonds differ from other materials. Thus, what makes a similarity interesting to a scientist is the difference that it makes. In effect, a scientist, whether he is an expert on physical diseases, or on rocks, or speech defects, or diamonds, or whatnot—a scientist is, first of all and after all, a master of discrimination. Differences are his stock in trade, and differentiation is the operation by which he performs his wonders.

True, he aims at making generalizations. He attempts to sort out the welter of facts with which he deals so as to group them according to the most useful scheme of classification. He looks for important relationships among various events. His great achievements are the broad theories and general laws that he succeeds in formulating. In fact, the more general the laws that he formulates the more important they are, provided they square with the facts, enabling him to account for past events and to predict events which have not yet occurred. It is common knowledge that the broad generalizations he achieves are precisely what make a scientist renowned.

But the results of science are not to be mistaken for the procedure of science. A classification is arrived at by determining, first of all, those things that *do not* belong together, that are not importantly related, that are not alike. It is easy enough to see that different things look alike somehow; a baby can do that—and does it to a great extent. Important and useful classifications are achieved by those who are able to look more closely and to see the subtle respects in which things that look alike to the untrained or careless eye are actually different. General laws are discovered by scientists who do not assume that "the exception proves the rule"; they are not entirely satisfied by rules to which there are many exceptions, because exceptions do not prove a rule. They tend to refute it. A competent scientist pays attention to exceptions—to the cases that are different from the average or usual case. It is precisely by studying these differences, and accounting for them, that he finally arrives at a sound general law. To choose a very obvious example, it would clearly be necessary for a medical research worker to know in considerable detail the differences among the various kinds of disease germs before he could arrive at a sound theory concerning disease germs in general.

One other very important point remains to be stressed. A thoroughgoing scientist is suspicious of his generalizations, his theories and laws. He has a certain attitude toward them; he regards them as being constantly subject to revision. As a matter of fact, although it appears that he is forever bent on arriving at some generalization or other, he is actually engaged in the business of deliberately making revisions in already established generalizations. Every experiment he conducts is deliberately set up not to *prove* that his hypothesis or belief is correct, but to discover whether there is some particular respect in which it is wrong. To a scientist a theory is something to be *tested*. He seeks not to defend his beliefs, but to improve them. He is, above everything else, an expert at "changing his mind."

ADAPTABILITY

This, then, represents the way in which a scientific person is tuned, so to speak. He has a nose for the new, the exceptional, the fine shades of variation in the world about him and in himself and his social relationships. In all this he differs from the prescientific sort of individual who is tuned to similarities and identities, who goes about pouring new wine into old bottles, who generalizes quickly and then tends to stay generalized. Not that all persons whom we call scientists behave consistently in terms of the process set, as here described; many who go by the name of scientist seem more inclined, indeed, to defend conclusions already drawn than to welcome sounder ones. Outside their laboratories, moreover, many so-called "scientists" are as static in their points of view as anyone could be. It is equally true that most people who do not claim to be scientific are probably not entirely static in their orientation to life. It would hardly be possible for them to be so and still function as tolerable members of society, or even survive at all. One who was utterly unprepared for change, or who unswervingly refused to change his beliefs or habits, would be quite unfit to meet the demands of human existence.

It is also to be well noted that survival would be difficult or unlikely for one who was very unreasonably changeable, wildly inconsistent, fitfully whipped about by every chance wind of circumstance and fancy. Such an extreme would be as pathological as the one just mentioned. What is desired, what characterizes a scientific orientation, as the term is here being used, is a realistic, an optimal —a "just right"—degree of adaptability.

This can be represented in a simple way by means of numbers. Let us suppose that an optimal degree of adjustment is represented by a constant value of 10. Then let us suppose that the world, or reality, changes in ways indicated by the numbers in the right-hand column below. The changes required of the individual, if he is to maintain optimal adjustment, may then be represented by the numbers in the left-hand column, so:

Changes in the Individual	Optimal Adjustment	Changes in Reality
2	10	8
5	10	5
1	10	9
3	10	7
7	10	3

The two top numbers in the right- and left-hand columns, 2 and 8, add up to 10; so do the next two numbers, 5 and 5, etc. In other words, what this simple scheme is intended to represent is the fact that optimal adjustment comes about when the individual changes his beliefs, behavior, etc., in such a way as to accommodate himself to changes that arise in the reality to which he has to adjust. If he refuses to adjust to these changes in reality, his resulting maladjustment may be indicated in the following way:

Rigid Constancy of the Individual	Resulting Maladjustment	Changes in Reality
2	10	8
2	7	5
2	11	9
2	9	7
2	5	3

Here, for example, is the wife with fixed ideas as to what any husband ought to be, and who, because she is a woman "of principle," refuses to change her ideas in order to make them correspond to the actualities represented by the real live husband who blinks at her from across the breakfast table every morning. Here, too, is the conservative or reactionary, including some of those who call themselves liberals or radicals (the basic thing, after all, is not the label but the degree of flexibility), who believes now, always has and always will believe whatever it is that he believes, in spite of any and all facts that make the year 1946 different from 1910. Here, then, is represented the "Maginot Line mentality."

On the other hand, the individual who changes his beliefs and his behavior willy-nilly, more or less without regard for the facts to which he has to adjust, likewise fails to achieve or maintain optimal adjustment:

Unrealistic Inconsistency of the Individual	Resulting Maladjustment	Changes in Reality
2	10	8
3	8	5
6	15	9
2	9	7
8	11	3

Here is represented the faddist, the shallow enthusiast over the newest fashion designers' fantasy or star-dusty economic panacea, who goes in for any movement that happens to waft by—whether it involves combing the hair down over one eye or eating rye crisp —not out of deep and mature convictions, but usually out of profound boredom, or a sort of exhibitionism. Back of it all lies, as a rule, an essentially infantile personality structure and a basic sense of insecurity.

In such ways we may represent two extremes of maladjustment and a more or less ideal form of optimal adjustment. Not many persons perform consistently in accordance with either of these extremes or with the ideal. Rather, we tend to range ourselves along a continuum like that in Fig. 1.

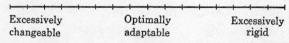

| Excessively changeable | Optimally adaptable | Excessively rigid |

FIG. 1.   Schematic scale of personal rigidity (adaptability).

In our culture, most of us probably veer considerably to the right of center on this continuum. If it were possible to measure each of us in these terms, and we were then to plot a graph showing the number of us falling at each point along the scale, the curve would probably look something like that in Fig. 2.

In a culture in which a scientific orientation had been rather thoroughly adopted, the curve would look about like that in Fig. 3.

Under each curve there is an area labeled A. Within A are to be found those persons who are regarded as most normal, or representative. They are often referred to as the "right-minded" or

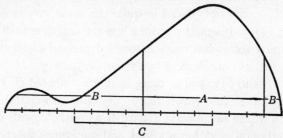

FIG. 2. Suggestive curve (not based on actual data) of distribution of individuals in a prescientific culture with respect to adaptability. *A* represents those persons who, in such a culture, are regarded as "normal." *B* represents extreme individuals regarded as maladjusted in that they are too changeable (left-hand end of scale) or too rigid (right-hand end of scale). *C* represents those individuals who would be regarded as "normal" in a scientific culture.

"better" people. A considerable proportion of those regarded as normal in our culture (Fig. 2) would not be so regarded in a scien-

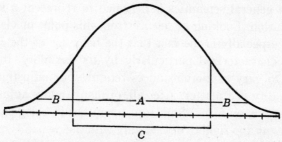

FIG. 3. Suggestive curve (not based on actual data) of distribution of individuals in a scientific culture with respect to adaptability. *A* and *C* represent those persons who, in such a culture, would be regarded as "normal." *B* represents extreme individuals who would be regarded as maladjusted in that they are too changeable (left-hand end of scale) or too rigid (right-hand end of scale).

tific culture (Fig. 3), because they are rather more set in their ways than would be considered desirable by scientific standards.

Under each curve there are two areas, at the extreme ends of the scale, labeled *B*. In these areas are to be found the individuals who are thought to be abnormal or pathological—seriously maladjusted. They are not placed in quite the same way in Fig. 2 as they are in Fig. 3. It would require a less extreme degree of rigidity and perhaps a somewhat more extreme degree of changeableness to be regarded as pathological in a scientific society.

In Fig. 2, as in Fig. 3 also, there is an area labeled *C*. It covers the region of the scale which represents optimal adaptability. In our culture we do not always regard it as pathological, but it is often looked upon as rather unusual, and sometimes we consider it "queer." The kind of behavior involved in optimal adaptability is not necessarily condemned, but sometimes it is not well understood, and it does not always appeal to the voters, for example. In a scientific society (Fig. 3) it would be the most common behavior and would be evaluated as most normal.

SCIENCE AND PERSONAL ADJUSTMENT

Now, science may be regarded usefully as a method of adjustment. It is in that sense that we are using the term. It is in such a sense that general semantics is designed to represent a scientific life orientation. Looking at science from this point of view, what we notice especially is the fact that the behavior of the scientific person is characterized particularly by its flexibility, its strong tendency to vary as circumstances require. For adjustment in a process reality is a matter, after all, of many, many adjustments. The most common form of maladjustment lies in being too stable, too consistent, too rigid to deal readily with the demands of changing situations brought on by the sheer fact that one grows older day by day in a world that does not stay the same from day to day.

Within the highly developed fields of physics, chemistry, geology, etc., are to be found specific applications of the general method of science. But if we think of science as being limited to such fields, and to the laboratories which have made them so important, we miss the point that means most to us as individuals and as a society. We miss the point that what is done by the physicist, the chemist, the geologist, etc., is something that practically all of us can do in our own daily lives in one way or another.

The fundamental thesis of this book is simply that science, clearly understood, can be used from moment to moment in everyday life, and that it provides a sound basis for warmly human and efficient living. This sounds fantastic, if it does, only because of the ways in which we define science.

THE MEANINGS OF SCIENCE

The term *science* has at least six general meanings. It refers, first of all—and this is perhaps not commonly recognized—to the basic set or orientation to reality that we have discussed. The fundamental scientific assumption is that reality has a process character; if you reject that, you remove practically all the purpose and point in everything the scientist does. In a perfectly static world the only requirement for perfect adjustment would be a good memory, and everyone would have that, if one might speak of memory as existing in a world in which tomorrow and yesterday would be identical. What most fundamentally characterizes the scientific, or well-adjusted, or highly sane person is not chiefly the particular beliefs or habits or attitudes that he holds, but rather the deftness with which he modifies them in response to changing circumstances. He is set to change, in contrast to the more rigid, dogmatic, self-defensive individual who is set to "sit tight."

There are other meanings of the word *science*, however, which do not serve nearly so well to indicate how science might be used in daily life—and these other meanings are the ones that are more commonly held. For example, *science* is often used to refer to certain techniques, usually involving the use of apparatus. If a man spends his time using such apparatus and techniques, we usually say that he is a scientist. It would ordinarily be more accurate, however, to say that such a man is a technician. One may be highly skilled as an operator of X-ray apparatus and yet have neither the set nor the wit of a scientist. As a matter of fact, many of our greatest scientists are not particularly competent or experienced as technicians. Einstein is probably our greatest scientist and to my knowledge he has never conducted a laboratory experiment in his life. Individuals who have a flair for tinkering with apparatus and for using certain techniques can be clearly differentiated from scientists by referring to them as "tinkerniquers." The term is not meant to be disparaging; competent tinkerniquers are extremely useful. The term does help, however, in making a very important differentiation.

In the third place, we frequently define science in terms of "the sciences." That is, we think of science as physics, or engineering, or biology, or chemistry, or some other field of science. In our high schools and colleges students "take" science; it is a number of courses or subjects, and it is not to be found in any other courses or subjects. The view seems to be that outside these specific fields there is no science. There is no science in history, for example. To say that, using the term *science* as it is used in general semantics, is to be rather uncomplimentary toward the historians! No doubt we have all read in magazines at some time or other, or we have heard lecturers declare, that a scientific approach to social, or economic, or moral problems is impossible. What they are saying is that one cannot use "atom smashers" or Boyle's law to feed the unemployed or to insure happy marriages. That seems obvious enough. That is not to say, however, that one cannot use science to do these things.

A fourth way in which we use the word *science* is closely related to the above usage. This is the sense in which we speak of scientific knowledge. To many people, science means essentially a body of knowledge. The advertiser is appealing to such people when he refers to something as a "scientific fact." Science news stories in the daily press and on the radio are almost entirely concerned with information (sometimes misinformation) allegedly resulting from the labors of laboratory men. It would usually be futile to examine such stories with a view to finding out *how* the information was obtained, and the procedure whereby it had been determined that the information was dependable. High-school textbooks of general science tend to be largely mere compilations of more or less reliable statements concerning such phenomena as water, fire, earth, and air. The student does not necessarily get from them any considerable understanding of what it is that scientists actually do, or by what means they decide to do it, or what difference it makes to anyone or to society. Certainly they can get no clear notion that science might be used by them in their own day-to-day living.

Then there is the common use of *science* as a word that refers not to sheer factual information or techniques but to theories and laws. In such a sense, science refers, for instance, to Newton's law of gravitation or to Einstein's theory of relativity. Science thus is made up of long words and mathematical equations that are very difficult to understand and that do not seem to have much to do with everyday life. You have to know mathematics in order to know what the scientists are talking about—from this point of view. Very few people have any such scientific theories of anything. They insist that such theories are over their heads. If, in addition, they assume that science means little else, they can hardly be counted on to have any deep interest in it or in its human possibilities.

There is, however, a more generally useful sense of the word— and the next several chapters are designed to elaborate it. We may regard science, as we have said, as a generally practical method of adjustment. Science *as method* in this general sense need not be confined to laboratories. It is not something that can be used only by men in white coats, wearing goatees, squinting at test tubes, and speaking six-syllable words in a strange dialect. It may be thought of simply as organized common sense. It is the method whereby ordinary individuals in their daily lives may forestall shock and disappointment, avoid or resolve serious conflicts, increase their efficiency and zest for living—in short, live sanely.

Calling it common sense might be a mistake. It is simple sense, but it may not be very common. It tends to be very obvious—once stated or demonstrated. It is so obvious that one has to be extremely careful not to ignore it. Scarcely anything is more difficult to learn than something that is obvious. It is very much like trying to learn nothing at all, and it requires tremendous alertness to learn nothing. For example, most people, according to experienced swimming teachers, find it very difficult to learn how to float—apparently because there is nothing to learn. You don't do anything in order to float. What you have to learn is to do nothing that would keep you from floating.

Learning general semantics—learning, that is, how to be scientific in the sense in which we are using the term—is very much like that. What you have to learn for the most part is to do nothing that will keep you from achieving and maintaining optimal adjustment. Science, as method, consists of behavior that is quite natural for human beings. One has to learn simply to permit that behavior to occur, to give it a chance to occur. Such learning is largely a matter of unlearning, or, if you start early in life, it is largely a matter of not learning what isn't so or what won't work. Most of us seem not to realize the extent to which we learn misinformation and adopt unsound theories. A bright child can be trained to act quite stupidly. It may be true that we cannot make a silk purse out of a sow's ear (although, as George D. Stoddard has remarked, we can often make a silk purse out of what we *thought* was a sow's ear), but it is all too true that we can make a sow's ear out of a silk purse. There is such a thing as trained inefficiency or cultivated confusion. The psychiatrist, Dr. Adolf Meyer, of Johns Hopkins University, has said that what ails most people is not that they are ignorant but that they know too much that isn't so. For such people, the better part of further learning is forgetting, and forgetting of well-learned misinformation and inefficiency is not easy as a rule.

In addition to the unlearning or forgetting that is usually required of the student of general semantics, or of scientific method, there is demanded of him, as we have indicated, much learning of the obvious. There are two common reactions that we tend to make to whatever we label as obvious. The first is that we feel as though we have always known it, since it is difficult to believe that we could have overlooked it. The second is that we feel that it must not be important, because it is so easy to "understand." In either case we tend to brush it aside, to spend little if any time pondering over it, and so we miss its implications. For example, probably all of us would feel that raising one's arm is childishly simple and obvious. Well—just *how* do you raise your arm?

It is reasonable to say that most inventions and advances in our knowledge have been mainly discoveries of the obvious. The wheel, the lever, the safety pin; Mendel's laws of heredity that summarized his experiments in raising peas; Pavlov's careful reports on the behavior of dogs, reports that have influenced modern psychology so greatly; Freud's observations of neurotic behavior; Lister's conclusions regarding antiseptic methods—these and thousands of other examples are on the whole a recital of achievements by men and women who "looked twice," who did not take such common occurrences as fears or pus or a crop of peas for granted. Anything that we have long overlooked but might easily have noticed usually seems simple and obvious, once we have it pointed out to us. We tend, therefore, to develop the illusion that we have always known it, and it is this that constitutes one of our greatest barriers to thorough and continuous learning.

The Basic Features of Science as Method

With this keynote of caution, we may examine briefly some of the more "obvious"—but very important and not at all commonly employed—features of scientific method.

We may say, in briefest summary, that the method of science consists in (a) asking clear answerable questions in order to direct one's (b) observations, which are made in a calm and unprejudiced manner, and which are then (c) reported as accurately as possible and in such a way as to answer the questions that were asked to begin with, after which (d) any pertinent beliefs or assumptions that were held before the observations were made are revised in light of the observations made and the answers obtained. Then more questions are asked in accordance with the newly revised notions, further observations are made, new answers are arrived at, beliefs and assumptions are again revised, after which the whole process starts over again. In fact, it never stops. Science as method is continuous. All its conclusions are held subject to the further revision that new observations may require. It is a method of keeping one's information, beliefs, and theories up to date. It is, above all, a method of "changing one's mind"—sufficiently often.

Four main steps are indicated in this brief sketch of the scientific method. *Three of them are concerned primarily with the use of language:* the asking of the questions that guide the observations, the reporting of the observations so as to answer the questions, and the revising of beliefs or assumptions relevant to the answers obtained. The things which we seem most commonly to associate with scientific work, namely, the apparatus and the observational techniques, these make up but one of the steps—and this is one part of the whole procedure that can be managed more or less entirely by technicians or laboratory assistants, provided there is a scientist to tell them what techniques and what apparatus to use. The recording, tabulating, and writing up of the observations can also be done in many instances and for the most part by assistants capable of following fairly simple instructions. But nobody else can take the place of the scientist when it comes to framing the questions and the theoretical conclusions. That, above everything else, is his work as a scientist, and that is work that requires the ability to use language in a particularly effective way. *The language of science is the better part of the method of science.* Just so, *the language of sanity is the better part of sanity.*

Of this language there are two chief things to be said. It must be clear and it must be accurate or valid. Whether or not it is grammatically "correct" is of secondary importance; certainly one can write with grammatical "correctness" and yet fail to achieve either clarity or validity. Scientific language need not, but may, embody what the literary critic would call good style. At least, it is generally agreed that there are many fascinating scientific books. Incidentally, at least the first fifty pages or so of Einstein's little book entitled *Relativity* might well be recommended to high school and college students as a model of English composition.

THE LANGUAGE OF SCIENCE AND OF SANITY

There is a cardinal principle in terms of which language is used scientifically: *It must be used meaningfully.* The statements made

must refer directly or indirectly (by means of interrelated definitions) to something in the realm of experience. It is not enough
that they refer to something for the speaker and that they also
refer to something for the listener. What is required is that they
refer to approximately the same thing for both the speaker and the
listener. In speaking meaningfully one does not just communicate;
one communicates something to someone. And the something communicated is not the words that are used, but whatever those words
represent. The degree to which communication occurs depends precisely upon the degree to which the words represent the same thing
for the listener that they do for the speaker. And the degree to
which they do is an index of the clarity of the language employed—
the clarity that is such a basic feature of scientific language. (It is
to be understood, of course, that what is here being said holds for
both spoken and written language.)

Clarity is so important in the language of science—which is to
say, in the language of sanity—because clarity is a prerequisite to
validity. It is to be considered that statements that "flow beauti-
fully" and are grammatically superb may be also devoid of factual
meaning, or meaningful but vague, or precise but invalid. Now,
scientific statements—that is to say, statements that serve to make
adequate adjustment probable—must be both clear and valid. They
can be clear without having validity, but if they are unclear their
validity cannot well be determined. They must then, first of all, be
clear or factually meaningful; they must be that before the question of their validity can even be raised. We ask, "What do you
mean?" before we ask, "How do you know?" Until we reach
agreement as to precisely what a person is talking about, we cannot
possibly reach agreement as to whether or in what degree his
statements are true.

Only to the extent that those who hear a statement agree as to
the specific conditions or observations required for ascertaining its
validity can the question of its validity have meaning. And the
extent to which they do agree in this sense is, of course, an indication of the extent to which the statement is clear or meaningful. If
a statement is such that those who hear it do not agree at all as to

how it might be verified or refuted, the statement may be "beautiful" or "eloquent," or grammatically irreproachable, but it is also, and above all, nonsense. It cannot be demonstrated to be valid or invalid, and is meaningful therefore, if at all, only to its author and to his psychiatrist. Otherwise it is mere noise, melodious and rhythmical, made up of more or less familiar words, perhaps, but taken altogether it is no more factually meaningful than the noise of a rattling steam radiator.

An example of such noise may be seen in the statement made by Dr. Pangloss in Voltaire's *Candide* that "this is the best of all possible worlds." Coming upon it as it stands, one would certainly have to do a considerable amount of inquiring in order to discover just what it is about. What, for example, does Voltaire's good Doctor represent by *this* world? Does he mean the world as he knows it, or "everybody's" world, or only as it is experienced by certain persons; or does he mean only part of the world as anyone might experience it? With the little word *is*, does he refer to the world as one finds it, or to its ultimate possibilities? Then, too, there are the spell-marks *best* and *possible* and *worlds*, to say nothing of *all*. It does not take much examination to see that the famous statement of Dr. Pangloss is hardly less noisy than Lewis Carroll's " 'Twas brillig and the slithy toves did gyre and gimble in the wabe." One may be pardoned for recalling, in this connection, the following which appeared in a 1939 Associated Press dispatch from Washington, D.C.: "Asked to interpret a statement in the president's message that the United States had no political involvements in Europe, Early [Secretary Stephen Early] replied that it meant exactly what it said."

QUESTIONS WITHOUT ANSWERS

What has been said above concerning statements holds also, and with particular emphasis, for questions. In the meaningful use of language it is a cardinal rule that the *terminology of the question determines the terminology of the answer*. One cannot get a clear answer to a vague question. The language of science is particularly distinguished by the fact that it centers around well-stated questions. If there is one part of a scientific experiment that is more important than any other part, it is the framing of the question that the experiment is to answer. If it is stated vaguely, no experiment can answer it precisely. If the question is stated precisely, the means of answering it are clearly indicated. The specific observations needed, and the conditions under which they are to be made, are implied in the question itself. As someone has very aptly put it, a fool is one who knows all the answers but none of the questions.

Individuals who suffer from personality maladjustments are especially well characterized by the fuzziness of the questions which they persistently ask themselves. What these individuals want, above everything else, are answers. What keeps them awake nights, what puts furrows in their brows and ulcers in their stomachs, is the fact that they cannot satisfactorily answer their own questions. They persistently stump themselves. Their failure to find the answers that would serve to relax them is not due primarily to their "stupidity," or to the general impenetrability of nature, as they rather commonly suppose. It is mainly due, instead, to the fact that they frame their questions in such a way that no amount of genius would enable them, or anyone else, to answer the questions. When maladjusted persons state their problems in the form of highly answerable—that is, clear and precise—questions, they frequently discover that their tensions are quickly and materially relieved. What they discover is simply that they knew the answers all the time; what they hadn't known was that those were the answers they were seeking. Their vague questions had obscured that fact.

I once received a letter from the president of a women's club. It seems that a very considerable dispute had left the club members in a virtual deadlock, and they had decided to seek elsewhere for any possible help in resolving their collective perplexity. The question they had been trying to answer was this: "Will democracy defeat religion?" It had arisen somehow in the course of a study project. The president of the club said they would like to have a scientific answer to it. Further correspondence indicated that it had not occurred to them that they were grappling with an impossibility—that they had asked themselves an unanswerable question. It was composed of familiar words and had an interrogation mark at the end. They had taken it for granted, therefore, that somewhere someone could somehow produce *the* answer.

In the first place, their question was unlimited as to time. *Will* could have meant next week, next year, or ten thousand years hence. Beyond that, there was no indication given as to how one might recognize "defeat" if and when he encountered it in the realm of actual experience. Moreover, anyone who has ever tried to indicate with even moderate clearness what he might mean by *democracy* or *religion* will recognize certain other defects in the question as stated. It is not that these words "don't mean anything." On the contrary, they mean too much. They very nearly mean "all things to all men." The question will be answered, therefore, in "all ways by all men," and what the club members wanted was one answer, *the* one. Such a question as they were asking has answer*s*, thousands of them, but it has no single answer. If they had asked, "Do persons who attend town meetings in our town attend church less often than those who don't?" they could have got a very clear answer. Whether that was what they wanted to find out is not known. What is quite certain is that it would have been to their advantage to decide just what it was that they did want to find out.

In the whole history of human knowledge, there is scarcely any other notion more liberating, more conducive to clearheadedness, than this notion that some questions are *unanswerable*. It is not a matter of our not having the information or the intelligence with which to answer them. It is simply that the questions do not imply just what particular information may be required. No amount of intelligence can overcome this. In fact, anyone who unhesitatingly and confidently answers such questions, or who persistently tries to answer them, exhibits thereby a profound lack of intelligence. When it has been said that such a question is unanswerable, there is practically nothing more to be said. Insofar as there is an answer, that is it. That disposes of the question.

This sounds incredible, perhaps. We are not to be so easily

silenced. When we ask what is the secret of success, for example, we do not readily understand, and we are likely to feel annoyed or even insulted, upon being told that our question is nonsense, or mere noise, or unanswerable. We might begin to understand a little better if we were told to restate the question without using the words *secret* and *success*. The request would probably puzzle us a bit, however; and until we began to catch on, we would be likely to come back with the retort that we didn't want to use any other words, because what we wanted to know was exactly what we said: "What is the secret of success?"

Outside such verbal circles lies wisdom. And the way to get outside of them is to shatter them by the simple method of classifying them as noisy or nonsensical. The way to stay outside of them is to ask questions clearly enough to indicate *where* and *when* one may reasonably expect to find the answers. That is utterly basic to any effective method of inquiry, and without effective methods of inquiry we can hardly hope to gain the answers that can make for wise social policy or adequate personal adjustment.

Human energy is never more extravagantly wasted than in the persistent effort to answer conclusively questions that are vague and meaningless. Probably the most impressive indictment that can be made of our educational system is that it provides the student with answers, but it is poorly designed to provide him with skill in the asking of questions that are effectively directive of inquiry and evaluation. It teaches the student to "make up his mind," ready or not, but it does not teach him how to change it effectively. Any attempt to improve our educational system that does not involve a clear recognition of this defect of it can hardly be expected to lead to substantial reform. In fact, any attempt to reeducate a maladjusted individual that does not leave him with effective techniques of inquiry cannot be trusted to result in substantial and lasting benefits.

Science, as sanity, consists largely in the language of science, particularly as it is to be seen in the scientist's manner of framing questions. Of his every question, the scientist asks, "By exactly what procedures might a reliable factual answer to it be found?"

If he cannot find such procedures, *he abandons the question.* That is why he is so efficient in solving problems; he confines his energies to questions that *can* be clearly answered. We can all follow his example—from moment to moment in our daily lives—and so insure ourselves more fully of personal growth and social development.

THE IMPORTANCE OF CLEAR ANSWERS

In later pages further discussion will be devoted to this extremely fundamental problem. It will suffice to conclude the present remarks by pointing out the reactions which we rather commonly make to the frustrating experience of trying to answer "riddles." After attempting for a sufficiently long time to achieve absolute answers to certain questions concerning free will, religion, ethics, broad social policy, self-appraisal, etc., we often arrive at the realization that our attempts appear to be more or less futile. True, the discussions which these questions generate are sometimes very interesting and enjoyable—provided we do not take them too grimly. But we can hardly miss the main point that such discussions tend not to be conclusive. As this begins to dawn upon us, sometime between the ages of fifteen and fifty, if at all, we seem to feel the need of taking some sort of attitude toward it.

There would appear to be four main attitudes that we adopt. There is the one that we express by saying that, after all, nature is mysterious; this is an important ingredient in most varieties of religion. There is another attitude that we express by declaring that men are fundamentally stupid. Vice President Curtis is said to have put this with dramatic brevity to a midwestern farmer with these words, "You're too damned dumb to understand!" A third attitude is represented by the common expression, "One man's opinion is as good as another's." We call this "tolerance," and there is a fairly general feeling, no doubt, that it is sound and desirable. From a scientific point of view it is—provided it is not an endorsement of sloppy thinking, a putting aside of our techniques for effective evaluation, a kind of semantic swooning under conditions of difficult decision. It is commendable from a scientific point of view provided it represents the policy of maintaining freedom for the efficient and unprejudiced investigation and revision of any man's opinion—including our own opinions.

A fourth attitude, and one that is not so common, is the one that we have been considering. It is the attitude which we express by asking, "To what degree does this question represent nonsense?" A scientist realizes that vigorous and stubborn attempts to settle with finality questions that are vague or meaningless are rather more than likely to result in confusion and bitterness, conflicts and cynicism, and other varieties of human misfortune. He does not blame these regrettable outcomes on man's basic stupidity, or on a sort of hopeless mysteriousness of nature. He does not merely urge his fellows to be tolerant—and condemn them if they are not. Rather, he looks for the sources of difficulty in the question itself, in the way in which it is formulated, and he seeks to make clear the simple principle that one cannot get a precise answer to a vague question. The good will and well-being which the patriarch and the moralist so often and so disastrously fail to achieve, the scientist would seek to gain by teaching people how to put to nature and to themselves *only* the kind of questions that *can* be answered with practical clarity.

Chapter IV

SCIENCE AND TOMORROW

$\mathcal{W}$E CONSIDERED, IN THE LAST CHAPTER, FIVE IMPOR-
tant aspects of science as method. We say they are important because they are fundamental in the scientific civilization that has
been developing with ever-increasing tempo during the past three
or four centuries. Within our own day, perhaps, and quite probably
within the lifetime of our own children, this scientific culture will
become relatively dominant. It will involve a way of life quite
different in many respects from that which to our fathers, and to
many of us, has seemed "right" and "natural." An old era appears
to be passing, and the extraordinary social upheavals of our day
become, in many respects, understandable from this point of view.

Between nations and groups of nations, within nations, and
within individuals in every quarter of the globe there is going on a
tremendous and turbulent conflict. New ideals, new beliefs, new
methods and ways of life are challenging old ideals and beliefs, old
methods and ways of life. The old is prescientific and authoritarian; the new is scientific. The question as to what is meant by
scientific in this sense—what is meant by scientific behavior and a
scientific society—is the question that concerned us in the last
chapter, and in the present chapter our discussion of it will be extended. And it is to be realized that what we are considering is the
background and basis of general semantics.

So far we have indicated, as we have said, five important features of science as general method and orientation, science as a way of life. In brief summary these are:

1. The basic notion that reality is to be regarded as a process. Process implies continuous change. Continuous change implies a never-ending series of differences in ourselves and in the various aspects of reality to which we must remain adjusted. No two things are exactly alike; no one thing stays the same. The point of view which such a notion represents is the fundamental point of view of science.

2. Adaptability, a readiness to change as changing conditions require, is fostered by such a point of view. Adaptability is a prominent feature of a scientific way of life.

3. Of the four main steps involved in scientific method, three are concerned primarily with the use of language: the asking of the questions that guide our observations, the reporting of the observations in such a way as to answer the questions, and the revising of beliefs to the extent that such revising is required by the answers obtained. (The fourth step, which is not directly concerned with language, is that of making the indicated observations.) *The language of science is the better part of the method of science.*

4. The language of science is meaningful, in the sense that it refers directly or indirectly to experience or observable actualities. As meaningful language it is clear and it is designed to be accurate or valid. It is continually directed by two great questions: "What do you mean?" and "How do you know?"

5. The language of science not only involves meaningful, clear, and valid statements, but also centers around clearly answerable questions. The use of language in a scientific way involves a peculiarly important rule: *The terminology of the question determines the terminology of the answer.* There is no place in scientific language, there is no place in the language of sanity, for vague or meaningless—that is to say, unanswerable—questions. Such questions are maladjustive, tragically misdirective of human energy. In a scientific way of life they are ruled out; they are frankly abandoned. As was said at the conclusion of the preceding chapter, the

good will and well-being which the patriarch and the moralist so often and so disastrously fail to achieve, the scientist would seek to gain by teaching people how to put to nature and to themselves *only* the kind of questions that *can* be answered with practical clarity.

PROJECTION

The discussion thus summarized may be further developed by pointing out that there is another very important feature of the scientific use of language. It is an important feature of the scientific orientation as a whole, and of general semantics. At first glance it may seem to be rather subtle. It is the degree to which the scientist is conscious of his language as an aspect of his own behavior. It is the degree to which he realizes that his statements are about himself as well as about something else that he is apparently talking about. It is the degree to which he understands that his language, any language, is man-made and is no more reliable and effective than the men who have made it and the men who use it. There is nothing foolproof and there is nothing superhuman about language, even scientific language.

Mencius, an ancient Chinese philosopher, said, in effect, that the mind works according to its own theory as to how it ought to work. In recent times, essentially the same observation has been expressed differently by Professor R. D. Carmichael in the statement that the universe, as we know it, is a joint product of the observer and the observed. In one way or another, philosophers and scientists have long been aware of this extremely basic principle. Modern psychologists have found a word for it. What Mencius was apparently talking about is referred to in modern psychology as *projection*.

Projection is as natural as breathing. It is another one of those things which, when pointed out, seems perfectly obvious, and so we have to be on our guard lest we overlook its far-reaching significance. Those who already "know" about it are especially prone to dismiss it as something which they "fully understand."

When, in the spring, a young man chances to look up and exclaim, "What a gorgeous blonde!" it should be recognized that his words tell us precious little about the young lady to whom he is presumably referring, but that they do tell us something about himself. He is projecting; the "gorgeousness" is inside him. When a hospital patient, somewhat the worse for imbibing, tells us in agitated tones that there are pink elephants on the wall, he is not telling us anything about the wall; he is informing us of his own internal state. He is projecting; the pink pachyderms are in his own head. When a friend greets you with the cheery announcement that it is a fine day, he is not informing you about the weather; he is only telling you that he has had a good night's rest and a satisfactory breakfast. He is projecting; the "fineness" is not of the day so much as it is of his own body. When a man says ruefully, "I didn't know it was loaded," he is informing you that he sometime previously projected his own notions about a gun into the gun.

Now, what a scientifically oriented person would have done in the above instances is very simple indeed. He would have added the words "to me," not out loud, perhaps, but "to himself" at least. He would have exclaimed, "What a gorgeous blonde (to me)!" and "It looks to me as though there were pink elephants on the wall over there. Can you see any?" We express our awareness of the degree to which our thoughts or statements are projections of our own internal condition, rather than reports of facts about something else, by such words as "it seems to me," "apparently," "from my point of view," "as I see it," etc. For convenience, then, we may refer to consciousness of projection as *to-me-ness*.

A scientifically oriented person exhibits a high degree of to-me-ness in his use of language. In reporting an experiment, a laboratory scientist usually qualifies his conclusions by warning the reader that unduly broad generalizations are not to be drawn from the reported findings, since they hold strictly only for the particular individuals tested and only for the specific conditions under which they were tested. He adds "to me" in capital letters, so to speak. His language, at its scientific best, represents a peculiarly high degree of consciousness of projection. That is a very large part of the reason why the generalizations he does eventually draw tend to be unusually valid.

A profound lack of awareness of projection, on the other hand, is to be seen in the language behavior of most patients suffering from grave "mental" illness. For example, it is strikingly evident in the disease known as paranoia, abnormal suspiciousness. This is brought out dramatically by William and Dorothy Swain Thomas in their book, *The Child in America*, in which they discuss the importance, in psychological case studies, of knowing not only whether the statements of the person interviewed are objectively true, but also the respects in which they are persistently distorted because of self-projection. They illustrate the point by means of the following:

Very often it is the wide discrepancy between the situation as it seems to others and the situation as it seems to the individual that brings about the overt behavior difficulty. To take an extreme example, the warden of Dannemora prison recently refused to honor the order of the court to send an inmate outside the prison walls for some specific purpose. He excused himself on the ground that the man was too dangerous. He had killed several persons who had the unfortunate habit of talking to themselves on the street. From the movement of their lips, he imagined that they were calling him vile names, and he behaved as if this were true. If men define situations as real, they are real in their consequences.

Unconscious projection is, indeed, one of the outstanding symptoms of personality maladjustment, even of the relatively minor types found in the common run of people. It is at the basis of innumerable petty quarrels and animosities, misunderstandings, anxieties and confusions, simple errors of judgment, and the hundred-and-one other tensions and frictions that keep life from being any nearer than it is to our hearts' desires. The lack of to-me-ness is to be regarded reasonably as due not to "human nature" but rather to the kinds of formal and informal education to which we are subjected in our essentially prescientific culture. And that would appear to be a very hopeful view of the matter. If the limitations are not in us so much as they are in our training, a great deal may be done about them.

Unconscious projection shows itself rather conspicuously in our use of the verb *to be* in its various forms *is, are, am,* etc. When we say, "This *is* a fine day," the *is* has the practical effect of identifying or confusing our private opinion or inner feelings with the objective realities outside ourselves. Again when we say, "The curtain *is* blue," the *is* operates to confuse our personal judgment with some sort of external fact. The color of the curtain is, after all, a joint product of our nervous system and certain characteristics of the curtain. The "blueness" may be said to be in our head. What the curtain *is* would seem to be something else again. So far as we know, there is no "blueness," as such, in the curtain; rather there are certain physico-chemical phenomena to which, *as we observe them,* we give the name *blue.* Our awareness of all this would be expressed by saying, for example, "The curtain appears blue to me," or "The curtain is blue as I see it."

Now, of course, unless someone comes along with pugnacious inclinations and says, "You're crazy! That curtain is green," we are not likely to get into serious difficulty by asserting that a curtain *is* blue, although most of us do waste a little time occasionally arguing about whether something is blue or green. But when we carry the same unconscious projection into various other situations, we tend to create for ourselves an impressive array of troubles, some of them catastrophic. When parents or teachers look at a child and say, "Wilbur *is* naughty and bad. He *is* a thief," they are likely to leave some scars on Wilbur's personality. They are not so likely to—they are not so likely to make such a statement in the first place—if they are aware that the statement conveys practically no information about Wilbur, but that instead it says something about their own standards of child conduct, gives some indication of the sort of books they have read, the kind of parents and teachers they themselves have had, etc. As for Wilbur, the statement tells him not "how to be good" but that his parents and teachers don't like him. Being as unconscious of projection as they are, he is likely to summarize his reactions by replying defiantly, "You're mean and I don't like you either!" And so another human life is started down the drainpipe of civilization. It doesn't take much if it happens often enough. Just as little drops of water will wear away a rock, so many little *is*'s will wear away a hope.

What we do with *is,* we do with other words and in other ways also, but we do it more easily and conspicuously with *is.* Human experience has been riddled with interminable and bitter disputes over whether something or other is or is not art, is good or bad, is successful or not, is wise or stupid. A great number of Supreme Court cases, for example, revolve around the question as to whether some law or other is or is not "constitutional," and not infrequently in these cases one man's use of *is* serves to swerve the course of history.

What is important in all this is not that we do indulge in self-projection or that *to be* is a "bad" word. There are no bad words; there are unfortunate ways of using any word. As for projection, it is perfectly natural; it is merely one characteristic of the way in which our nervous systems work. In and of itself, it is neither "good" nor "bad." Like digestion, another natural bodily process, its results can be harmful or beneficial, depending on whether or not it is abused. Digestion is often abused by people who do not understand it. Something similar can be said of projection; it is abused by those who are not clearly aware of it and of the role it plays in the use of language, and so in the development of individuals and of societies.

The problem is not so much that of revising the language or of eliminating some of the words; our language is so heavily an *is* language that it would be practically impossible to talk without using the various forms of *to be.* (In a recent investigation of over 200,000 words of the written language of adults, one of my research students, Miss Grace Shattyn, found that approximately one-fourth of all the verbs used were forms of *to be.*) The problem is simply that of developing a keen awareness of projection, and of the peculiar significance of certain terms such as *is* in this connection. It does help, it is conducive to greater awareness of projection, to replace *is* by such terms as *appears, seems,* etc., whenever it proves convenient, and to indicate to-me-ness by such expressions as "in my judgment," "from my particular point of view," and the like.

But the essential thing is *awareness* of projection. We need not always, by any means, express this awareness in so many words out loud or in writing. We can say, "It is a blue curtain," or "It is art," and know quite clearly what we are doing.

In scientific language at its best, the importance of projection is clearly recognized and adequately indicated so that the listener is amply warned of it. It is not something that can be dealt with by rules of thumb. The person who is highly conscious of projection will tend to take it into account and to allow for it as circumstances require. Insofar as he does this, he is using language and behaving generally in a scientific manner, as the term *scientific* is here being used.

VENTRILOQUIZING

Closely related to unconscious projection is another aspect of prescientific language behavior. It is to be seen in a particularly interesting form in the case of Edgar Bergen and Charlie McCarthy, and as we observe this pair of echoes we have our most important lesson to learn from Charlie McCarthy. He exemplifies something that has been of crucial significance in the history of the race, and that is still of the greatest importance in the lives of all of us. He exemplifies what we might well call *ventriloquizing*.

To ventriloquize is to speak *as if* with the voice of another. One of the most obvious, important, and altogether amazing examples of this is to be seen in His Honor the Judge, who speaks as if with the voice of The Law. So successful is this particular sort of ventriloquizing that it seldom if ever occurs to us that the voice we hear is quite undoubtedly the voice of the Judge himself! What we see in the instructive case of Mr. Bergen and Charlie McCarthy is a burlesque reversal of this historic and gravely significant process: the voice of Charlie McCarthy is actually the voice of Mr. Bergen, but the voice of The Law is actually the voice of the Judge

Ventriloquizing has occupied and still occupies a major place in the bag of tricks by which we strive to solve our problems, individually and as societies. It is the trick whereby we speak, to ourselves or to those whom we seek to control, *as if* we were speaking with the voice of the Old Man. It is the trick whereby Authority, the authority of age and precedence, is exercised in the molding of the young and in social control generally. The great ventriloquizers who have shaped and who continue to shape our destinies are the Judge, the Priest, the Teacher, and the Parent. They speak as if with the voices of The Law, The Almighty, The Wise, and The Good. They represent the great cornerstones of the structure of our culture: the State, the Church, the School, and the Home. Together they amplify what we harken to solemnly as the voice of the Old Man.

It was against this grave and booming voice that Galileo raised his persistent and disturbing cry. It was as though, in Galileo, humanity struggled with new vigor against the stifling forces of tradition. And the rise of the state in certain parts of the world in our own day serves to remind us that it was in the same period, since Galileo, the period in which the individual found new and powerful methods of self-assertion in the techniques of science—it was in this same period that the individual found, also, new and powerful methods of self-assertion in the techniques of democracy. In a general sense, there has been going on a great cultural change in which the individual has gradually gained a measure of independence from the Old Man—a revolution in which, as it were, the wooden dummy has mutinied and now willfully distorts and suppresses the voice of the ventriloquist.

Some men have learned, for example, that the voice of the Clergyman does not come from beyond the North Star but from the Clergyman's own throat. It is no doubt, in many cases, the voice of a kindly man from whose words a degree of wisdom may be distilled. Some men have learned, too, that the voice of the Judge belongs to the Judge, that what he speaks of as The Law is, at bottom, the voices of other judges not altogether unlike himself and mostly long since deceased. And although we have not all kept pace with George Bernard Shaw, who once declared that any child who believes what his teachers tell him is an ass, we have for the most part learned to wonder at the Teacher who, for $3000, instructs his students, as if with the voice of Wisdom, how to make $50,000. Nor is it to be overlooked that in these latter years the Parent has tended to become less the patriarch and more the companion, awkward, perhaps, but yet becomingly humble.

In brief, some men, increasing numbers of them, have seen the trick in ventriloquizing. For them, the voice of the Old Man has come to sound for all the world like the voice of Mr. Fosdick, of Felix Frankfurter, of Robert Hutchins, and of just plain Dad. It is getting to be a bad day for oracles. Of the ventriloquizers, of the voice of the Old Man, the children of science ask, without awe, "What do you mean?" and "How do you know?" And when the ventriloquizers roar their answers, as if with the voice of the Old Man, the children of science reply with unnerving calm, "Let's see." The children of science are from Missouri.

Ventriloquizing is usually an unconscious process, but it may be done deliberately by men who know quite well what they are doing. In fact, since the time of Aristotle it has been honored as an art and it has been taught in the universities as a part of rhetoric. In the principles of rhetoric, as Aristotle formulated them and as they are still taught for the most part, an important place is given to what is called "ethical proof." Now, what teachers of rhetoric mean by ethical proof is largely what we mean here by ventriloquizing. To present ethical proof of a statement is to show that it keeps good company and has good parents, so to speak. That is to say, for example, an American political speaker presents ethical proof of his views by declaring them to be the views of Washington and Lincoln and the very essence of sound American policy. He speaks, thus, as if with the voice of the Founding Fathers and of Great American Statesmanship. As the advocates of Aristotelian ethical proof contend, it works. Indeed, it does. In a prescientific society ventriloquizing is an amazingly successful language technique. An effective speaker is able to make the illusion stick for most listeners, to create the impression that his own voice is actually the voice of another whom the listeners accept as Authority.

It is in advertising that the technique is especially easy to observe. The advertiser knows that we are not likely to pay much attention to his voice. Who is Frederick P. Chumberwaith to us? So he speaks to us as though with the voice of Mrs. Martin K. Vandevan, III. He shows us a colored picture of her in a lovely evening gown, saying, "I smoke Whiffies all the time. They're so exceedingly genteel." Now that doesn't sound like Fred Chumberwaith at all. But it's he, all right. He put the words into Mrs. Vandevan's mouth—or, more accurately, under her photograph.

In thoroughly scientific language behavior there is, of course, no ventriloquizing. Whether as speaker or listener, the scientist, conscious of projection in himself and in others, realizes very well that the voice of the Judge is indeed the voice of the Judge himself. The scientifically oriented person understands that what the Judge calls the voice of The Law is simply the Judge's own interpretation of the facts of the case at hand and of statements that other men have made. He understands, further, that what the Judge does is to project his own interpretation into the mouths of other men more highly regarded than himself or even into an Institution that is somehow above and beyond mere men. The illusion thus created is that it is these other men who are doing the speaking, or that it is the great Institution making itself heard.

It is as though Edgar Bergen were to project his voice so effectively into Charlie McCarthy's mouth that people would quite forget that it was Edgar Bergen who was doing the talking. Most of us do not entirely forget this in the case of Bergen and McCarthy. But some people do—some people actually send Charlie flowers and candy and holiday greetings! Practically all of us, however, revere The Law. A scientific person, of course, respects the *laws*. He holds them subject to revision, but he respects them until they are revised. He regards them as necessary in social organization. He understands, however, that they are man-made, and that if they are to be revised, as frequently they must be, men will have to do it. He realizes that The Law, on the other hand, as something beyond men and which men have not created, is a sheer illusion, a semantic by-product of unconscious projection. He realizes that such illusions as this are a characteristic product of ventriloquizing. This is part and parcel of his clearheadedness.

PREDICTION AND EVALUATION

In our discussion of what science involves, we have one more fundamental point to cover. This has to do with the ultimate objective of science. Whether in the laboratory or from moment to moment in everyday life, what one aims to accomplish through scientific method can be summarized in one word: *prediction*.

Here again it is easy to see that science, viewed in terms of its main objective, certainly need not be confined to the laboratories. Relatively accurate and dependable prediction is as much to be sought after in the town hall or the living room as it is in connection with test tubes or condensers. Certainly the objective of science is essentially the objective of any attempts we make to achieve personal and social adjustment. In this respect, as in so many others, science and sanity merge.

Accurate prediction is important for two outstanding reasons. The first is that it serves as the basis for any *control* we may gain over the processes of nature or over our own personal and social development. The second is that prediction is the basis of *evaluation;* a theory or policy is "good" insofar as it enables us to predict accurately, and thus prepare effectively to meet coming events. As a matter of fact, the ability to predict, or what we commonly call foresight, makes up a very great share of all that we usually mean by intelligence.

Scientific method, then, is specifically and deliberately designed and used not only to explain events that have already occurred, but also, and more importantly, to predict events that have not yet occurred. The purposes, the procedures, the lines of interest, the terminology, the attitudes—in fact, everything about a scientist, as scientist—makes sense, clearly and systematically, only in relation to this primary objective of science as method.

What is there about scientific method that makes it peculiarly useful as a means of achieving predictability or foresight? We have already answered this question in general terms. Science makes for predictability because, first of all, it expresses, as we have emphasized, a "set" to recognize change and differences, a "set" that makes for alertness and adaptability. Beyond that, science represents a respect for the authority not of mere age or tradition or vested interest, but of systematic observation, of tested assumptions and evaluated experience. Moreover, and this is extremely important, the language of science is aimed at precision. Its questions are factually meaningful, as are its answers, and its general theories are grounded securely in these factually meaningful answers. The scientifically oriented person operates efficiently with such a language because he is highly conscious of his own self-projections, allows for them, and avoids deceptive ventriloquizing.

It is by means of his carefully drawn general conclusions, his theories and assumptions, that the scientific person is able to make his predictions. These theories and assumptions tend to be reliable because they are developed through a careful study of their usefulness. The scientist's theories are "good" simply because he is constantly revising them, bringing them up to date. He would rather be right than steadfast. Therefore he does not defend his theories, he tests them. He makes predictions on the basis of them, and then carries out the necessary observations in order to evaluate the theories by finding out how "good" his predictions were. They are practically never perfect, so he is practically never satisfied. Consequently he changes his theories, then makes new predictions, and again checks to see whether they were better than the earlier ones. So he goes, from youth to old age, never stopping at any point to exclaim, "Here is Truth, final and absolute!" Better theories are achieved by those who do not worship old ones.

BEHIND THE WATCH FACE

Now, in some of their more general theories scientists employ terms of a special kind. These terms do not refer to anything that can be seen, heard, touched, tasted, or in any other way observed. They refer to what are called "constructs." A construct is something or some event that the scientist simply assumes to exist. He is not capricious about this, however. It is a matter of assuming something that he cannot observe, in order to explain what he does observe. This is a bit difficult to make clear in general terms; an example or two will be helpful.

Practically everyone, no doubt, has heard of electrons, atoms, and molecules. These are constructs. That is, no one has ever seen an electron and, as in the case of the purple cow, no one ever expects to see one. Scientists talk about "shooting a stream of electrons," and they discuss the speed with which electrons travel. They tell us that electrons make up atoms, and they speak, for example, of the mass of an atom. Incidentally, the mass of a hydrogen atom, as stated by Einstein and Infeld in *The Evolution of Physics*, is— careful now—0.000,000,000,000,000,000,000,0033 grams! From such remarks we tend to gain, if we and the scientists are not careful, the notion that electrons and atoms are rather like tiny marbles perhaps, that we might be able to see under a microscope. From the way certain physicists talk about "smashing atoms," it might be possible to conclude that it is more or less like cracking walnuts. After all, however, such language does not refer to anything real in the sense that little marbles are real. It refers to what are called inferential data—that is, particles and processes that are not observed and are not observable, but are inferred.

Why do scientists make such inferences? Let us go back to the year 1827 and look in, so to speak, on the famous Scottish botanist, Robert Brown. It was in that year that he made one of those great discoveries of the obvious that have so vastly increased our knowledge. One day in 1827, Mr. Brown was quietly looking at some pollen grains, peering down the tube of his microscope in order to observe their shape and size. In order to observe them better, he had placed the grains in a droplet of water. So there he was, deeply absorbed with his view at the bottom of his microscope tube— when it dawned on him that the grains were moving!

Now there is scarcely anything more perplexing, and sometimes unnerving, than the movement of something that is not supposed to be moving, and Robert Brown certainly had not expected his pollen grains to move about in the droplet of water under his microscope. It is not difficult for us to imagine his mingled uneasiness and restrained excitement as he tried one way and another to understand his strangely fitful pollen grains. He determined that the restlessness of the particles was not caused by any vibration of the microscope, or by currents in the fluid, or by its gradual evaporation. Then he wondered whether the particular pollen grains he was observing at the time might possess some unusual characteristic, but he found that other pollens behaved in like manner. In fact, he discovered that sufficiently small particles of any material presented the same agitated and incessant motion when suspended in liquid and viewed under sufficient magnification.

Robert Brown was not, as a matter of fact, the first man ever to observe this curious phenomenon, but he was the first one ever to *see* it. He was the first, that is, to "look twice," to become sufficiently curious and dissatisfied with his ability to account for it, to seek persistently for an explanation. But such an attitude is very rare in our culture, and it was not until about sixty years later that significant scientific attention was given, particularly by the Frenchman, Jean Perrin, to this peculiar *Brownian movement*. In recent years, however, it has been studied intensively, with results that have been of the greatest importance in the development of the physical sciences. Incidentally, it is an experience that one long remembers to see, as Robert Brown saw, this astonishing unceasing fitfulness of tiny particles in liquid under a microscope. Again by the way, the Brownian movement has been observed in liquid carbonic acid contained in a cavity inside a transparent quartz crystal, and it is assumed that in this particular instance it has been continuously active for millions of years!

If we contemplate Robert Brown's predicament for a moment, we shall begin to realize why scientists feel the need of constructs— the need of assuming some kind of processes that cannot be observed, in order to explain what they do observe. Robert Brown and the other investigators who followed him could in no way account for the movement of the little particles solely in terms of what they could actually observe. They could, and did, rule out several possible explanations. They ruled out the possibilities that the particles moved because of their own chemical composition, or because of their gradual solution or other chemical changes, or because of the intensity of the light under which they were being examined, etc. Moreover, they could get no adequate explanation solely from the information they gained by photographing the moving particles, studying the paths they followed, their speed, changes in direction, and the known conditions under which all this occurred.

The investigators found themselves in the position so aptly described by Einstein and Infeld in *The Evolution of Physics:*

> In our endeavor to understand reality we are somewhat like a man trying to understand the mechanism of a closed watch. He sees the face and the moving hands, even hears its ticking, but he has no way of opening the case. If he is ingenious he may form some picture of a mechanism which could be responsible for all the things he observes, but he may never be quite sure his picture is the only one which could explain his observations. He will never be able to compare his picture with the real mechanism and he cannot even imagine the possibility or the meaning of such a comparison. But he certainly believes that, as his knowledge increases, his picture of reality will become simpler and simpler and will explain a wider and wider range of his sensuous impressions.

"If he is ingenious he may form some picture of a mechanism which could be responsible for all the things he observes...." Such a "picture" is what we mean by a construct, or it may be made up of several constructs in some sort of relation to each other. Robert Brown needed such a picture of the "mechanism inside the watch" —inside the water droplet, as a matter of fact. Without it he was simply unable to explain why the pollen grains did not remain quiet. And in such a sense he faced the problem that confronts every man who attempts an ultimate explanation of any observable aspect of reality or life. This is true for the simple reason that whenever one sets out to observe any aspect of reality, one sooner or later reaches the limits of the ability to observe. After all, the human organism is very definitely limited in its observational capacities; and even with the most efficient apparatus we can devise, we cannot observe absolutely everything about anything. There is

always a limit beyond which all our sense organs and all our apparatus cannot take us. There is, in this sense, a *submicroscopic* realm.

What we call the history of human thought is, in its deeper sense,
a recital of the pictures that men have imagined in order to account
for reality, of men's notions concerning the unobservable in terms
of which the observed might be made comprehensible. We need not
be elaborate in examining the kinds of pictures men have formed,
but if we are to appreciate clearly the difference between a prescientific and a scientific orientation to life we do need to understand the main features of the two chief contrasting kinds of such
pictures, or theories, that underlie present day points of view.

The one, the scientific, is represented reasonably well by the notions, or constructs, that have been devised in order to account for
the Brownian movement. Briefly and in simple terms, the explanation is that the particles move about unceasingly because they are
being constantly bombarded by innumerable molecules, much too
tiny to be seen, and darting about at enormous speeds. Each particle tends to move in an irregular path, because the force of the
molecular bombardment varies, being greater now on one side of
the particle, now on another. According to the theory, larger particles suspended in liquid are also bombarded by the tiny molecules, but they do not move because a sufficiently large number of
molecules continually strike against all sides of such a larger particle, so that the force of the bombardment from one side is can-
celed, or equaled, by that from any other side at the same instant.

The ceaselessness of the agitation of the Brownian particles is
taken as evidence of the corresponding ceaselessness of molecular
activity in the apparently quiet fluid. The motion of the particles
which can be observed is interpreted as the effect of the motion of
smaller particles that not only are not observed, but which are also
unobservable—no one has actually seen a molecule, much less an
atom, to say nothing of an electron. (By definition, they vary in
size from largest to smallest in that order, molecules being made
up of atoms, and atoms of electrons.)

The major significance of the Brownian movement lies in the
fact that it serves as a particularly vivid, easily observable illustra-

tion of processes which are apparently characteristic of the physical world in general, including our own bodies. The theories which have been worked out to account for the Brownian movement, therefore, are assumed to have a *general* validity. That is to say, they are not merely theories of Brownian movement. They are *theories of reality*. The care with which they have been constructed, the tremendous number of precise observations by which they have been tested, the accurate predictions, and therefore the tangible achievements (such as radio, for example) to which they have led —all this gives to these molecular, or electronic, or quanta theories a remarkable security. There are many unsettled disputes, of course, as in science there are always open questions; but the basic theory that what we call reality, whether in the form of gas, liquid, or solid, constitutes a continuous process—this basic theory can hardly be impressively challenged by anyone.

It is this notion of process that is fundamental to a scientific orientation, whether in the laboratory or in everyday life. To be familiar with the details, the specific constructs, the interlocking definitions by means of which these constructs can be precisely tested against observation—to be familiar with all this is advantageous. (For a particularly interesting recent account of nuclear physics, see the official report of the development of the atomic bomb under the auspices of the United States government, 1940–1945, *Atomic Energy for Military Purposes,* by Henry D. Smyth, Princeton University Press, 1945.) A great fund of such scientific knowledge is not, however, absolutely essential to sane living. What is essential is a sure "feel" for process in whatever one has to deal with and in oneself. An elementary knowledge of electronic or molecular theory, in such general terms, at least, as we have used above in discussing Brownian movement, does give one a means of visualizing processes, and it also provides one with assurance that the whole process notion is essentially well founded. The most important thing is a generally dynamic orientation, a set to expect the differences and changes which continually occur in a process reality. With such an orientation one is better prepared and adapted for life in this "restless universe."

THE PLOGGLIES

The other main type of theory or picture of the "mechanism inside the watch," the prescientific picture, is entertainingly represented by a little story about the "plogglies." According to this story, there were once two very perplexing mysteries, over which the wisest men in the land had beat their heads and stroked their beards for years and years. But nothing came of all this. The two mysteries continued to plague everyone.

The mysteries were that whenever anyone wanted to find a lead pencil he couldn't, and whenever anyone wanted to sharpen a lead pencil the sharpener was sure to be filled with pencil shavings.

It was a most annoying state of affairs, and after sufficient public agitation a committee of distinguished philosophers was appointed by the government to carry out a searching investigation and, above all, to concoct a suitable explanation of the outrage.

One can hardly imagine the intensity of the deliberations that went on among the august members of this committee. Moreover, their deliberations were carried out under very trying conditions, for the public, impatient and distraught, was clamoring ever more loudly for results. Finally, after what seemed to everyone to be a very long time, the committee of eminent philosophers appeared before the Chief of State to deliver a truly brilliant explanation of the twin mysteries.

It was quite simple, after all. Beneath the ground, so the theory went, live a great number of little people. They are called plogglies. At night, explained the philosophers, when people are asleep, the plogglies come into their houses. They scurry around and gather up all the lead pencils, and then they scamper over to the pencil sharpener and grind them all up. And then they go back into the ground.

The great national unrest subsided. Obviously, this was a brilliant theory. With one stroke it accounted for both mysteries. The only thing wrong with it was that there aren't any plogglies.

The theories which we speak of as prescientific, or magical, may be regarded as plogglie theories. They are of many kinds. In general, however, and for purposes of rough differentiation, they may be divided into two types, those that assert that there are "big people" and those that assert that there are "little people" inside the "closed watch" of reality. The big plogglies are gods, demons, devils, various kinds of monsters, etc. The little plogglies are fairies, brownies, elves, gremlins, and other charming and lively creations of human fancy. These plogglies, big or little, are the spirits behind the "watch face" who turn the cranks that move the hands around the dial. They all have one very important quality: *they are not predictable.*

That makes them very useful—to those clever people, the witch doctors and medicine men, ancient and modern, who contrive to make use of them. In the first place, their unpredictability makes for the perfect alibi. No matter what happens, it can always be explained *after it has happened* by saying, as solemnly as possible, "Well, that's how it goes with plogglies." And to say that something happened because it was the plogglies' will that it should happen sounds quite all right to anyone who believes in plogglies and has been taught to understand that plogglies are like that and to have a proper respect for their impetuosity.

Among the most impetuous and most commonly invoked of all the plogglies are the ones we honor in the name of Luck. Of late we have taken to calling them gremlins; they are pictured in the comic strips as mischievous little men persistently bent on getting motors out of order, blowing dust in the batter's eye, rolling dropped nickles out of sight, and in other ways keeping life generally unpredictable. In another form plogglies flourished a few short centuries ago—and for some unenlightened people they still do—as devils. Robert Burton's *The Anatomy of Melancholy,* written in Shakespeare's time, is a detailed catalogue of sober beliefs, then current, concerning the demonic causes of insanity. He described the public torments to which the deranged were subjected and the horrible punishments administered to them on the theory that the devils by which they were possessed would be thereby persuaded to take flight. When such treatment failed, physicians and public officials excused themselves by saying more or less elaborately—or simply by letting it be taken for granted—that there was precious little to be done about devils. Apparently it occurred to very few besides Burton that the devils might be simply the physician's alibi.

It is this same quality of impetuosity, of not being very predictable, together with another very interesting and closely related quality which plogglies have, that makes them useful in another and quite practical way—useful, that is, to the medicine man. This other quality may be expressed by saying that their unpredictable impulsiveness is patterned along human lines. The plogglies are imbued with a sort of rarefied "human nature." Man has created them in his own image—by a process of unconscious projection.

The medicine man can argue therefore, as he does, that since plogglies are so humanly unpredictable and impulsive, it pays to take no chances with them. One can't be too careful. If there is anything that one might be able to do to get the plogglies to listen to reason and throw the next good corn crop one's way, so to speak, it wouldn't be a bad idea to do what one could. The medicine man knows how these things can be arranged—something on the order of taxes, or what in urban centers these days is called "protection." Nothing too forward or obvious, of course, for the plogglies are quite fastidious and there are only certain ways in which these things are to be done—rites, they are called, ceremonies or rituals. The medicine man has undergone arduous training in the performance of these ceremonies, and it is his business to perform them, always of course for a suitable fee or honorarium. So everything is arranged and every possible effort is made in order to get the plogglies to make things come out right. If the plogglies hold up their end of the bargain and the corn crop is unusually good, the medicine man gains prestige and a larger following—and a share of the corn crop. If the plogglies don't deliver, if there is a drought and the corn is hardly fit for fodder, it is the duty of the medicine man to point out that the plogglies plainly have been displeased with one's conduct, and that greater devotion and contributions are called for.

With plogglies, then, everything can be explained very satisfactorily—to anyone who believes in plogglies. There are many plogglies scurrying all around us today, although some of the modern plogglies are much more subtle than brownies, for example. One might say that they are more abstract. They are not always personified—that is, they are not imagined to exist as persons. Thus, they are not so definitely human-like, but they do have quite the same unpredictability, and interpretations made in terms of them are calculated to give one more hindsight than foresight. In this more modern sense, "heredity" is often a plogglie, for example, and sometimes "environment" is another, and between the two of them they lick clean the platter of human frailty and fortune. What cannot one explain by asserting that it *was* due to "heredity" and "environment"—until someone rudely asks, "Precisely what are you talking about?" "Human nature" is a plogglie on constant call by "wise" men busy interpreting the things people do to the people who do them. It is a peculiarly interesting plogglie in that it can't be changed, not by any amount of political and social reform, or of education, or of ceremony. It works out its relentless plot. It is "fate." It explains all human conduct very simply: Whatever people are going to do they are going to do; whatever they have done they have done; because that's "human nature" and you can't change "human nature." It is to this particular plogglie that Popeye pays his somewhat nasalized respects when he says, "I yam what I yam and that's all I yam."

We shall see more and more clearly that plogglies—that is to say, theories of the plogglie type—are consistent with our whole traditional prescientific culture. To anyone outside that culture, or to anyone among ourselves who has never entirely absorbed it, there is something almost unthinkable, however fascinating and amusing and tragic, about plogglies. But to those who have never stopped to evaluate such matters, who have accepted more or less without question the creeds, beliefs, methods, etc., which their fathers have passed on to them, there is nothing particularly strange about plogglies. In fact, it is difficult for them to see how we could ever get along without them. They are inclined to feel a deep distrust of anyone who does not believe in plogglies and who does not participate in the ceremonies by means of which the plogglies are allegedly appeased.

ELECTRONS AND BROWNIES

The most important difference between prescientific plogglies and scientific constructs lies precisely in their respective values for purposes of prediction. The plogglies give one a certain kind of hindsight. If one accepts the necessary assumptions, then it constitutes an explanation of a sort to say that it rained last night or that a child died of diphtheria because the plogglies, in some form, willed it and made it happen. But if, in an attempt to make it rain again or to prevent another child from dying, one indulges in a ritualistic dance or burns a candle, one performs not a technique of prediction and control, but a mere act of uncritical and unreflective faith. One indicates by means of such a ritual that one does not have and does not propose to develop a really adequate explanation.

In one sense, of course, plogglies and scientific constructs, such as electrons, are alike: they are both imaginary. No one has ever seen a plogglie. No one has ever seen an electron. Then why do electrons make for prediction, while plogglies do not? Because they are defined differently, and they are defined differently because we have different attitudes toward them. This is to say, chiefly, that the scientific person is highly conscious of the fact that the electron, for example, is the product of his own imagination, and he is clearly aware of the further fact that he projects it into reality. The prescientific person, on the other hand, is not conscious of the fact that the plogglies are the products of his own imagination, and so he projects them quite unconsciously into reality. Consequently, the scientific person controls his electrons, and the prescientific person is controlled by his plogglies.

The scientist therefore defines the electron, and his other constructs also, very deliberately. He says they have certain characteristics as to shape, size, internal structure, their relation to each other, their speed of movement, etc. He gives them the particular characteristics that they must have if they are to account for events which the scientist observes. But having defined the electron, say, he does not hesitate to change his definition whenever the events he observes cannot be accounted for in terms of electrons as he had already defined them. After all, he made the definition in the first place, and there is nothing sacred about it. He is perfectly free to revise the electron any way he pleases, in order to use it as effectively as possible in explaining reality. He forms a picture of a "mechanism inside the watch," such a mechanism as will explain the way the hands have been seen to move around the watch face. If now the hands begin to move differently, or if now he notices something about their movement that he had previously overlooked, he must, and he does without hesitation, form a picture of a different sort of "mechanism inside the watch." After many such revisions of his picture, his constructs, he can predict rather well how the "hands of the watch" will move for the next few minutes at least, if not for the next few days or even years.

Now, this is not at all the way the prescientific person carries on with regard to his plogglies. He does not revise his plogglies. He does not feel free to do so. He does not imagine that it could be done. He sees no point in doing it anyway. He feels no need for making better predictions; it does not occur to him that one can predict. So far as he is aware, the future is in the lap of the gods. He is resigned to it. All he knows or cares or understands of prediction is that the plogglies will be angry with him unless he does what he has been taught that the plogglies require him to do. Even though he does these things, of course, he may be punished for sins he wasn't conscious of committing, or he may suffer the wrath of the plogglies who have their own supernatural reasons for moving in their "mysterious ways their wonders to perform." With the prescientific person life is a matter of hindsight, hope, and dread —and always the hindsight is intended to be comforting and to make the dread more bearable, to make it seem even a little foolish and unnecessary, since "everything is for the best in the best of all possible worlds" anyway. Whatever may happen will be the plogglies' will; whatever has happened was the plogglies' will. Since nothing can be done about it, by definition, the most gracious way to behave is to be humble, patient, and uncomplaining and to remember always that things could be worse, that, in fact, by definition, they couldn't possibly be better. Thus, prediction is not achieved, because none is attempted. Plogglies are not supposed to enable one to foresee the shape of things to come; they are supposed to enable one to explain events that have already occurred, to explain them in the most consoling sort of way.

THE IMPORTANCE OF FORESIGHT

It is not altogether important, of course, that we fill our heads with details about the specific theories scientists have worked out concerning the various kinds of inferential, or submicroscopic, events in terms of which they make their seemingly uncanny predictions about the observable world. It is important that we realize that scientists do such things, that they work at forming pictures of the "mechanism behind the watch face." It is important that we understand that their scientific theories are in substantial agreement on the point that reality, including ourselves, is fundamentally a continuous process. It is important that we be able to appreciate this basic process in such common and practical terms as growth, development, decay, and changes of various kinds.

It is important that we realize that because reality is process-like it presents a never-ending series of differences to which we must adjust. We can predict generally that as we live from day to day we will change, the world about us will change, no two things will be exactly alike, and no one thing will stay exactly the same. It is this fundamental set that is important. Without it our predictions tend to lead us to expect a greater degree of constancy and similarity than tomorrow is likely to bring. The result is that we are frequently caught off guard, with consequences more or less grave, varying all the way from the tragedy of Pearl Harbor to minor annoyance at biting into an occasional bad peanut.

False knowledge and false assumptions make for false predictions. As we predict, so we adjust to reality. Whether we expect a given event to occur or not to occur ten years, or ten days, or ten minutes from now, or within the next split second, insofar as our predictions are in error we shall be unprepared for what actually does happen. Being unprepared, being in fact prepared for something quite different, the actual events will be disappointing to us, or irritating, or frightening—even disastrous at times. The emotions and conflicts involved may amount to definite shock, "nervous breakdown," etc., the effects of which may be lasting. Errors in prediction frequently of course incur physical injury, sometimes death. In the social realm they occasionally lead to depressions, widespread unemployment, international frictions, and wars.

Predictability then is not only the polestar of the scientist, around which revolve all his purposes, theories, and procedures; it is also the bedrock foundation of sanity, of adequate everyday social and personal adjustment. It is not to be implied that science, in its highly refined technical aspects, is to be mastered in its entirety before one is to be considered sane. What is implied is that science, as *general method* and as basic *orientation,* does tend to make for foresight and general adequacy in the behavior of individuals and of groups.

Two Worlds

By way of bringing together and high-lighting what we have considered in this and the preceding chapter, we shall list in parallel columns the main features of a scientific orientation, or way of life, as we have presented them, and the contrasting features of a prescientific orientation that has been dominant for many centuries and that is indeed prominent even today.

BASIC FEATURES OF PRESCIENTIFIC ORIENTATION	BASIC FEATURES OF SCIENTIFIC ORIENTATION
1. Fundamental notion of the static character of reality. A static reality involves essential constancy (there is nothing new under the sun). Main attention is given to similarities; differences are minimized or ignored. Consequently, the individual is not especially important except as he represents a type.	1. Fundamental notion of the process character of reality. A process reality gives rise to a never-ending series of differences. As much or more attention is paid, therefore, to differences as to similarities. As one important consequence, the individual is regarded as an individual, not merely as an example of a type.

2. Rigidity, or conservatism, the tendency to maintain established beliefs and habits regardless of changing conditions, is fostered by these basic notions of static constancies. Thus, traditions are cherished, and the authority of age and precedence is extolled, seldom challenged; experimentation is discouraged. The Old Man is honored and obeyed. As a result of all this, individual infantilism and social retardation are fostered.

3. The basic method of problem-solving, which we call authoritarian, involves mainly the practice of abiding by advice obtained from some vested authority, such as a parent, teacher, priest, or judge. Authority sometimes resides also in a book or code of rules. The pronouncements of such authority are not to be revised. This authoritarian method works in practice to maintain unchanged the traditional beliefs, customs, and rules of conduct. If problems are not solved, they are "explained" in terms of "fate," or "nature," or the "supernatural"; and toward the *language* used in such "explanations" there is a dominant attitude that is naïve and unreflective.

4. The language of a prescientific orientation is designed to control behavior by virtue of the vested authority it represents. If it is not clear, a properly appointed authority will interpret it, and his interpretation is to be believed. The validity of authoritarian pronouncements is not to be questioned. Statements of assumption and statements of fact tend to be regarded as the same.

2. Adaptability, a readiness to change as changing conditions require, is fostered by these basic notions of process differences. Thus there is a tendency to challenge authority systematically; to experiment, to test traditional beliefs and customs against actual observation and experience. The Old Man is respected, but evaluated critically. As a result of all this, individual and social maturity is stimulated.

3. The basic method of problem-solving, which we call scientific, consists of four main steps; (a) the asking of questions that direct one's (b) observations so as to (c) answer the questions clearly in such a way as to test one's beliefs or assumptions, (d) which are revised accordingly. Of these four steps, three (a, c, and d) involve mainly the use of language. This scientific method works in practice toward the continual improvement of specific techniques, refinement of beliefs, and "modernization" of customs and rules of conduct. If problems are not solved, new theories and methods are devised to solve them.

4. The language of a scientific orientation is designed to be factually meaningful, directly or indirectly, and clear and valid. It is intended to satisfy two important tests: "What do you mean?" and "How do you know?" Moreover, assumptions are sharply differentiated from statements of fact.

5. Prescientific language tends to make for questions that are frequently vague and quite often meaningless factually. Attempts to answer such questions give rise to misunderstandings and disagreements, to misinformation and misleading theories, with the result that predictability and foresight are achieved slowly, or not at all, and individual and social maladjustments are thereby fostered.

5. Scientific language is oriented around factually clear, answerable questions. Vague or meaningless questions are abandoned as being misdirective of human energy. On the principle that the terminology of the question determines the terminology of the answer, only clearly stated questions are tolerated. Because of this, mutual understanding and agreement are facilitated, predictability and foresight are improved steadily, and individual and social adjustment is thereby fostered.

6. In a prescientific orientation, the natural process of projection is carried out unconsciously (relative lack of "to-me-ness"). It is realized only vaguely, or not at all, that every statement conveys information about the speaker as well as information about whatever the speaker may seem to be talking about; and the degree of self-reference is largely ignored in evaluating the statement's factual significance.

6. In a scientific orientation, the natural process of projection is carried out with a high degree of awareness (consciousness of projection, or "to-me-ness"). It is realized that every statement conveys information about the speaker as well as information about whatever the speaker may seem to be talking about; and the degree of self-reference is reckoned in evaluating the statement's factual significance.

7. In a prescientific orientation, there is a marked tendency to speak as though with the voice of another (ventriloquizing). For example, the voice of The Law is not recognized as the voice of the Judge himself. The speaker tends to ventriloquize both unconsciously and deliberately (as in the planned use of "ethical proof"). Only the more artful and deliberate ventriloquizers seem to realize that, after all, it is their own evaluations that they are expressing.

7. In a scientific orientation, there is little or no tendency to speak as though with the voice of another (ventriloquizing). For example, the voice of The Law is recognized as the voice of the Judge himself. The speaker tends not to ventriloquize either unconsciously or deliberately; he realizes that what he expresses are his own evaluations—even though he may quote another man's words.

8. Accurate prediction, or foresight, is not a particularly well-recognized objective in a prescientific

8. Accurate prediction, or foresight, is a clearly recognized objective in a scientific orientation. The-

orientation. At least, theories and specific statements are not evaluated primarily in terms of their usefulness in making predictions. In a prescientific orientation there are, strictly speaking, no scientific submicroscopic theories; there are, rather, *beliefs* regarding the "supernatural." These tend not to be changed, because they are considered not as theories but as statements of fact. Faith in these beliefs and obedience to the authority which represents them— obedience expressed by participation in prescribed rituals, for example— are prized as the means of control over natural and human events.

ories and specific statements are evaluated primarily in terms of their usefulness in making predictions. The value of a scientific submicroscopic theory (such as a molecular theory of matter) lies in the accuracy of the predictions which it makes possible. Changes in such theories, as also in theories that do not clearly involve submicroscopic constructs, are made in the interests of more adequate prediction. Theories of high predictive value are prized as the means of control over natural and human events.

We may gain a clearer notion of what we mean by a scientific orientation or way of life by contrasting it in this way with a prescientific orientation or way of life. It is to be realized, of course, that we are referring here to science not as highly specialized and refined laboratory techniques but as general method. What technical laboratory science adds to the above features of the scientific orientation are, in the main, three things: (a) precision apparatus and techniques of measurement, (b) a high degree of control over the conditions under which the observations and measurements are made (experimental controls), and (c) quantitative or mathematical reporting and analyzing of the data obtained. These are *refinements*. They have made possible the highly developed sciences, such as physics and chemistry. They characterize science in its most efficient forms. But they are not to be mistaken, as they so often are, for the fundamental method of science. We cannot use these refinements to any important degree in our ordinary daily conduct, but science, as method, we can use from moment to moment in our everyday affairs.

Against this background, we shall now turn to a consideration of general semantics as a system of basic premises, general principles, and specific practical techniques. On the basis of our considerations of science as method, we can more clearly understand and more deftly apply general semantics, because it is a system which has been distilled from all that we signify by science. It is the scientific method reduced to simple and practical terms. It is science made teachable—even to children. In it we may hope to find a means to hasten the development of a scientific civilization, and a means to prepare ourselves for its problems and its opportunities.

PART III

Words and Not-Words
Outline of a General Semantics

THE WORLD OF NOT-WORDS

𝒥T HAS BEEN SAID BY MANY, AND IN VARIOUS WAYS, THAT the problems of knowing and of understanding center around the relation of language to reality, of symbol to fact. These ink marks over which your eyes are racing, these ink marks that we agree to call words, and these words that we agree to accept as "legal tender" for the exchange of information, by what magic, or by what humdrum rules, do they serve their strange functions? If you stare at a word long enough, it does indeed become, for you, mere ink marks, a peculiar pattern of lines. At first it looks as though it were spelled correctly, then you cannot be sure, and finally you are overcome with the feeling that to consider its spelling at all is to enter into the most entangled mazes of humanity.

Of course if you stare at anything sufficiently long and thoughtfully, as a calf stares at a new gate, it tends to appear at last as though it were utterly unaccountable. A great philosopher once remarked that the strangest invention in all history was that peculiar covering for the human foot that we call a sock. He had been looking at one for several minutes. There are times when it seems impossible, however, that any other human invention could be more astonishing and strange than a word—the word *sock,* for example.

One may wonder how words came to exist in the first place, and how they "get" their "meaning." One may wonder, as C. K. Ogden and I. A. Richards wondered throughout a sizable book, about "the meaning of meaning." And we can be sure that at least one would discover sooner or later that a word "means" something more than other words. People who are accustomed, for example, to look in a dictionary for the meanings of words proceed under a great delusion if they suppose that what they find in a dictionary is a word's full meaning. What they find is that the dictionary definition of a word consists of other words. Moreover, a dictionary is a closed system. In it, not only is a word defined in other words, but these, in their turn, are also defined in other words— and if you follow far enough this trail of definitions of words, you find that it is a trail that goes in a great circle, so that finally you make the enlightening discovery that the words are defined by each other. *Space* is defined in terms of *length* and *length* is defined in terms of *space, beauty* is defined in terms of *good* and *good* in terms of *beauty,* etc. When you have energetically explored a dictionary, what you know are words, and what you know about them are words, too. And if all you know are words, you are left with the question with which you started, the question of what words "mean"—besides other words.

The question is incredibly complex, and our stupidity has been expressed persistently in the unduly simple answers we have given to it. We can avoid a repetition of that stupidity, at least in part, by the easy means of announcing that we do not propose here to exhaust the subject. Our aims are modest. We are concerned chiefly with three aspects of "meaning": with the non-verbal *facts* which words represent, with the *evaluations* which they express, and with the *effects* which they have on those who hear or read them, including their effects on the persons who speak or write them. The word *blonde,* for example, may refer to a particular person, or it may be spoken in such a way as to express evaluations ranging all the way from love to disgust, or its utterance may lead to any reaction from cheery smiles to homicide. What *blonde* "means" according to the dictionary is something else again, and it is not our primary concern. It is the primary concern of certain other students of language, and the work they do is important. Moreover, there are many other ways of considering the "meaning" of a word. The problem is as profound and as intricate as the problem of humanity itself. Certainly we shall not attempt to exhaust it. Within the limits of our major interests, however, we shall deal with it in an orderly way.

WHAT IS A FACT?

Let us begin by looking briefly at the main steps involved in the seemingly simple process of Mr. A. speaking to Mr. B—the process of communication. First, there is a "fact," which is to say that something happens to stimulate Mr. A. He feels it and interprets it. He speaks, verbalizing his interpretation. In speaking, Mr. A produces sound waves which serve to vibrate certain membranes and fluids in Mr. B's ear. This sets up activity in Mr. B's auditory nerve, and so in his brain cortex, and then he interprets what goes on in his cortex. Finally he says something or does something—to which Mr. A in turn reacts, and then Mr. B reacts again to Mr. A, etc. This sort of thing has been going on among hundreds of millions of people for thousands of years, with the result that human society has been growing more and more complex. Mr. A talking to Mr. B is a very important matter. Around it center practically all our problems of human understanding and disagreement, of cooperation and conflict, of knowledge and stupidity, of peace and war.

Just what goes on when Mr. A speaks to Mr. B? We said that, to begin with, there is a fact. It is this part of the process that we shall consider in the present chapter. The basic question we have to examine is simply this: What is a fact? Propaganda experts, so-called, keep warning us about the dangers of what they call emotional appeals. They urge us to look at the facts, to insist on the facts, to keep our eyes on the facts. This advice is so disarmingly simple. It leaves so much to chance, takes so much for granted. Behind it lies the assumption that a fact is a fact, and that everyone knows a fact when he sees one. In the meantime, there are some very elementary considerations to be taken into account. One is that knowing the facts is impossible if one means knowing *all* the facts about anything. Whenever anyone advises you not to act until you know the facts, he puts you under a spell of inaction forever unless he indicates which facts and how many of them you are to know, because you will never know them completely. Then, too, what we call facts have a way of changing, so that yesterday's statistics become today's fairy tales. Furthermore, a fact appears different depending on the point of view; your facts are not exactly like those of someone else. Actually, one man's fact is not infrequently another man's fiction. This means, finally, that facts are, in important measure, a matter of social agreement. Unless these elementary points are clearly recognized, telling people to stick to the facts is usually a sure-fire way of getting them embroiled in hopeless argument.

If you would recognize a fact when you see one and make the most of it, there are, then, four things about any fact that you must be clear about: It is necessarily incomplete, it changes, it is a personal affair, and its usefulness depends on the degree to which others agree with you concerning it.

A fact is necessarily incomplete. There are definite limitations to our ability to observe the world about us, to say nothing of our ability to observe ourselves. There are certain air waves that we do not register as sound. There are energy radiations that we do not see, or feel, or in any other way recognize. In order to see beyond certain limits of magnitude we must use microscopes, and even microscopes have their limitations. In other words, we get only as much of the facts as we can with the sensory organs—and the magnifying devices—we have to work with. Beyond the directly observable lies the microscopic world, and beyond even that the submicroscopic realm extends to limits, if there are limits, that we can imagine scarcely better than a blind child can imagine the appearance of trees in autumn.

What we observe as a fact is necessarily an abstract, an expurgated version, so to speak, of something concerning which we can only conjecture. "If he is ingenious he may form some picture of a mechanism which could be responsible for all the things he observes. . . ." Thus, indeed, and inescapably, "in our endeavor to understand reality we are somewhat like a man trying to understand the mechanism of a closed watch" which he has no way of opening. So far we may go and no farther in our explorations of reality. Our "facts" are incomplete. The argument against intolerance and dogmatism is not, in the final analysis, a "moral" argument; it rests solidly upon the simple consideration that it is humanly impossible to know *all* the facts, or even all of any one fact. The carrier of dogma is deluded; he may or may not be "immoral."

We can know something, however. Facts change, and yet a semblance of yesterday remains in today's sounds and visions. Facts change, but sufficient unto the day are the facts thereof. Indeed change itself would appear to be the most important fact of all. Facts as we observe them are little more than quick glimpses of a ceaseless transformation—as if we viewed the separate frames of a moving picture without quite realizing that what we were viewing was, in fact, a *moving* picture. Looking closely at a motion-picture film we see that each successive frame is slightly different from the last. Just so, looking closely at a "fact" we see that it appears slightly—or markedly—different from time to time. The grasses grow, the fruit ripens, the boy becomes a man. A person, as we know him, is a kind of average, a fusion or blending, an abstract, of many different observations that we have made of him. Like the sting of a bee, each fact occurs but once. Because *facts* change, any one fact is unique. Actually, to say that facts change is to say simply that no two facts are completely alike. Generally speaking, however, all the facts within our range do not change so utterly or so suddenly as to leave us dumb with surprise. True, there are times when change takes us quite unawares; that is the basis of comedy—and of tragedy. But so long as we remain responsive to the fact of change itself, the ever-changing facts are not, as a rule, unnerving.

In a basic sense a fact is an observation. An observation is the act of an individual. So it is that a fact is a personal affair. After all, that is why a fact (considered as a personal observation) is necessarily incomplete: The individual who observes it is limited in observational capacity. And that, in part, is why a fact changes: The individual who observes it is himself changing continuously, and so he observes differently from time to time. To paraphrase

Heraclitus, the same man cannot step in a river twice. Having learned this lesson for the first time, we bewail our disillusionment, and having learned it well, we treasure our foresight. We do not merely discover facts; in some degree we fashion them. "The world as known to us is a joint product of the observer and the observed." The basic importance of the personal equation in what we call facts is illustrated in homely and effective terms in the following passage from the introductory chapter in the fifth volume of *Colloid Chemistry*, edited by Jerome Alexander:

Lest we be too confident of all our sensory knowledge, let it be recalled that Blakeslee and Fox demonstrated that the ability of persons to taste phenyl-thiocarbamid is heritable as a Mendelian recessive, and that even those who get any taste at all from it (about 70 per cent) describe it variously as bitter, sweet, salty, or sour. This indicates that there is a relativity of sense impressions. H. C. Moir tested sixty persons as to their ability to recognize by taste four simple flavors—orange, lemon, lime, and vanilla. Only one person had a perfect score. Five had records of over 75 per cent, but forty-eight failed to reach 50 per cent. Vanilla was variously identified as black currant, lime, apricot, greengage, damson, lemon, pineapple, orange, tangerine, almond, red currant, strawberry. Only a limited number of persons can taste sodium benzoate, and wide differences exist in the ability to detect and recognize such odors as verbena and to distinguish between wines. R. J. Williams reports (*Science*, Dec. 11th, 1931) that a man whose sense of smell appeared otherwise normal could not detect the odor of a skunk, while *n*-butyl mercaptan, the "perfume" carried by skunks, had no unpleasant odor for him. Laselle and Williams in attempting to identify a substance as creatinine, found it tasteless, though the literature states that creatinine is bitter. It was not until they had tried the sample on several others that they located someone who found it bitter. Since lean meat contains much creatinine (about 2 grams per pound), and soups made from lean meat contain extracted creatinine, we have another possible basis of differences in taste. Williams believes that the problem is associated with the more general one of individual metabolic idiosyncrasies, which crop up at times in medicine (*e.g.*, reactions to morphine, novocaine, iodoform) or in industry (reactions to cosmetics, "chemicals," etc.).

There is, indeed, no accounting for taste, unless we recognize the fact that it is an individual matter in a fundamental physiological sense. And the individual differences, great as they are to begin with, become tremendously confounded when the factors of training, or so-called psychological conditioning, are brought into play. What is true in this respect of the sense of taste is likewise true in varying degrees of all the other sense modes. Individual differences in sensory capacity in its various aspects have been heavily documented by scientific investigators in many laboratories. This is to say that a fact, as an observation, is a personal affair, to be trusted as such and not as a universal truth.

What this means, in practical terms, is that a fact is useful, or dependable, to the degree that other persons agree with you concerning it. (We are referring here, of course, to first-order facts, not to conclusions that might be drawn from them. One man's conclusions can be better than those of the people who disagree with him.) If the majority say something is green every time you say it is red, you had best take their word for it. If a doctor, two internes, and a nurse all agree that there are no grasshoppers on your suit jacket, you might as well quit trying to brush them off. Generally speaking, the larger the number of people who agree as to a fact, the more dependable the fact is.

This is to be said, however, with two qualifications. The first is that some observers are more reliable than others. If you were a factory personnel manager hiring inspectors whose job was to detect flaws in metal plates, you would not employ applicants indiscriminately. In a sample pile of 100 metal plates there might be 27, for example, that were defective as determined by ten experienced inspectors. An applicant who would find only 17 or as many as 36 defective plates in the pile would not be as reliable an observer as one who would find 27. Modernized factories use various kinds of so-called aptitude tests in determining the reliability of applicants for work requiring observational ability. The general principle underlying such tests is that the reliability of an observer is to be measured in terms of his agreement with other observers. Fundamentally, what we mean by a good observer is one with whom other observers of experience and established competence tend to agree. It is not necessarily true that one man's report of a fact is as good as another's.

Another aspect of this general point is that agreement in making observations depends in part on similarity in the conditions under which they are made. If you have a microscope and I have none, you may disregard my disagreements with you. But if I use the same microscope as you, our disagreements become important. Every newly discovered microbe, every new synthetic substance, every newly discovered fact of any sort is for a time known to only one person. No one else may dispute it simply because others have not observed it, so long as these others have not used the proper method for observing it. Its dependability as a fact increases, however, as more and more other persons do observe it. In fact, until it is observed by at least two individuals, it remains unsubstantiated. What all this amounts to is that some observers are more reliable than others, not only because of differences in ability to use the same equipment and techniques, but also because of differences in available equipment and technique.

The other qualification is that some observations simply cannot be verified *directly* by a second party. If I tell you that I have a toothache, you have to take my word for it so far as any direct confirmation by you is concerned. You cannot feel my toothache. Nor can I tell you the toothache; I can only tell you about it. How, then, is a fact of this sort to be verified? Indirectly. We commonly say, "He says he has a headache, but he doesn't act like it." Or "He says he has a headache, but there certainly doesn't seem to be any reason for it." Physicians distinguish two major types of condition of this kind: malingering and hysteria. When a person says that he is unable to hear, he may be deaf in the ordinary sense, but also he may be pretending (malingering), or he may be suffering from hysterical deafness. The proper examination methods give strong indirect evidence as to whether the condition is one or the other of these types. Essentially, if it can be shown that the accepted physical causes of deafness are absent and, further, that the person can hear, we say he is malingering—not only is he giving a false report, but he knows he is. If, however, the accepted physical causes are absent and the person cannot hear, at least not under conditions sufficient to demonstrate hearing in a malingerer, we say he is either genuinely deaf, or else hysterically deaf. Absence of the accepted or known physical causes of deafness is strong evidence that he is not genuinely deaf, of course, but there remains in such a case the possibility that medical history is on the verge of being made by the discovery of some physical cause of deafness not previously recognized. Generally speaking, hysterical deafness is the diagnosis made when, so far as can be determined, physical causes are absent and the person is honest in reporting that he cannot hear. What we mean essentially by saying that a person is hysterically deaf is that, although he has the physical equipment for hearing, he does not hear because of emotional conflicts which make hearing intolerable for him. The fact that, when the emotional conflicts are cleared, the person hears and freely admits it is taken as good evidence that he is not, or was not, malingering.

The report of any so-called inner experience—as of an ache, pain, itch, etc., that cannot be observed directly by a second party —may, then, be (a) reliable, (b) deliberately false, or (c) hysterical. Whether it is the one or the other has to be determined by indirect evidence. We accept it as reliable when it is consistent with the conditions and the behavior associated with it. Whether or to what degree it is consistent, and so reliable, depends, even in this case, on agreement among the persons who are in a position to observe its consistency.

With these qualifications granted, therefore, we may say that a fact is an observation agreed upon by two or more persons situated, qualified, and equipped to make it—and the more persons agreeing, the better.

The Process of Abstracting: Non-Verbal Levels

We have said, then, that a first-order fact, as an observation, is incomplete, an abstract of a fuller, more detailed reality which we can only partially observe directly. We have also said that observations made with the naked eye, as it were, can be extended by means of magnifying devices, such as microscopes, telescopes, high-speed cameras, etc. (We call these extra-neural means of observing, because they provide the nervous system with extra stimulation beyond that afforded by the unaided sense organs.)

A simple diagram will serve to summarize these statements. We shall begin by presenting only part of the diagram (Fig. 4), expanding it later and explaining it as we go along.

Macroscopic level of neural
    abstracting

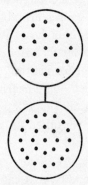

Microscopic level of
    extra-neural abstracting

FIG. 4.   Schematic diagram of macroscopic and microscopic levels of abstraction.

Figure 4 represents what we call facts in our common everyday speech. Facts, in this sense, are anything that we observe, anything that we see, hear, smell, taste, touch, or feel kinaesthetically, internally. Thus, anything from a hippopotamus to a microbe, anything from a fever to an itch, is a fact, as here diagrammed, so long as it is directly experienced. The diagram represents two levels of facts: the macroscopic, or level of direct neural observation, and the microscopic, or level of extra-neural observation. We refer to these as levels of *abstraction*, because, as we have said, observations are necessarily incomplete. They are abstracts, and observation is a process of abstracting.

We can make this more clear by adding a third level to our diagram (Fig. 5). The third, or lowest, level represents, in terms of Einstein and Infeld's analogy, "the mechanism inside the watch." It represents the reality that lies beyond the reaches of our observa-

tion, the submicroscopic realm, which we know only by inference.
That is why we refer to it as the level of *inferential* data. The word
data is important. It says that this submicroscopic realm is to be
regarded as factual. From a scientific point of view, we talk about

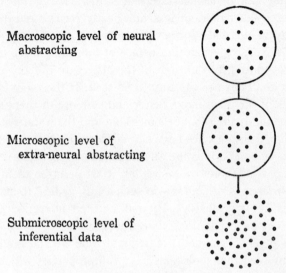

Macroscopic level of neural
  abstracting

Microscopic level of
  extra-neural abstracting

Submicroscopic level of
  inferential data

FIG. 5.   Schematic diagram of non-verbal levels of abstraction.

it in terms of atoms, electrons, etc., and our talk does not express
mere fantasy. With it we make the best sense we can.

Suppose, for example, that you fill a glass with water and leave
it on your desk. Now, you can observe the water in the glass just
as it stands there, or you can place a droplet of it on a glass slide
and view it under a microscope. On the basis of such observations
you can say certain things about the water, and you will be "talking facts." One of the observations you will make, however, if you
leave the water on your desk for a few days, is that the amount of
it decreases. The glass does not leak, nobody drinks from the glass,
you do not see the water leave. Yet it gradually disappears. You
say this is a fact. You call it evaporation. If you are ingenious you
may form some picture of a mechanism which could be responsible
for evaporation. Scientists have done so—in submicroscopic terms.

Of course, you might "explain" evaporation in terms of unpredictable plogglies. Scientists explain it in terms of a molecular theory of matter. They *infer* that what we call water is made up of tiny particles in constant motion at high velocities. The particles, which they call molecules, are electrically charged so that they attract each other more or less, and partly for this reason most of them stay in the glass for several hours. A certain proportion of them, however, approach the surface of the water while moving at terrific speed and fly right out of the glass into the air. You don't see them go. They are too tiny to be seen. If the room is hot, the molecules in the glass move faster and so more of them fly out of the glass; and if the room becomes cold and the water freezes, this means that the molecules have slowed down a great deal and very few of them escape into the air. In other words, scientists do not merely say that there are molecules; they describe them—on the basis of inference, of course—in such a way as best to account for what they actually observe. By making their inferences this way, they can make predictions that would otherwise be impossible. With mere plogglies such predictions could not be made. Thus, having inferred that molecules have the properties which will account for increased evaporation at high temperatures, scientists can predict rates of evaporation at lower temperatures, or under different atmospheric pressures, etc. So often have scientists been able to verify predictions made on the basis of such inferences that they have built up elaborate dependable theories about the submicroscopic world of inferential data.

The development of the scientific theories which describe this vast submicroscopic world of inferential data is like a fascinating detective story serial, in many ways the most engrossing in our literature. It is the story of the creative imagining, later confirmed in many instances by actual discovery, not only of electrons, molecules, and atoms, but also of hormones, vitamins, antitoxins, bacteria, allergies. In the field of psychology the story has been worked out in terms of so-called unconscious conflicts, drives, wishes, and other mechanisms supposedly underlying our behavior. It has been worked out, too, in terms of motives, habit strengths, inhibitory states, and other inferential conditioners of learning and forgetting. From another direction the sleuths of science have moved in to discover chromosomes and genes, and so to write, paragraph by paragraph, the strange story of heredity. Growth and senility, health and disease, contentment and misery, genius and stupidity are understood today, insofar as they are understood at all, in terms not of facts in the ordinary sense, but of facts of an inferential kind.

In the most general sense, the submicroscopic realm is to be described in the dynamic terms of process, radiations, vibrations, a whirling dance of unobservable particles and wave motions. It is from this realm that we abstract the shadows and colors, the out-lines and tangible facts that we know so incompletely, and some-times misleadingly, through observation. And of these facts directly known to us, the most pervasive and the most dependable is the fact of change, seen as an interminable array and never-ending series of differences, which we can know from experience and by which experience teaches us, if we permit it to teach us anything. By observing the differences and predicting the changes in the world about us and in ourselves, we learn, as well as we can, how to form a picture of a mechanism that will account for what we can observe. By forming such pictures and by revising them as our predictions prove false and our new observations disclose our old mistakes, we achieve increasingly an understanding of the facts with which we must daily contend. What this amounts to is that the significance of a fact lies chiefly in the theory by which we seek to explain it, for the theory by which we seek to explain it de-termines the use we will make of it.

There was a time, not so long ago, when even in the western world men assumed that insanity, for example, was to be accounted for on the basis of spirits and devils resident within the body of the afflicted individual. The observable facts of insane behavior were doubtless much the same then as now. What we do about those facts, however, is very considerably different today, and the reason for this is simply that today we no longer assume the presence of devils. The demonic plogglies have been replaced—not merely eliminated, but replaced—by other forms of inferential data, and correspondingly the older cruel methods of dealing with the insane have given way to more humane and more effective procedures. Even today psychiatrists differ in their methods of treating "mental" disease, because they differ in the assumptions which they employ in trying to account for it. Roughly, there are two major points of view. There are those, on the one hand, who lean toward the belief that insanity is hereditary, or that at least it is due primarily to so-called biological factors. On the other hand, there are those who favor the view that "mental" disease is primarily a product of training, or environmental factors. These two general types of theory, or inference, tend to result in different examination procedures, the making of different sets of observations, and different kinds of treatment. All of which is to emphasize that the significance of an observed fact lies mainly in the theory, the ultimate submicroscopic data, by which we seek to explain it.

For everyday practical purposes the most important consideration is simply this: the observations we make are incomplete. They are abstracted from something—from what we have represented in our diagram as the submicroscopic level of inferential data. We had best be aware, at least, of this general level of reality. We had best try, however crudely, to picture to ourselves what we assume it to be like. And if our picture does not serve to predict and account for the facts we do observe, we had best revise the picture. These are the minimum requirements for any person who would seek to behave scientifically, and to understand, even in an elementary fashion, the world about him and his own reactions to it.

It is to be noted that in our diagram we have placed a larger number of dots, representing details, in the microscopic circle than in the macroscopic circle. This is intended to indicate simply that with the unaided eye, or other sense organs, we cannot observe many aspects of an object or phenomenon which do become apparent to us when we employ extra-neural means or special techniques of observation. Water observed in the ordinary way may appear motionless and clear. A droplet of the "same" water viewed under a microscope would not appear so inert. We might see tiny forms of life darting about in it, for example. And if we were to place a pollen grain in the droplet we might observe the strange Brownian movement that we discussed in the preceding chapter.

The facts of human behavior, of anger, or weeping, or laughter, viewed without reference to the factors, the inferential factors, underlying them, can hardly be understood at all. On the basis of ordinary observation, such behavior can be described more or less, of course. The conditions under which it occurs can be described also, and a kind of explanation of our behavior can be made in terms of the conditions under which it occurs—of the stimuli to which we respond. Yet our observations of the behavior and of the stimulating conditions are so woefully incomplete that we can hardly achieve any significant understanding merely in terms of these observations, as such. As a matter of fact, whether or not we clearly realize it, we seldom state explanations of our actions simply by describing those actions or their environmental settings. We go beyond the obvious facts and attempt to account for our behavior in terms of "human nature," "heredity," "divine will," "instinct," "habit," etc.—or, in a more modern scientific way, we speak in more adequately defined terms of physiological, psychological, and semantic factors, largely inferential. The consciousness of self, upon which personal adjustment ultimately depends, lies in a consciousness, a clear awareness, of the inferred factors, or assumptions, by which we try to understand ourselves. Unless we are clearly aware of these assumptions, we cannot be critical of them, we cannot test them and revise them so as to make them more useful in the prediction and control of our own behavior.

In order to test such an assumption, it is necessary to determine (a) how well it accounts for past behavior, (b) how well it enables you to predict future behavior, and (c) whether there are other factors or assumptions that make for better explanations and predictions. If, for example, you assume that your irritability in response to noise is hereditary, you will first of all recall as accurately as possible your past reactions to noise. Hereditary characteristics are, by definition, relatively constant. The pattern of your fingerprints, the color of your eyes, the texture of your hair are presumably hereditary features, and they vary hardly at all from minute to minute or from year to year. If your reactions to noise vary considerably, you can hardly account for them, or predict them, in terms simply of heredity. Further study may indicate that your irritability is a learned reaction associated with only certain kinds of noise. Or perhaps you will discover that you are made irritable by noise only when you are hungry. A medical examination may reveal that you have stomach ulcers. If so, the physician will probably prescribe some form of treatment. If the treatment works, any understanding of why it works will depend upon the assumption of some kind of physico-chemical processes, for a full account cannot possibly be given in terms of what can actually be observed.

Thus, an object, or event, or human reaction, as observed directly on the macroscopic level, may be regarded as an abstract of what might be observed on the microscopic level. This is to say that our eyes do not give us a complete picture of an apple or a pencil, or a fit of anger, for example. And, as we have considered, the picture we get even on the microscopic level is likewise incomplete. It is an abstract of whatever there may be on the submicroscopic level. In our diagram we represent the submicroscopic level with a broken-line spiral in order to differentiate it sharply from the other two levels. The broken-line spiral is also intended to indicate the relatively more dynamic character of the inferred processes as compared with the facts which we abstract from them by observation. Moreover, our notions concerning the inferential data are not fixed with finality but are constantly held subject to revision; and we assume that the submicroscopic events serve to generate the differences and changes in reality as we observe it. All this we represent by the open end of the spiral and by drawing it with a broken instead of a solid line. It is to be noticed, too, that there are more "dots" in the spiral than in the circle above it. This is meant to indicate that even on the microscopic level we do not observe, or abstract, everything. Certain details are necessarily left out.

FIRST-ORDER FACTS

What we have represented on the macroscopic and microscopic levels may be regarded as first-order facts. What we mean by a first-order fact is simply a reliably observed fact. Objects fall, trees have bark, paper burns: these are first-order facts. There is a delightful little story for children in which this line recurs many times: "That is the way ducks do." The main character is a little yellow duck that swims, sticks its head under the water with its feet in the air, and in general carries on "the way ducks do." To the question, *"Why* do they?" a rather sensible answer, on the level of observable facts, is, "That is the way ducks do." It is a first-order fact about ducks. It states a norm. Why do we breathe, and why do our hearts beat? In a practical sense—that is to say, on the macroscopic and microscopic levels—there is no *why* about such things: they are simply first-order facts. Life and reality, as we experience them directly, are matters of first-order fact. Our ultimate understanding of life and reality, however, is basically in terms of the inferential processes by which we strive to account for first-order facts. It is extremely important, therefore, that we do not confuse our factual data with our inferential data.

We began our discussion by referring to the process of Mr. A speaking to Mr. B. This common and frequently momentous process begins properly with a fact. This is a way of saying that the study of language begins properly with a study of what language is about. The understanding of any symbol depends in large part upon a knowledge of what it symbolizes. In order to understand language it is necessary to know, at least in general terms, what it may be used to represent. That, essentially, is what we have been considering in terms of the macroscopic, microscopic, and submicroscopic levels—the non-verbal levels of abstracting.

HOW THE LEVELS DIFFER

We shall add more parts or levels to our diagram in the next chapter. Up to this point we have diagrammed what we might call the world of not-words. We have sketched a schematic representation of "reality," of the "physical world," of observable sense data, and of unobservable inferential data in terms of which we may know about the world in which we live and also about the life processes going on within ourselves. This world of not-words may be observed, or known, or abstracted, on different levels, of which we have recognized three for the purposes of our diagram.

There are certain summary statements to be made about these *levels of abstraction:*

1. One level is not the same as any other level. As we built up the diagram, we considered briefly how the levels differ, one from another, and these differences, as stated, seem quite obvious, no doubt. It is very important, however, that in regarding them as obvious we do not also regard them as of no particular significance. Our disposition to take such things for granted, without considering their consequences and implications, constitutes an important aspect of the semantic disorders which we shall take up in later chapters.

Some of the clear implications of the fact that one level of abstraction is not the same as any other level are to be seen in an investigation of what occurs when this fact is disregarded. And it is disregarded not only by the primitive who reacts to the inferential ghosts of his ancestors as though they were objective, live, present creatures, but also by the so-called "modern" individual who refuses to eat eggs, for example, because he evaluates the submicroscopic *process* egg as if it were the same as the macroscopic egg which he sees, smells, and tastes rarely if at all. Some persons should not eat certain foods because they are allergic to them, but ordinary food dislikes are as good an illustration as one could want of the confusion of one level of abstraction with another—of the failure, that is, to differentiate the levels, and to *act* as if one knew that the sense-data levels were different from the inferential-data level. We shall return to this point later. It is sufficient for the present to say only enough to give some significance to the basic statement that one level of abstraction is not the same as any other level.

2. The lower the level of abstraction, the more detailed and dynamic, the more process-like does reality appear to be. Thus, as we go to lower levels we gain a more nearly complete picture; we approach what Einstein and Infeld mean by the "ideal limit of knowledge"—we approach it but never reach it. We never reach it simply because we are physically limited, and also because we are investigating a process when we investigate reality or any phase of reality; and before we could achieve *complete* knowledge of a process it would at least be necessary for the process to stop. But if we cannot achieve complete and final knowledge of the process which we call reality, at least the knowledge we can obtain can be kept relatively *up to date*. Moreover, an awareness, even a rough awareness, of the submicroscopic level of abstraction, as inferred by modern scientists, renders one less susceptible than one would otherwise be to believing all and only what one sees. To believe all one sees and that one sees all is to entertain sheer delusions. That such delusions may often be apparently harmless should not be permitted to obscure the plain fact that they are always potentially harmful and even disastrous. In certain "mental" diseases their effects are dramatically apparent.

3. Abstractions on all these levels are *unspeakable*. We can speak about them, but we can never transform them completely into words. A statement about direct experience can never be a duplicate of, or a full substitute for, the experience. Bite your tongue—not too hard. Now, try to *say* the feeling! Whatever you may say, the words you speak are not the feeling you speak about. The feeling, as such, is clearly *unspeakable*. This means, for example, that another person can never convey to us *all* that he feels, *all* that is occurring within him. He can only convey as much as words or other symbols will "carry." Therefore we can never be sure that we "know" how he feels. Recognition of this fact constitutes the very germ of anything we might call tolerance or humane understanding. Indeed, a consciousness of abstracting, as we shall see, gives a basis for a science of values, for adequate evaluation in social and personal affairs as well as in the physical sciences.

CONCERNING DEFINITION

With this, we shall leave the world of not-words for a moment, in order to enter the world of words. For this purpose we shall return to our diagram, and after we have completed the building of it, we shall have more to say about the levels of abstraction and the process of abstracting.

It will be noted that we have not yet attempted to give a concise, verbal definition of *abstracting*. We are not neglecting to define the term, however. We are defining it, as we go along, in terms of the diagram which we are constructing, and in terms of what we say about this diagram. As we proceed in this way, we shall come at last to a point at which we might be ready to consider profitably a brief verbal definition of *abstracting*, but when we are ready for it, we shall have little need of it. We shall know by that time, as well perhaps as words and a diagram can enable us to know, what *abstracting* refers to and what it implies. And when we know that, we shall find that we can discuss quite clearly and effectively an impressive variety of human problems, including our personal problems, in terms of the process of abstracting.

It is with this process that general semantics is fundamentally concerned. The principles of general semantics are statements of the normal functioning of this process; and what we call semantic disorders are the confusions and inefficiencies that result when these principles are violated. Philosophers and psychologists have dealt all through the centuries with the process of abstracting, but they have tended to deal with it much as the six blind men dealt with the elephant. They have tried to understand it from their respective points of view, each point of view being more or less limited to some one aspect of the whole process. Thus, for the most part, logicians have confined themselves to the study of word-word relationships, giving far more attention to the verbal than to the non-verbal levels of abstraction. Philosophers have traditionally stressed the importance of one part of the abstracting process to the exclusion of other parts, and by doing so, they have developed so-called schools of philosophy, devoting an appalling share of their time to quarreling with each other. Psychologists have tried to split up the process into "thought," "emotion," "feeling," "motor functions," "higher mental processes," etc. In the meantime, any such splitting would appear to be quite artificial and arbitrary, at best a convenience for purposes of study and discussion. So far as one can observe, the process of abstracting is an integrated, unitary affair; it is regarded as such in terms of general semantics. Its organization can be most clearly seen in the form of levels of abstraction. In the present chapter we have discussed the non-verbal levels. In the chapter that follows the verbal levels will be considered.

Chapter ᠁᠁᠁᠁᠁᠁ VI

THE WORLD OF WORDS

———

So THOROUGHLY DO WE TAKE SPEECH FOR GRANTED AS an exclusively *human* characteristic, so thoroughly do we take it for granted as a *personal* characteristic, that it scarcely ever occurs to us to "speak about speaking." We learn to speak, for the most part, without conscious effort, and by the time we are old enough to understand in any mature fashion those strangely powerful and direful noises that we call speech and that give us, somehow, control over others from a distance, it has become so much like reflex behavior, like breathing or chewing or coughing, that it hardly occurs to us that there is anything about it to be understood. Consequently most of us, by far, never do come to understand our speech in any deep or comprehensive manner. Mostly we just talk. As a noted professor once expressed it, "I seldom know what I am going to say until I hear myself saying it." Most persons could add to that that sometimes they don't know what they have said a moment or so after they have said it. A day after they have said it, it has, except for a few stray fragments, become lost in the mists of nomore.

One of the advantages of writing over speaking lies, as a matter of fact, in the increased awareness of language that writing involves. At least, language that is written is not so likely to be forgotten, and it is not so likely to be uncritically accepted, as is language "writ in the water" of speech. Certain primitive societies have managed to achieve rudimentary forms of culture and to survive for centuries without written language, but no advanced civilization was possible until the invention of writing and other methods of making more or less permanent records of symbolization, such as painting, geometry and other mathematics, etc. Professor John Dewey once declared that the invention of symbols was the outstanding event in human history.

Our world of words, to which we become so unreflectively accustomed, is indeed not something to be taken for granted. Our common belief that language is an exclusively human characteristic is for all practical purposes true, and precisely because it is true we have to face the fact that our problems, as individuals and as social groups, insofar as they are *human* problems, tend largely to arise out of the nature or structure of our language and the ways in which we make use of it. Whether we speak of our problems as economic, or political, or educational, or personal, we imply that they are to be described and understood and solved largely in terms of various methods of dealing with symbols.

The crucial point to be considered in a study of language behavior is the relationship between language and reality, between words and not-words. Except as we understand this relationship, we run the grave risk of straining the delicate connection between words and facts, of permitting our words to go wild, and so of creating for ourselves fabrications of fantasy and delusion. The importance of these considerations is heavily underscored by the fact that we obtain the overwhelming bulk of our information and convictions by purely verbal means. It is also to be recognized that by far the greater part of what we communicate to others in the form of language is not words about facts in a direct sense; rather, it is predominantly made up of words about words. Firsthand reports of direct experience comprise a relatively small proportion of the speech of most of us. Nevertheless, firsthand reports of direct experience must form the basis of our entire language structure, unless we are to live in a world of words that bears a gravely disordered relationship to the world of non-verbal reality.

This does not mean that our statements must always refer directly to immediate experience, to facts that can be pointed to or tangibly demonstrated. The referents of *electron,* for example, are not tangible things. The referents of *if, to, and, yet,* etc., are seldom very obvious. Just where does one usually find the referent of such a word as *ability?* One cannot, while speaking in Boston about rice culture in China, point to the referent of *China.* We should be as clear as possible about this. The "tyranny of words" does not lie chiefly in the fact that frequently referents for them cannot be found immediately in the form of solid objects or well-defined events. What is important is that *eventually,* by means of some sort of interlocking definitions, some rules for using one word in relation to another, we tie our statements down to first-order facts. These facts will not as a rule be observable at the moment they are referred to, but they should be observable in principle. Language is never so boring, however, or so ineffectual, as when it is kept on the level of sheer enumeration of first-order facts. In order to say anything significant, one simply has to rise above that level, and the higher above it one can rise the more significant one's remarks become—provided the steps taken in rising, so to speak, are taken in an orderly fashion and can be readily traced back to the level of factual data.

The relationship between language and reality is a *structural* relationship. For purposes of personal adjustment or effective social organization, the structure of our language must correspond essentially to the structure of reality. Structure, in this sense, can best be discussed under three headings: (a) degree of differentiation, (b) variability, or extent and rate of change, and (c) relationships among the parts (organization). In these respects, how does the structure of our language compare with the structure of reality? This is the fundamental question to be asked, from the point of view of general semantics, concerning the relation of words to facts.

LANGUAGE STRUCTURE: DEGREE OF DIFFERENTIATION

As we have said before, a fact occurs but once. This is a way of stating that no two things are exactly alike and no one thing remains exactly the same. It is a way of expressing the process character of reality. Thus, the structure of reality shows a practically infinite degree of differentiation.

The structure of our language, on the other hand, is much less highly differentiated. Even though the English tongue, for example, contains many thousands of words and many of these have more than one recognized dictionary meaning, yet we are far from having one word for each fact. Each word, and even each dictionary meaning of each word, must do heavy duty, representing a great number and variety of facts.

In this respect, then, there is a fundamental lack of correspondence between the structure of our language and the structure of reality. It is a lack of correspondence that makes for considerable difficulty. Much of our more apparent confusion is due to this simple fact: that there are more things to be spoken of than there are words with which to speak of them. A rather large share of our misunderstandings and disagreements arises not so much because we are constitutionally stupid or stubborn, but simply because we have to use the same words to refer to so many different things. Thus, the word *intelligence* has been used—and is currently used— to refer to a most bewildering variety of activities and assumed qualities. Discussion about intelligence therefore drips with controversy, invective, and obfuscation: animals have intelligence; animals cannot have intelligence; intelligence is hereditary; it is environmentally determined; the rate of mental growth is increased in an enriched environment, decreased in an impoverished one; it is not; intelligence is comprised of a general factor together with a number of specific factors; it consists of specific factors only; of a general factor only; it is mainly a verbal affair; its verbal aspects are relatively unimportant, etc. To ask innocently, "Just what is all this talk about?" is to cry into the teeth of a typhoon. Such a question, if recognized at all, is met by a gale of definitions and variegated examples. It is only by painstaking care that one might conduct an "intelligent" discussion of intelligence.

Moreover, what is called intelligence by one person may be called by one of many other names by someone else. The general principle in this connection is that not only may the same word be used to refer to many different things, but also many different words may be used to refer to the same thing. Two witnesses in a court trial, one five feet in height and the other six feet five inches, are likely to disagree, one contending that the suspect was tall and the other insisting that he was short. What is sauce to the goose may be soup to the gander. The deacon glowers when the alderman laughs.

The difficulties in communication—and in understanding—thus created are due, fundamentally, to the structural difference, with respect to degree of differentiation, between language and reality. So far we have considered this structural difference in its more apparent aspects. It has a still more serious form: our language, as used, tends strongly to be two-valued at best, seldom more than three-valued. That is to say, we deal largely in terms of black and white, good and bad, beautiful and ugly. Our language, in other words, tends to assume an either-or form, to provide for differentiation into only two categories. We talk, not always but often, and particularly in decisive matters, as though there were only two alternatives, so that anything must be classified as *either* A *or* B (the so-called law of the excluded middle). We pride ourselves on being willing to consider *both* sides of a question, as though a third, or even a tenth or a fifty-fourth, were inconceivable. Not infrequently, of course, we do recognize a third possibility: high, low, and medium; good, bad, and so-so. In such a case, our language assumes a three-valued structure. This makes possible a middle-of-the-road policy, the so-called golden mean. The view that moderation in all things is a virtue expresses the conviction that an either-or form of language is not conducive to wisdom. Many a man's claim to immortality rests fundamentally on his recognition of the undue limitations imposed upon us by a two-valued language, and his counsel that we avoid extremes by choosing a middle course, a third alternative. Even this slight break with linguistic tradition, however, has so far been achieved by few, and leaves most of us with a feeling of verbal awkwardness, at least in many situations.

In American politics, for example, a third party seldom makes a strong appeal. The great majority of the voters find it difficult enough to decide between two parties; a third complicates matters beyond the practical capacity of our common language. Our racial conflicts, to choose another obvious example, operate within the well-worn grooves of a verbal frame of reference within which people are sorted into opposing groups of black or white, Jew or Gentile, Catholic or Protestant, etc. In the first chapter we mentioned still another illustration of the practical consequences of our two-valued orientation: the personal maladjustments we tend to create for ourselves by restricting our self-evaluations to the two terms of "success" and "failure." In the meantime, reality consists of *degrees* of political belief, of "racial" or religious difference, of personal accomplishment. The actualities to be dealt with in political, or religious, or personal terms present a highly differentiated structure. Our inability to deal effectively with these actualities stems in no small part from our misguided persistence in attempting to order and understand an infinite-valued reality by means of a two-valued or three-valued language structure.

As we shall see in Chapter X, certain simple devices are used in general semantics to counteract in some degree the ill effects of this particular lack of structural correspondence between our world of words and the world of not-words.

LANGUAGE STRUCTURE: VARIABILITY

All our words are in some measure "abstract" or generalized. In part, as we have seen, this is because there are at any given moment more facts than there are words with which to refer to them. The word *chair,* for example, names no one unique object, but a very large array of objects. Even such a supposedly exact term as *$10.51* does not specify *which* $10.51. The "abstractness" of our words is due to another reason, however. This other reason is the difference between language and reality with respect to the variability of structure, or rate of change. Reality is process-like; language, by comparison, is static. The world in which we live and we who live in it change faster than does the language we use to speak about our world and ourselves. So it is that words become generalized because the conveyer belt of time brings under their spell a changing inventory of "meanings."

Even a proper name, such as *National Broadcasting Company,* which we may at first glance take to be unambiguous on the ground that there is only one National Broadcasting Company, is seen on closer examination to refer to something different every day, every hour, every minute. Your own name signifies something at least slightly different every time it is used by you or by anyone else. These considerations become particularly important with reference to the pronoun *I*. "I was a shy and homely child" involves, as it stands, a fantastic misstatement of fact. I_{1946} never was a child. It was I_{1910} who was shy and homely. Certainly I_{1946} and I_{1910} are not the same. When *I* is used without a date, however, it tends to express identity, or lack of difference, between clearly different stages of a growing, changing individual. This is one of those perfectly obvious things that we so commonly overlook. When we do learn to take it into account, it is impressive how often we find beneath a festering point of personal maladjustment an unqualified, undated, generalized personal pronoun.

It is true that with the passage of time our language changes in some degree. That is why dictionaries are revised and brought more or less up to date occasionally. A perennial complaint of the older generation is that the younger generation is vulgarizing the language, is rudely deficient in respect for the mother tongue. Even the imposing and reverently preserved bulwarks of Shakespeare, the King James version of the Bible, Wordsworth, and Matthew Arnold do not completely stay the tide of linguistic innovation. The teachers of English struggle valiantly against an avalanche of jive. Migrations and wars, conquests and colonizations, new experiments in government, increased diversity of industrial and professional pursuits, and the rise of the sciences have all served to introduce new words and to alter the sense of old ones. In each professional field with which I am associated there are one or more special dictionaries, and as this is being written still newer glossaries are being compiled; and each of these will be, on its date of publication, in some measure out of date. If Benjamin Franklin could return tomorrow to Philadelphia, not only would he see all about him the imprint that he long ago left upon the city, but he would also find, even in the pages of his own *Saturday Evening Post*, a vocabulary strange to his tongue.

Yet it would not be the language of Philadelphia that would seem most strange to Benjamin Franklin, were he suddenly to re-appear in its streets tomorrow. What he would find most unfamiliar would be the responses of the people to their new language—and to the old terms once known to him. The general countenance of the city, the activities of its inhabitants, their tools, their aspirations, from these he would gather most clearly the impression of being in a foreign land. Even the loaf of bread under his arm would be dif-ferent from the one he carried in the Philadelphia of the pre-vitamin eighteenth century. Our language in its codified forms changes at a tortoise pace compared to the hare-like transformations of ma-terial and social reality. In driving his third automobile, my father still said, "Giddap" and "Whoa." In 1946 jitterbugging is essen-tially a mystery to people who call it dancing. Under the spigots of cultural evolution the old categories bulge, spill over, and collapse.

Viewing reality through the lenses of language we get at best a blurred and jerky picture. Against a misty background a few bulky shapes appear, and as the winds of living history play upon the mists the shapes seem suddenly to change, or they disappear and new ones come into view. But it always takes us some time to see the changes; it is as though we remain unaware of them until some time after they have occurred. We experience an irregular series of greater and lesser surprises, for astonishment is only the child of miscalculation imposed by words which have come to imply what no longer recurs. The moving finger of actuality writes faster than the tongue can herald. The structure of language is less fluid than the structure of reality. Just as the thunder we hear is no longer sounding, so the reality we speak about exists no more.

Maladjustment, for the individual or for society, lies in mis-taking the verbal record of the past for the description of the present. Because the words we speak today are quite the same as the ones we spoke yesterday, we tend to create the illusion that what we speak about is also quite the same. It can be serious enough when change takes us by surprise; what is even more serious is to have change escape our notice entirely. That is the condition of persistent delusion. There is a theory that schizophrenia in the adult consists of a reversion to childhood modes of behavior. What would seem to be a more apt statement of the case is that the disorder lies in a failure to recognize and take into account the changes that constitute the passage from childhood to maturity. There are maladjusted individuals—and societies—who live as though they looked upon the present as a temporary deviation from the past. Their norm being as of yesterday, they treat the here and now as though it were a condition of abnormality. The new wine sours in their old bottles.

The essential forms of our language were devised by ancient men who were remarkably unfamiliar with present-day knowledge. The pictures they imagined of "the mechanism inside the watch" appear today as a fanciful mythology. Because they had not been driven to assume the superdynamics of the submicroscopic realm which we accept, the world in its visible aspects seemed far more static to them than it does to us. In devising our language, they created a world of words that implied a relatively static world of not-words. That language, still with us so far as its basic structure is concerned, still plagues us. It is reflected in our institutions, our customs, our common modes of conduct and evaluation: we prepare ourselves rather better for a history that might repeat itself than for brave new days.

It is one of the purposes of general semantics to stimulate basic revisions in our language structure, revisions that will provide for evaluative reactions of greater adjustive value in a world which we now know to be far from static and unchanging. These revisions will be discussed in the chapters that follow, particularly Chapter X.

LANGUAGE STRUCTURE: ORGANIZATION

As we have seen, a structure may be described in terms of its degree of differentiation (number of parts) and its fluidity or rate of change. It may be described also in terms of its organization, the relationships among its parts.

There are a few very important features of the organization of our language which all of us have learned from our grammar books. Of course, we learned them as grammar and perhaps we find it easier to recall the distractions of the classroom than the details of the lessons. For our present purposes, however, memory need not be unduly sharp and clear. It will not be difficult to recall that in our grammar books words were classified, in part, as nouns and adjectives, as verbs and adverbs. One of the verbs was *to be,* which took the forms of *is, was, were,* etc. These particular few details of grammar are the ones that most concern us here. In fact, a large part of what we have to say with regard to the organization of our language structure can be illustrated by the simple statement: "John is smart."

We classify *John* as a noun, *is* as a verb, and *smart* as an adjective. To put it simply, a noun refers to a thing, an adjective refers to a quality of a thing, and a verb refers to a relationship between a quality and a thing, or between one thing and another. Now, one might take off from this modest beginning and whirl away into an elaborate dissertation on the intricate complexities of grammar, but this will not be necessary for our purposes. In keeping it simple, however, we should appreciate the fact that a tremendous number of details are being left out of account. They are being left out only because they are not crucial to our discussion.

To say that *John* is a noun is to say, according to the traditional rules of language usage, that John is a thing of some sort. To say that John is smart, and to say that *smart* is an adjective, is to say that smartness is a quality of John. This leaves *is* implying a relationship of inclusion, or possession: the smartness is possessed by John, or is included in him. This sort of language structure implies that reality is made up of things that possess qualities. In other words, the qualities—the colors, shapes, odors, etc.—*belong to the things.* The ancient men who devised our language doubtless regarded this as a "self-evident" truth. They probably constructed the kind of language they did simply because they took for granted that just such a language was needed in order to give a true account of reality. So far as they could see, it was true that reality consisted of things with attributes.

So it was that a great delusion came to be embedded in the very structure of our language so that, simply by using the language, we maintain the delusion, working it continuously into our beliefs and attitudes, our habit systems, our institutions and culture patterns. Probably this was not emphasized, perhaps it was not even mentioned, in your grammar book. It is likely that you were, as I was, permitted to acquire the uncritical view that grammar is a fact of nature rather than a creation of human beings. What impressed us most when we were school children was that the more "correctly" we used grammar, the better marks we got. It escaped our notice, in all likelihood, that using grammar "correctly" might involve certain disadvantages. We should be clear on the point, however, that the errors made by our teachers, innocent of them as they must have been, were errors chiefly of omission. It was not that we were taught too much grammar; rather, we were not taught enough of it. We were not brought up to date.

We were not made sufficiently aware of the fact that, contrary to the incomplete grammar books, reality does not consist simply of things with attributes. The relationships that characterize the structure of our common language are not altogether like those which characterize the structure of reality. The ancient wise men notwithstanding, the sort of language that appears to be needed in order to represent the relationships to be found in the world of not-words is one which expresses a space-time order among facts, and between the observer and the observed, between the speaker and what he speaks about. To put it quite simply, the venerable designers of our language left out of account, in large part, the human beings who were to use the language. And in conceiving of the nature of reality they overlooked the part which they themselves played in abstracting it. They were like a potter who bows down before the idol he has made with his own hands, forgetful that he himself has fashioned it. Even today we continue to revere the semantic apparitions molded in the contours of our verbal forms.

"John is smart" leaves out of account, or seems to deny, two very important considerations. One is that the smartness is not entirely *of John;* it is "a joint product of the observer and the observed." The other is that *John* and *smartness* properly represent, respectively, not a thing and a quality of that thing, but a comprehensive on-going series of events (John) and some part of that series (the smartness). It is not to be proposed that we abolish nouns and adjectives and *is.* At least, I shall leave that to someone far less impressed with the forces of tradition than I am. It is rather to be suggested that in using our language we remain aware of its structural implications, and where they tend to mislead we avoid being misled by seeing steadily those facts which the language would obscure and distort. In saying, "John is smart," let us remember that we are not simply calling attention to a quality of John; in part, we are reporting our personal evaluations. The same consideration holds when we say that John is good or that he is wicked. In judging others we express to an important degree simply our own standards of judgment.

We run a slighter risk of delusion, of course, if we replace *is* with certain other verbs. When, for example, we say, "John appears smart," we more definitely indicate that, in part, we express a private judgment. If, to go further, we say, "John appears smart to me," we indicate still more definitely that the judgment is personal and not necessarily universal.

Our language is made still more adequate if we replace *smart* with other terms more nearly descriptive of John's behavior. Thus, what is to be communicated is more clear if we say, "John scored an I.Q. of 140 on Form L of the 1937 revision of the Stanford-Binet intelligence test yesterday," or "John is only eight years old and he can name and locate all of the forty-eight states." It is simply a matter of being more or less clear. Adjectives like *smart, good,* etc., tend to imply qualities of things and to fall into a two-valued usage, and so what they imply in the way of events or behavior is not always apparent. It is with an appreciation of this fact that they are to be used.

One further point is to be emphasized. "John is smart" tends to imply something about John besides his alleged smartness. As it stands, the statement strongly indicates that John is always the same. Nothing is said about when, where, in what respects, or from what point of view John is smart. One is left with the implication that John is smart all the time, everywhere, in all respects and from any point of view: John is John. Beneath the particular words used we see the basic structure of identity: A is A. In the meantime, John $_{today}$ *is not* John $_{yesterday}$. John playing tennis is not John computing his income tax. What is meant by *John* depends in some measure on who speaks the word and on who hears it; it depends on time, place, and circumstance. *John* refers ultimately to a series of events. To the extent that this is appreciated and reflected in our statements about John, they tend to imply and create more and more effective understanding.

LANGUAGE STRUCTURE: SUMMARY

The problem that is posed by these remarks is essentially that of making our language sufficiently expressive of differences and change, in a shifting structure of where-when relationships. In no small part the formula of effective writing and speaking lies just here. Illustrations are to be seen in the characters created by such writers as Shakespeare, or Anatole France, or Joseph Conrad. Representative as his actions may be of experiences that are in some form almost universal, there is only one King Lear. There is only one Hamlet, one Lord Jim, one Thaïs. These characters are great in a literary sense because, while we feel that we share their experiences, we know that we do not duplicate them. They are neither types nor caricatures. They have the unique significance of individuals. The language in which they live serves not only to make clear what we have in common with them, but it also accentuates the differences between them and ourselves, between each of them and any other characters we might imagine or encounter in the flesh. Hamlet as an individual, a responsive, motivated individual, with ever-changing relationships to other individuals, is a linguistic achievement of high order. What he means to you is necessarily different from what he means to me, and what he means to either of us differs from time to time. That, in part at least, is what we speak of as the genius of Shakespeare. There is more to it than that, of course; there is more to it than we can say with any certainty.

The language of science in its more highly developed forms illustrates quite as well or better than the language of great literature the fundamental importance of the structural features we are discussing. Regardless of the fields in which they work and of the specific techniques which they use, scientists employ a language which expresses relationships that reduce to the data of differences and change. Theirs is the language

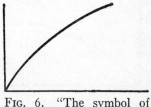

FIG. 6. "The symbol of science."

which, more than any other, corresponds in structure to the known structure of reality.

The essential structure of the language of science can be represented by a very simple diagram, one that is familiar to all of us. We may regard it as a universal symbol of science and of the scientific way of life. It may one day supersede the many other symbols by which men have tried for so long to focus their energies and fashion their wills. The many forms that it takes may be reduced, for symbolic purposes, to that shown in Fig. 6.

Let us call it the sign of the curve. It is to be found in the textbooks of all the sciences. It represents what any scientist strives to express: a variation of one kind, a variation of another kind, and the relationship between them.

In order to discuss it as clearly as possible, we shall present it in a slightly more detailed form (Fig. 7).

Along the x axis, or ordinate as it is called, we represent differences, or variations, or changes, or successive increases of something—let us say the height of an individual. Along the y axis, or abscissa, we represent differences, or variations, or changes, or successive increases of something else—let us say the age of an individual. Let us suppose that each year on his birthday we measure his height, and we record each measurement by placing a dot above the point on the y axis representing his age in years, and to the right of a point on the x axis representing his height in feet and inches. We do this once a year for seven years. Then we draw a line joining the seven dots. We read along the y axis how much the individual has changed in age, along the x axis how much he has changed in height, and in the curve joining the dots we read that

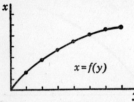

the two series of changes are related— that change in height is a function of change in age, $x = f(y)$, or height varies with time. Along the two axes we may represent large differences or small ones; along the curve we may place the dots close together or far apart, representing a gross or a finely detailed relationship between x and y.

FIG. 7. Illustrative curve showing relationship between two variables (not based on actual data). Variables are represented by x (along the ordinate) and y (along the abscissa). The relationship between them is represented by the curve, and by the equation: x is a function of y.

This basic form of scientific symbolism, then, has a structure quite similar to the structure of reality. It allows for the expression of differences, or changes, in very fine detail, and it allows for the expression of relations between changes with high degrees of precision. It provides fundamentally for two kinds of statement: the description of differences or changes in x and y (in height and age, for example), and the prediction of changes in x in relation to changes in y (changes in height, for example, in relation to changes in age).

Scientific language is designed for talking about curves of this general sort. This is to say that it is designed (a) for describing facts in terms of differences or changes, (b) for expressing relationships between facts in terms that relate one set of changes to some other set of changes, and (c) for predicting facts in the sense of predicting a change in one thing relative to a certain change in something else.

It is not to be implied that for a statement to be scientific it must be concerned with exact numbers or precise measurement. It is doubtless true, as Professor Edward L. Thorndike and others have pointed out, that if something exists it exists in some amount and can be measured. But it cannot always be measured *yet*, or here and now, or in precise numerical terms. There are many, many differences which we can express only in the rough terms of *more* or *less*. There are many changes that we can describe only as faster or slower than certain other changes to which we are accustomed. There are likewise many relationships that we can observe and speak of only in the general terms of *positive* or *negative, high* or *low*. What is fundamental is that scientific language deals directly or ultimately with differences, changes, and relationships. In general, it tends, therefore, to correspond in structure, more closely than does our "common" or prescientific language, with the structure of reality—with respect to (a) degree of differentiation, (b) variability, or extent and rate of change, and (c) relationship among the parts (organization).

In Chapter X we shall consider a number of practical "devices" for making our so-called common language more effectively scientific in structure than it usually is, and therefore more adjustive in both a personal and a social sense.

THE PROCESS OF ABSTRACTING: VERBAL LEVELS

With this introduction we may now consider the verbal levels of abstraction. In the last chapter we dealt with the non-verbal levels. The relationship between the verbal and the non-verbal levels is of major concern in general semantics, and up to this point in the present chapter we have been discussing it in the general terms of the structural differences and similarities between language and reality. The relationship between language and reality can be made still more clear by reference to our diagram of the process of abstracting.

As presented in the last chapter, the diagram consisted of three levels. We shall now add a fourth, as in Fig. 8.

We shall call this fourth level a representation of the first-order verbal level of abstraction or, briefly, the level of description. It might also be referred to as the label level, indicating that on this level we employ mainly labels for first-order facts or individuals. It is the level on which we name things, events, feelings, occur-

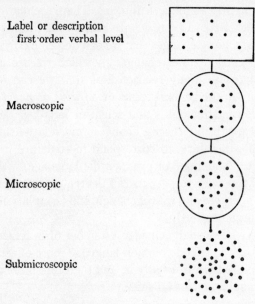

Label or description
first order verbal level

Macroscopic

Microscopic

Submicroscopic

FIG. 8.   Schematic diagram of the non-verbal levels and the first-order verbal level of abstraction.

rences—observables generally. An abstract on this level is called a first-order verbal abstract.

As we go from the non-verbal levels to the descriptive level, we leave out certain details. We do not say *all* about anything. It is extraordinarily instructive to try to tell someone *all* about something, such as a teacup, or a sandwich, or a snowstorm. There are no exhaustible subjects! The fact that details are left out in the abstracting process is indicated by the smaller number of dots in the rectangle which stands for the descriptive or label level.

We cannot with language go "below" the first-order verbal level. When we have said all we can in describing something we have reached this level of abstraction, and if asked to go further we can only point to, or demonstrate, or act out, or somehow exhibit tangibly what we "mean." We have reached the point where there is nothing more to be said. In this connection it is to be considered that definition can proceed in either of two directions, so to speak. It can move up or down the scale of abstraction: *baseball* can be defined in more general terms as a type of *spheroid,* or in more specific terms as a spherical object with a cork center wound with string and covered with horsehide. Now, suppose we are asked to define descriptively each of the terms used in this definition—and then each of the terms used in these definitions. After all, there are only so many words in the language that would be suitable, and eventually we shall find that we have used them all. There would then be no more to *say* about the "meaning" of *baseball.* We would have reached the first-order verbal level, and if pressed further we could do nothing but exhibit a baseball. (By that time, of course, our questioner would be fortunate if we didn't heave it at him!)

Words are used on this level, then, as *undefined terms:* undefined in the sense that they can be defined no further by words, and so can be defined only by example, by demonstrating or exhibiting what they are used to name, or to stand for. *Baseball* can be used as an undefined term in this sense. That is, we can use the word *baseball* without defining it except by example. Any so-called concrete noun can be so used. So can a verb like *run* or *jump;* or an adjective such as *yellow* or *wide;* or an adverb like *rapidly.* Without undue difficulty we can employ such terms on the first-order verbal level as basic undefined terms.

The case is not so clear, however, with certain other words like *if, now, yet, of,* etc., or *electron,* or *supernatural.* When you have defined *if* as fully as you can, what do you exhibit as a tangible example of what you mean by it? Likewise for *of?* There is a sense, of course, in which such words can be given factual reference, but we understand them mainly as words which we use in order to construct sentences or phrases. They are fasteners and hinges in the language chain, as it were. We use them primarily to express relations between other words, and so ultimately between facts. Strictly speaking, relations between facts are not expressed on the first-order verbal level; they represent abstractions of higher order.

Words like *now* and *yet* are "time words." Time is a higher-order abstraction. It is a bit difficult to point to a parcel of time, a chunk of "now." Time words express relations between events. As undefined terms they can hardly stand for tangible objects or observable events. At best, they stand for whatever we experience as the feelings of longer or shorter durations, or as "now" and "then." *Future* is a curious word in this respect. It refers to something that hasn't happened yet. It represents an abstraction definitely above the non-verbal levels.

Electron is an example of those words that stand for constructs, as we saw in Chapter IV. There is no first-order fact to which *electron* might refer directly. It refers to something we construct in imagination in order to explain and predict first-order facts. When pressed to define the term, the best we can do is to state the accepted rules for its use, and finally to present specific examples of its use in particular statements. These statements will refer in part, of course, to demonstrable facts, and only in this indirect sense does *electron* have an observable reference. It may not be used, strictly speaking, as an undefined term on the first-order verbal level.

The peculiar thing about *supernatural* is that, by definition, it refers to something beyond, or "above," or outside nature. It refers, that is, to something that is independent of anything "natural." It differs in this respect from *electron*, for example, the definition of which is rigorously dependent upon observable data and has been gradually revised in accordance with such data. Not only is it true, therefore, that such a term as *supernatural* cannot be used as an undefined term on the first-order verbal level, but also it is not clear as to just how it might be used so as to refer indirectly, like *electron*, to observable data. It represents not only a verbal abstraction, but one which bears an apparently loose and uncertain relationship to the non-verbal levels of abstraction.

It is to be understood, then, that there are certain words which, according to their accepted usages, may not be used on the first-order verbal level of abstraction. They do not serve to name or label particular observable facts. They represent relationships among facts, or they refer to constructs of inferential data. All other words, however, may serve as names for first-order facts and may be used, therefore, on the descriptive level. They need not be, of course. Almost any word can be used metaphorically, or to state an analogy, and most words lend themselves to statements on relatively high levels of generalization, or inference. We shall discuss the higher verbal levels presently.

In order for the process of abstracting to go on normally or efficiently, it is essential that the verbal and non-verbal levels be kept sharply *distinct* and closely coordinated. This is to say that the difference between symbol and symbolized, word and fact, map and territory, speakable and unspeakable—this difference is to be recognized clearly and its implications thoroughly understood. One of its basic implications is that the verbal and non-verbal levels must be kept coordinated: the structure of the language must be made similar to the structure of reality.

We have already discussed this matter of structure, but in terms of the process of abstracting it can be illustrated particularly well in terms of map and territory. (The map-territory analogy has been developed by Korzybski in *Science and Sanity*.) What we call a map is an example of a kind of language, symbols arranged in some kind of order. Now for a map to be useful to a traveler it must be coordinated with the territory, its structure must be similar in certain respects to that of the territory it represents. The arrangement of the symbols, the dots, lines, etc., of the map must accord with the arrangement of the actual cities, roads, rivers, etc., of the territory. For example, if in the territory we find, from west to east, Denver, Omaha, Chicago, then on the map we must find these places correspondingly represented. If on the map they are represented in the order of Denver, Chicago, Omaha, the order or structure is faulty, the map is not coordinated with the territory, and the traveler who tries to follow such a map is likely to suffer consequences which may range from mere annoyance to utter calamity. Among other experiences, he will be likely to suffer shock more or less, depending upon the degree to which he maintains awareness of the difference between map and territory. If, like a savage, he

scarcely recognizes any difference at all between symbol and fact
—map and territory—he will be gravely confused for some time
after discovering that he is in Omaha instead of Chicago. If, however, like a scientist, he has practically no tendency to identify
symbol and fact, practically no readjustment at all will be required
of him when he discovers that the map was wrong. He will merely
change his map and go on his way. The trouble with the more
primitive traveler is that he would hardly understand what was
wrong. Assuming as he does that map and territory are practically
identical, he places undue confidence in the map and so he is not
semantically prepared to handle his difficulty with the obvious (to
us) solution of changing the map. Such a solution would occur only
to a person to whom map and territory were distinctly different—
on different levels of abstraction—and who understood that the
usefulness of a map depends precisely on the degree to which it
corresponds structurally with the territory.

What we have said about map and territory can be said, also,
about any symbol and whatever it is supposed to symbolize. It can
be said about a statement and whatever it is supposed to represent.
It can be said about any theory and the facts it is supposed to explain and to predict. People who cling to theories that explain little
and predict nothing are like the primitive who "believes in" his
map even though it brings him to the wrong destinations. Such
people persist in the use of home remedies that don't remedy anything. They cling to business practices that lose money for them.
And we are not necessarily talking about "uneducated" people. As
a society we continue to believe that punishment counteracts crime,
in spite of the plain fact that the penitentiaries we have built for
the purpose of punishment must ever be enlarged to accommodate
the growing number of offenders. Likewise, we talk again of coer-
cive disarmament and reparations and the other old methods of preventing war, having learned little, apparently, from the wars they
have not prevented. Once we have learned to love a belief, we trust
it fondly and forgive it its shortcomings. We seem to resent the
facts that cast doubt upon it. Certainly it is to be abundantly observed that maladjusted people tend to rely more on their beliefs

and theories, on words generally, than on the experience and observation by which they might be tested.

What is important at all times is a consciousness of abstracting, an awareness and understanding of the fact that a symbol is not the same as what it symbolizes, that the verbal and non-verbal levels are to be kept distinct and coordinated. The price we pay for the lack of such awareness of our abstracting processes, and for the consequent lack of predictability, is to be counted in terms of shock, confusion, and maladjustment in our personal lives and in our social organizations. The price we pay is to be measured in terms of the social policies and personal beliefs that lead us over and over again into grief and waste. All too often we fiercely defend the very policies and beliefs that serve to create our difficulties. We defend, and even revere, institutions and customs that make for conflict. We do not like to have our attitudes criticized, even when they are attitudes that make us miserable and inefficient. We become sentimental about our maps, as it were, even when they lead us over and over again into blind alleys.

We can hardly overestimate the importance of this grave and pervasive result of a lack of consciousness of abstracting, this reluctance to change our maps—our beliefs, theories, policies, etc. Only insofar as we are conscious of abstracting, conscious of the levels of abstraction and of the relations among these levels, does it even occur to us that there is any point in "changing the map" when difficulties are encountered. An extreme example of this is seen in the ants, creatures which, according to William Morton Wheeler, have not developed a new social idea in sixty million years. The degree to which we resemble ants—that is to say, the degree to which we retain unrevised the beliefs, creeds, customs, etc., passed on to us from our forebears or adopted during our own infancy and childhood—that is in general an index of the degree to which we are not conscious of our abstracting processes.

This means that there is potentially a trace of the pathological in undue consistency of behavior, and in our traditional culture we have placed, and still place, a very high value on consistency. It was Sinclair Lewis who once snorted, "Consistent? A cockroach is consistent!" True it is that the highest degrees of consistency in behavior are to be found among the more lowly forms of life; and on human levels the most consistent behavior is to be found, perhaps, among such gravely sick individuals as those suffering from certain forms of insanity, who speak and act in stereotyped ways. Adjustment to a process reality must necessarily involve a degree of flexibility, of changeableness. In terms of our diagram, the map, the verbal abstracts, must be changed as nonverbal reality changes, and reality changes continuously. This is not to say that there is "nothing to cling to." We shall be reassured on that point before we are finished.

INFERENCES AND *Etc.*

Without further discussion at this time, it will be well to bring our diagram to completion, in order that we may gain a more comprehensive view of the process of abstracting and its implications. Up to this point, our diagram consists of four levels. One of these represents verbal abstracting. We shall now add the remaining verbal levels (Fig. 9).

Verbal levels above the first-order level of description or labeling are called inference levels. We join one level to the next by a single line, in order to indicate that the process proceeds from level to level. We represent the details left out (the increasing generality of statement) simply by decreasing the number of dots in the rectangles as we go to higher levels. (It is to be understood, of course, that the terms *higher* and *lower* have no fundamental significance as used here. The diagram could be turned upside down or sideways without changing its essential character.)

We arrange the levels in our complete diagram, starting—in an entirely arbitrary manner—with the submicroscopic level and proceeding upwards. We end at the top with *Etc.*, in order to represent that we deal here with an infinite process of generating abstracts. The fact that the diagram contains three levels of inference is by no means intended to indicate that there are never more than three. On the contrary, any abstract can be further abstracted; from any inference further inferences can be drawn. It is this that we repre-

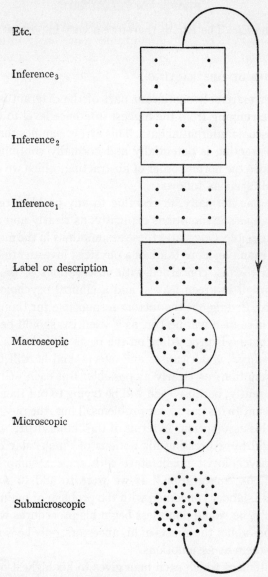

Etc.

Inference$_3$

Inference$_2$

Inference$_1$

Label or description

Macroscopic

Microscopic

Submicroscopic

FIG. 9. Schematic diagram of the process of abstracting. (Adapted from A. Korzybski, *Science and Sanity: An Introduction to Non-Aristotelian Systems and General Semantics*. Lancaster, Pa.: The Science Press, rev. ed., 1941.)

sent by the *Etc.* The *Etc.* is therefore a very important part of the diagram.

THE ORDER OF ABSTRACTING

Another extremely significant part of the diagram is the arrow in the line running from the highest inference level to the level of submicroscopic inferential data. This arrow signifies that the process of abstracting is potentially and normally continuous, and it suggests also the normal order of abstracting, which we may sketch in general terms as follows:

One begins normally, in reacting to any problem or situation, by stating one's assumptions explicitly, as clearly and as much in detail as possible. One states these assumptions in the most relevant way. For example, let us think of a physicist investigating the speed of light, a chemist concerned with observations of the formation of chlorophyll in green leaves, and a clinical psychologist preoccupied with finding out the factors responsible for thumb-sucking. Each of these men will be (or, as a scientist, should be) aware of the fact that he is proceeding on the basis of certain assumptions about "reality," about causes and effects, and he will try to state these assumptions as clearly as possible. But each man will state them differently, because each will be trying to put them in a form most relevant to his particular problems. Thus, the physicist might verbalize his assumptions in terms of the "ether drift," the chemist might begin by expressing his notions of "molecular dynamics," and the psychologist might start with some assumptions about "heredity" or "maturation." If we were to add to the group a Trobriand Islander concerned with the problem of maintaining his food supply, he would doubtless begin his procedures with certain assumptions about the ghosts of his ancestors, only he would hardly recognize them as assumptions.

The statement which each man gives to his highest-order inferences—the way, that is, in which he describes the unobservable aspects of reality, the inferential data—determines his manner of investigating what is observable on the microscopic and macroscopic levels. The particular observations he makes and the particular observations that he fails to make are determined mainly by the assumptions on the basis of which he undertakes to make observations. The more clear he is about these assumptions, and the more aware he is *that they are assumptions,* the more decisively is he able to check them against relevant observations.

In the case of the Michelson-Morley investigations of the speed of light, for instance, the investigators' inferences about the submicroscopic "ether" were so explicitly stated that a decisive test of them could be made. According to these assumptions, the speed of light should be greater when the light is traveling in the direction of the earth's rotation than when it is traveling counter to that direction. Starting with these assumptions—starting, that is, in terms of our diagram, with high-order inferences about the submicroscopic level—the experimenters constructed special apparatus by means of which they could observe the speed of light. And their observations, on what would be considered as the microscopic level in this case, enabled them to say definitely that their inferences about submicroscopic "reality" had been in error. Consequently they abandoned the notion of a submicroscopic "ether." By carefully describing their observations, and by abstracting inferences from their description, and then by abstracting further inferences from these inferences, etc., new and different high-order inferences concerning submicroscopic "reality" were eventually abstracted, on the basis of which further observations were carried out, etc. Thus goes science. The process of abstracting, in science, works continuously.

The trouble with the Trobriander is that to him, apparently, the ghosts of his ancestors are not inferences at all. To him, in all probability, there just *are* ghosts. He is not conscious that his word *ghosts* is merely a name for an abstraction inside his own head, for an inference, an assumption. So long as there just *are* ghosts, so long as the Trobriander is not even conscious of having assumptions, he does not, of course, proceed to make any observations that would serve to test the validity of his assumptions. So it is that we abandon our "ether," and any other assumptions found to be false or defective, and, by so doing, gradually change our civilization, while the Trobriander retains the "ghosts of his ancestors" and, by so doing, in almost complete measure perpetuates the beliefs and customs of those ancestors. It is something of this sort that we refer to when we say that our civilization advances, while in backward cultures there is little or no progress.

Indeed, a cardinal aspect of the method we call science, and of the everyday life orientation that we call scientific, is the consciousness of, the clearest possible statement of, one's assumptions, and especially one's assumptions regarding submicroscopic phenomena. We all have some notions as to what there is "behind the watch face." We express these notions in terms of "heredity," or "human nature," or the "supernatural," and in many other ways; they represent in one sense or another our notions of "causes" and "effects" and the relations between them. But when, like the Trobriander, we do not recognize the fact that these notions are inferential, are assumptions, and not statements of tangible fact, we quite effectively short-circuit our abstracting processes, so far as these notions are concerned. For all practical purposes we convert the process of abstracting from the form represented by our above diagram to something that might be diagrammed as in Fig. 10.

Thus, we do not state our highest-order inferences *as inferences*. We treat them as true statements about the "supernatural," or whatnot, and so any observations we might make on the macro and micro levels are not relevant to them, nor are any descriptions we might make of such observations relevant either. They are not relevant, that is, in the sense that they would tend to verify or refute the statements or beliefs. We appear to adopt an inference, together with a few other inferences to which it is related, and then we never *test* it. Any abstracting we do in terms of it tends to be quite independent of non-verbal or lower-order verbal abstracting. It is this that we have diagrammed here as "short-circuited" abstracting. This is the mechanism of the "closed mind," of the old dog that cannot learn new tricks. It is represented in the behavior of the Indian who dances in a particular way in order to make the corn grow well, regardless of the corn crops that have followed his dancing in the past. To him the god who will refuse to make the corn

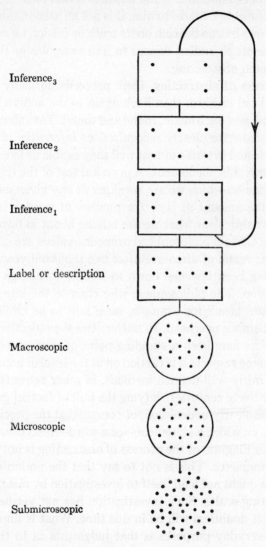

FIG. 10. Schematic diagram of "short-circuited" abstracting, illustrating the mechanism of semantic blockage.

grow if he does not dance is not an assumption to be tested but a fact to be respected. Since, to him, it is not an assumption, the way the corn grows has no bearing on its truth or falsity. Of course, one need not resort to Indian dances to find examples of this sort of short-circuited abstracting.

The process of abstracting, then, proceeds normally from any particular level upward, then back again to the non-verbal levels, then upward, and back again, round and round. The submicroscopic inferential data are clearly recognized *as inferential*, as assumptions to be tested in terms of how well they enable us to explain and predict observable phenomena. A practical test of the relative level of abstraction on which we are speaking at any given moment lies simply in the amount of time (or number of words) required to make reasonably clear what we are talking about in terms of first-order facts. Certain philosophical pronouncements are still floating about in the realm of discourse after two thousand years or more, never having been fastened down to a solid anchorage in.factual demonstration. The philosophers who cling to the kite strings of Plato's "pure idea," for example, seem still to be circling a considerable distance overhead. In universities the objective of higher education has long been a standing point of controversy, and although in some respects it is carried on at the level of actual courses taught by fairly well-defined methods, in other respects it is still, after many lively centuries, defying the pull of factual gravitation.

It is to be clearly understood, of course, that the precise level of abstraction on which a statement—or a word—rests cannot be designated. Our diagram of the process of abstracting is not to be read like a thermometer. This is not to say that the notion of level of abstraction might not lend itself to investigation by means of fairly reliable rating scales. Such investigation has not yet been undertaken, but it doubtless will be in due time. What is important for practical everyday purposes is that judgments as to the relative difference in abstraction of any two statements are not, as a rule, difficult. You can become quite adept at recognizing when you are going to a higher or to a lower level of abstraction in the course of a discussion. You can learn to appreciate a relatively high level of abstraction, or a moderate level, or a low one. It is this sort of practical awareness of *relative* level, and of shifts from higher to lower levels, that is significant in the moment-to-moment use of language, whether as speaker or listener. And this can be deliberately cultivated through attentive practice. Concerning this important matter more will be said in later chapters.

One more point remains to be further clarified. In our diagram, a line with an arrow in it connects the highest-order verbal level of inference with the lowest, or submicroscopic, level. This can be made very mysterious, or quite simple. We have already made the point that what we see, hear, etc., on the levels of observation is necessarily incomplete: there is a submicroscopic realm. One might ask, "Where does it come from?" We must be careful that in asking such a question we do not create for ourselves a tiger that we cannot ride. So far as general semantics is concerned, there is this to say: We infer, on the basis of what appears to be mandatory evidence, that there is "something" beyond the limits of our observation. Since we cannot observe it, we have no choice but to make inferences about it. And the only basis we have for these inferences are the observations we can make. This means that it is only by reporting our observations as reliably as possible, and by drawing inferences from them in more and more general terms (on higher and higher levels of abstraction) that we can arrive at any notions or statements about the submicroscopic realm. It follows that the only tests we have of these inferences are the further observations by which we check how well they explain and predict observable facts as we find them occurring. What all this amounts to is that the process of abstracting is circular. That is why we draw a line with an arrow in it connecting the highest-order verbal inferences with the submicroscopic level. In the following chapters the practical significance and applications of this will be indicated.

A DIAGRAM OF SCIENCE

All this may sound rather academic, rather remote from the everyday affairs of anyone. It may be so—as an abstract discussion. But in at least two respects, what we are here discussing is by no means academic, or "merely abstract." In the first place, what we have sketched above constitutes the general method of science. As applied in various technical fields, it produces results that contribute to a continual alteration of our material environment. It has been the use of this general scientific method that has produced such things as radio, aviation, moving pictures, the sulfa drugs, X-ray, etc. For example, modern scientific technology has made transportation and communication more and more efficient. If the earth was 24,000 miles around at the equator in 1800, then, in terms of the time it takes to travel around the globe, it is now scarcely more than 300 miles in circumference—and in terms of the time it takes to convey a message around the earth, it has all but vanished entirely. Do these facts affect your daily life, your plans for the future, etc.? Are these academic matters? Is the atomic bomb that fell on Hiroshima—instead of on you—an academic proposition? Indeed, in terms of its practical, material, industrial consequences, there is hardly anything less academic than science.

In the second place, what has been sketched here as the general method of science may be viewed as the essential basis of an *orientation* to life in its moment-to-moment aspects. Science as technology in the narrow sense, as seen in various specialized laboratory techniques, affects our daily lives most tremendously, but it cannot be used directly to a very important degree in our ordinary hour-to-hour behavior. Science as general orientation is another matter, and it is science as general orientation with which we are mainly concerned in this book. As general orientation it can be described and understood in terms of the process of abstracting, a process that is inherent in life itself, to be used or abused in the daily life of common people no less than in the esoteric activities of men engaged in highly technical research.

It is from such a point of view that we shall consider in the following two chapters, some of the basic characteristics of the process of abstracting and certain of the fundamental principles involved in efficient abstracting—in terms of which a general scientific orientation toward life becomes possible.

THE PROCESS OF ABSTRACTING

$\mathcal{M}$ARK TWAIN'S OBSERVATION THAT EVERYBODY TALKS about the weather but nobody does anything about it is not merely funny. As was true of so many of his ostensibly humorous remarks, this one about the weather has a "gear shift" attached, so that one chuckles and then reflects. Why don't people do anything about the weather since they do talk about it so much? One clear reason would appear to be that they scarcely talk about it at all.

They talk about themselves. When you remark to the mailman, as he gives you your daily quota of bills and circulars, that it is certainly a grand day, you do not, of course, report a meteorological observation so much as a gastro-intestinal one. You merely tell the mailman that you have no headache, that your rheumatism is not bothering you, and that your favorite baseball team won a double-header yesterday. Certainly if you are trying to inform the mailman about the weather, you are carrying coals to Newcastle; he has been pushing himself around through the weather for the past two or three hours.

The point is that any statement you make about anything at all refers in some measure to yourself. It may, up to a certain point, convey information about geraniums, or the Brooklyn Dodgers, or even the weather, but it also constitutes evidence of your own inner state. The remarks we make range along a continuum in this respect. At the one extreme we find the sort of utterances which have scarcely any external factual reference whatever—even though the person who utters them may seem to assume that they do have. A lady in a "mental" hospital once told me at great length about a boat trip she had been forced to take. She had been bound hand and foot and placed on a cot in the hold of the ship. Throughout the voyage a lion kept leaping across her cot, now from one direction, now from the other. It was all very exciting, but of course it referred only to a drama going on inside her own head and it was meaningful chiefly to her psychiatrist.

At the other extreme we find statements that have a minimum of self-reference such as "Fresh eggs 30 cents a dozen," or "It is five miles from here to the nearest post office," provided, of course, that these remarks turn out to be reasonably true or reliable. Even such statements, however, are not entirely free of self-reference, and would properly be terminated with "so far as I know" or "to me." While it is true that figures can lie, yet it is with the language we call mathematics that we can make statements that are most precisely descriptive of reality. Provided we all agree to abide by a few rules, such as $1 \div 1 = 1$ (a statement which is not "true" but merely conventional), we can place considerable confidence in such remarks as, "The time is now 8:15, and the temperature in downtown Chicago is 42 degrees." While we realize that this may not be absolutely true, still, for all practical purposes, we can afford to treat it as a statement of fact rather than opinion; we can with reasonable safety have another cup of coffee before dashing for the bus, and wear a topcoat when we go out. If everyone concerned abides by the rules of mathematics and of scientific observation and reporting, we can even accept as "fact" rather than sheer opinion, for the time being at least, the statement that one gram of hydrogen contains 303,000,000,000,000,000,000,000 molecules! It is clear, nonetheless, that such a remark certainly refers to a great deal that is to be found inside someone's head, as well as to something characteristic of the external physical world.

THE OBSERVER AND THE OBSERVED

This whole point has been brilliantly summarized, as we have mentioned previously, by Professor R. D. Carmichael: "The universe, as known to us, is a joint phenomenon of the observer and the observed." Translated into the language of general semantics, this statement says that the process of abstracting is personal or private, and projective. The moment you say of any word or statement, or any object, that it constitutes an abstract, you imply that it is abstracted *from something by someone*. The words "by someone" represent the fact that an abstract is personal or private. This is true of the process of abstracting generally, since to say that *any* abstract of yours is personal to you is to say that they all are. And if abstracting is a personal process it must also be projective. That is to say, for example, insofar as the pipe, which you speak of as lying on your desk, constitutes an abstract "manufactured" by your nervous system, then you must project that abstract outside your nervous system if you are to speak of it and react to it as lying on your desk. This is really not as complicated or strange as it may sound. Actually, once projection is well understood, it is recognized as one of the processes inherent in living organisms, quite as common as breathing. And the abuse of this process can be quite as harmful as the abuse of any other natural life process, such as breathing, for example.

We have already discussed briefly the process of projection in an earlier chapter. Perhaps a story about a certain university dean will serve to illustrate it more clearly. This particular dean, a beloved gentleman of rather ripe age, was riding one day on a train, returning to his home from a convention which he had attended in a distant city. He had been up late the night before and was finding it rather difficult to remain alert and to converse with a professor friend who was sitting beside him. At one of the stations along the way a young lady who had been a student in one of the dean's classes boarded the train and, with respectful and friendly greetings, sat down facing him. They exchanged remarks about this and that, but after a time the dean's drowsiness became more assertive than his sense of decorum and he dozed off. Within a few moments, however, he came to with a mild start and resumed the conversation. In reply to his remarks the young lady started talking again in a very animated manner—and again the dean dozed off. This was repeated several times, each time the dean falling asleep while the girl was speaking.

A few days later the professor who had seen this contest between wit and Morpheus told the dean's wife about it, much to her amusement. The same evening at dinner she asked the dean about the young lady he had met on the train.

"You know," the dean replied, "I don't know what's the matter with that girl. She would begin to say something and would go along all right for a while, but then she would stop right in the middle of a sentence. After a time she would start talking again, but then she'd stop. I really couldn't make her out."

Another incident in point was related recently by a professor of very considerable repute. He said he had had a dream. He had dreamed that a burglar came into the bedroom, and he had sat up in bed and shouted at the burglar, "Get out of here!" He shouted so loudly that he woke up. As he sat there staring wide-eyed around the room, he happened to look down beside him and see his wife, who had turned on the bed-light, smiling up at him.

"I had a dream," he said.

"Did you?" she asked. "What did you dream?"

"I dreamed a burglar came in the room, and I shouted at him, 'Get out of here!' I shouted so loudly I woke up."

His wife smiled more broadly. "Do you want to know what you really said?" she asked.

"What I really said? But I told you what I really said."

"What you really said—and you said it very softly and sweetly— was, 'Hello.' "

Other less dramatic but equally pointed illustrations of the process of projection are to be found in the study of optical illusions. One that is widely known is the Müller-Lyer illusion (Fig. 11).

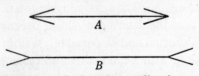

FIG. 11.   The Müller-Lyer illusion. Is one line longer than the other? An illustration of unconscious projection.

If you were to bet a friend five dollars that line *B* is longer than line *A*, you would soon learn what is meant by projection, and you would also learn that it is to your advantage to be as fully conscious as possible of your projections. According to measurement with an ordinary ruler, line *A* and line *B* are the same length. According to your nervous system, unaided by a ruler, line *B* is the longer.

The person who says, "Line *B* *is* longer than line *A*," speaks a language quite different in structure from that of the person who says, "Line *B* *looks* the longer *to me.*" The first individual would appear to regard his abstract not as an abstract at all, but as a simple fact, obvious to everyone, universally and absolutely true. Not recognizing it as an abstract, he does not recognize it as personal and as projective. He is the person who would bet five dollars he was right, who would be amazed that anyone would take his bet, and who would be dumbfounded and would probably suspect someone of cheating upon discovering that he had lost the bet. He is the "practical" person for whom seeing is believing, impractical because he does not realize also that believing is seeing!

The individual who says, "Line *B* *looks* the longer *to me,*" on the other hand, uses a language which indicates a degree of awareness that what he sees when he looks at the two lines is an abstract, structured by his own nervous system, and therefore personal or private. As such, it is not necessarily true for anyone else, and it is not true in any absolute sense. Its "truth" is relative to the particular nervous system by which it is abstracted, and to the particular conditions under which it is abstracted. That is, whether or not it is true depends to a significant degree upon these other factors, and not just upon the line "itself." The Müller-Lyer pattern, as known to you, is, as Professor Carmichael would say, a joint product of the pattern itself (a tricky phrase) and of your observations of it. This is merely a way of saying that what you see depends not entirely upon what there is to be seen, but also upon the particular way in which your seeing apparatus, your nervous system, works. It is therefore a way of saying that anything you see—the Müller-Lyer lines, for example—is in part something that exists independently of your seeing it and it is in part something projected by you, so that what you call its characteristics are in some measure determined by the characteristics of your own nervous system. The individual who says, "Line *B looks* the longer *to me*," thereby indicates some degree of consciousness of all this. Therefore, his predictions would be better. He probably would not bet five dollars that he was right, and, bet or no bet, he would not suffer any particular shock in finding out that he was wrong.

Unconscious projection is one of the hallmarks of the primitive, the stupid, and the maladjusted. To paraphrase an apt passage in Hayakawa's *Language in Action,* the importance of being conscious of one's projection mechanisms lies not only in the fact that it tends to make one more fair and tolerant and generally efficient, but also in the fact that it tends to keep one from making a fool of oneself.

This general point is extravagantly illustrated by the story of the hillbilly wife who was rummaging one day through some things that her husband had brought home from town and had tucked away among his private belongings. In the course of her pawing about she came upon a mirror, an object she had never seen before. Her only possible interpretation was that it was a photograph. As she stared at it sullenly, she muttered, "So that's the old hag he's been steppin' out with!"

You will remember the fable of the greedy dog who was carrying a bone in his mouth and chanced to look into a brook where he saw what he took to be another dog, also with a bone in his mouth. Thinking to have two bones for himself, he began by barking at the other dog, and the bone he did have dropped from his mouth into the brook. This fable always ends, apparently, with a moral about the wisdom of not being greedy. Such a moral has its points, no doubt, but it is to be suggested that a more fundamental moral concerns the advantages in awareness of projection. The dog was not only greedy, but he was also, and more basically, a dimwit. The fable neatly suggests, incidentally, the impossibility of treating "character" and "intelligence" as though they were unrelated to each other.

The personal and projective character of abstracting is so clearly illustrated by another example that it will be worth our while to consider it briefly. Consider the words *hot* and *cold* and the ways in which we use them. The degree to which one is conscious of abstracting tends to be revealed by one's casual, offhandish use of such common words. For example, we commonly make such remarks as, "It (meaning the weather, the world outside one's skin) is hot today," or "This drink is nice and cool." When such remarks are quite lacking in "to-me-ness" they indicate a lack of consciousness of abstracting. A simple experiment serves to make this more clear. Suppose we have three pails of water (Fig. 12). If for five minutes you hold your left arm in the pail on the left and your

| 35 degrees | 70 degrees | 140 degrees |
| Fahrenheit | Fahrenheit | Fahrenheit |

Fig. 12.   Drawing representing pails containing water of indicated degrees of temperature. (See accompanying text.)

right arm in the pail on the right, and then plunge both arms into the pail in the middle, will you find the water in the middle pail "hot" or "cold"? Through your left arm you will abstract "hot" or "warm" water, and through your right arm you will abstract "cold" or "cool" water! Now the question arises (if you are not careful of the way you ask questions), "Well, which is it? Is the water in the middle pail *really* hot or *really* cold?" And if you talk the way a great many people do, you will add, with a suggestion of a snort, "It can't be both!"

Thus, sense meets nonsense with a resounding crash. Let us examine the collision and the wreck. Every school child "knows" that hot is hot and cold is cold and that that's that—and every traditional Teacher of Logic beams upon every school child who "knows" so much. For it has been told by wise men since the days of Aristotle that A is A, that everything is either A or non-A, and that nothing can be both A and non-A. These three premises, as we have seen, known as the Law of Identity, the Law of the Excluded Middle, and the Law of Non-Contradiction, respectively, have been extolled for over two thousand years as *the* inexorable Laws of Thought. It is from the pattern framed by these Laws that we have in large measure designed the basic structure of our culture, our civilization, and our individual personalities. All this, of course, sounds very classroomy, and it might be well to refer it back to our three pails of water.

You will recall that through your left arm you abstracted "hot" water and through your right arm you abstracted "cold" water in the middle pail, and that some Aristotelian onlooker had exclaimed, "Come now! Make up your mind. What is it, hot or cold?" You find his question difficult, and he finds your indecisiveness, as he calls it, very annoying, for well he "knows" that hot is hot, that water is either hot or it isn't hot, and that water can't be both hot and not hot at the same time. That is nothing more or less than a translation of the great Laws of Thought. It is common sense, pure and simple. "Do you mean to stoop there with your arms in that bucket," he persists, "and tell me that the water is both hot and cold? What's the matter with you?" So he thrusts his own hand into the water and says with disdain, "It's cool, of course. Can't you tell when water is cool?" And if you inform him that water never *is* cool, he will seriously conclude, quite probably, that you have "lost your mind."

In the meantime, what are we to say about this curious situation? It is clear that our Aristotelian friend is identifying one level of abstraction with another. His word "cool" does not refer to the water in the pail, as he naïvely assumes it does, but to the abstract "manufactured" by his nervous system. His failure to realize this is an example of what we mean by unconscious projection. His common sense, his "laws of thought," constitute a generalized formula which tends to perpetuate such unconscious projection as a habitual mode of reaction. It is a formula which summarizes a kind of orientation that makes for the abuse of natural life processes, the specific process of projection and the general process of abstracting. And when natural life processes are

abused persistently the consequences tend to militate against individual and social survival.

FIVE BASIC POINTS

In the last chapter and in this one, then, we have considered
several of the general characteristics of the process of abstracting:

1. It may be regarded as a process of leaving out details.
2. It proceeds normally from "lower" to "higher" levels.
3. It is potentially continuous, since changes on one level normally generate changes on the level "above" it, and since on the
submicroscopic level there is continuous change.
4. It is personal: an abstract on any level is abstracted *from
something by someone.*
5. It is projective—one's evaluations are necessarily projected
outside one's nervous system and are perceived as "reality." Such
projection is potentially conscious and therefore useful in prediction and control of reality. As an unconscious process it is potentially or actually harmful.

ABSTRACTING IS SELF-REFLEXIVE

We have now to consider other characteristics of the process of
abstracting: it is (a) self-reflexive, (b) multiordinal, and (c) potentially self-corrective, and (d) its results can be communicated.
We shall discuss each of these in turn.

You will recall that in our diagram of the process of abstracting
a few pages back there was an *Etc.* It was at the top of the diagram
and it represented the fact that any abstract can be further abstracted. In this connection the process of abstracting is seen to
resemble our number system. With our number system there is no
such thing as *the* largest number, because no matter how large a
number you choose you can always add 1 to it and make a larger
number. Likewise, with regard to the process of abstracting, there
is no such thing as *the* highest level, because you can always make
an abstract of an abstract—"there is always room at the top for
one more." It is with reference to this "abstractableness" of any

abstract that we speak of the process of abstracting as self-reflexive.

There are many common illustrations of self-reflexiveness. Bob Burns, the radio comedian, once told about his uncle's invention designed for dealing with a particular type of self-reflexive process. His uncle's invention consisted of a spot remover for removing spots left by spot removers. Another radio comedian, Bob Hope, commenting one time upon the remarkable new automobile models, said that in order to operate them all you had to do was to push a button that pushed a button. Then there was the cartoon published some years ago which showed two candid-camera fans pointing their cameras at each other, the one candid-camera fan taking a picture of the other candid-camera fan taking a picture of the first candid-camera fan taking a picture, etc. Essentially the same self-reflexive process is to be seen in some of the controversies that go on—and on—in certain scholarly journals: Professor Vorstein's reply to Professor Hatton's reply to Professor Chatterton's reply to Professor Svendson's criticism of Professor Willoughby's translation of Homer's *Odyssey*—a series in which Professor Vorstein's is the most recent but by no means the last word.

The picture on the old Post Toasties box provides another example of self-reflexiveness. You will recall that it was picture of a Post Toasties box on which, of course, there was picture of a Post Toasties box so that it formed a picture of a picture of a picture, etc.

We bring all this a little nearer to the problems with which we are most concerned if we talk about self-reflexiveness in the terms which Professor Josiah Royce of Harvard used in a particularly significant discussion of this matter. He spoke of the self-reflexive character of the ideal map. His notion may be stated simply in this way: If you are making a map of a territory that is to cover everything in the territory, it must include you and the map you are making, since, of course, you and your map are in the territory you are mapping. In other words, your map must be, in part, a map of your map if it is to be complete. And it follows that if the map of the map is to be complete, it must include itself, in turn—and so you will have a map of a map of a map, and so on, indefinitely.

This means that there can be no such thing as an absolutely complete map.

As with maps, so with language generally. Suppose you attempt to describe what you are doing at the moment. Obviously, if you are to describe what you are doing at the moment, you will describe the description you are making at the moment. And, as with the map, if your description is to be complete it must necessarily develop as a description of a description of a description, and so on. This, as was true of our statement about the ideal map of the map, is simply a way of saying that such a thing as an absolutely complete statement—the Last Word—is inconceivable. The structure of our language, the structure of the world, and the structure of our nervous systems appear to be such that any sort of symbolizing, on human levels at least, whether speech, writing, maps, pictures, numbers, or whatnot, turns out to be potentially self-reflexive indefinitely.

It is of interest, and in some cases it is of great value, to know that the self-reflexive character of our language, of abstracting generally, is what makes possible the paradoxes and seeming paradoxes around which interminable philosophical disputes, as well as certain parlor games, have long revolved. You may have devoted a few evenings to perplexity, trying to figure out whether the statement "All Cretans are liars" is true or false, since it was spoken by Epimenides who was himself a Cretan. Then there is the famous one about the barber who shaved everyone in the village who did not shave himself. The question is whether the barber shaved himself, for if he did he didn't! To recognize these as self-reflexive problems at least relieves one of the suspicion that one is imbecilic.

A closely related problem is that of infinite regress. An example of this is found in the well-worn story about the five-year-old girl who asked her mother who made the world. Upon being told that God made it, she asked, "And who made God?" Out of the mouths of fools and babes come our most distressing questions—because they have not learned to stay within the well-beaten verbal pathways of "right-minded" people. Any child who persists long enough in asking "Why?" or "What for?" or any philosopher who drives himself far enough into the dim recesses of the problem of cause runs the risk of falling at last into the bottomless well of infinite regress.

These Cretans who are truthful liars, these barbers who do and do not shave themselves, these paradoxes, and these questions that catapult one into the tailspin of infinite regress, what are we to do about these? A poll would probably reveal the most popular answer to be, "Why do anything? If philosophers want to fiddle away their time on such puzzles that's their business." Unfortunately, these do not happen to be mere puzzles, or topics for spirited but futile debate in the belfries of ivory towers. They are evidence of the very stuff of which human misery is made.

Because of the simple fact that we *can* use language for talking about language, that we *can* make statements about statements about statements, *ad infinitum*, we have to contend not merely with paradoxes such as the above, but also with the maladjustments and catastrophes that result from gossip, rumor, daydreaming, suspiciousness, delusions, and a host of other symptoms of self-reflexiveness gone wild. This is no academic matter. We must not allow talk about Post Toasties boxes and prevaricating Cretans to deceive us. It is not too much to say that anything resembling a satisfactory understanding of personal and social adjustment is out of the question unless it includes an adequate understanding of the role of self-reflexiveness in such adjustment and in maladjustment.

It is not to be implied that this peculiar characteristic of our abstracting processes makes only for confusion and hardship. These consequences occur only when it is abused, and it is abused when it is not recognized and consciously employed. Self-reflexiveness not only has made possible millions of inferiority complexes and thousands of jealous homicides, but it has also made possible the theory of relativity and the other revolutionary achievements of modern mathematical physics. It makes possible practically all that we mean by cultural advance. It gives a basis for the science of engineering, including *human* engineering. If our language, our abstracting processes generally, were not self-reflexive, whatever there is of significance that we mean by the word "human" simply would not exist. Abstracting, like digestion, is a natural bodily function (as a matter of fact, digestion too is a variety of abstracting process), and the continuous, projective, self-reflexive aspects of that function represent natural, normal aspects of our whole bodily economy. It is as dangerous to be misinformed about them as it is to be misinformed about nutritional or reproductive functions.

MULTIORDINALITY

A key to a more adequate understanding of self-reflexiveness is afforded by Korzybski's notion of multiordinality. According to this notion, many of our most important terms are multiordinal, and as such they have no general meaning. What a multiordinal word "means" is determined by the level of abstraction on which it is used; in a more familiar but partial sense we may say that what such a word "means" varies with the context. Thus when we speak, for example, of a statement about a statement, we use the word "statement" in two different ways. Let us refer back to our diagram of the process of abstracting, and let us say, hypothetically, that we make a statement on one level and then on "the next higher" level we make a statement about that statement. For example, we may say, "Blue pigeons fly faster than white pigeons." Now we may go to "the next higher" level of abstraction and make one of a number of statements about this statement, such as, "It is true" or "It is false" or "It is interesting if true" or "To the extent that this statement is true, it implies a relationship between pigmentation and muscle structure." These statements are on a higher level of abstraction than the first statement because they are statements about the first statement. But we can say of the first one and of each of the others, also, that it is a statement. Thus the word *statement* is seen to be multiordinal in that it can be used on different levels, or orders, of abstraction, and its particular meaning varies from level to level. Consequently, to the question "What is a statement?" no general, absolute answer may be given.

It will be well to consult Korzybski's original discussion. On pages 14 and 15 of *Science and Sanity* he says:

The reader should be warned from the beginning of a very fundamental semantic innovation; namely, of the discovery of the *multiordinality* of the most important terms we have. This leads to a conscious use of these terms in the multiordinal, extremely flexible, full-of-conditionality sense. Terms like "yes," "no," "true," "false," "fact," "reality," "cause," "effect," "agreement," "disagreement," "proposition," "number," "relation," "order," "structure," "abstraction," "characteristic," "love," "hate," "doubt," etc., are such that if they can be applied to a statement they can also be applied to a statement about the first statement, and so, ultimately, to all statements, no matter what their order of abstraction is. Terms of such a character I call *multiordinal terms*. The main characteristic of these terms consists of the fact that on different levels or orders of abstractions they may have different meanings, with the result that they have no general meaning; for their meanings are determined solely by the given context, which establishes the different orders of abstractions. Psycho-logically, in the realization of the multiordinality of the most important terms, we have paved the way for the specifically *human* full conditionality of our semantic responses. This allows us great freedom in the handling of multiordinal terms and eliminates very serious psycho-logical fixities and blockages, which analysis shows to be animalistic in their nature, and, consequently, pathological for man. Once the reader understands this multiordinal characteristic, this semantic freedom does not result in confusion.

Accidentally, our vocabulary is enormously enriched without becoming cumbersome, and is made very exact. Thus a "yes" may have an indefinite number of meanings, depending on the context to which it is applied. Such a blank "yes" represents, in reality, "yes" ("yes unlimited"), but this includes "yes_1," "yes_2," "yes_3," etc., all of which are, or may be, different. All speculations about such terms *in general*—as, for instance, "what a fact or reality is?"—are futile, and, in general, illegitimate, as the only correct answer is that "the terms are multiordinal and devoid of meaning outside of a context." This settles many knotty epistemological and semantic questions, and gives us a most powerful method for promoting human mutual freedom of expression, thus eliminating misunderstandings and blockages and ultimately leading to agreement. . . .

With the introduction of the multiordinality of terms, which is a *natural* but, as yet, an unnoticed fact, our ordinary vocabulary is enormously enriched; in fact, the number of words in such a vocabulary *natural for man* is infinite. The multiordinality of terms is the fundamental mechanism of the *full conditionality* of *human* semantic reactions; it eliminates an unbelievable number of the old animalistic blockages, and is fundamental for sanity.

From such a point of view, jesting Pilate asking, "What is Truth?" becomes a simple fool. As soon as we recognize the multiordinality of the word *truth*, "What is Truth?" turns out to be as nonsensical as the most noisy lines in *Alice in Wonderland*, and we have one thing less to worry about. "Am I inferior?" and "Does he *really* love me?" are seen to be as "harmless" as "Who made God?" The general problem of meaninglessness—meaningless or unanswerable questions and meaningless or untestable statements—is bound up with self-reflexiveness and with the multiordinality of terms which this involves. If we abandon the futile attempt to give a term a *general* meaning, we then devote ourselves clearly and consciously to making adequate the context from which the term derives any particular meaning that it might have. The fact that the meaning of a term is seen to shift and change does not disturb us; rather, it gives us a freedom of expression and a flexibility of interpretation that are strongly conducive to mutual understanding and agreement. A thorough consciousness of self-reflexiveness and multiordinality tends to make, also, for a degree of "clearheadness," an accuracy of statement, an awareness of the whole evaluating process, that go far to counteract the befuddlement involved in worry and fear, resentment and anxiety, and other disabling semantic reactions.

Examples of multiordinality may be found in abundance, once we begin to look for them, and the disregard of multiordinality may be observed in most cases of personality maladjustment. To select an amusing instance, you may recall the old saying, *"Never* and *always* are two words one should always remember never to use." In other words, "Always avoid always" and "Never say never." These are self-contradictory, until we recognize that in each case the "same" word is used on different levels of abstraction, and in this way the statement is made, in effect, that on lower levels of abstraction *always* and *never* are less likely to be "true" than they are on the higher levels. That is, "in general," "on the average," or "for practical purposes" something may never or always be true, but "actually" or with reference to specific facts it is likely to be true only partially, or only sometimes, or under certain conditions. We speak, for instance, of exceptions that "prove the rule," and often what we are talking about are the individual facts that "make no difference" so long as we are interested only in the general average or trend. In light of such considerations, such a statement as "Never say never" makes sense, and in this case *never* serves as an example of a multiordinal term. However academic and mouth-filling the words may sound at this point, the multiordinal character of the process of abstracting appears to be anything but academic when we come to consider practical problems of getting along in everyday life.

NOT THE SAME MISTAKES

Another fundamental characteristic of the process of abstracting is that it is normally self-corrective. Someone has said that it is all right to make mistakes, so long as you don't make the same fool mistake twice. The implication of this is frequently expressed in this way, that it is all right to make mistakes because that is how we learn. We seem to be talking about the same thing essentially when we say that experience is a great teacher.

As everybody "knows," however, experience does not necessarily teach us anything. Sometimes we do make the "same" mistakes over and over again, and it apparently does not always occur to us that there is anything to be learned from our blunders. But there is one general type of human behavior concerning which such remarks cannot be made. There is a certain area of behavior in which experience is a great teacher and in which we do learn from our mistakes. This is the area of behavior which we call science.

Some people are very much puzzled by this. As a matter of fact, some people lose confidence in scientists just because scientists are "always changing their theories." "Why don't they make up their minds?" "One says one thing and one says another!" Even among "scientists" it is usually great news when some scientist renounces a theory he formerly proposed. "I see Thorndike has gone back on his own law of frequency!" If in his later years Freud had agreed with certain of his critics, one can well believe that there would have been big, black headlines in the newspapers: "Freud Admits Sex not Everything." And no one would have been more shocked, or incredulous, than some of Freud's followers themselves. Early in World War II we witnessed a similar state of affairs (not among scientists): the hectic turmoil among Stalin's disciples when he signed the famous pact with Hitler, and the equally perplexed reactions of many people when they discovered at a later date that they were Stalin's allies.

In our culture, consistency is highly respected, so much so that most people even feel self-conscious for some time after they stop using *ain't*. "Self-improvement" requires considerable "will power" and a thick skin in our civilization, if one is to remain poised and undiscouraged when greeted with: "You think you're pretty smart don't you?" or "You mean you want me to go with you to hear those longhairs sing Italian?" An amazing number of books on "psychology," "mental hygiene," and "happy marriage" are read surreptitiously behind drawn blinds, and books on etiquette are seldom left out where guests might see them. Many a successful politician never drives a new car in public until he has first got it good and muddy along some out-of-the-way country road. Perhaps the most obvious form which this general tendency takes is to be seen in the fact that very few people can take criticism. That, in fact, is the secret of the appeal which Dale Carnegie makes with his "psychology" in which the basic tenet is "never offend anybody" or "never criticize." "The customer is always right."

Much of what we mean when we speak of our commercialized civilization is summarized in that appalling slogan. In those five fateful words, "the customer is always right," is caught up and crystallized a basic personal and social philosophy through which we condone and nourish our habitual weaknesses. Applied in business, it makes for the peculiar sort of sense of values according to which we spend as much for candy and cigarettes as we do for schools, and pay a baseball player or a radio comedian more lavishly than a Supreme Court justice or a director of medical research.

But it is not in business affairs that we find the most striking results of this point of view. Applied in education, this policy of "the customer is always right" forces a leveling and retarding process. It makes for a kind of school in which what is taught and what is learned are in large measure determined by what taxpayers, as represented by trustees and school-board members, want taught and by what immature and mediocre children and adolescents prefer to learn. It becomes an actually important aspect of educational policy that what the schools teach or the ways in which they are conducted shall not imply criticism of established community beliefs and customs!

It is, of course, a matter of well-known historical record that the main purpose of our schools has been that of safeguarding and transmitting to each new generation the ways of its elders. While this is particularly clear in the training given the young in primitive societies, it is not an inconspicuous aspect of education in our time and in our culture. The directors of a large metropolitan university were prevailed upon a few years ago by "public opinion" to cancel an agreement whereby the renowned Bertrand Russell was to become a member of the faculty. It seems that Mr. Russell not only had developed some of the most advanced thought of our day, but had also applied that advanced thought to some discussions of "sex" —and the customers of that particular university didn't want any of Bertrand Russell's "sex." So Mr. Russell went to Harvard, and the students there were probably as disappointed by what Mr. Russell told them about "life" as were the young of Manhattan in being let down after the exciting build-up, because the lectures around which all the furor swirled have been published under the title of *An Inquiry into Meaning and Truth,* and there is not enough in them about "sex" to make it worth while even for a police investigator to read them. Besides, they are not easy reading.

In one's personal adjustment, as well as in business and education and other aspects of our social structure, application of the point of view summarized in "the customer is always right" leads to tremendous confusion, conflict, and generally infantile personalities. It shows itself in a resentment of criticism, touchiness, a high degree of insultability, all of which make for tensions, ill temper, selfishness, and a general lack of serenity. What lies behind all this is an abuse of the process of abstracting. What lies behind it is an essentially static notion of reality, with a consequent disinclination to recognize differences and a lack of adaptability or preparedness for change. What lies behind it is a relative lack of consciousness of abstracting, little or no awareness of the continuous, personal, projective, self-reflexive, multiordinal character of the abstracting process at its best, by means of which we achieve individual growth and social progress. What lies behind it, then, is an abuse of the process of abstracting, by virtue of which the normal self-correctiveness of that process is not permitted to operate.

In this lies a crucial difference between much of our everyday behavior, on the one hand, and that behavior which we call science, on the other. In science as general method, at its best, the process of abstracting is cleared of semantic blockages and proceeds freely. Under such conditions it is self-corrective. It is this that is particularly represented by the arrow in our diagram of the process. Any theory, assumption, belief, opinion, etc., is automatically referred back to reality to be tested against relevant observations and experience, and to be corrected accordingly. In this sense, any *scientific* theory contains the seeds of its own revision. That is why scientists are "always changing their minds." A scientific "truth" is always tentative, subject to change in accordance with the further observations to which it invariably directs us. This is what we mean when we say that a theory is good if it stimulates research, because if it stimulates research it directs us to the making of further relevant observations on the basis of which the theory can be tested and improved. In other words, a theory is good if it points the way to a better theory. And it is in this general sense that we speak of the process of abstracting as self-corrective. It provides a basis, a mechanism, for the innumerable specific adjustments necessary for constantly effective adjustment.

Time-Binding

Finally, the results of the process of abstracting are communicable. In this particular character of the process lies its value as a time-binding mechanism: A means of enabling one person to benefit from the knowledge of other persons, of enabling each new generation to bind into its own time, so to speak, the wisdom of times past, and so of avoiding the blunders and of extending the achievements of previous generations. It is by virtue of this time-binding characteristic that the process provides a basis for social coordination, for what we call culture, for the development of civilization. Symbolisms, written and spoken language, art, mathematics, maps, blueprints, graphs, etc.—these results of abstracting are such that they can be communicated not only in "space" but also in "time," not only from New York to London but also from the Egypt of Cleopatra to the modern America of Radio City. And, what is also extremely important, statements can be conveyed not only from a speaker to his listeners, but also from a speaker *to himself*. The relation of language behavior to personality development is high-lighted in this obvious but curiously underestimated fact that a speaker is generally his own most responsive and deeply affected listener. The old codger who said that he figured it was all right to talk to himself so long as he didn't answer back was inadvertently calling attention to a universal phenomenon. We all talk to ourselves, even when we are talking in public, and we all "answer back." That is the technique of madness—and of genius.

By virtue of the communication of symbols it is possible for one person to use other nervous systems as well as his own. Hayakawa, in *Language in Action,* gives a simple example of this. If Jones and Smith are walking and Smith is about to be struck by a stone which Jones sees, Jones can transform his lower-order abstract into the symbol, "Duck!" Smith ducks and avoids injury, because a communicated symbol enables him to make use of Jones' nervous system in addition to his own.

This represents, in very simple form, the fundamental formula of civilization, which is essentially a matter of each person utilizing the nervous systems of other persons. To a limited extent, animals and lower forms of life generally are capable of this sharing of communicable abstracts. The rabbit thumps his hind feet on the ground, the hen cackles, the elephant trumpets, and other rabbits, hens, and elephants respond accordingly to the signals thus communicated. But there are important differences between the process as it operates in human beings and in lower forms of life. These differences can be represented in a slightly exaggerated way, in order to make the differences very clear, as in Fig. 13.

The right-hand side of the diagram you will recognize as representing the process of abstracting; but it represents this process as it operates potentially on the human level. The process of abstracting as it operates on subhuman levels is represented, in an admittedly exaggerated way, by the left-hand side of the diagram, labeled *A*. A dog, for example, knows nothing of microscopic or submicroscopic reality, and has comparatively no world of words. In this latter point lies the exaggeration in our diagram, but it helps to emphasize the fact that although a dog may be capable of some "language," his capacities for verbal abstracting are certainly very limited in comparison with our own capacities. His are mostly first-order "verbal" abstracts. He can signify some

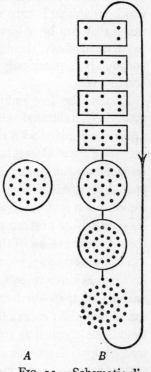

A   *B*

FIG. 13. Schematic diagram of process of abstracting in human and subhuman forms of life. *A* represents limited, essentially one-valued abstracting process of animals. *B* represents potentially infinite-valued abstracting process of humans (see Fig. 9).

types of facts by various first-order barkings and tail-waggings. He can respond with certain movements to the words of his master, or to the barkings and tail-waggings of other dogs. But chiefly he responds directly on the macroscopic level.

The range of even these first-order and second-order symbols of which an animal is capable is very limited in comparison with the range that can be achieved by adult human beings. As has been pointed out above, the number of different words in a multiordinal vocabulary is practically infinite, and this is true even on the low verbal levels.

Finally, the tremendous variety of possible symbols and the potentially unlimited self-reflexiveness of the human abstracting process, combined with the fact that human beings are capable of *recording* their abstracts or symbols, make for an enormous difference between human and subhuman abstracting. It is a difference that definitely makes a difference. Thus, men can both build a civilization and wreck it, but all a dog can do is to stick chiefly to his own private abstracts, making comparatively little use even of the nervous systems of the other dogs around him, and making no use of the nervous systems of the dead dogs that have lived before his time. For this reason, Korzybski would classify dogs and other animals as *space-binders*, capable of moving about, of "binding space" into their experiences. By sharp and significant contrast, he would classify men as *time-binders*, capable of "binding time" as well as space—capable, that is, of "binding" into their own experience the abstracts of other persons, other nervous systems, not only those now living but also those who lived in times long past.

Men are time-binders, because for human beings abstracts on verbal or symbolic levels are communicable not only directly but also in recorded form. We can write. We can take the recorded abstracts of Aristotle or Newton or Washington and abstract them further. In this sense we can make progress. Each human generation can for this reason start where the last generation left off. An American boy in 1946 can aspire to be not *like* George Washington but better than George Washington; he can go on from where Washington stopped. Therein lies the key to human advance. But the fact that it can be done, that time-binding is humanly possible, does not serve to guarantee that it will be done. It is accomplished effectively only by those who are conscious of the process by means of which it may be accomplished. The fact that a relatively conscious use of this process is an integral part of scientific method accounts for the amazing time-binding, or progress, that has been achieved in the areas in which science has been vigorously applied during the three short centuries since Galileo pointed the way.

This fact serves to raise an extremely significant problem. In scientific areas we have abandoned traditions; by virtue of the conscious use of scientific method we have sought deliberately to abandon traditions. We have succeeded to a degree undreamed of by our prescientific ancestors. Even the world of your grandfather was quite effectively bounded by its visible horizons, but in the few years since then men in laboratories have destroyed the tranquillity that was possible to your grandfather. The visible horizon of your world is merely one of its physical decorations; it no longer serves as an effective boundary. Man has become a wonder-working space-binder as well as time-binder. Each afternoon you can listen to men speaking in Ankara, in London, in Bern. Each evening the newspaper enables you to make use of nervous systems in Tokio and Cairo and Buenos Aires. And as you sit by your loud-speaker men all over the world, hot in pursuit of their own interests, can and do make use of your nervous system!

Communication, transportation, industrial processes, the tool-using aspects of everyday life, military methods, and commercialized recreation—these have been transformed as if by witches through the applications of experimental techniques. The materialistic aspects of our world have been enormously revamped. Since Galileo, but particularly during the last hundred years, we have been binding time like racing tailors, until all is changed and all is changing faster and faster—in those areas where we have applied and are applying scientific method.

In other areas? The Roman law, the Greek logic, the Roman church, the medieval moralities and philosophies, the economics of at least two centuries ago, the political customs of uncertain but long record, and an education in which all these are preserved and extolled—that is the other half of the disjointed world in which we live. It is as if Athenians, ancient Egyptians, Romans, and the subjects of Ghengis Khan had appeared again to push the buttons and spin the dials, to drive the motor cars and pilot the airships, to man the tanks and bombers and submarines of a world of magic which they had "discovered" but did not understand. With laws and customs, with social traditions and personal designs for living, fashioned and in some ways fashioned well for a world and a mode of life that have all but vanished, we find that habits hinder where they used to help and beliefs bring turmoil where they once made for comfort.

All this is simply to say that with old maps we traverse a new territory. The issue is sharp. If we cannot or will not make the territory old again to suit the maps, we must make the maps new to suit the territory. If we cannot or will not cease to use science in some areas of our experience, we must begin to use it in those other areas where we have so long preserved and cherished the old ways. If we cannot or will not cease to experiment upon our material world and our physical things, we must begin to experiment upon ourselves, our beliefs, and social customs, our ways of living together in a world that has shrunk to the size of a small state. For when the world changes faster than do those who live in it, they become, by definition and inexorably, increasingly maladjusted to it.

Indeed, the results of the process of abstracting can be communicated, and thus time-binding and progress become possible. But if we so employ the process of abstracting that in some respects we "bind time" while in other respects we block the process of changing our abstracts, we inevitably produce a personality that is out of joint. And if men generally do this, they create a kind of social or cultural schizophrenia, affecting civilization with a mighty internal stress that leaves no individual undisturbed. Lincoln insisted that his country could not exist half slave and half free: "A house divided against itself cannot stand." It can be said, and with greater compass and more profound foreboding, that a civilization cannot exist half scientific and half medieval. Men who cherish the past and seek steadfastly to preserve it can only disintegrate as the past they cherish recedes ever farther away from them into oblivion. As time-binding creatures we cannot with impunity seek to emulate our fathers. It is not in their world that we must live.

This does not mean that civilization must end. This is no theme of woe and torment. We are a time-binding class of life. Since Galileo we have learned, as we had never learned before, what that can mean! The growing force of that realization can hardly serve otherwise but to generate hope and zest. The river of Heraclitus rises, and the flood brings not desolation but fertility and a renewal of life and abundance.

In Brief

The implications of the process of abstracting, the basic premises and the general principles which it involves, and their varied applications will be more fully developed in the chapters that follow. At this point it will be well to restate briefly the chief characteristics of the process, as we have discussed them in the past several pages. In summary, then, we may say of the process of abstracting that it is:

1. A process of leaving out details
2. A process that proceeds normally from "lower" to "higher" levels, and that is
3. Potentially continuous
4. Personal
5. Projective
6. Self-reflexive
7. Multiordinal
8. Self-corrective
9. Productive of results that can be communicated

As a natural life process of such character it provides a basis for time-binding, for human progress, for personal and cultural adjustment. Effective abstracting involves the application of certain principles which we shall discuss presently. The abuse of the process of abstracting gives rise to an array of symptoms of personal and social maladjustment. A discussion of these will follow in later chapters. And so we shall pursue our study of man the map maker, attempting the neat self-reflexive trick of putting ourselves through the fine-grinding mill of our own evaluative processes.

THREE BASIC NOTIONS

THE AFTER-DINNER SPEAKER'S QUAINT SPECIALIST, who came to know more and more about less and less until he knew everything about nothing, serves well as a model of what a general semanticist is not. Ideally, a general semanticist comes to have fewer and fewer misconceptions about more and more things, until finally he no longer has any delusions about anything.

This is to suggest that the prime objective of general semantics is to make one conscious of abstracting, and so in the last three chapters it has been our concern to discuss abstracting as a natural life process, diagramming its structure and indicating its salient characteristics. If one is to be conscious of one's process of abstracting, one needs to know something about it, at least as much as might be learned from Chapters V to VIII. What is important now is the follow-through, a working out of the implications of the process of abstracting as we have so far described it. We need to state as clearly as we can the general premises and principles involved in the adequate functioning of the process. And we need to understand the consequences of the proper use and of the abuse of these principles, consequences not only in the broad terms of cultural tendencies and world affairs, but also in the specific and intimate terms of everyday successes and failures, ecstasy and grief, zest and ennui.

You may recall A. A. Milne's delightful story in *Winnie the Pooh* about what happened one morning when Pooh Bear went tracking in the snow in the woods. Piglet saw him going along with his head down and asked what he was doing, and Pooh said, "Tracking." When Piglet wanted to know "Tracking what?" Pooh said he didn't know because you never could tell with paw marks. So Piglet joined him, since he didn't have anything to do until Friday anyway. The paw marks they were following led them round a spinnet bush, and there they were going along wondering whether what they were tracking might turn out to be a Woozle or a Wizzle, when suddenly it appeared that whatever it was had been joined by another Woozle or Wizzle—and to their mounting astonishment they found as they continued that they were evidently pursuing more and more of both Woozles and Wizzles!

In fact, Piglet became so very astonished that, judging the time to be twelve o'clock, he was moved to recall of a sudden something he had almost forgot to remember that he had to do between the hours of twelve and twelve-five, and so he left Pooh Bear to his tracking. He who tracks and runs away will live to track another day seems to have been Piglet's way of sizing up the situation. And so it was Pooh who made the great discovery. After a while he stopped going round the spinnet bush, and looked closely at all the tracks made by the many Woozles and the many Wizzles, and he looked at them for a long while because he was a bear of very small brain. Then he very carefully placed his own paw snugly down into one of the Woozle tracks! And when Pooh Bear did that he did a very remarkable thing from which he learned a very important lesson. Pooh Bear had got wise to himself.

What Pooh Bear had learned, only very partially no doubt, we *can* learn in significant measure as we become more and more aware of what we are doing, going round and round the spinnet bush of human knowledge, engrossed in the feverish and sometimes frightening pursuit of the inky paw marks of Truth. As with Pooh and Piglet, so with us, as we go round and round, the tracks—the spell marks—become more and more numerous, and we are joyed and disturbed, by turns, as we excitedly contemplate catching a Truth. And when wisdom comes, as very occasionally it does, it reveals itself in the wry smile with which we admit that the tracks we follow are the tracks that we ourselves have made.

Wisdom comes with the realization that what we see and what we look at are not the same, that what we know and what we know about are different, that "the universe, *as known to us,* is a joint phenomenon of the observer and the observed."

NON-IDENTITY

This fundamental wisdom is summarized in the basic premise of general semantics, the *premise of non-identity.* In its most general form, it is stated as A *is not* A. So stated, it is likely, perhaps, to strike most persons as strange or incomprehensible, or even non-sensical. We are accustomed to the teachings, the language struc-ture, and the semantic influences generally which tend to make us feel that there is something more natural about the basic Aris-totelian premise of identity, A is A. When we say that this seems more "natural," however, we indicate simply that it is more familiar to us. The premise of non-identity becomes more and more under-standable as we formulate it in various ways and as we apply it in specific instances.

We have made a specific application of the premise in connection with our discussion of the three pails of water a few pages back. It turned out, as you will recall, that "A is A," in the forms of "hot is hot" and "cold is cold," did not correspond with the actual, living, extensional "facts" that the "same" water was abstracted as "hot" through one hand and as "cold" through the other hand. Thus, "A is not A" applied in the forms "hot is not hot" and "cold is not cold." The prescientific premise that A is A is seen to involve, in such a case, a disregard of certain essential conditions of the ab-stracting process.

Now, it is well for us to realize that for many years a considerable controversy, and an impressively confused one, has been going on with regard to the "validity" of the premise of identity and the con-trasting premise of non-identity, respectively. Without entering into the more intricate mazes of this controversy, it would seem that our present purposes will be achieved most readily by stating as clearly as possible what is meant by non-identity, and by a rejection of identity, within the context of general semantics. We can state the matter quite simply.

Let us consider, then, some of the ways in which a more specific form may be given to the general premise, A is not A. It may be stated, first of all, in terms of the process of abstracting, as "the word is not the object." That is to say, the name given to a fact, or any statement made about the fact, is not identical with that fact. Korzybski has put this in an engaging way by saying that whatever you say a fact is, it is not. Nothing, of course, could be more obvious. But apparently it is precisely because of its glaring obviousness that its enormous importance, its far-reaching and systematic implications, are sometimes difficult to appreciate. Since "the word is not the object" is so utterly indisputable, we tend very strongly to develop an illusion of complete understanding. Moreover, we find it most difficult to believe that anyone has ever doubted it, that we ourselves have ever doubted it or have ever believed that the word is the object.

A noted professor of philosophy has on occasion contended, for instance, that no one, except possibly rare psychiatric cases, ever tries to sleep on the word *bed*. Therefore, he insists, to talk of any such identification, to say, that is, that anyone believes that the word is the object, is to talk nonsense. Now, within the context of general semantics, it is not contended that identification, or application of the so-called "law of identity," ever, except in very rare psychiatric patients, takes any such literal, bald form. But this is not to say that identification plays a negligible role in human behavior in our culture. The identification of which we speak is that seen, for the most part, in those instances in which people *act as if* the word were the object.

They do not try to sleep on the word *bed*, but they blush upon hearing the word *syphilis*. They not only blush. For many years after men in laboratories had shown the way to a drastic reduction and even the possible elimination of this dreadful disease, the primitive verbal taboos of our supposedly enlightened culture operated effectively to stifle discussion. Without discussion, little was accomplished. People acted toward the word *syphilis* very much as they did toward what it presumably represented. They sought to avoid not only syphilis, but also the word *syphilis*. Their behavior was remindful of primitive word magic, in accordance with which it is naïvely assumed that by controlling the word one controls the thing it stands for—that by not speaking *syphilis* one somehow prevents syphilis. Identification of word and object, in this general sense, is no abstract professorial nonsense. Identification of this sort constitutes one of the most serious aspects of our social, as well as our intimately personal, problems of adjustment, growth, and survival.

Such tragic identifications are found most frequently in exactly those areas of experience where we continue to be most authoritarian, where orientation by vested precedent has not yet been forced to give way to the scientists, the Word Testers. These last strongholds of the Old Man are those which we discuss in hushed and restrained tones, or not at all, under the general headings of sex, religion, finance, and social controls as they operate in government and in the codes of caste, class, status, etc. It is no accident that the problems encountered in "mental" hospitals are so largely concerned with sex, morality, religious confusions, money, and those human relationships involving superiority and inferiority— the governing and the governed, the "censors" and the repressed, the whole matter of social control. It is with regard to just such problems that we have not learned to be effectively scientific. It is with regard to the words that symbolize experience in these areas that we have maintained our most consistent taboos.

If we were to teach the multiplication table the way we teach matters of "sex," the world would be filled with an interminable dispute as to what six times five might be. Scarcely anyone would be willing to venture an opinion on the matter in mixed company. The result of all this word-shyness, this essential identification of ink marks and sound waves with the actual experiences they are assumed to stand for, is that most of us are more or less "feeble-minded" and maladjusted so far as "sex" is concerned. The attitude of many new mothers is not too remotely remindful of the pussycat, described in a short story by Stella Benson, who turned to look upon its new litter of kittens with an expression that seemed to say, "Gee whiligers! Look what's happened!"

The extent of our verbal subterfuges in this general connection can be gauged roughly by the fact that some nursery-school teachers found by actual count that they had to learn approximately forty different polite expressions which children used to say that they wanted to go to the toilet! The flouncing gyrations that we go through in trying to skirt around certain four-letter Anglo-Saxon words, and even some technical anatomical terms, is one of the semantic wonders of the world. Only a professor of "philosophy" could believe that no one acts as though the word were the object!

Two Kinds of Language

As a matter of fact, it is as if we used two different kinds of language in dealing with our ordinary problems. This oversimplifies the case, but in so doing it serves to clarify an important point. If your radio, your car, or your electric ironer does not function properly, you consult a tradesman, a mechanic of some sort, and in the conversation that is carried on by you and the mechanic a language is used that is remarkable for its straightforward effectiveness, its expression of sheer sanity on the part of both of you, and especially on the part of the mechanic. You do not call a spark plug by forty different "respectable" names, and neither of you blushes when talking about the generator, or even when touching it. Nor do you consider it a personal insult and become angry when the mechanic tells you that one of your tubes is dead. There is a minimum of identification of the words you use with the facts you are talking about, or of "self" with the realities to be dealt with.

At any moment, however, all this can change appallingly. If it turns out that the mechanic has forgotten some of his tools and it is too late in the day for him to go after them, the conversation might turn into other channels. The two of you might fall to talking about politics or religion, for example. The mature sanity which both of you had been exhibiting a moment before may well vanish like a startled dove. A kind of sparring attitude is likely to reveal itself in your conversation, expressive of a vague understanding each of you has of the verbal reflexes which the other fellow is likely to display. And unless one, or preferably both, of you is very tactful, one, or probably both, of you is going to identify "yourself" with the remarks being made, and the remarks being made with that about which they are presumably being made. If you come out of it with any conclusion other than the conviction that the mechanic is a fool, it is likely to be due to the mechanic's business sense which prompts him to try not to offend you unpardonably. You will be fortunate if one, or probably both, of you does not secretly or openly conclude that the other is a "red" or an "atheist." In short, you are likely to end up discussing—and cussing—not politics or religion but each other, and if you do not go entirely "unsane" in the process, it may occur to you to wonder why this did not happen when you were talking about the radio or the car. It may, in fact, occur to you to realize that as soon as we learn to talk about politics and religion the way we talk about vacuum tubes and generators, we shall probably begin to manage our political and moral affairs as efficiently as we now deal with receiving sets and automobile engines.

Psychiatrists long ago discovered that patients in "mental" hospitals are variously confused, disoriented, deluded, out of touch with reality. They long ago learned that their main task in treating such patients is that of somehow getting them to face reality and to deal with it "objectively." They have found, for instance, that many of the patients can be helped significantly through what has come to be known as occupational therapy. This is a name for being busy with one's hands at a job that requires one to deal directly with facts or materials of some sort in a systematic, organized way and with more or less significant results. This is by no means the whole of modern psychotherapy, but it is one of the more direct ways in which psychiatrists have come to take advantage of the fact, generally true, that men do not "go crazy" in response to facts as such. They tend to "go crazy" as they get away from facts, out of touch with reality—when what they say and think no longer stands in an adequate relationship to their world of not-words.

Words About Objects and Words About Words

Now, if one is to coordinate words and objects, maps and territories, beliefs and realities, one must first of all clearly differentiate them. Insofar as one fails to make this special application of the premise of non-identity, one runs the risk of utter confusion in which delusions are as plausible as valid statements, since the essential difference between them is not recognized. Unless the word and the object are very definitely not identified, words about objects and words about words are all one. One's higher-order abstractions are reacted to, or evaluated, as if they were the same as one's lower-order abstractions, unless the differences between them and the nature of the relations between them are clearly recognized. The person who does not recognize these differences and these relations—who is not conscious of abstracting—tends therefore to identify different orders of abstraction, words with objects, objects with submicroscopic events, higher-order statements with those of lower order. For such a person, seeing is believing, reading or being told is believing, thinking or telling himself is believing. The details of such considerations have been summarized succinctly by Korzybski in the statement, "The pathological processes of 'mental' illnesses involve identification as a generalized symptom."

This, then, constitutes one way of elaborating the bare premise of non-identity, the premise that A is not A. It is one of the ways of indicating what is meant, within the framework of general semantics, by the statement that identity, that A is A, is false to facts. For example, it is false to facts to say that money is money if you mean that a bond with "$100" printed on it is the same as a hundred-dollar bill, or that a check for $100 is necessarily the same as 100 silver dollars. One hundred dollars in one form may not be at all the same as one hundred dollars in some other form. And certainly the "same" hundred-dollar bill has different value, different "meaning," under different circumstances. At one time it may "mean" fifty bushels of potatoes, at another time it may "mean" a surgical operation. At one time you would rather have the bill than the potatoes; at another time you would much rather have the potatoes or the operation. A hundred-dollar bill is not always valued the same. It is *evaluational* identity and non-identity that we are talking about. It is the identification involved in talking and acting *as if* the word were the object, the inference were the description, the coin were the meal it might—or might not—buy, etc. In the sense intended, then, truth is not truth (A is not A), for example, in the sense that what truth refers to on one level of abstraction is not identical with that to which it refers on some other level. To put it in homely terms, a theoretical statement about hamburger is not the same as the label *hamburger*, which in turn is not the same as hamburger you can stick a fork into and put in your mouth, which again is not the same as hamburger acted upon by your digestive juices and assimilated into your body.

Thus, within the framework of general semantics, we may indicate a broad denial of identity, and a relatively general application of non-identity, by giving the premise of non-identity the following form: A given abstract is not the abstract from which it has been abstracted, nor is it an abstract of itself. This is a general way of saying that the word is not the object or that an inference is not a description, etc. For example, the experience of having a toothache is by no means completely represented by any amount of verbal description of it, and the more general statement, "I had a toothache yesterday," leaves out most of the details covered in the more full description. The experience comes first and the description is an abstract of it; the general statement is an abstract of the description. An abstract represents a previous abstract and may be represented by a further abstract. The premise of non-identity is one way of expressing a recognition of this general character of abstracting.

HORIZONTAL NON-IDENTITY

If we refer to what we have been discussing as vertical non-identity and vertical identification (in terms of our diagram of the process of abstracting), then we may recognize, also, what we may call horizontal non-identity and horizontal identification. Thus, when applied extensionally the formal law of identity, A is A, becomes, for example, "man is man," or even "man is an animal." On the other hand, the formal premise of non-identity, A is not A, becomes "man_1 is not man_2," or "$Smith_1$ is not $Fido_1$." In such a sense, of course, the premise of non-identity would be impossible to deny. It is extraordinarily secure. In order to deny it, one would have to produce two men, for example, or a man and an animal, or any two things that were identical in all respects—exact duplicates. If you care to, you may try it. The premise of non-identity is secure, indeed, on non-verbal grounds. In some relatively abstract sense one may say that A is A, that man is man, boys are boys, "pigs is pigs," man is an animal, etc. But in terms of "facts," of first-order unspeakable phenomena or experience, one cannot make such statements legitimately.

Not only is it evident that $Smith_1$ is not $Smith_2$, for example, but it is also apparent that $Smith_1$ ^{today} is not $Smith_1$ ^{yesterday}. Not only are no two things alike, but also no one thing is ever twice the same, ever identical with itself. "One cannot step in the same river twice." Thus, the premise of non-identity is seen to be entirely general, within the frame of reference of general semantics. With reference to a process reality, it appears to be structurally correct.

The law of identity sometimes holds sufficiently for practical purposes, in spite of its structural defectiveness. Therefore we can use it many times, but we should always be aware of our use of it. When eating peanuts, for example, we may proceed on the practical assumption that peanuts are peanuts, that $peanut_1$ is $peanut_2$, that they are the same. Even so, we should remember that they are not, that ultimately peanuts are not peanuts, that is, $peanut_1$ is not $peanut_2$. The differences, generally speaking, make no important difference, of course, and we can for the most part disregard them. But if we are basically oriented to non-identity, we will bite into the bad peanut that may be found in almost any bag, without bursting into invective against *"these* damned peanuts." We will merely discard peanut$_1$ and go on to enjoy peanut$_2$, since basically we had not assumed that they would be the same anyway. Therefore, an occasional bad peanut is no cause of shock, no generator of tensions.

It is "in principle" that different things are the same. This is to say, it is on relatively high levels of abstraction, "in general," "on the average," "for practical purposes," "in main essentials," with regard to certain more or less important respects (not in *all* respects) that two different things may be evaluated, spoken of, or dealt with as though they were identical. For certain purposes specific differences may not make a difference; what is important is that we realize that differences exist and that we recognize the conditions under which they do make a difference. This is to say that what is important is that we be fundamentally oriented to non-identity so that we shall be prepared for differences at any time. It is precisely the differences we least expect that tend to make the biggest difference, that have the gravest consequences and demand the most difficult readjustments.

What all this amounts to is that, within the system of general semantics, the law of identity becomes a special rule, more restricted in its range of application than is the premise of non-identity. This means that it is to be applied, when applied, under conditions involved in the orientation of non-identity. Let us put this simply by saying that similarities are as valid or dependable as the ever-present differences allow. The differences are more basic; it is by ignoring some of them, by leaving out details, that we recognize similarities. It is by our being aware of those details that we leave out, by recognizing those differences that we disregard, by being basically oriented to non-identity, that the similarities we abstract, the generalizations we draw, the "identities" we assume "for practical purposes," may be safeguarded and made as dependable as possible. On the basis of a non-identity orientation, we may tentatively, and with awareness of its limitations, employ the law of identity with reasonable safety. This is consistent with what we have said about the natural order of abstracting, in which differentiation provides both the basis and the test of generalization.

NON-ALLNESS

There are two other fundamental premises closely related to the one we have been discussing. The first of these may be stated as "A is *not all* A." This is much more understandable in its more specific form, "the word does not represent all the object," or "the map does not represent all the territory." This premise expresses the fundamental notion that abstracting is a process of leaving out details. One can never say all about anything, just as one can never observe all of anything. This may be succinctly stated as the *premise of non-allness*. It is supplementary to the premise of non-identity.

In terms of ordinary human behavior, the law of identity tends to generate an attitude of *allness*, a way of evaluating an abstract as if it were not an abstract but as if it were, rather, all there were to be evaluated. This is to be seen generally in connection with rumor or gossip. People evaluate second-, or fifth-, or tenth-hand statements (abstracts) as if they were sufficient and conclusive. They form judgments of the individuals concerned, and even take action, often with grave consequences, on the basis of such high-order abstracts. Urging people not to spread rumor, appealing to their "sense of fairness," etc., usually is quite ineffective, since the basic orientation of identity makes it practically inevitable that people so orientated will identify different levels of abstraction, and quite "innocently" react to high and low levels as though they were alike. It is not that gossipmongers are inherently "bad," "vicious," etc. In a sense, they are simply uneducated (no matter how much schooling they have had). Unconscious of abstracting, unaware of the differences and relations among levels of abstraction, they mistake high-order inferences for first-order descriptions, and descriptions for facts, and "facts" (as personally abstracted) for realities. They do not maliciously mean to do this. Doing it is simply an integral aspect of an identity orientation. All the preaching and teaching on earth, including threats of punishment and death and promises of heaven, are essentially powerless against it, unless that teaching results in a basic orientation to non-identity and the supplementary non-allness.

Individuals thoroughly trained to non-identity and non-allness do not suppress their impulses to indulge in gossip. They just don't have such impulses. They have not learned, lo and behold, how to be good. They have simply become conscious of their abstracting processes. Like Pooh Bear a few pages back, they have got wise to themselves. They have learned that what they say is not what they say it about, and that what they look at is not what they see. The moralist would say they have achieved tolerance and understanding, or that they have been "reborn," or have "found the light." The fact is that they have learned the difference between a *signal* and a *symbol*. An abstract, evaluated as such, is recognized as a symbol. A symbol represents something other than itself, and a *symbol reaction* is a reaction that is made not to the symbol directly, but to the something else which it represents or symbolizes. A rumor evaluated as an abstract, and so as a symbol, is not reacted to directly. What is reacted to are the facts back of, or supposedly represented by, the rumor. And if no facts can be found, no reaction is forthcoming. There is no mysterious "sense of fairness," or "strength of character," or "inhibition," or "will power" involved. It is simply that no adequate stimulus to action is found, so no reaction is made.

On the other hand, a rumor evaluated not as an abstract, and therefore not as a symbol, but as a fact, tends to be reacted to directly, as though it were a signal. And to signals, we tend to react, as do animals, in relatively undelayed, thoughtless, stereotyped ways. Thus, insofar as words or statements are evaluated as signals rather than as symbols, our reactions to them tend to become abnormally prompt, unreflective, and pathologically consistent. We become hoop-jumpers, responding faithfully and in set patterns to the words and slogans that are thrown at us. We can be depended upon like so many trained seals. Levels of abstraction are identified by us, and the words we hear or read are *all* that is required to get us to react. Under such conditions, when symbols become signals, it is fatefully true, as Korzybski has stressed, that "those who rule the symbols rule you."

Identity and allness go hand in hand, as do non-identity and non-allness. If rumor $_{macroscopic}$ is rumor $_{description}$ is rumor $_{inference}$, then rumor $_{inference}$ is all that is required for a reaction to rumor $_{macroscopic}$. If rumor $_{inference}$ is not rumor $_{macroscopic}$ one cannot react promptly and in a stereotyped manner to rumor $_{inference}$. One must wait and find out what there is to react to as rumor $_{description}$ or, better, as rumor $_{macroscopic}$. And even this latter will not be reacted to except as it is understood to be an abstract of rumor $_{submicroscopic}$, and so not absolutely dependable.

If, for example, stutterer$_1$ is stutterer$_2$ is stutterer$_3$, etc., if a stutterer is a stutterer, then all one needs to know in order to react to an individual is that he *is* a stutterer, and the reaction will be made quickly, with relatively no delay, since essentially the same reaction is to be made to stutterer$_1$ as to any other stutterer. But if stutterer$_1$ *is not* stutterer$_2$, one cannot react to the label with prompt finality; one must know more than the fact that the individual is called a stutterer. He may be also the King of England or the Russian Foreign Commissar. He may even be, by any ordinary standards, a normal speaker.

All this may sound so much like common sense and common knowledge that it would appear necessary to guard against the deceptive illusion of utter familiarity. To say, "That is nothing new" is all too often to say, in effect, "I have stopped learning about that." It is one of our most common and effectively paralyzing ways of expressing an attitude of allness. To call something "old stuff" frequently indicates nothing about what we so label; rather, it reveals simply that we do not intend to make any effort to increase our knowledge, to improve our understanding, or to change our habits. "Old stuff" means, "I know it *all* already." An attitude of this kind—"You can't tell me anything about that"—has an effect quite similar to that of a pus sac in the brain.

What there is for most of us to learn, beyond what we already know, about non-allness is simply that an ever-clear awareness of non-allness *as a principle* provides us with greater assurance that we will behave as if we knew that our knowledge and our statements are never complete and final. This consciousness of non-allness is part of the "know-how" of adequate behavior. And "know-what" without "know-how" is generally futile.

The case of Henry is a good illustration of this. Henry was a behavior problem. Everyone who was supposed to deal with him finally gave up and called in a psychologist. The psychologist came, examined the school records, talked long and in detail with Henry's teachers, his school superintendent, his distraught parents. He talked with Henry, he gave him tests, he observed him at work and at play. Then he called Henry into private conference and delivered his considered judgment: "Henry," he said, "you've simply got to control your temper."

Henry blew up. "Control your temper! Control your temper! My pa and ma have told me that, over and over again. My teachers have all told me that, my superintendent, the preacher, everybody, they've all told me I have to control my temper. Now you tell me. Listen. Just *how* in hell do you control your temper?"

It is useless, sometimes to the point of disaster, to know something without knowing how to act as though you knew it. The purpose of being clearly aware of basic principles, such as those of non-identity and non-allness, is that they make for more intelligent, adaptive regulation of one's behavior than any rules of thumb and routine habits ever could. They provide one with an important measure of know-how.

SELF-REFLEXIVENESS

A third basic premise of the system of general semantics is that language, and abstracting generally, are self-reflexive. We have already discussed this, and it is sufficient here simply to indicate its fundamental place within the system. Its close relation to the premises of non-identity and non-allness is plain enough to require no elaborate statement. As a self-reflexive process of making abstracts of abstracts of abstracts, potentially *ad infinitum,* the abstracting process necessarily involves non-identity and non-allness.

IN BRIEF

For practical purposes, it will be well to summarize these basic premises of general semantics in the following forms:

Non-identity: The word is not the object; the map is not the territory; an abstract on one level is not the same as an abstract on any other level.

Non-allness: The word does not represent all the object; the map does not represent all the territory; what is abstracted on one level does not represent all that is abstracted on a lower level.

Self-reflexiveness: We use language for talking about language, we make maps of maps, statements about statements, evaluations of evaluations; we make abstracts of abstracts of abstracts indefinitely. In other words, abstracting is self-reflexive.

These, then, constitute the basic premises, the bedrock, of the whole system of general semantics. If these are accepted, the rest follows. And their implications turn out to be surprisingly varied and general, touching life, your life, in its many trivial and major aspects. What we have said in this chapter will be more adequately understood and more effectively applied, incidentally, if it is remembered that what we have said *is not all* that could be said. As we go round and round the spinnet bush of human knowledge and experience, there is much more tracking yet to be done before we find ourselves—as we shall see still more clearly in the next chapter.

WORKING PRINCIPLES

$\mathscr{I}$N THE PRECEDING FOUR CHAPTERS WE HAVE DISCUSSED
the process of abstracting and the basic premises of non-identity,
non-allness and self-reflexiveness. In these terms we have presented the system of general semantics in its more fundamental
aspects. This system is applied in accordance with certain principles, and the following discussion concerns these principles. It is
in terms of these that general semantics may be used more or less
generally in dealing with personal and social problems.

We shall consider three main principles, those of *probability*
(uncertainty), *symbol reaction* (conditionality) and *extensionalization*. In connection with symbol reaction, we shall deal with the
two supplementary principles of *delayed reaction* and *optimal
tonicity*. In a general way the principle of extensionalization implies and serves to integrate all the others; for this reason it will
be last in order of presentation.

PROBABILITY

The *probability principle* follows directly from the three basic
premises of general semantics. It sums up the wisdom that truth is
tentative, because all things change even though some things may
change slowly and by imperceptible degrees. Truth is tentative,
because it is abstracted by human beings who are not infallible.
The principle may be stated simply in some such words as these:
In a world of process—and by creatures of process—predictions

can be made and reports can be given only with some degree of probability, not with absolute certainty.

In other words, and bluntly, one cannot be absolutely certain of anything—except, it would seem, uncertainty. Einstein has very aptly expressed this general notion: "As far as the laws of mathematics refer to reality, they are not certain; and as far as they are certain, they do not refer to reality." This is equally true of languages other than mathematics. It is not to be denied, of course, that sometimes probabilities are very great; one can be very nearly certain that somewhere tomorrow the sun will shine. Death and taxes are practically foregone conclusions. And as Will Rogers said as he stared at the French menu, "When you get down under the gravy, it has to be either meat or potatoes." But even about such seemingly invariable matters one speaks from experience, and experience has the tantalizing character of incompleteness. There is always at least a small gap between the greatest probability and absolute certainty.

"Then," you may well ask, "is it absolutely certain that nothing is absolutely certain?" As we answer this, let us remember the levels of abstraction. It is certain that statements about reality cannot be absolutely certain. This statement of certainty is, however, a statement about other statements; it does not refer to reality. "As far as the laws of mathematics refer to reality they are not certain; and as far as they are certain, they do not refer to reality." To put it simply, it is certain that $2 = 2$, *because we say so;* it is certain, that is, unless we are referring to 2 pigs and 2 pigs, for example. Ellis Parker Butler notwithstanding, 2 pigs is not 2 pigs, provided they are real pigs. To paraphrase Einstein, as far as $2 = 2$ refers to reality, it is not certain; and as far as it is certain, it does not refer to reality. We have to deal here not with a mysterious paradox, but simply with the fact that the levels of abstraction are different, that a statement about reality is different from a statement about that statement. The one is not certain; the other may be, at least so long as we treat it as such. The essential point is this: a statement such as $2 = 2$ is certain, when it is, simply in the sense that we agree to treat it as certain. The elementary fact, so easy to forget, is that language and the rules of its use are man-made—and they are still in the making.

The great importance of the principle of probability (or uncertainty) lies in the fact that our living reactions are on the low, non-verbal levels of abstraction. It is on these levels that "all things flow." On higher levels we can *say* they do not. We can *say* what we like. As Hayakawa has so vividly expressed it, we can put up a sign that says "Free Beer Here" when there is no free beer here. The levels of abstraction are potentially independent. In the meantime, we and the world about us do not remain absolutely fixed and static and are not, therefore, absolutely predictable. We can be sure that $2 = 2$ in principle, but not in a horse trade. The next oyster is not the same as the last oyster if you have just eaten twenty-seven oysters. Since no two things are the same and no one thing stays the same, your inability to adjust to reality will be in proportion to the degree to which you insist on certainty as to facts— and believe that you have achieved it.

In a practical sense, in terms of behavior, this principle can be reduced to a sort of motto: "I don't know—let's see." That is to say, whenever one is confronted by a new situation one does not unhesitatingly respond to it in some way definitely decided upon in advance. It is rather as though one were to say, "I don't know— let's see," with a sensitiveness to any respects in which *this* situation might be different from previous ones, and with a readiness to make appropriate reactions accordingly.

It is to be clearly recognized that such an approach to new situations does not involve indecisiveness. It does not represent failure to "make up one's mind." Rather it represents a method for making up one's mind without going off half-cocked. It provides a measure of insurance against the blunders we make in judging people by first impressions, in applying to individual women drivers our attitude toward *the* woman driver, in condemning a person—or in committing ourselves to his support—on the basis of hearsay or on the basis of very brief acquaintance. We make such blunders by reacting to the individual not as though he were an individual, different and variable, but as though he were merely a member of a type and the same as all other members of that type—and then we react inappropriately because we are so very sure of our opinion of the type.

From time to time in the Sunday supplements there are articles concerning the type of man *the* college girl wants for a husband— "Betty Co-ed's Ideal Soul Mate." It frequently happens that such an article is written by a reporter who has gone about some university campus asking a dozen or so girls what type of man they prefer. It appears that usually the girls' answers are very positive and in some respects they are more or less specific. Dorothy, for example, says she wants to marry a man who is tall, blonde, a good dancer, and popular. That description is fairly specific, and still sufficiently vague to apply to any one of thousands of men. Let us suppose Dorothy meets one of them. To her, he's "the type," so it is a case of love at first sight. She does not love him, she loves "the type." Being sure that he is "her type," she is equally sure that he is "her man." It will not be until sometime later, after her life has become rather thoroughly enmeshed in his, that she will discover—with great unhappiness and shock, and perhaps resulting bitterness about "men"—that besides doing a neat rhumba and being tall, blonde, and popular, he is also "lazy," "quick-tempered," and "unfaithful." Since it will not occur to her that she had no basis for being so sure in the first place, it will occur to her that she has been cheated, and that "men are not to be trusted." And she will be just as sure of that as she had been sure that she had found her "soul mate."

Maladjusted people almost universally *complain of* feelings of uncertainty—or else they express their unfortunate condition in dogmatic pronouncements and attitudes of sure finality from which they refuse to be shaken, in spite of the mistakes and miseries into which they are plunged because of them. It appears to be quite incomprehensible to such persons that there could be anything amiss so far as their basic assumptions are concerned. Most of them seem not to consider that they have any *assumptions* at all. They have been taught and have never questioned that certainty is desirable, even necessary, and altogether attainable. Most school children are early taught a sense of shame at having to say, "I don't know." From their prim and impeccable teachers they acquire the amazing notion that the proper ideal is to know everything correctly, absolutely and forever. In a grading system in which A means "perfect," a grade of B can and very frequently does leave children in a state of chagrin and demoralization! Such children grow up with feelings of profound distrust of politicians who waver in their judgments on national and international issues. As they themselves enter into the councils of men they bring with them the "virtues" of resoluteness and dogmatic conviction—or, as it is sometimes called, pigheadedness. They tend to become what someone has referred to as "men of principle and no interest."

In some unreal "higher" realm, certainty might be possible and, as a working principle, it might be useful. But unreal "higher" realms do not exist except inside our heads and on high levels of abstraction. If one attempts to live on these levels as though they were the same as the non-verbal levels of reality, one forfeits any chance of adequate adjustment to the world and to the people in it. In the realm of direct experience whether we look backward in memory or forward in anticipation, nothing is absolutely certain. Each new situation, problem, or person is to be approached, therefore, not with rigidly fixed habits and preconceived ideas, but with a sense of apparent probabilities. It is as though one were to say, "I don't know *for sure*, but I'll see what there is to see." Above all, this principle of probability, or uncertainty, is not merely something to "know" or to touch upon in a classroom lecture. It is a principle to be *acted upon* from minute to minute, day in and day out.

SYMBOL REACTION

A closely related principle is that of *symbol reaction* (conditionality). A symbol reaction may be recognized by contrasting it with a *signal* reaction. Consider the runner, to whom the crack of the official starter's pistol is a signal, to which he is tensely set to make one and only one response, and to make this response with the least possible delay. The runner's response to the sound of the starter's gun is an example of a signal reaction. Other examples may be seen in the amenities of social relationships: "Thank you," "You're very welcome," "I've had a lovely time," "Do come again," sometimes but not always followed by "when you can stay longer," etc. Still other examples are to be seen in such common behavior as the persistent voting of a straight ticket; the devout churchgoer's bowing of the head as the minister begins intoning *The Lord's Prayer;* our shocked reactions upon hearing certain four-letter Anglo-Saxon words—outside the places where they may be heard without the social requirement that we be shocked by them; undelayed and stereotyped reactions of rejection, or approval, made to certain names, such as *communist, capitalist,* etc.

In fact, signal reactions figure prominently in most ritual and ceremony, whether in the church, the court, polite society, or wherever. Our most strongly held beliefs, preferences, and prejudices are usually expressed as signal reactions. Also, in moments of anger, dejection, and other states of deep feeling, we tend to react with practically no reflective hesitation and according to fairly rigid patterns of speech and behavior. The language used at such times is likely to be extreme, involving considerable allness, as expressed by such words as *always, never, nothing, nobody, everybody, everything, entirely, absolutely, of course,* etc. It is language going all out.

From such examples we may draw the general statement that signal reactions are relatively undelayed, more or less unvarying or stereotyped, and that they indicate an underlying overreadiness to react. In other words, to a stimulus which one evaluates as a signal, one is likely to react too soon, too much, and in too limited a pattern. The "too-muchness" indicates an underlying state of tension. As I have stated previously in *Language and Speech Hygiene,* "The tendency to show undelayed reactions is consistent . . . with a condition of hypertonicity. We rather expect a tense individual to be jumpy, nervous, irritable, quick to take offense, etc., to show hair-trigger reactions generally. It is the relatively relaxed individual whom we rather expect to be thoughtful, patient, tolerant, to suspend judgment, to consider the many sides of a question, to be collected and unexcited in an emergency."

Symbol reactions are to be contrasted with *signal* reactions, then, in being more variable, more delayed, and involving a more nearly optimal degree of tension. Associated with the symbol-reaction principle, therefore, are the supplementary principles of *delayed reaction* and *optimal tonicity*. They are integrally related and no attempt will be made to separate them to any considerable degree in the following discussion. Methods of relaxation will be discussed in some detail in Chapter X.

DELAYED REACTION

To be conscious of abstracting is to realize that any word or statement, as well as any object or event, any stimulus, is an abstract of *something else*. In that sense it is a symbol, representing something other than itself. One does not, therefore, react to it directly, as though it were a signal; rather, in reacting to a symbol, one reacts to the "something other than itself." But this "something" is not always immediately obvious; it takes time, a fraction of a second up to very long periods, to find out what a symbol represents most reliably and relevantly. This is true in part because what it represents is never two times the same. One's reaction, therefore, is to be correspondingly delayed and variable, since there is clearly a disadvantage, as a rule, in being overly ready to react in any rigidly set way. The person who consistently shows symbol reactions tends to be relatively relaxed—not too relaxed to act at all, but not too tense to be reflective and flexible.

Some of our old folk maxims express this principle of delayed reaction to some degree: "Look before you leap." "When angry count to ten." "Don't count your chickens before they are hatched." Also, there is the familiar warning, "Stop, Look, and Listen!" It would appear that the reason why these wise sayings have no more effect on behavior than they do is that—and this is scarcely realized—they are profoundly inconsistent with the basic prescientific assumptions by which we live. If certainty is a desirable ideal, why not count your chickens before they are hatched? If love is love, A is A, regardless of the level of abstraction on which you experience or evaluate it, why look before you leap? If truth is truth, if truth$_1$ is the same as truth$_2$, if truth $_{inference}$ is the same as truth $_{observation}$, there is no point in delayed and conditional reactions.

To a mouse, cheese is cheese. That is why mouse traps are effective. To many human beings Right is Right, Wrong is Wrong, Capital is Capital, and Labor is Labor. That is why propaganda is effective. In this connection, it is interesting to consider what we call conditioned responses. A dog, as the Russian physiologist Pavlov demonstrated some fifty years ago, can be trained, or conditioned, to produce a flow of saliva at the sound of a bell. This is one example of the so-called conditioned response which has received so much attention from modern psychologists.

Since farmers first began to call their hogs, essentially the same phenomenon had been demonstrated daily for centuries before Pavlov "discovered" it. What the farmers and Pavlov did was to train their animals in identification. They got them to the point where they behaved toward a bell or some other sound in the same way that they behaved toward food itself. If you call the hogs and then give them corn they will, after a few feedings, come even if you don't give them corn, provided you call them. For the pigs, "A is A" becomes "the farmer's call is corn." The stupidity of a pig is to be measured in terms of the number of times he comes in response to your call after you have discontinued the corn—and in terms of the promptness and speed, the lack of delay, with which he continues to come.

In our culture what Pavlov and the farmers have demonstrated to be true of animals is not infrequently true of human beings as well. As a matter of fact, it is appallingly true of human beings—in our culture. In a book dealing with "the psychology of totalitarian political propaganda," Serge Chakotin points out with discouraging thoroughness the similarity between the methods used by Pavlov in training dogs to salivate alike to bells and beefsteaks, and the methods used by Hitler and other authoritarian leaders in training their followers to be followers—to respond to swastikas and other convenient signals with monotonously *consistent* and *undelayed* gestures, attitudes and elaborate courses of action. Political propaganda, as well as commercial propaganda (advertising), depends for its effectiveness upon the degree to which people can be induced to react to slogans, names, designs, colored lights, etc., in essentially the same way that dogs can be induced to respond to bells and buzzers. The degree to which people can be induced so to respond is indicated by the vast amount of political and commercial propaganda to which we are subjected. There is so much of it because it pays—in our culture.

The phrase, "in our culture," has been stressed in this discussion because it is by no means certain that it is necessary for human beings to behave in these respects as do dogs or pigs. So-called laws of learning, based on studies of relatively unconditional animal behavior, have been advanced by many psychologists as laws of *human* learning. They may well be for the majority of people—*in our culture*. We too, as well as Pavlov's dogs and the farmer's pigs, have been, and still are, trained in identification. Consequently we too characteristically respond to words and to certain other stimuli in undelayed and stereotyped ways. We too can be trained to develop highly conditioned or, rather, highly *un*conditional responses. To put it simply—and disagreeably—we too can be easily fooled.

After all, the way we classify, or label, an individual or a thing determines very largely how we will react toward it. When our classification, or labeling, of an individual determines, entirely and without exception, our attitudes and reaction toward that individual, our behavior is scarcely distinguishable from the behavior of Pavlov's dogs.

Now, it is to be clearly recognized that in our still fundamentally prescientific culture we tend strongly to deal with individuals and things in terms of classes, categories, or types. The very structure of our language largely insures this, without our having to attend to it. That structure, patterned as it is on the A-is-A premise, implies that reality consists of types of things, each type having its distinguishing attributes or features. Thus, we speak of our language as having a subject-predicate structure. That is to say, it is designed to classify objects or actions according to their supposedly intrinsic and absolute qualities. It performs this function quite automatically. Almost any common noun, for example, denotes, when used uncritically, not a particular or unique thing, but a whole class. "This is a book" represents the more nearly complete statement: "This particular, unique object belongs to that class of objects we call *book* and is to be reacted to accordingly, as we react to other objects in this class." It is a statement of classification serving to assign a particular thing to a given category or class of things. Then, as we have learned to react to that category, so we react to the particular thing. In such a sense, any statement of the form, "This is a book," is an expression of *identification*.

Such a statement of identification says, in effect, that a number of different objects are the same. Any common noun serves this function of identifying, of expressing the *sameness* of, all the different, particular things which it names. *Chair, hat, shoe, virtue,* and so on, are words which imply that in this world there are large numbers of things that are the same. All you have to do is to talk, using such words as they are customarily used, and you will automatically indulge in varying degrees of identification.

In varying degrees—because, while the structure of our prescientific language would tend to enforce almost complete identification and thus render us practically incapable of intelligent behavior, most of us exercise some degree of "horse sense" in using language. Actual experience with hard facts teaches us, in varying degrees, that A is not A, that all examples of *hat* or of *virtue*, of *democracy* or of *physician,* etc., are not the same. To the degree that we learn this, we learn to *delay our reactions,* in order to vary them—in order to make each reaction appropriate to the particular example of *hat* or *virtue* or whatnot. We do this because we have learned that some hats are crowns, some crowns are phoney—and occasionally a very intelligent individual among us has learned that no two crowns, no two hats even, are exactly alike in all respects, in all their effects, and in all that they may represent.

An awareness of this leads to a certain set, or reaction tendency, which is seen as a tendency to delay reactions to words and to things, insofar as these are evaluated as abstracts or symbols. This delay is essential to adequate evaluation. If all *Jews*, or all *physicians*, or all *blondes* are not the same, then we cannot have one response, to be made without hesitation, to every *Jew*, or to every *physician*, or to every *blonde*, on every occasion. Then we must have various possibilities of reaction, and we must delay them in any particular instance until an appropriate response becomes apparent. The important fact is that we can do this.

Of course, it has been clearly demonstrated, over and over again, that men *can be trained* to behave essentially like animals, to make undelayed reflex-like signal reactions instead of the delayed, evaluative symbol reactions of which they are naturally capable. Just because they can be so trained, it is all the more essential that they be highly conscious of the basic principles and methods by means of which their behavior can be so grossly perverted. The way to avoid a danger is to learn how it occurs. If you want to avoid being fooled you should find out how the fooling is done. The way to convince yourself that the magician did not saw the woman in two is not to shut your eyes and tell yourself resolutely, "He couldn't have!" The way to convince yourself that he didn't is to learn his technique.

Just so, the way to keep from behaving like Pavlov's dog is to find out just what Pavlov did to the dog. He merely took the premise of identity, A is A, and trained the dog to behave in terms of it to an absurd degree. That is to say, he got the dog to the point where two different things meant the same thing. What Pavlov did in his laboratory, we do in our homes and schools and in everyday life situations with words. We simply call different things by the same name. Then we learn to respond to the name. So doing, we come to make the same response to many different things.

We do not have to behave in such unconditional ways, however. We are able to respond on many different levels of abstraction. In this we differ from dogs and other animals, and the difference is crucial. Because of it, we can avoid identifications, but dogs apparently cannot. We can associate, or classify together, any facts whatever, or we can avoid doing so, as suits our purpose. We need not form condition*ed* responses, as dogs seem destined to do. We can keep our responses condition*al*. That is to say, we can vary our responses with the conditions under which we make them, in accordance with the principle of non-identity. In order to do this, we have to delay our reactions more or less—and we can.

To put it simply, we can avoid learning an invariable reaction to a class. We can recognize the differences among the individual members of a class, and vary our reactions to them accordingly. We can understand that a given individual may be classified in any number of different ways, depending on the purposes of classification, and that he does not absolutely belong in some particular class. Moreover, we can recognize that classes on higher levels of abstraction are more inclusive than are classes on lower levels. Class reactions —that is to say, identifications—on the higher levels have more widespread effects, therefore, than do class reactions on lower levels. If you have a condition*ed* response to the word, and therefore to the class, *Negro,* it affects your relations with several million individuals. A condition*ed* response to the label, and the class, *northern Negro,* will affect fewer of your human relationships. You can, however, avoid forming or retaining either of these conditioned responses. You can react to $Negro_1$ and to $Negro_2$ differently. You can do more than that: you can react to man_1 and to man_2, not as members of the class, *Negro,* at all, but as individual human beings. Not only can you do this, you have to be trained not to do it. In other words, if you are to have conditioned responses, they have to be conditioned. Otherwise they will tend to be conditional. You are not one of Pavlov's dogs.

We can respond on different levels of abstraction. But we may not know that. We may not be conscious of abstracting. In our prescientific culture we do not tend to become conscious of abstracting. If we do not know that a word names a whole class of things and implies identification of them, if we do not evaluate the difference between words and objects, if we do not clearly differentiate inferences from descriptions, we tend to behave the way animals do, because they too are ignorant of such matters. Under such conditions, we react to lower-level abstracts, to individual persons, objects, or events, as though they were the same as higher-level abstracts, classes, categories, or generalizations. We react to the word *educa-tion*, for example, as though it were the same—to be reacted to the same—as actual education; and, so, as though education₁ were the same as education₂. There actually are people who are in favor of "education," and others who are opposed to "education"! Such people have condition*ed* responses on a high level of abstraction.

THE LIMITATIONS OF HABIT

It is to be heavily emphasized that the foregoing discussion is not meant to imply that all classes, categories, and generalizations are to be done away with, that no habits are to be formed, that nouns and adjectives are to be abandoned—or anything of the sort. We must have generalizations, and classifications, and we must have a degree of regularity in our behavior, call it habit or what-ever you like, if we are to maintain any semblance of organized society. Many times, moreover, we must have prompt and de-cisive action if we are to survive at all.

What the foregoing discussion stresses is simply that generaliza-tions are not always dependable or useful and are therefore to be evaluated in relation to specific circumstances—and circumstances vary. Classifications are necessary, indeed, in human society, but they can, and frequently do, become too rigid, as applied. More-over, just how any particular thing is to be classified is not a fore-gone conclusion. It depends upon the purposes, necessities, and possibilities of the moment. A person is not altogether and forever a "stupid" or a "brilliant" individual, for example. All of us behave sometimes as though we were feeble-minded, and most of us have occasional flashes of very creditable insight. To talk of a person as belonging to this or that type, or possessing this or that quality, seldom does justice to the complexity and ever-changing character of the facts about him. At best, he is to be typed only for a specific purpose, and then not with absolute finality.

We need names, and language generally. We need class names, but we need also to realize that they are class names. We need to understand that what they name is variable, often greatly so. Realizing that, we are likely to use words with the care—or carelessness—appropriate to any particular situation. It is not language, as such, or any word, as such, that is "good" or "bad"; it is rather our attitude toward language, our degree of consciousness of what its use involves, that makes the difference between adjustive and maladjustive discourse.

We need regularity to some degree in our behavior. There are certain advantages in having people obey traffic regulations, in having trains run on schedule, in serving meals at fairly regular intervals, in handling certain situations by means of stereotyped public ceremonies or polite conventions. Etiquette, for example, is a great convenience. There is something to be gained from habitually shaving and otherwise grooming oneself. A general semanticist would most assuredly grant all this. In fact, he would favor a policy of routinizing as much as possible the relatively unimportant but unavoidable, and the necessary, regulations of personal, domestic, and community living. If you insist on using only the blue toothbrush and on hanging it always on the second hook from the left, he will thank you for it if he must share the same bathroom with you. He will not object if you say nothing more original than "Good morning" as you greet him at the start of each new day. But there is a limit.

Habit can be an accessory to progress, but it is not the chief means to it. It should be regulated from that point of view. It is an accessory to progress insofar as it saves time and conserves energy—but there is no progress, even so, unless the time so saved and the energy so conserved are used in the intelligent modification of other behavior. The more habitual shaving becomes for you, for example, the more free you are, while shaving, to consider problems that are of some importance to you. There is much advantage in this—unless, in considering these problems, you always arrive at the same conclusions.

No two things are alike, and no one thing stays the same. If you are clearly aware of this, it is quite all right to act as though some things were alike, and to act as though some things stayed the same —to act according to habit. It is all right, because a difference to be a difference must make a difference, and some differences don't, sometimes. So long as you realize that there always are differences nonetheless, and that you have to judge whether they do make any difference, you can be trusted with a habit, because you will know when to set it aside. No habit is foolproof. Habits are useful to people who do not depend on them, or insist on following them, regardless of circumstances; for less judicious individuals, habits tend to make for inefficiency, stupidity, and danger.

It seems necessary to make the above few remarks of warning, because in our culture there is such a widespread respect for dogmatic and positive statement, unhesitating action, and consistency. We like "men of action" who are sure of their views and are not "always changing their minds." We like to "have things settled," to "know where we stand," and to "get going." We like to be "practical." It seems necessary, therefore, to state very definitely that the principles of probability and of symbol reaction are by no means designed to make for indecisive dawdling or a policy of changing horses in the middle of every brook. On the contrary, they are designed to insure decisions that are not foolish, and action that is appropriate, in a world where things do not come in neat packages and stay put. It was once said of a certain politician that he had an extremely dirty mind because he hadn't changed it in years. "Minds" that stay put in a world that doesn't may not get dirty, but they do become inefficient. Only a process can stay adjusted to a process. The working principles of general semantics are designed to gear the process that is you to the process of reality with which you have to mesh.

EXTENSIONALIZATION

The principles of probability and symbol reaction may be integrated and in some measure extended in terms of the more general principle of *extensionalization*. The term is used in two chief ways in general semantics, the one very general, the other more specific. In its more general sense, *extensionalization* refers to what we have otherwise described as the scientific method, and as the process of abstracting, carried on consciously and adequately. To behave in accordance with the principle of extensionalization is to behave scientifically, keeping the levels of abstraction distinct and coordinated, maintaining adequate word-fact relationships, abstracting in the proper order from lower to higher levels and back again to lower, maintaining effective relationship between inferences and facts. As the psychiatrists would say, the extensional individual is in touch with reality, faces the facts, and has a good understanding of himself. He is relatively free from semantic blockages, tensions, and disabling moods. He is good company, for himself as well as for others.

In its more specific sense, *extensionalization* refers to orientation on the non-verbal levels of abstraction. It will be helpful to consider this matter from the standpoint of extensional and intensional definitions. In a rough sense, a dictionary definition is intensional. In Webster the word *stutter* is defined as "To hesitate or stumble in uttering words: to speak with spasmodic repetition or pauses; to stammer." (*Stammer* is defined as "To make involuntary stops in uttering syllables or words; to hesitate or falter in speaking; to speak with stops and difficulty; to stutter.")

This definition of *stutter* is obviously designed not to describe or to denote any particular example of stuttering, but to indicate a whole class of events. It does this by suggesting the characteristics which all the members of the class tend to have in common. In the definition there is no mention of those details by means of which one example of stuttering might be distinguished from any other example of it. It was precisely by leaving out these details that the dictionary editor was able to write the definition. As far as this definition goes, all stutterings are alike. The definition represents the editor's attempt to state the essential *quality* that makes a stuttering a stuttering, instead of a house or a tantrum.

An extensional definition, on the other hand, is quite different. Strictly speaking, it is entirely non-verbal. You define *stuttering* extensionally by pointing to, or demonstrating, examples of it, not by talking about them. Two persons might agree thoroughly to accept Webster's definition of *stuttering,* as given above, and yet disagree widely in their respective extensional definitions of the word. The Extensional Agreement Index (EAI) is a measure which

I have devised to express the degree of agreement among two or more individuals in defining a word extensionally. In the University of Iowa laboratory, Dr. Curtis Tuthill carried out an investigation in which he found that even among experts the number of agreements in defining *stuttering* extensionally (by indicating which words on a phonograph record and on a sound film were "stuttered") was only about 38 per cent of the number that would have been involved in perfect agreement.

This is an extremely important matter, but detailed consideration of it would carry us too far afield. What such studies as Dr. Tuthill's serve to emphasize is that agreement as to how we should define our terms, intensionally, by no means insures agreement as to what the terms are to stand for, so far as actual examples are concerned. When a speaker has defined his terms, he is not justified in supposing that his listeners will relate those terms to the same specific actualities as the ones to which he himself relates them. Professor Quine, of Harvard, has pointed out that much of our failure to make headway in solving certain problems has been due to our "uncritical assumption of mutual understanding," and in doing so he has put a finger on one of the most serious obstacles to cooperation and progress with which we have to contend. It seems likely that our custom of defining our terms intensionally, and our naïve belief that this makes our "meanings" clear, are in no small degree responsible for our widespread "uncritical assumption of mutual understanding."

Verbal definitions can be, however, a very effective aid in extensionalization. In *The Mask of Sanity,* for example, Dr. Hervey Cleckley has presented what amounts to a very detailed verbal definition of *psychopathic personality*. His descriptions of a number of specific cases are sufficiently vivid that, on the basis of them, one might point to other actual individuals as examples of *psychopathic personality* with some assurance that Dr. Cleckley, at least, would agree. Such a definition is sometimes spoken of as an extensional definition; this is not strictly legitimate, and it would be more in keeping with standard usage to call it a descriptive, or perhaps an operational, definition.

Intensional, highly abstracted definitions are useful to the degree that they have been abstracted from detailed descriptive or operational definitions. They are useful, that is, provided those who use them know the lower-order definitions from which they have been abstracted. It is useful to say that to stutter is "to speak with spasmodic repetition or pauses," provided you can describe or demonstrate in considerable detail several actual instances of such speaking. If you cannot do that, then for all practical purposes you do not know what you are talking about. When an intensional definition is not based firmly on lower-order abstractions but floats about on thin air, so to speak, it is worse than useless— unless one can laugh at it. Taken seriously, such a definition, or the term that it represents, can block one's evaluative processes so effectively that one may become quite incapable of clear and intelligent discourse.

In modern science there is a general insistence on operational definition. Much of the credit for this must go to Einstein, but perhaps the physicist Bridgman brought the importance of operational definition before the public most effectively in his book, *The Logic of Modern Physics*, published in 1930. As a matter of fact, the notion was quite well expressed by Charles S. Peirce back in 1878 in an essay entitled, "How to Make Our Ideas Clear," which is available in a more recent volume bearing the intriguing title, *Chance, Love and Logic*. It is sufficient to say here that a term is defined operationally by describing the operations involved in applying the term extensionally. For example, an operational definition of *weight* would include a description of just what one does in making an observation of how much something weighs. An operational definition of *stutter* would include an account of how stuttering is to be performed, or by what procedures one might observe stuttering. In the sciences such definitions refer usually to specific operations of measurement.

On verbal levels, descriptive or operational definitions are most fundamental. They constitute the verbal groundwork upon which may be erected the superstructure of inference and theory, by means of which the achievements of science and sanity become possible. In their absence science and sanity tend to be replaced by non-sense and insanity. But operational definitions are not magic and they are not everything; they are simply an important and frequently neglected step in the process of abstracting. Unless they lead to higher-order abstracting, they are fruitless; unless they are derived from adequate extensional, non-verbal definitions, they are misleading. Moreover, they are necessarily relative—a term may be defined operationally in many different ways—and when taken in an absolute, now-and-forever sense, they tend to lead to the same difficulties that result from the use of absolute intensional definitions. When employed in a relative manner, they are fundamental, on verbal levels, but they are not as fundamental as extensional definitions.

The non-verbal levels provide the data of experience from which our verbal abstractions are derived and against which they are ever to be tested and evaluated. The gathering of these data, the "having of" experiences, from which one may draw conclusions and against which one may test them—this, in the more specific sense, is what is known in general semantics as extensionalization. And the principle of extensionalization may be stated simply by saying that adequate evaluation depends upon the continual testing of one's beliefs and assumptions, one's knowledge, against non-verbal experience, or "hard facts."

But the "hard facts" are understood in the light of modern submicroscopic, inferential data, as indicated by the diagram of the process of abstracting. It is not a matter of proceeding by the blind rule that seeing is believing. The extensional person realizes that there are limits to his possibilities of observation or direct experience. The "object," as he perceives it, is not all. But he does not say that beyond his observational limits lies a "supernatural" realm, a somewhere or something "beyond nature." In trying to form a picture of "the mechanism behind the watch face," he does not lose sight of the watch face. What he infers about that which he cannot observe or experience directly must, after all, be relevant to what he can observe directly. Otherwise his inferences would go wild, and he would have no way of judging their value to him in his overwhelmingly engaging business of dealing with the world of actual experience. We have already discussed the problem in dealing with the place of constructs in scientific method. We mention it here again, however, in order to make clear that extensionalization is not a naïve matter of believing everything one sees and that one sees everything—and that it is not an equally naïve tendency to allow belief to run wild without systematic reference to direct observation and experience. The principle of extensionalization ascribes a proper significance to the non-verbal levels of direct experience in the process of abstracting.

A child trained in extensionalization would, like Adam in the Garden of Eden, see the animals before naming them. As Eric Temple Bell has cleverly put it, in our traditional educational system children name the animals before they see them. We could add, in fact, that they name a good many animals that they never will see—they can't see them, they don't exist, even in a legitimate submicroscopic sense. As soon as children are able to read, and before many of them are ready to read, we turn upon them the trickle of words that gradually becomes a veritable torrent through which they must fight their way back to the world they left when they entered the school. But when they finally get back to that world of reality, if they ever do, they see it through an opaque screen of words, a sort of intensional filter. Most of them leave the world, when death comes at last, never having "discovered" it. What they see, as the world, is not at all what they look at, and might see, could they but remove the words from their eyes, so to speak.

General semantics, as seen in terms of its working principles, is designed to help you "get the words out of your eyes." In the next chapter some of the more practical ways of doing this will be discussed. The place of extensionalization in science and in sanity will thereby be made more clearly apparent.

$\mathcal{C}hapter$ ﹏﹏﹏﹏﹏﹏﹏﹏﹏﹏﹏ X

PRACTICAL DEVICES AND TECHNIQUES

$\mathcal{T}$HE PRINCIPLES WE HAVE BEEN DISCUSSING ARE OF value, of course, only as they are applied effectively in the details of our moment-to-moment behavior. It is a devastating and tragic weakness of many so-called intellectuals that they are long on "know-what" and short on "know-how." As a matter of fact, it is fashionable among a relatively large proportion of academic and literary people and other professional wordmongers to abstain from the tedious business of putting ideas to work. There are a number of theoretical psychologists, for example, who actually pride themselves on knowing little or nothing about the detailed use of psychology in the school, factory, home, or clinic, and they speak of applied psychology with an air of condescension. Just so, many physicists regard themselves as definitely superior to the engineers who make practical use of physics. In our colleges and universities the attitude is not uncommon that those courses are of greatest value which are least practical. It is probably a very rare student who graduates from a university with a clear understanding of just what he is to *do* with most of what he has been taught in the lecture rooms and laboratories.

This is all a way of saying that to a considerable degree talking, writing, and reading tend to become regarded as ends in themselves. In our culture you can actually become famous as a *speaker* or as a *writer*. You can even acquire a measure of renown as a *reader*. Many people claim a kind of distinction because of the

205

books they read, and in our schools a great deal of emphasis is placed on teaching pupils to read fast. Some persons actually make a hobby of collecting books, not in order to read them at all, much less to make any use of their contents, but just to possess them— and they are respected for it! All too often we forget that books unread, or read but disregarded, are of no value except as items of interior decoration or as means of killing time. This holds whether the books are new or ancient, profound or superficial, paper-bound or leather-bound. The value of a book is not in the book, it is in the subsequent behavior of its readers.

To evaluate knowledge without regard to its effects, as these are to be seen in the everyday behavior of those who have the knowledge, is to disregard the most elementary principles of abstracting. To claim that you know something while acting as if you didn't know it is simply to be semantically blocked. This is not to let ourselves in for the old futile argument about whether you can understand how something is done if you yourself cannot do it. Of course, you can understand on different levels of abstraction. Such terms as *know* and *understand* are multiordinal terms. You can know something *verbally*. The point is that when it comes to matters of personal adjustment, it does precious little good to know something verbally if you do not also know it extensionally. There is scant consolation in saying that you understand the principles of adjustment so long as your behavior shows that you are mal-adjusted.

It is particularly absurd to claim that you understand the processes of abstracting and evaluating if you do not behave accordingly. Either to criticize general semantics, or to endorse it verbally, while violating its principles, is to invalidate your criticism, or to render your endorsement ineffectual. Your understanding of general semantics is to be revealed, therefore, not so much in what you say about it, as in how you say it, in how you use language for talking about anything, and in your non-verbal behavior from moment to moment every day.

The principles of general semantics can be applied in many ways, of course. Since they are, at bottom, the principles of scientific method, they are used in some fashion by any competent research worker, and by anyone who solves any problem whatever on the basis of factual investigation and clear statement. This means that general semantics is applied in some measure, at least sometimes, by millions of people who have never heard of general semantics and who haven't the slightest notion that they are applying it. It is used to some degree by physicians, engineers, teachers, psychologists, skilled tradesmen, farmers, housewives, editors, lawyers, artists, etc. The point is, however, that these principles, like any others, are used most effectively by those who know they are using them, and who understand their limitations and the details of their possible applications. What might be called unwitting horse sense is far better than nothing, or than tutored nonsense, but it is no substitute for the conscious application of a sound principle clearly understood.

So far as ordinary personal adjustment is concerned, the principles of general semantics are most commonly applied by means of the extensional devices, delayed reaction and semantic relaxation. The discussion that follows is designed to make these terms clear for practical purposes.

THE EXTENSIONAL DEVICES

We speak of individuals as being tall or short, smart or stupid, honest or corrupt, beautiful or homely, etc. Some wag has said that there are two kinds of people in the world: those who always divide the people of the world into two kinds, and those who don't. It appears that those who do are in the majority. The number of adjectives which we use to describe people and their behavior may be taken as the approximate number of traits in terms of which we attempt to classify people. We tend, however, to use these adjectives two at a time, in pairs of opposites. This is one of the most striking and important aspects of our language behavior. C. K. Ogden has written a fascinating little book about it, entitled *Opposition,* from which one may gain a practical sense of the far-reaching significance of this either-orish tendency in our use of language.

From a general semantics point of view, this matter is particularly important in the following respects. First, we tend to use these adjectives as though they referred to absolute qualities or attributes. Often and to a large degree we forget that when we classify a person as stupid, for example, we are making a statement about our own personal standards—perhaps even about our own lack of understanding—quite as much as we are making a statement about the other person. We are not usually very conscious of the self-projection in which we are indulging. Therefore we tend to forget that what is expressed in such a statement is a matter of inference rather than description, of personal judgment rather than fact, and that it is relative rather than absolute.

In the second place, our use of these adjectives serves generally to emphasize similarities among people rather than the differences among them. This effect is heightened by our practice of using the adjectives in pairs. If we say that Smith is smart, we say in effect that he is like all other persons who possess smartness; and we tend to imply that the rest of the people are alike in possessing dullness. We do not indicate those respects in which Smith appears to be unique; we do not indicate how he differs from everyone else. In other words, we do not speak of him as an individual at all; we cannot with a two-valued language that emphasizes similarities. If, as in a democracy, we are to focus attention upon the individual, his uniqueness, his importance as an individual, we must use a language that emphasizes the *differences* among individuals.

Finally, it is to be noticed that when we apply a trait adjective to an individual, we make a sort of diagnosis of him. When we "explain" the conduct of little Wilbur by saying that he *is* mean, we say, in effect, that he possesses meanness. In the Middle Ages it would have been said that little Wilbur was possessed of the devil. Nowadays, of course, we are more enlightened; we would say that Wilbur *has* the trait of meanness. We might be even more enlightened than that, and say that he possesses this trait in some degree, that he has much or little of *it*. In the Middle Ages there were techniques for casting out the devil from within a person who was so unfortunate as to be possessed of him. We understand now, of course, that it is foolish to have a technique for casting out something that isn't there. It is all right, however, to use the same techniques—they were mostly methods of punishment—to cast out the meanness. Could it be that the meanness and the devil are the same thing? And what sort of thing is this?

Briefly, it would appear to be one of the products not of "human nature," but of the subject-predicate structure of our common language. That is to say, we talk about people as though they possessed attributes, or traits, in an absolute sense, and as though they were to be classified according to these traits which they have somehow inside of them. The assumption, usually unspoken, is that a trait, such as meanness, for example, is, always has been, and always will be a quality of the person who possesses it. Not only is this assumption scientifically defective and unnecessary, but also, and what is more important, it renders the problem of individual development quite hopeless. It focuses attention on something which is, by definition, essentially unalterable. In an extensional view of personal problems and individual development, attention is focused on alterables.

In an extensional orientation, then, differences are emphasized as well as similarities. A person, say Smith, is evaluated not merely as a member of some type or class, to which he may legitimately be assigned, of course, for a specific purpose but not for all time, but he is also evaluated as an individual. We recognize his individuality insofar as we see Smith as different from his fellows. There is here no denial of the fact that, from this or that point of view, Smith appears to be quite similar to many other persons. He appears to have much in common with his fellow lodge members, his political bedfellows, his professional colleagues, etc. Our group loyalties, family ties, and fields of interest represent the fact that we feel something in common with others, we regard ourselves as similar to other persons and are so regarded by them—we "belong." All an Elk wants to know about you is that you are a brother Elk— unless, of course, you ask him for a loan.

It is extremely easy to see similarities among people. It is so easy that to most people all babies look alike—and at the same time, even so, every baby looks just like its mother or its father. It

is so easy that for most of us the world comes to be made up of
Jews and Gentiles, of Catholics and Protestants, of Harvard men
and non-Harvard men, of friends and outlanders, etc. Even in the
democracies the problem of class and caste is ever present and difficult. It appears to be very hard for us to regard Smith as an individual. We want to know who he *is*—meaning the class to which
he belongs. Then we react to him accordingly, as we react to others
who belong to the same class.

As a means of overcoming the difficulty of giving adequate emphasis to differences, Korzybski has introduced what he calls extensional devices. The problem of taking due account of differences
is, of course, only part of the more general problem of relating
language and reality, of representing a world of process by means
of a static language. We have seen that extensionally there is no
identity, but at the same time practically every word in our language implies identity. A name, for instance, such as *elm* or *Henry*,
implies something to be named, something that remains the same
from one time to another, so that the same name will serve to
represent it from one time to another. Moreover, a name like *elm*
implies that there are many elms, many individual trees that are
alike and can be designated by the same word—and the word *tree*
implies identity on an even broader scale. Yet on non-verbal levels
there is no identity, and so the use of our language, because of its
identity-static structure, creates tremendous difficulties in our attempts to make sufficiently accurate statements about a world of
process differences. It was in consideration of this basic problem
that Korzybski proposed the extensional devices. They are designed to effect a change in the structure of our language, to make
that structure correspond more nearly to the structure of the "territory." How this is done can best be indicated by presenting the
devices and explaining their use.

In *Science and Sanity* Korzybski presents five extensional devices. Three of these he calls working devices: indexes, dates, and
the *etcetera*. The other two he calls safety devices: quotation marks
and the hyphen. We shall indicate several in addition to these, but
first we shall discuss these five.

WORKING DEVICES

The working devices serve to make our ordinary language much more representative of a reality of process, in which no two things are alike and no one thing stays the same, and about which one can never say all there is to be said. The three devices go together; each one implies the other two.

When you studied algebra you learned to deal with such symbols as x_1, x_2 and the like. The numbers were called subscripts, meaning that they were written under the x. These subscripts are indexes, or index numbers. They are not merely something thought up by some mathematician in a fit of whimsy. They are very useful to the mathematician whenever he wishes to remind you, and himself, that x is a variable term—that is to say, x can be used to represent any number whatever. Thus, at one time it may be used to represent 9, at another time 118, etc. In other words, x_1 is not x_2.

Now, after all, x is like any ordinary word. The word *house,* for example, is a variable term. It can be used to refer to my house, or to your house, or to any one of all the possible buildings one might want to talk about. And house$_1$ is not house$_2$. Interestingly enough, the extensional device of the index had been applied to the word *house* long before the extensional devices, as such, were thought of; we have had house numbers for centuries. They represent a kind of indexing—and in their social effects they are far more remarkable than most of us have ever dreamed them to be. Communication makes civilization possible, but communication itself would not be possible, except for the most part in chance face-to-face situations, were it not for the extensional device of the index, in the form of house numbers, apartment numbers, office numbers, telephone numbers, etc. Without such indexes modern communication by mail, telegraph, and telephone would be out of the question, and without modern communication civilization as we know it would also be out of the question.

Other common forms of the index device are to be seen in social security numbers, automobile license numbers, the elaborate systems of numbers used in cataloguing books in public libraries, the numerals worn on the backs of football players—anyone can recall a great number of other examples. Indeed, life as we know it would simply not be possible without indexes.

It is astonishing that we have applied this ingenious device to almost everything except our language. In general semantics we apply it to that, too. If we can say house$_1$, house$_2$, etc., we can say man$_1$, man$_2$, etc., or love$_1$, love$_2$, etc. We can use indexes with any word whatever. And notice that when we do, we use the *etc.*, also.

Your English teachers may have told you not to use *etc.* If so, they were, without meaning to perhaps, teaching you that you live in a world about which you can know everything and say everything. That being true, the only ones who say *etc.* are the ones who have not studied their lessons. It is to be considered that when you learn a language, such as English, you are also learning a kind of physics and psychology, a knowledge of the world and of yourself. It is the failure to realize this that would appear to account for the more or less common assumption that English is a "tool subject." To regard English as a "tool subject" is to assume that when you learn to write and to read, you do not learn anything except how to write and to read, and that, having learned to do these things, you possess the "tools" with which to learn.

People who suppose—and many educators do suppose—that you can teach reading and writing merely as "tool subjects" appear to overlook the fact that a tool implies something to be tooled by a tooler. They appear to assume that there actually are subjects without content, and to ignore the obvious consideration that a tool implies something about that which it is to be used on, the purpose it is to be used for, the person who is to use it, and the wisdom or lack of wisdom of the persons who designed it. That is to say, they appear to overlook the fact that you cannot learn a language without also learning the *structure* of the language—and without learning to impose that structure onto reality, a reality which includes yourself. When you learn English, as it is sometimes taught, you learn, among other things, that reality involves no *etcetera*'s. To learn that is to prepare yourself for innumerable shocks and disappointments, and regrettable and foolish mistakes occasioned by absolutistic allness and dogmatism. There is not space enough in this book for a thorough elaboration of the above statements, but what has been said will have served its purpose if it helps to suggest that such an innocent-looking device as the *etc.* is by no means a triviality.

What the *etc.* represents most definitely is the basic premise of non-allness; it provides a practical means, a device, for applying that premise in a very general way and in specific instances. Just so, the index represents most definitely the basic premise of non-identity, and constitutes a device for making it effective in everyday living.

The other working device is the date. Dates are a special kind of index; they serve to index times. It may be said that there is no time, as such, in nature, but there are times. Dates enable us to represent this fact, and to remind ourselves quite automatically, because no two dates are the same, that no two times are identical. By means of dates we commonly index letters, newspapers, magazines, legal documents, etc. But we can use them much more generally than has been our custom. Just as $Smith_1$ is not $Smith_2$ (no two individuals are the same), so $Smith^{1940}$ is not $Smith^{1942}$ (no one individual stays the same). The French people learned the hard way that war_1 is not war_2, that war^{1918} is not war^{1940}. Likewise, the British learned that war_1 is not war_2, that war^{1941}_{Malaya} is not war^{1918}_{Europe}. It is this extensional orientation that is foreign to the Maginot Line mentality, to conservatives and sentimentalists generally. Dates as indexes to words, like the other index numbers, serve to represent particularly the premise of non-identity. They help to give to our language a structure that more nearly corresponds to the process structure of reality. They serve to remind us—and we seem to require constant reminding—that all things change.

SAFETY DEVICES

These working devices are supplemented by two safety devices: quotation marks and the hyphen. These are used as expedients. It is a consequence of our prescientific orientation that we tend often to use words elementalistically. It is this matter to which the mathematician Keyser refers in speaking of "the postulate of elementalism, underlying the wellnigh universal practice of employing such phrases as 'soul' *and* 'body,' 'space' *and* 'time,' 'matter' *and* 'spirit,' 'emotions' *and* 'intellect,' and so on, as if the meaning of either term of any such couple differed ultimately and radically from the meaning of its mate and admitted of separation therefrom." Such terms, used in this way, involve a verbal splitting of events which, on the non-verbal levels, cannot be split. They imply a reality of absolute, non-related, independent entities or elements.

It is, nevertheless, frequently expedient to use these words, either because no other terms are readily available, or because our listeners would find other terms too unfamiliar. So the terms are used, but they are placed in quotes, actually or by implication, as a safety measure to remind both speaker and listener that they are to be evaluated with regard to their false-to-fact implications. Thus, we may speak of "emotional" maladjustment, or of "intellectual" development, employing the quotes to remind ourselves that maladjustment is never exclusively "emotional," or that development is not solely "intellectual" and in no sense "emotional." Likewise, we may use the hyphen, and speak of emotional-intellectual maladjustment, or development. Just so, we may speak of space-time, rather than space *and* time. To speak of space *and* time is to imply that it is possible to demonstrate something nowhere at some time, or somewhere at no time!

Thus, the hyphen and quotes are used to counteract the elementalistic use of language. They represent and foster a non-elementalistic orientation, a recognition of the fact that John Gunther has expressed by saying that everything has a cause and the cause of anything is everything. Reality has a structure, and structure is a matter of ordered relations. The apparently trivial little marks that we call quotes and hyphens serve, then, to remind us of this basic structure of reality, of the fact that events are functionally related to one another.

Quotation marks and hyphens have been used fairly systemati-

cally in this book and, although from various points of view there
are doubtless inconsistencies, an examination of the specific instances in which they are here employed will indicate reasonably
well the various ways in which they may be applied as extensional
devices.

THE EXTENSIONAL BARGAIN

The general application of these devices is mainly a matter of
agreement, a kind of bargain between speaker and listener that
they are being implied continually. In writing one can make a
limited use of the devices in the sense of actually writing in the
indexes, dates, *etcetera*'s, quotes, and hyphens, but there is a practical limit. In speaking, one can actually speak the words as indexed and dated, with *etcetera*'s, one can speak words as hyphenated, and one can indicate quotes by means of appropriate gestures,
perhaps. One can also express a good deal by means of vocal inflection, timing, bodily gesture, and facial expression. But, as with
writing, the practical limits are easily reached. In reading silently
one can read as though the page were sprinkled with the devices.
In the main, however, one finds any considerable overt use of the
devices to be quite impractical and unnecessary, as well as in-
sufficient. Their use is, as has been said, largely a matter of mutual
understanding, a bargain, between speaker and listener, writer and
reader. It is simply to be understood that words are used and are
to be evaluated as though they were indexed and dated, and, where
necessary, quoted and hyphenated, with *etcetera*'s indicating non-
allness wherever appropriate. Thus, with no considerable outward
or obvious change in language, a tremendous change in language
structure and in neuro-semantic reactions is accomplished.

In fact, it would appear to be quite impossible to talk very adequately about a process reality without using the extensional devices. Without the "extensional bargain" between speaker and
listener, even such a common statement as "Jack Benny is a great
comedian" involves gross identifications, elementalism, unconscious
projection, allness, etc. But with the understanding that the words
are indexed and dated, that at least *is* is quoted, and that the state-

ment is followed by *etc.*, these ill effects are largely eliminated. With the extensional bargain, one may make such a statement and run little risk of starting an argument, because the statement conveys scarcely more than, for example, "I laughed at something Jack Benny said last night."

This will appear to be a trivial example. It has been deliberately chosen for that very reason, because anyone who has observed carefully the conversations that occur at bridge parties, on buses, in cafés, in family living rooms, etc., doubtless realizes how tiny are the acorns of seemingly inconsequential chatter from which enormous oaks of social friction grow. It is precisely in the common speech of every day that the lack of the extensional bargain leads to the greatest number of semantic irritations and hurts for the great majority of people. You do not seek in the halls of parliament, the board rooms of great corporations, or the lecture rooms of noted professors for the semantic blunders of the man in the street. He very frequently disturbs his domestic peace or incurs the distrust of his bus companions by saying something no more momentous than "Jack Benny is a great comedian."

Indeed, it is a never-ending source of astonishment, even to many experienced clinical psychologists and psychiatrists, that the maladjustments from which most people suffer are in the main trivial almost beyond belief, when viewed impersonally. The experiences that most children and adults evaluate as tragedies certainly lack the Cecil B. DeMille touch. Only as one grasps the overwhelming significance of this simple fact can one appreciate the corresponding significance of such apparently trivial adjustive devices as indexes, dates, *etcetera*'s, quotes, and hyphens. It has been the writer's experience that to most people the value of these devices is quite entirely beyond comprehension on first acquaintance. From a prescientific point of view, they simply are not to be taken seriously. Most people are inclined to stare blankly when told that these devices represent the very crux of extensionalization, of science and of sanity, that to know general semantics without knowing how to apply these devices readily is to possess a knowledge that is fairly useless.

In part this incredulity seems to arise from the lack of a clear notion as to just how the devices might be used. It is important, therefore, that one undergo a period of fairly intensive training in their use. For a few days, or for brief periods of only a minute or two from time to time, one should rather consistently index and date the more important words in everything that is spoken, written, read, or heard. One should index objects—$tree_1$, $tree_2$, $tree_3$, $tree_4$, etc., $chair_1$, $chair_2$, etc., noting differences all the while. One should index people, whether acquaintances or strangers—$Smith_1$, $Smith_2$, $Smith_3$, etc., observing how they differ one from another—observing, that is, what the *1, 2, 3,* and *etc.* represent. The use of dates should be greatly increased for a time—the boss $^{10 \text{ A.M., Oct. } 3}$ seems very irritable, Mary $^{\text{evening of Oct. } 4}$ is not very affectionate, the news $^{10 \text{ P.M., Nov. } 6}$ is not encouraging, etc. For a while one also should deliberately avoid as much as possible the elementalistic use of terms, replacing such words as *emotion* and *thought* with some non-elementalistic term like *evaluation,* or any other words descriptive of behavior.

There is little point in attempting to *say* more about these devices. They are to be understood, not on verbal levels, not as something to be talked about, but on non-verbal levels, extensionally, as something to be used. When Galileo invented the telescope, some of his friends refused to look through it. They didn't especially object to looking at it and talking about it, but, after all, according to Aristotle, Jupiter had no moons, and it was simply nonsense, therefore, to say that if you looked through Galileo's gadget you would see the moons of Jupiter. One can easily imagine these friends of Galileo saying to him, disdainfully, "Surely you do not expect men of learning and authority, men of our position, to take your toy lenses seriously. Who are you to contradict Aristotle? You had best put that toy away and stop talking about the moons of Jupiter. People will think you have lost your mind. Look through it? Really!" Doubtless they would not have used the extensional devices, either. Is it not common sense that A is A? A_1, A_2, A_3, etc., indeed! Well, there is little point in talking about it. If you look through Galileo's telescope you do see the moons of Jupiter. If you *use* the extensional devices, you do apply the principles of general semantics and you discover what you discover. It is different from that to which you have been accustomed. The proof of the pudding is in the eating.

So far as personal adjustment is concerned, the use of these five extensional devices is both a preventive and a corrective measure. Remembering the people in quandaries of Chapter I, their idealism, frustration, and demoralization, their feelings of inferiority and their vague questions and fuzzy answers, we can see the value of the extensional devices. For rough practical purposes we may regard adjustment as a matter of defining our goals in accordance with our possibilities of achieving them, of making our questions answerable and our answers clear, and of evaluating ourselves realistically. What this amounts to is the dating and indexing of our goals, our opportunities, and limitations, and so our successes and failures—the defining of them with an *etcetera* at the end of each definition. Quotation marks around "success" and "failure," "superiority" and "inferiority," help us to avoid misdirective or paralyzing generalizations about ourselves. And "causes" turn out, as a rule, to be hyphenated: not "mental" *or* "physical" but neurosemantic, or organismic-environmental; not "emotional" *or* "intellectual" but a combination of both, and of other things, too; not "economic" *or* "moral" but socio-economic in a matrix of semantic environments comprising a general culture structure. Thus, the simple little hyphen helps us to avoid simple-minded explanations. The extensional devices do not usher us into the millennium, but they do make it possible for us to reduce materially the agonies we create for ourselves out of loose talk and wild generalizations. They do, that is, provided we use them consistently in talking about ourselves, the world we live in, and the other people who make up such an important part of that world.

SPECIAL TERMS

Besides the five devices which we have presented above, there are several others which tend to have similar effects. For the most part, these additional devices consist of certain types of words: *plurals, quantifying* terms, *actional* and *operational* terms. There are, in addition, *conditional* terms which indicate the particular context or conditions under which a statement may be valid, terms such as *in our culture* or *in our time*. Also there are terms which express *consciousness of projection,* such as *to me, appears, seems, as I see it,* etc. Finally, the device of *underlining* (italics) can be used as an aid in extensionalization. Each of these supplementary devices will be discussed briefly.

Plurals, in certain instances, tend to have an effect similar to that of indexes. For example, to speak of the cause*s*, rather than the cause, of war is to imply an awareness of the extensional variability among factors related to war. Likewise, to speak of falling*s* in love*s*, rather than falling in love, is to suggest by implication that $love_1$ is not $love_2$ and that there are many ways of "falling." And to use language in this way is to make for greater conditionality of response, to avoid undue rigidity of belief and conduct.

Quantifying terms lend an exactness to language which is lacking in vague statements. "Casualties Were Heavy" produces a somewhat different effect from that produced by: "Of ten thousand troops, five hundred were killed and twelve hundred injured during the attack."

A stutterer once told me that he was sure people were inclined to make fun of his speech. He had apparently held to this notion ever since an incident which occurred one day in the second grade, when, according to his report, his classmates had laughed at him. Inquiry brought out that there had been about thirty pupils present at the time, and that of these only two had laughed, and these, he recalled, were regarded as somewhat slow-witted. The teacher had not laughed at him, and he could not, in fact, recall that anyone else had ever definitely ridiculed him. This simple exercise in quantitative statement was unquestionably of some effect in changing his general attitude—in bringing him "down to earth." Accuracy of statement is one of the cardinal principles of science and of sanity, and the effect of quantification is to make for greater accuracy. We cannot always, of course, achieve quantification in precise terms, but we can often be more accurate than we usually are and so make our conclusions more reliable and of greater adjustive value.

The value of *actional* and *operational* terms lies in their tendency to counteract the subject-predicate form of statement. To say that Henry is mean implies that he has some sort of inherent trait, but it tells us nothing about what Henry has done. Consequently, it fails to suggest any specific means of improving Henry. If, on the other hand, it is said that Henry snatched Billy's cap and threw it in the bonfire, the situation is rendered somewhat more clear and actually more hopeful. You might never eliminate "meanness," but there are fairly definite steps to be taken in order to remove Henry's incentives or opportunities for throwing caps in bonfires.

Psychiatrists sometimes complain that when their patients come to them they have already diagnosed themselves. Such a patient greets the doctor with the statement, for example, that he is suffering from an inferiority complex, or that he is an introvert. What the psychiatrist has to do in such a case is to get the person to tell him not what he *is* or what he *has*, but what he *does*, and the conditions under which he does it. When he stops talking about what *type* of person he *is*, what his outstanding *traits are*, and what *type* of disorder he *has*—when he stops making these subject-predicate statements, and begins to use actional terms, to describe his behavior and its circumstances—both he and the psychiatrist begin to see what specifically may be done in order to change both the behavior and the circumstances.

The major advances in psychology that have been achieved during the past thirty years or so have been due largely to the increasing use of a language more highly descriptive of behavior. The older psychologists, of the tradition of Wundt and Titchener particularly, concerned themselves mainly with the so-called elements of "mind" or consciousness, and with the so-called qualities of the various types of sensation, perception, and thought. A similar linguistic tendency was evidenced in the writings of such psychologists as McDougall, who "elementalized" man into a mosaic of instincts and corresponding drives. The more recent "trait psychology" appears to have been a sequel to these earlier static, subject-predicate approaches to the study of human beings. The same basic approach seems to underlie much of the recent effort to explain behavior in terms of personality "types."

Even Pavlov, who did so much to free psychology from this sterile tradition, was not entirely guiltless of the same tendency. He spoke in terms of inhibitory and excitatory types of reaction, and even of inhibited and excitable types of animals and men. But it was Pavlov and, later, Thorndike, Carr, Watson, Seashore, and other "behaviorists" and "functionalists" who gave some degree of impetus to the newer leanings toward a non-Aristotelian psychology. The change which they stimulated was a change in language, fundamentally a change in the structure of the language used for representing personality and behavior. It has by no means taken hold entirely, but it has influenced most psychologists to talk less about types and traits, and more about the on-going, interrelated processes of behavior in functional relationship to specific patterns of stimulating and limiting conditions. From certain branches of modern psychology it is but a short step to general semantics, and the reason for this lies in the linguistic revolution stimulated, though not completed, by the "behaviorists" and "functionalists."

Actional terms, descriptive of what is done and "what goes on," are called by some writers *operational*. The physicist Bridgman did a great deal with his book, *The Logic of Modern Physics,* to stimulate the use of operational terms and of operational definitions. This point was discussed in the last chapter, and it is mentioned here again by way of rounding out the discussion of extensional devices. Operational terms represent not entities that *have* qualities, but operations, or actions, or behaviors. Operationally considered, sociability, for example, is not an instinct, or a trait, or a quality; it is what one does, the reactions one makes, under certain conditions. Operationally considered, "thought" is not an attribute of "mind," or a "thing" with attributes of its own; it is behavior, the performance, largely, it would seem, of certain manipulations of symbols. Actional, behavioral, functional, operational terms and statements serve to direct attention to actualities, about which something might be done, rather than to things with attributes, highly abstracted qualities, which exist by definition and "logical fate." Such notions tend to paralyze our potentialities for behaving in ways that are adaptive.

Another aid to extensionalization is to be found in terms which serve to *qualify,* to state *exceptions* and to specify *conditions.* Among such terms may be listed *except, but, under conditions of,* and various adjectives and any other words which serve to specify limits of generalization. We may speak of these as *conditional* terms. Of special interest are two particular phrases: *in our culture* and *of our time.* The title of one of Karen Horney's books is *The Neurotic Personality of Our Time,* and the significant words in that title are *of our time.* They imply Karen Horney's basic point of view, that personality maladjustments are to be most fruitfully considered in relation to the conditions of society or of culture under which they occur. Such a point of view represents, in some measure at least, a relativistic and extensional orientation.

A great deal of argument concerning socio-economic issues would be tremendously clarified if the statements made were concluded with *in our culture.* For example, private enterprise is essential to industrial development—*in our culture;* a sufficiently high national debt will lead to national economic ruin—*in our culture;* wars are inevitable—*in our culture;* etc. The service performed by this phrase, as here used, is that of reminding us that the statements are not necessarily valid pronouncements concerning "human nature," or "reality." They are statements that might not be valid at all under cultural conditions different from our own. What is more important, they imply that different cultural conditions are at least conceivable.

Extensionalization is furthered also by terms expressive of *consciousness of projection,* terms such as *to me, in my opinion, as I see it, from my point of view,* etc. In an earlier chapter we discussed consciousness of projection as to-me-ness, and it is the purpose now to emphasize the value of such terms as *to me* in making consciousness of projection effective. The sometimes harmful effects of the *is* of identity and of predication can be counteracted in large measure by means of *to me,* or its equivalent. Semantically there is a great difference, for example, between saying, "Poetry is silly" and "Poetry is silly—to me." The latter leaves poetry a leg to stand on, as it were. It reminds both the speaker and the listener that the speaker is necessarily talking about himself as well as about poetry.

It is important to observe that this device of *to me* rarely occurs in the language of advertising, political bombast, and in strongly affective states, such as those of anger, grief, or discouragement. Unconscious projection appears as a fundamental mechanism underlying such language, and that accounts for much of its disintegrative and demoralizing effect. It is difficult to imagine advertising and political speech-making, as we know them, under conditions created by a new generation trained to be clearly aware of projection. It is quite as difficult to imagine, under such conditions, any widespread use of the language of misery, resentment, and general demoralization so common—in our culture.

It is not to be implied that the mere use of *to me,* or its equivalent, will insure a highly effective consciousness of projection. Like the other extensional devices, it is to be used with an understanding of its general semantic implications. A parrot-like utterance of it has no adjustive value. Any of these terms and devices that *can* aid extensionalization *can* be used just as pointlessly and meaninglessly as any other words. It is not the words, but the neuro-semantic reactions represented by them, that are important.

If printed words were never capitalized and if no punctuation were used it would be relatively difficult to read them. The conventions of writing and printing—variations in size of type, capitalization, punctuation, etc.—are designed, after all, to further evaluation and understanding on the part of the reader. To the general semanticist, one of these conventions is of special interest, and he tends to use it somewhat more than is customary. This is the convention of *underlining*—or, in printing, of italicizing—certain words.

Underlining is generally used for such purposes as that of referring to a word as a word—as in referring to the word *word*—and to indicate titles of books and foreign terms. The general semanticist uses underlining for these and other customary purposes, but he stresses particularly the use of underlining in emphasizing the special importance of certain terms in particular contexts. When the general semanticist uses underlining (or italicizing) in this way, he is saying to the reader, in effect, "Be sure to give special attention to the extensional sense of this word, as the present context indicates its extensional sense." In other words, "Please don't take this word for granted. Try to make a special effort to visualize and to feel what I am talking about." The examples of underlining (italicizing) in the present book will serve to illustrate its use as an aid to extensionalization.

PRACTICAL EFFECTS

By means of the effective use of these extensional devices a very considerable change in the structure of language is achieved, and this change serves to foster a generally extensional orientation. As has been said, they need not be used overtly at all times, and it is not possible to use them overtly to a sufficient degree. A considerable amount of practice in using the devices is essential, however, if one is to develop a "feel" for their semantic significance. Once this "feel" is acquired to a reasonably high degree, one need not use the devices outwardly or actually, except now and then when they are especially to be stressed. Otherwise, their use is a matter of mutual understanding between speaker and listener (writer and reader), an agreement, or bargain. The "extensional bargain" is that the devices are continually implied in speaking and writing—that words are used as though with the devices. Outwardly one's language may seem little different from what it has been. Semantically, structurally, it is, however, tremendously different.

It is different in ways that can, in some respects, be fairly easily noted. In the first place, language involving consistent use of the extensional bargain tends to emphasize differences to a greater extent than is customary. Consequently it serves to qualify and refine one's generalizations, to make one more aware of exceptions to any rule, to make one note more carefully the individual case, and to render one's statements generally more accurate. For these reasons the extensional bargain automatically fosters what we call tolerance, open-mindedness, fairness, etc., and it counteracts dogmatism, unjustified conservatism, and prejudice. It tends to promote learning and to improve adjustment. Moreover, it does these things quite as a matter of course, without any need for special pleading or trumped-up motivations.

In line with all this, the extensional bargain fosters the realization that truth is relative. Scarcely anything is more tragic in its consequences than the belief in and the search for absolute Truth. In order to believe in absolute Truth, one must reject the premises of extensional non-identity and non-allness and ignore the implications of the self-reflexiveness of language. If one is not willing to do that, then one must abandon, without quibbling, the quest for universal and final Truth. Truth with a capital T serves as fact, unchanging, unalterable. Nothing can be done about it. One cannot progress beyond it. It is incompatible with a world of change. It belongs only in a static orientation. But truth with a small t, so to speak, relative truth, truth that is consistent with non-identity, non-allness, and self-reflexiveness, truth that is indexed and dated— truth in such a sense serves the purposes of growth and adjustment in a reality of process. It is a guide, rather than an obstacle, to progress. Relative truth is truth regarded as assumption. One so regards it because one is conscious of the processes by which it is abstracted. As assumption, it is as dependable as observation and experience indicate. Truth in such a sense is constantly refreshed, brought up to date, kept useful. It does not serve to block learning, but to direct it.

In another respect the extensional bargain promotes a relativistic orientation. As was said near the beginning of this chapter, in an intensional, absolutistic orientation, human behavior comes to be viewed as representing traits and types of personality or character. One's behavior, then, is taken to indicate what traits one *has* and what type one *is*. And that's that. In an extensional, relativistic orientation, on the other hand, the situation is quite different. One's behavior is regarded not as trait, but as *technique*. That is to say, it is evaluated in relation to the situation in which it occurs; it is evaluated with regard to its effects on that situation. Behavior *does* something. A technique is simply a way of doing something. Thus, stamping your foot and shouting, "Shut up, you!" is a technique sometimes used for certain purposes. Or to smile and say, "Good morning," in a friendly way is to use another technique. Both are forms of behavior. To say that they represent personality traits or types of temperament is to speak of them in a subject-predicate fashion, and so to dismiss them as essentially god-given, mysterious, and unchangeable. To say that they are techniques is to imply an entirely different attitude.

According to customary usage, a trait is evaluated as a quality of a particular type of person, and a type is a rather hopeless matter. You *are* a certain type, or you are not. Types are born. They will out. There is precious little one can do about them. But a technique is evaluated with regard to what it is designed to do, how effectively it does it, and the effects of doing it. A human reaction, regarded as a technique, is, therefore, to be evaluated with reference to what it accomplishes, the efficiency with which it accomplishes it, and the consequences of the accomplishment. This constitutes an extensional evaluation; and when behavior is talked about with a language involving the extensional bargain, it is this sort of evaluation of behavior that tends to result.

Because this is true, the extensional bargain serves to direct attention to *alterables*. That is to say, when we speak with the extensional devices we tend to speak of behavior as technique, and the object of evaluating a technique is to alter it. For this reason, techniques tend to be revised. The object of evaluating a personality trait is to bemoan it or to rejoice over it. But techniques are to be altered—or discontinued—in view of how well they accomplish what they are designed to do, and in view of the consequences of what they accomplish. Thus, in working clinically with maladjusted people, from an extensional point of view, we seek to discover not what traits they *have* or what types they *are*, but what they do. We ask concerning the behavior in question what it is designed to accomplish, how well it accomplishes it, and what consequences it has. We then proceed to alter the behavior accordingly.

And in seeking to alter the individual's behavior, we search also for possible alterations in the conditions that give rise to, and limit, his behavior. The emphasis is on alterables, not on unalterable qualities of unalterable things.

The difference between an absolutistic, subject-predicate, intensional language structure and a relativistic, functional, extensional one is thus sweeping and revolutionary. They imply and foster vastly different tendencies in personality development, in educational policies, in social customs. They imply and foster nothing less than different kinds of civilization. The one we have tried for many centuries, but even though we are familiar with it we seem at times to understand it insufficiently. The other we are attempting to glimpse in the pages of this book.

THE LANGUAGE OF SCIENCE

Consistent use of the extensional devices tends to make for language behavior consistent with the general method of science. We have discussed the language of science in Part II, and we shall give further attention to it, as it relates to problems of personal adjustment, in Chapters XI and XII. There is no need, therefore, to discuss it in detail at this point. It is important, however, to remind ourselves that just as the better part of science is the language of science, so the better part of sanity is the language of sanity—and that the language of sanity is, in its basic structure, the language of science.

What this language provides is the means to meaningful inquiry and clear statement. It is to be recalled that the general method of science, stripped of its technicalities, lies in (a) asking questions that can be answered on the basis of observations, (b) making the relevant observations, or using those made by others, (c) reporting the observations accurately so as to answer the questions asked, and (d) revising conclusions previously held in accordance with the answers obtained—and the asking of further questions that are prompted by the new conclusions. Now, aside from the making of observations, this is seen to be a method of using language. The observations themselves are directed by the questions asked, just as the questions asked are determined by the conclusions previously drawn.

The extensional devices are important in this connection because they tend to make for questions that are indexed and dated— questions that can be answered by observations specified as to time, place, and conditions. They tend also to make for answers similarly indexed and dated, and for conclusions that are relative, expressive of non-allness. An *etcetera* at the end of a conclusion says, in effect, that the conclusion is not final and dogmatic, that further observations may lead to its revision. It is conducive, therefore, to continued observation and learning, to an on-going search for more and more knowledge and better and better explanations and predictions. The understanding, prediction, and control of events, essential to personal adjustment, are facilitated, therefore, by the extensional devices. Their use tends to make for a language of science and so of sanity.

DELAYED REACTION

Two other techniques that are fundamental in the application of general semantics are those of *delayed reaction* and *semantic relaxation*. They are closely interrelated and in discussing them more or less separately the impression is not to be left that they operate independently.

We discussed delayed reaction in some detail in Chapter IX, because by doing so we were able to illustrate more clearly the principle of symbol reaction. The difference between fully conditional symbol reactions and stereotyped signal reactions is, in large part, a matter of the greater delay in making symbol reactions. It is simply the difference between going off half-cocked and taking enough time to size up a situation before responding to it.

The important practical point about delayed reaction is that it is something one can practice. It is a rather definite aspect of behavior. One can be clearly conscious of *doing* it. What we call the voluntary control of behavior lies to an important degree in regulation of the delay in responding; in other words, it lies in *timing*.

Delay, in and of itself, of course, is of no particular value. It is what goes on during the delay that matters. If all you do during the delay is to count to ten, for example, you gain nothing as a rule, and you may lose valuable time. Being slow to respond may indicate stupidity, or confusion, or fear. The point is to be greatly stressed, therefore, that delay of reaction has adjustive value only to the extent that you carry on effective evaluation during the delay, evaluation of the situation confronting you and of the likely consequences of this or that reaction to it. It takes time to make such evaluation—that is why delay is important.

Moreover, there is no virtue in dawdling; a reaction is to be delayed only long enough to make adequate evaluation possible. This means that the vast majority of one's everyday reactions will involve delay that is hardly perceptible, or no delay at all beyond what is "ordinary." Many things will be done, and should be done, by habit, promptly and in a reflex-like manner. For practically any individual, however, there are many situations in the course of an ordinary day that cannot be dealt with adequately in any such fashion. Even well-established habits and routines have to be modified occasionally in response to changed circumstances, and occasionally one meets up with circumstances in which practically any of one's accustomed behavior is quite inappropriate. At such times conscious evaluative delay is essential to adequate response. The necessary evaluation is fundamentally a matter of noting the crucial differences between the situation confronting one and the other situations with which one is inclined at first glance to identify it. It is a matter of meaningful indexing and dating, of differentiating this from that, then from now. One matures as a person by responding differently today from the ways in which one responded yesterday—and so by delaying the reactions one makes today in order to keep them from being identical with those one made yesterday.

In the so-called breaking of habits delay is particularly important. Probably the most essential step in eliminating a habit, such as that of excessive smoking or of quick temper, is that of deliberately postponing customary actions. Actually you "break" a habit eventually by substituting some other form of behavior for it, but the other behavior never gets a chance to occur unless the habitual behavior is held in abeyance. As a matter of fact, the speed with which a reaction is made is an integral aspect of it; one of the easiest ways to change a habitual response is to change its rate. When you do this you change its whole structure more or less. Likewise, when you delay a response you tend to change the nature of it, because the nature of it depends in part on the promptness with which it is made. If, for example, you are used to having lunch at twelve o'clock and you miss your lunch one day, you are likely to be not as hungry at two o'clock as you were at twelve. A response is a series of events and if any part of the series is eliminated, postponed, or otherwise disturbed, the whole series is affected. On this fact depends the effectiveness, at least in part, of delayed reaction in the "breaking" of habits.

Personality maladjustment consists, in substantial measure, of what might be called habits. That is to say, it is largely a matter of holding to the same beliefs, expressing the same attitudes, making the same reactions, without due regard to differences in purpose and circumstance. In order to stay adjusted, one has to react differently to different situations. This means that one has to see differences and evaluate them. This takes time. That is why an essential technique of adjustment is that of evaluative delay of reactions.

SEMANTIC RELAXATION

Delayed reaction, and adequate evaluation generally, are facilitated by a state of semantic relaxation. The word *semantic* as here used is meant to emphasize the basic importance of evaluation, of feelings and attitudes, in relation to one's state of tension. It is important to differentiate clearly between the sort of muscular tension that results from trying to lift a piano, for example, and the tension that expresses fear or discontent. There is nothing undesirable about the muscular exertion of useful work or joyful recreation. The tensions we are considering here are those due to worry, resentment, anxiety—self-defensive tensions; and the relaxation we are considering is characterized by freedom from tensions of this kind. That is why it is called *semantic* relaxation.

Relaxation of this sort is most thorough and stable when it comes about simply as a result of adequate personal adjustment in a general sense. Effective application in everyday living of the principles we have been discussing tends to make for semantic relaxation. To the extent that this is true no special methods of relaxation are necessary. As a matter of fact, so long as one is basically maladjusted it is not likely that any direct attempts at eliminating one's self-defensive tensions will prove very successful. The relaxation you achieve by deliberately relaxing is not quite as "genuine" as that which you achieve simply by living according to sound principles.

This view of the matter is not to be carried too far, of course. There is some value in direct methods of relaxation. We have to deal here with a two-way relationship: personal adjustment fosters relaxation, but relaxation tends also to foster personal adjustment. To the degree that one is tense one is likely to behave inappropriately and to cultivate maladjustive attitudes. Anything that can be done directly to reduce tensions is likely to result, therefore, in more adequate behavior.

In order to understand relaxation and tension in relation to personal adjustment, it is necessary to be clear on the fact that for practical purposes there are two kinds of relaxation, and they are vastly different. The one is relaxation for rest; the other is relaxation for work. The one involves a deeply restful state, even sleep; the other involves simply optimal or "just right" tonicity, a freedom from tensions that are excessive or unnecessary, and from tensions due to conflicts, anxiety, and maladjustment generally.

If your objective is rest, if what you want is to get to sleep at night, or to take a noon nap, or to rest as completely as possible for ten or fifteen minutes, you might be able to make use of such a technique as that described by Dr. Edmund Jacobson, Director of the Laboratory of Clinical Physiology, Chicago, in his books, *Progressive Relaxation* and *You Must Relax*. *Progressive Relaxation* is the more technical book; the other is addressed to the general public. Very briefly, the method involves two main features. The first is that of tensing a muscle and then suddenly releasing the tension, in order to become well acquainted with the sensations of excessive tonicity as contrasted with states of slight tension, or relaxation. The second is that of relaxing one part of the body at a time, and in a systematic order from feet to head and head to feet. You know how ineffective it is to tell yourself, or to have someone else tell you, to relax. In fact, Dr. Raymond Carhart, in a study reported in the 1943 volume of *Speech Monographs,* has presented evidence that verbal instruction to relax tends to result in a noticeable *increase* in tension. With Dr. Jacobson's technique you get around this difficulty, one might assume, simply by telling yourself to relax, not all at once and nothing first, but a piece at a time, as it were. You "tell" your toes to relax, then the soles of your feet, your ankles, the calves of your legs, the big muscles of your thighs. In this way you continue until you reach your forehead. Then you return, part by part, to your toes again, and then you go back toward the head, keeping it up until you are relaxed enough, or until time is up, or you have fallen asleep. At least in the beginning stages of training you would follow some such instruction as this: "Think of your toes; tense them; feel the tension; now let go; feel the relaxation." And so for the other bodily parts to be relaxed. Details will differ more or less from instructor to instructor; in essentials the procedure is as here described. One can learn by means of it to relax quite profoundly and to achieve relatively deep rest.

In fact, if your aim is rest you can make use of a great many commonly practiced methods of relaxation: listening to music, taking a warm bath, simply trying to become as limp as possible, passively watching and feeling yourself breathe while lying down, sun-bathing, massage, etc. Children can be calmed down a great deal—temporarily—by getting them to pretend that they are rag dolls, sacks of flour, and the like. Lying at ease while recalling and visualizing an unusually peaceful scene will sometimes help you to get the most out of a ten-minute rest. Soft wind blowing off a lake and gentle rain falling on the roof of your bedroom are among the many natural aids to drowsiness and relaxation.

It is relaxation for work, however, that we want most of the time, and it is this with which we are here chiefly concerned. Utter relaxation would be an intolerable handicap to a normally busy person; in fact, it would be as pathological as very extreme tenseness. The objective of semantic relaxation is not a state of rag-doll limpness, but optimal tonicity. An optimal or "just right" degree of tension can be defined for practical purposes in this way: you are optimally tense when either increased tension or further relaxation would not increase, but would tend to decrease, your efficiency.

There is a direct method of bringing about optimal tonicity, or semantic relaxation. It has been developed by Korzybski. It is still in the experimental stage, and until more research on it has been published one is justified only in describing it briefly and tentatively for whatever interest and value there may be in it at its present stage of development. Although as a systematic procedure it is quite new, its basic features are probably as old as the race. It is, in its essentials, the method that mothers have used from the Stone Age up to now in order to calm their fretful babes. When a baby cries and shows other signs of discontent its mother does not say to it, "Think of your toes. Make them tense. Now relax them!" Nor does she resort to vigorous massage. Mainly what she does is simply to *hold* the baby. And the calming effects of this holding, effects that are often impressively dramatic, can hardly be explained on any mechanical basis, in terms of sheer physical pressure, for example. The quieting appears to be an evaluational, a semantic, reaction to being held in a reassuring manner. Thus, a mother holding her babe in order to calm it illustrates in a fundamental sense the direct method of semantic relaxation.

It is a bit difficult to describe the actual procedure. In fact, it is not advisable to do so in any detail in this book. It is not advisable for two main reasons. In the first place, as has been said above, the method is still in the experimental stage and any exhaustive description of it would be premature. In the second place, it is not as simple as it tends to appear when put into words; one should learn it through demonstration by a trained instructor. Trying to learn it from the printed page would be somewhat like trying to learn how to play baseball by correspondence. Nevertheless, something more or less definite can be suggested as to the procedure, and because it is likely to be of some interest to the reader we shall attempt, somewhat gingerly, to describe it at least roughly.

We shall limit our discussion to relaxation of the hands and face, although it is to be understood, of course, that any of the other "muscular parts" of the body, such as the calves, thighs, arms, and shoulders, can be relaxed by this method. In some measure it may prove possible to make the procedure clear by contrasting it with massage. Probably anyone who has ever carried a heavy object with one hand for some distance has found pleasure and relief after his labor in massaging the numb and tired hand and fingers. This massaging is done rather vigorously as a rule, with the application of considerable pressure. The purpose of it is to achieve relief from feelings of muscular fatigue and numbness.

The technique of semantic relaxation is strikingly different from this sort of massage. In fact, it does not involve massage at all. With one hand you simply feel the palm and fingers of the other, holding the hand gently without pinching or squeezing it, slowly and with light pressure bending the fingers under and back again, noting how the hand feels. Is it soft, warm, and dry, or stiff, cold, and moist? Do the fingers bend readily? You hold the hand with firm but light pressure for a few seconds, then release even this light pressure, then apply it again. Now you bend the fingers gently again two or three times. You reverse hands and repeat the process. That is essentially all there is to it. Whât it amounts to is simply feeling with one hand the state of tension of the other, and "loosening up" the one with the other, not so much by physical pressure and active massage as by direct manual expression of calmness, ease, warmth, reassurance. It is the semantic rather than the mechanical aspect that is important.

In relaxing the face you place the hand over the face so that the thumb on one side and the fingers on the other are just below the cheek bones. The palm will be cupped lightly over the chin. The hand and fingers should be quite relaxed. Now slowly bring the thumb and fingers together, gently pulling the upper lip outward with the thumb and forefinger. The lower lip also will be gently pulled forward. See that the lower jaw hangs loosely and that the neck is not held in a rigid position. Work the palm and fingers slowly and gently so as to pull the mouth and cheek muscles outward, then release them, repeat the process, etc. Be careful not to dig in with the finger tips. Do not pinch or press hard. There are two objectives: to feel directly through the hand the state of tension of the face, and to "loosen up" the facial muscles by means of the gentle, calm use of the hand.

It is to be appreciated that one is not directly aware to any great extent of the degree of tension in any part of the body, unless the tension is extreme. Through the hand, however, one can directly feel the state of tension in the face, or the forearm, for example, and so become more acutely aware of it. This heightened awareness of tension through feeling it with the hand and fingers is probably responsible, in large measure, for the relaxation that follows. Everyone is doubtless familiar with the fact that when we become aware that we are tense we tend to relax. The procedure here described simply makes one more aware than usual of any tension that may exist, and so it increases one's natural tendency to reduce excessive tension. It is, in this sense, little more than a technique, apparently rather effective, for reminding one quite vividly of excessive tensions, and so of inducing one to eliminate them as much as possible. By using the technique for brief periods a few times a day, one tends to cultivate a more or less consistent state of optimal tonicity.

Insofar as this is true, the procedure is, of course, of great practical value. Once learned, once the tendency to be awkward, or too vigorous, fast, or perfunctory about it is overcome, it is extremely easy to use. The method tends to produce not the deep relaxation that is conducive to sleep or profound restfulness, but simply an optimal degree of tension. It does help one, perhaps, to sleep more soundly and to benefit more fully from periods of rest, but its chief advantage lies in the fact that it gives one relaxation for work, so to speak. It counteracts our common tendency to make hard work of whatever we do, to frown and grimace unduly, to overreact, to carry on our daily activities with a greater degree of tension than is necessary.

As we have previously stressed, optimal tonicity is closely related to delayed reaction. It is conducive to evaluative delay and is, in turn, reinforced by it. Jumping to conclusions, flying off the handle, going off half-cocked—these are familiar expressions used in describing the behavior of ineffective and blundering people. Irritability, oversensitiveness, quickness in taking offense, undue certainty of first impressions—these are generally recognized signs of maladjustment. On the other hand, poise, patience, and self-assurance are hallmarks of adequate adjustment. They involve effective delay of reactions and freedom from excessive, self-defensive tensions. The well-adjusted person reacts neither too soon nor too much.

SUMMARY OUTLINE OF GENERAL SEMANTICS

These practical techniques—the extensional devices, delayed reaction, and semantic relaxation, or optimal tension—are to be used with a clear understanding of what they represent. They represent and make effective the principles of general semantics. In order to indicate more clearly the place of these practical techniques within the system of general semantics, it will be useful to summarize that system at this point in brief outline form:

OUTLINE OF GENERAL SEMANTICS

1. Basic assumption of the process character of reality, and of the fundamental importance of change and differences
    A. Basic premises
        1. Non-identity
        2. Non-allness
        3. Self-reflexiveness of language and of the process of abstracting
    B. General semantics, based on the above premises, as a systematic formulation of the process of abstracting, as
        1. A process of leaving out details
        2. A process that proceeds normally from "lower" to "higher" levels, and that is
        3. Potentially continuous
        4. Personal
        5. Projective
        6. Self-reflexive

7. Multiordinal
8. Self-corrective
9. Productive of results that can be communicated
C. Working principles of general semantics
  1. Probability (uncertainty)
  2. Symbol reaction (conditionality)
     a. *Delayed reaction*
     b. *Optimal tonicity (semantic relaxation)*
  3. Extensionalization
     a. Order of abstracting
     b. Extensional definition
     c. *Extensional devices*
        (1) Indexes, dates, *etcetera*'s
        (2) Hyphens, quotes
        (3) Extensional terms
            (a) Plurals
            (b) Quantifying terms
            (c) Actional and operational terms
            (d) Conditional terms
            (e) Terms which express consciousness of projection
            (f) Underlining (italics)
D. Practical devices and techniques—selected for special discussion in the present chapter
  1. Delayed reaction
  2. Optimal tonicity (semantic relaxation)
  3. Extensional devices

THE IMPORTANCE OF APPLICATION

The extensional individual, employing the extensional devices and exhibiting delayed reaction and semantic relaxation, provides a living example of science as a way of life. Free from the self-defensive tensions which are due to semantic blockages, conscious of abstracting, aware of his own projective mechanisms, able to learn easily from criticism and from his own mistakes—such an individual is neither quick in taking offense nor long in holding a grudge, inclined neither to jump to conclusions nor to dawdle when action is necessary, neither frustrated unduly by difficulties of his own making nor demoralized by circumstances beyond his control. This is not to say that he has no problems; it is only to say that he is relatively efficient in dealing with them. It is not to say that he has achieved adjustment; it is only to indicate that he makes adjustments.

By applying the extensional devices, optimal tonicity, and effective delay of reaction, one tends to cultivate a scientific approach to problems of whatever kind. Such an approach involves, first of all, as has been indicated, the asking of questions that are indexed and dated, meaningful relative to specified conditions. It involves the making of reliable observations, or the using of observations made by others that are relevant to the questions asked. It involves the ordering and reporting of these observations so as to answer the questions as well as they can be answered with the means available at the time. And the answers so obtained are held to be true or dependable only within the limits of probability justified by the observations on which they are based. The answers are to be checked against further observations. In the meantime they are to be acted upon if action is necessary.

That, stripped of its technical refinements, is the method of science. It represents, in brief outline, the process of abstracting. It describes the mechanism of personal adjustment. What we call maladjustment sets in when questions become vague, when observations become irrelevant and unreliable, when answers become ambiguous or are no longer subjected to revision. Maladjustment sets in when the principles of probability, symbol reaction, and extensionalization are violated. And when violation of these principles becomes institutionalized and is enforced by the authority of age and precedence, whole societies are misdirected. Their progress is curtailed and the time-binding potentialities of their citizens are stifled and distorted.

It is the promise of general semantics, of science as method, to free the time-binding process of the blockages arising from vested interest and belief, to render effectively continuous and self-corrective the natural human processes of abstracting and evaluating. It aims to stimulate the consciousness of self that counteracts the ravages of self-consciousness. It strives to carry the individual beyond any present stage of development, to enable him to start tomorrow where he left off, not where he began, today. By so doing, it endeavors to insure the necessary revisions by means of which our culture may provide continuously the semantic environments essential to the adjustment, the health, and the creativeness of each of us as individuals.

Toward this end the principles that have been discussed and the techniques that have been described may be effective only to the degree that they are applied. The details of application of these principles and techniques must necessarily vary from person to person and for each person from time to time. In any case it is application that matters. Without it the techniques are useless and the principles are sterile verbal forms. The index of understanding, here as elsewhere, is the behavior by which it is demonstrated.

PREVIEW

The principles of science and of sanity and the techniques of personal adjustment which we have considered are to be more fully understood by examining the ways in which they are commonly abused, and the consequences of their neglect. In the chapters that follow we shall consider, therefore, the confusions and conflicts, the frustrations and inefficiencies, of people in quandaries. By reviewing the parade of perversities which will move through the pages that lie ahead, we shall see more clearly, perhaps, how to forestall and counteract the ungainly creations of man's cultivated ineptitude. Thus, having learned in some measure how to apply the principles of general semantics, we shall now consider some of the more important problems to which, and some of the more significant purposes for which, the principles may be applied. In the main, we shall do this by investigating what happens when they are not applied.

PART IV

The Making of a Difference

THE LANGUAGE OF MALADJUSTMENT

$\mathcal{I}$T WILL BE RECALLED THAT IN THE OPENING CHAPTER it was said of people in quandaries that they exhibit, in relation to their other symptoms, a more or less pronounced difficulty in stating clearly the problems by which they are troubled. There is something peculiarly significant about their language. We did not elaborate on this point very much in the opening chapter, because we had not yet laid out a language for talking about language. But it is precisely this, in large measure, that we have done in the intervening chapters, and we shall now use that language for talking about the language of maladjustment.

Korzybski has said that if you destroy the terminology of a science you destroy the science. Observing the generalized sense in which *terminology* is here used, we can say, likewise, that if you destroy the terminology of maladjustment you destroy the maladjustment.

This is to say, there is a language of personality maladjustment. You have to use a certain kind of language—or you have to use language in a certain way—if you are going to worry, or to regret, or to hate, or to develop and maintain an inferiority complex. Leaving any consideration of language behavior out of a discussion of personality would be somewhat like leaving the cheese out of a cheese soufflé. As a matter of fact, most of the key terms that we customarily use in talking about personality are seen, on close scrutiny, to refer somehow to reactions that are made to and with words and other symbols. To speak of attitudes, fears, hatreds, anxieties, conflicts, likes and dislikes, self-evaluations, delusions, etc., is to indicate, even though obscurely as a rule, those kinds of behavior in which language plays a heavy, often a very dominant, role.

There are many ways to talk about language. That is to say, there are many dimensions of language behavior, many ways in which it can be observed and in which people can be differentiated with respect to it. For our present purposes some of these are more important than others, and those that are more important will be stressed. We shall be concerned only slightly if at all, for example, with those aspects of language which are emphasized in grammar books. We shall be more concerned with those aspects of language which make the difference between confusion and efficiency, between misery and zest.

Verbal Output

Some people talk a great deal; others speak hardly at all. This is one of the most obvious ways in which people differ so far as language behavior is concerned. The amount of speaking done by an individual varies greatly, of course, with the circumstances in which he finds himself. This makes it very difficult to arrive at any precise estimate of the amount of talking that might be regarded as normal. But if one gives attention to the matter in the course of everyday observations, a fair sense of the normal range of verbal output can be acquired One soon becomes sensitive to those persons, at least, who talk much more and those who talk much less than the general run of people, and these extreme individuals are of considerable interest.

Among the definitely maladjusted there would appear to be a disproportionate number of these ororverbalized and underverbalized individuals. Both appear to have great difficulty in expressing themselves with any considerable degree of satisfaction either to themselves or to their listeners. The ones who talk too fast, too soon, too vigorously, and too much seem to say scarcely more, after all, than do those who speak too little, too late, too slowly, and with scant enthusiasm. Both seem to have an inordinate respect for words. The excessive talkers act as though they were sure that anything may be understood and controlled if only it is talked about sufficiently, and they seem not to notice that mostly their own talk goes in great circles, bringing them over and over again back to the same bewildering starting point. The tight-lipped and the awkward-tongued appear to be constantly in awe of the power of speech, seemingly overwhelmed by a fear of its consequences.

High Verbal Output

For practical purposes, verbose individuals may be classified roughly into three categories. There are those who talk mainly to avoid silence. There are others who use language chiefly to conceal truth. And, finally, there are those whose incessant talking appears to serve the function of a great nervously twitching proboscis with which they explore unceasingly in search of certainty.

Among the people with whom I have worked there was one gentleman who exhibited what amounted to a phobia of those awkward silent periods which occur even at the best-regulated dinner parties. He would grow tense and become all but panicky, not infrequently breaking the silence by blurting out some inane remark which only added to his discomfort. It appeared that he felt a sense of guilt about these silent interludes, interpreting them as glaring evidence of his own conversational ineptitude. And back of this, so far as could be judged, lay a general sense of inferiority, which he attempted to conceal by permitting nothing to occur that might reveal his inadequacy.

One of the most striking cases I have ever known is that of a lady who seems to have no terminal facilities whatever. It is quite probable that she could talk all day; I have never felt up to making the experiment. An interesting thing about her speech is that a little of it is not unpleasant. Listening to her talk is somewhat like watching a six-day bicycle race; the first few laps are even a little exciting, perhaps. It is the five-hundredth lap that gets you. She seems to be motivated by a profound sense of frustration in her social and professional activities; in any prolonged monologue she eventually settles down to a steady outpouring of criticism and pained astonishment concerning her real and imagined rivals. In common parlance, she is a "cat." Her denunciations of other people, given usually in confidential tones, seem to serve as a crutch with which she supports her own tottering self-esteem.

There are other persons who appear to use speech not so much for the positive purpose of gaining approval and of bolstering their own self-regard, as for the negative purpose of concealing facts or motives. It is rather common experience in clinical practice to have a person talk all around a point, and only after exorbitant verbal smoke-screening finally come through with statements in response to which the clinician can say, "Now we're getting somewhere." People will pay a psychiatrist ten or fifteen dollars an hour, and then for hour after hour conceal from him the information which he seeks and needs in order to help them. In psychoanalysis, a procedure in which customarily the patient does practically all the talking and is encouraged to talk a very great deal, the phenomenon of "resistance" is rather taken for granted. Resistance, in this sense, is a matter of the patient talking about irrelevancies, if at all, by way of refusing to reveal crucial information about himself. Many commencement speeches are characterized by the same sort of thing; they are significant with respect to what the speaker does not discuss. This is remindful of the two Vermonters, one of whom was hard of hearing, who were standing one day on the edge of a crowd listening to a soapbox orator. The one who was hard of hearing nudged the other and asked him what the speaker was talking about. After listening closely for another moment or two, the other replied, "He don't say."

Individuals who move, as it were behind verbal smoke-screens do so, as a rule, because they fear the consequences of revealing certain information. In a basic sense they are perfectionists where their own social status is concerned. Perhaps it is that they have too well absorbed from their semantic environments the ideal of "the good boy" and "the nice girl." At any rate, they seem to be desperately conventional, to care almost painfully about public opinion. They appear to have been taught that to be silent is to be of no importance, but also that to reveal oneself to others is to run the dreadful risk of social rejection. So they talk, busily but sur-reptitiously, covering the dusty windows of truth with flowing cur-tains of words.

There are other verbose individuals, however, who seem actually unable to recognize what is relevant. They go about hustling up verbal blind alleys in all sincerity and with genuine expectations of reaching an exit from their perplexity. Their most obvious motiva-tion appears to be simply a desire to escape from confusion into a realm of eternal verities. They manifest a kind of dogged per-sistence in trying out one line of discussion after another. Never satisfied with their conclusions but retaining a wonderful faith in the power of words, they do not often rest, but strike out again and again on what might be likened to a search for a semantic northwest passage to the India of Truth. They wear themselves out on seemingly endless verbal treadmills. The field of philosophy is worn bare with the tracks left by these unwearying verbal hunters of the Absolute. But they are not all professional philosophers by any means. They bob up not infrequently in psychological clinics, stopping on the way, as it were, for linguistic repairs.

We must not, of course, permit ourselves to make an over-generalization. There are certain quite talkative individuals who are by no stretch of imagination seriously maladjusted. They are merely alert and sociable. They like to share with others their feelings, their views, their experiences and information. Their con-versation seems to be motivated to an important degree by a genuine interest in other people. These normally verbose individuals tend to show their normality in two very important characteristics: they know they are talkative, and they can be, and frequently are, good listeners. It is the compulsiveness and distractibility, and the gen-eral lack of insight into what he is saying and why he is saying it, together with his essential lack of interest in the listener, that indi-cate maladjustment in a verbose individual.

With these qualifications, then, it may be said that, in general, people who talk excessively appear to do so because they feel a need for talking a great deal. And they feel this need because, in spite of all the talking they do, their problems remain unsolved. Actually, their problems remain unsolved, their problems are, in fact, in large measure created and complicated, not in spite of their excessive verbalizing, but because of it. Ovververbalization appears to be, for these reasons, a fairly reliable indicator of personality maladjustment. The disorienting language of verbose individuals will usually be found to express, in more or less conspicuous degrees, idealism, frustration, and the varieties of aggression that take the form of criticism, vengefulness, and vigorous self-defense. It expresses, also, a naïve faith in words, something quite remindful of primitive word magic.

Low Verbal Output

People who talk very little are equally interesting, and, in part, for different reasons. As a broad generalization, to which there are many exceptions, it can be said that they have progressed more deeply into the stages of demoralization. They seem rather more conscious of their feelings of inferiority, more convinced that they *are* inferior. And they appear to be baffled, and conspicuously disheartened. In making these statements we must remember, of course, that not all quiet people are maladjusted. Quietness, like anything else, is to be interpreted in relation to the circumstances under which it occurs. Remembering this—and only by doing so— we can make good use of the generalization we have stated.

One young man who was sent one time to my office replied, when asked what his difficulty might be, "Why, I can't—that is, I'm not—I'm not sure I know. That is—well, a professor of mine, one of my professors, he said that he thought that I—maybe it was that—he feels that—well, that I have trouble expressing what I want to say." It turned out that he had been a star athlete in college, but that his unusual abilities along such lines were regarded with a fine disdain by his father. The family, first-generation immigrants, lived in a neighborhood in which there was a generally accepted standard for the young men: they should all become lawyers, doctors, professors, or something equally respectable. In the "old country" such professions had been virtually closed to them or to their fathers, and the families were fiercely ambitious for their sons. But this particular young man had failed to pass the scholastic requirements for medical school. His family, particularly his father, had not permitted him to give up, however.

At the time he came for assistance he was attempting to earn an advanced degree in physical education. He had two purposes. His immediate objective was to obtain a position as an athletic coach, in order to improve his financial situation. His main purpose, however, was to include in his study program certain courses which were required for admission to a medical college. His father, his father's friends, his own friends would simply never understand if he failed to become a doctor. He felt that he could never again look anyone in the face if he did not achieve this goal. A battery of intelligence, reading, and language tests indicated beyond any practical doubt, however, that he might as well have been trying to jump over the hospital. He was referred to the clinic because he was failing all his courses.

This individual did not simply exhibit a vocabulary deficiency, a reading disability, or some other specific language inadequacy. He was generally bewildered. In ordinary terms, his level of intelligence was below average and his vocabulary was rather limited; but there are a great number of individuals who have such characteristics who are very talkative, nevertheless. The trouble with our young man seemed to be that he had been trying for so long to talk "over his head," to compete verbally on a level where he had neither the words nor the information necessary to function easily, that he had become overwhelmed with his "inability to express himself." He had failed so many times that he had come at last to feel that there was something mysteriously difficult about even the most simple remarks. He gave the appearance of having almost completely lost confidence in his ability to deal with language. Words, whether to be spoken or read or heard, seemed almost to paralyze him. He appeared to go blank, to be suffering from a kind of neuro-linguistic stupor. To opportunities or necessities for speech he responded with manifestations of apathy and discouragement.

Other reasons, however, sometimes appear to underlie excessive silence. Some individuals, overcome by feelings of inferiority and of guilt, appear to project these self-evaluations on to others, and so to take it for granted that these others regard them as unworthy. They do not feel welcome. In some cases they are literally ashamed of themselves. They feel that if they say anything their listeners too will be ashamed of them and for them, and will more completely reject them. In varying degrees, such individuals show histories of having been ridiculed, criticized, and even punished for expressing their views as children. They have been led to feel that what they have to say is unimportant, or uninteresting, or unintelligent, or uncouth, or generally inappropriate. So they are neuro-linguistically fearful, shy, and retiring. And the fact they are so serves to deepen the very sense of inferiority from which their seclusiveness springs.

Behind such reticence, in still other cases, there often lurks a burning but concealed hostility toward a mother, or father, or some other person with whom the individual has been very intimately associated. Not infrequently this hostility appears as a reaction to fundamentally sexual frustration. The moral codes of our culture are, in some homes and in some communities, quite brutally strict, as enforced. Permitted no clearly approved outlet for powerful natural drives, children tend to react with hatred of their parents and of other persons who frustrate them. But the same culture that brings about this reaction also condemns it. Children are instructed, even by means of threats, scoldings, and painful punishment, to love their parents and to cherish their homes—the very parents who threaten and punish them and the very homes in which they undergo all this misery. The profound conflicts thus generated leave many individuals all but speechless. This speechlessness appears as a method of self-defense—what you don't say can't be held against you. But it is seldom a highly conscious self-defense. What the individual is directly aware of is that verbal expression is very difficult and unsatisfying.

Another type of case is of particular interest from a general semantics point of view. In the universities candidates for the degree of Doctor of Philosophy are customarily subjected to an oral examination before a committee made up of members of the faculty. The language behavior of certain candidates in these oral examinations provides an unusual source of fascinating observations. One type of such behavior is of special interest in the present connection. It has been clearly exhibited by many students whom I have known, but most particularly by one who, in response to every question throughout a two-hour examination, spoke with extreme caution, choosing his words with elaborate deliberation. He was somewhat like a clinical case with whom I once worked, who would characteristically spend several hours in composing a rather brief letter to his parents, revising and revising as though with restrained desperation. Both he and the Ph.D. candidate were linguistic perfectionists who labored under the belief that to every question there is one and only one right answer, that for every situation there is but one appropriate remark, and that therefore there is always the problem to be faced of choosing the precisely right word. Such an attitude represents the Aristotelian orientation with a vengeance. The absolute, identity, two-valued language structure, carried to extremes as in these cases, makes for quite obviously pathological language behavior. What is most conspicuous about the resulting behavior is the painfully slow, tentative, cautious manner of speaking, or writing, with a great deal of implied or actual revision.

MEMO FOR DEANS

It is worth special comment that, while it is probably widely recognized that people who talk very little are likely to be not altogether well adjusted, it is not so generally understood that glibness is quite as significant in this respect. In fact, it seems to be commonly accepted that sustained and flowing speech is a mark of capability and intelligence. The very fact that in our culture a high value is placed on "the gift of gab" accounts, in no small part, for the nervous striving for volubility which some persons exhibit. It accounts also for the tendency of other individuals to lose confidence in their ability to speak acceptably and so to become relatively quiet. In our schools and universities speech is usually taught from the point of view that the ability to speak anywhere on any subject for any required length of time is very desirable. And yet every teacher doubtless has encountered many students whose verbal facility is found, on close examination, to represent a pathological or nearly pathological state. Educators might well give very serious consideration to this problem. In this connection, it is of more than minor interest that often one of the most noticeable effects of the study of general semantics is to be seen in a tendency to delay one's verbal reactions, and to talk less, more slowly, with less agitation and more accuracy—and so with greater self-assurance and general effectiveness.

NEURO-LINGUISTIC RIGIDITY

Personality maladjustment is reflected in, and fostered by, certain other aspects of language behavior besides that of verbal output. One of these aspects may be spoken of as *rigidity*. It is to be seen in the range and variability of the topics about which one speaks—*content* rigidity; in the degree of monotony of sentence form, style, word usage, mannerisms, etc.—*formal* rigidity; and in the persistence of verbally expressed beliefs, attitudes, etc.—*evaluational* rigidity.

Under carefully controlled conditions and with much tedious labor, these phases of language behavior can be actually measured in the laboratory; I have directed several studies along these lines, and in the Appendix certain aspects of them are discussed. At this point it is enough to say that in part the statements to follow are based on the findings from these investigations. For everyday purposes what is important is not so much the ability or opportunity to make elaborate research studies of language behavior, as the ability to make significant observations in the school, the clinic, the office, the home and in life situations generally. One can make such observations to the extent that one knows what to look for, and rigidity is one of the aspects of language behavior that is worth observing carefully.

CONTENT RIGIDITY

One of the most common examples of content rigidity is what goes by the name of "talking shop." The doctor who talks about his operations, the banker who talks money, money, money, the housewife who explains in detail far into the night the best ways to wash linen, clean enamelware, and can tomatoes—such individuals exhibit content rigidity in their language behavior. Many are the hostesses who say, for example, in planning a dinner party, "Let's not ask the Smiths! He'll bore everyone all evening long talking about what's wrong with Congress." When you find yourself harping on one thing over and over again, you can best regard it as a danger signal so far as your personality adjustment is concerned. A topic of conversation, unlike early morning sounds in the country, is not something that most people find it easy to get used to when it recurs persistently.

Content rigidity indicates a sort of semantic constriction. It is somewhat like eating too much meat and potatoes. The trouble with eating too much meat and potatoes is not that they are harmful, in and of themselves, but that if you eat your fill of them you don't eat the other foods you need in order to have a well-balanced diet. Just so, if you talk about nothing but money, you will suffer from "semantic malnutrition." It is not that talking about money is harmful, but if you talk about nothing else you do not provide yourself with a sufficiently broad base from which to draw any adequate conclusions about the general business of living. It is not only that one talks about that which one knows; it is also true that one comes to know chiefly what one talks about. The person who exhibits content rigidity, therefore, tends to operate with restricted knowledge and to make misevaluations in many situations as a consequence.

Rigid-content speakers are, as a rule, rather poor listeners. When the conversation veers away from their pet topic, they tend either to become bored or else to try to bring it back again to their own special field of interest. Either way they rather effectively insure themselves against learning anything. It appears that they would rather talk than be informed. This sort of language behavior is to be found, in varying degrees, almost universally among persons of middle age or older, and it constitutes one of the most serious problems of our culture, since it is from these age levels that our leadership is drawn for the most part. In our society it is a mark of rare distinction for an elderly individual not to show signs of rigidity and boredom. The person who, at sixty, undertakes the study of a new subject is almost as newsworthy as the proverbial man who bit the dog.

The most serious aspect of content rigidity is that it indicates, and fosters, a relative lack of responsiveness to situations. Oblivious to what is going on around him, the individual pours out the spume from within his private world of words. There are persons who, in the presence of a gorgeous sunset, a beautiful girl, or the outbreak of a war, can go on discussing the relative merits of canned versus bottled beer, or the respective backfields of Notre Dame and Georgia Tech, exhibiting the obliviousness of their surroundings that distinguishes the well-conditioned crossword puzzle addict. A Spanish painter once wrote in his diary, "Eleven of the fourteen children have whooping cough. I finished two full-length portraits today." That's the spirit. It is that sort of detachment from reality, remindful of the schizophrenic's intense unconcern with his environment, that marks in some degree the person who exhibits in his speech a one-track "mind," verbal monomania. It is not merely a mark of "culture" or a badge of leisure, it is downright healthy, to express and cultivate a wide range of interests. The most highly developed verbal specialists in the world are to be found in the insane asylums.

 Oververbalized shop-talkers do not, as a rule, make good companions. They are not the people with whom one is likely to strike up deep and close friendships. They tend to be too heavily absorbed in their own few interests to feel any genuine concern for the personal interests and points of view of other people. When they do show sympathy for others, it is likely to be a spur-of-the-moment sympathy, a matter of form much more than of feeling. They can conduct themselves "appropriately" at a funeral or wedding, for example, but while they are bowing their heads they are likely to be thinking along their own private lines. Such individuals are easily bored by others who speak intimately of their sorrows or personal aspirations. In fact, they are easily bored by what they read or by public speeches that do not fit snugly into the grooves of their own verbal patterns. If they read at all they are inclined to limit their reading to only a few authors, or fields of interest, or types of books and magazines. One case in my experience had read one particular novel twenty-seven times! Such verbally self-imprisoned individuals are hardly well fitted to serve as husbands or wives, as parents, as confidants and friends. For this reason, they tend to talk themselves into lives of loneliness and general maladjustment.

FORMAL RIGIDITY

Usually, though not always, associated with content rigidity is formal rigidity. Some of the more common examples of this are to be seen in the people whose language is bookish, the society matrons to whom practically everything is "just lovely," and the individuals whose speech is heavily loaded with profanity or slang. A case in point is that of a girl who, according to a rather widely traveled story, was secretary to Professor Einstein. Her language was a persistent source of unrewarding amazement to the great physicist, and at last he said to her one day, "Miss Blank, there are two words in your vocabulary that you use a very great deal. I would be so grateful if you would please refrain from using them in the future. One of them is *lousy* and the other is *swell*." "Well, that's sure okay by me, Professor," she replied. "What are they?"

Another outstanding illustration of this sort of language is afforded by newspaper and radio commentators in discussing musical concerts. A particularly amusing example, taken from *The New Yorker* (March 20, 1943, page 51), is the following:[1]

[1] Permission, *The New Yorker*. Copyright, 1945, The F-R Publishing Corporation.

It was particularly worth while and, as the event proved, very exciting to hear again the familiar symphony of Sibelius. . . .

More than ever impressive is the primitive freshness and originality of the writing; the power of its simplicity; the new use to which familiar chords are put; the new conception of instrumental coloring, so singularly evocative of Northern nature, and, above all, the grandeur and heroism of its spirit. . . . And there is nothing untouched with grandeur and pathos, and the sense of a spirit heroically alone, self-communing and, most fortunately, apart from the patent insincerities and affectations, the feebleness and empty pose which, in the field of composition, have especially infested this age.—*Olin Downes in the* Times, *February 15th.*

Even the finest performance in the world of the Second Symphony of Sibelius, however, can scarcely mitigate the antipathy one feels toward a work so basically anti-musical. Such a conscientious rendition as was given last night merely emphasized its pretentious conception and the academic fashion in which the composer carried out that conception. Listened to as the accompaniment to a Western film, the second movement, for instance, might be pleasurable; alone it is altogether hateful.—*Paul Bowles in the* Herald Tribune, *February 15th.*

Comment seems hardly necessary.

Formal rigidity is further illustrated by a story that is told concerning a society leader of prominence in her local community. She often occupies the place of honor in reception lines, and it is said that under these conditions the one response that she gives, like a broken record, to any and all remarks is, "Oh, how lovely!" The story has it that one of the younger and less "regular" matrons of the town decided one evening to test the lady's reputed invariability of verbal response. As she approached the head of the reception line she prepared herself for the experiment and, upon reaching the town's social lioness, she smiled sweetly and said, "Today I gave my husband arsenic." And she received the graciously lilting reply, "Oh, how lovely!"

In ceremony, ritual, the phrases of etiquette, and much polite conversation, verbal mannerisms are particularly evident. Ceremony, etc., does not always, of course, have great time-binding value; often quite the contrary is the case. The more thoroughly ridden a culture is with ceremony and ritual, the more rigid its structure and the less it provides for change in custom and belief.

To the extent that the individual interiorizes this rigidity of his culture structure, to the extent, that is, that he becomes conventional, to that extent his own language comes to consist of set verbal patterns. "Frozen" language of this sort represents semantic blockages which quite effectively prevent the development of revised attitudes and improved methods.

Moreover, as the individual whose language patterns have become "congealed" assumes positions of authority in the institutions (the courts, governmental agencies, schools, churches, business establishments, etc.) of his culture, he contributes, in his turn, to the rigidity of the culture structure. This is seen in the tendency of conservative men and women to dominate in the older, ripened societies, except under conditions of great stress when the demands of survival itself force the adoption of new policies and procedures. Societies which are too heavily traditional to make these changes tend to disintegrate. Individuals are like societies in this regard; when their language habits become too thoroughly fixed to permit effective evaluation of changed and changing circumstances, they tend to exhibit more or less grave nervous and "mental" disorders. When the "map" no longer fits the "territory," disorientation in some degree is the inevitable result unless the "map" is revised.

It is in this connection that slang, profanity, and clichés generally become important. Slang is undesirable not simply because it is offensive to grammarians. In fact, grammarians who steadfastly resist changes in language usage are rather more unhealthy semantically than are those who use slang and other unconventional constructions whenever they do make communication more effective. It is slang that has become habitual and no longer serves to render expression sharp and directive, it is this "day-old" slang that is undesirable. It is undesirable because it constitutes words gone wild—maps drawn by doodlers. After all, slang words, profanity, set phrases of any kind, are like other words in that they have no meaning in and of themselves—the meaning of a word is not in the word, it is in you. The communicative value of a word, slang or not, depends upon the context in which it is used, context in a broad sense—verbal, situational, cultural. Just as dots on a map are irrelevant or misleading when not properly related to the rest of the map, so words are ineffective or confusing when not well fitted to the context in which they are placed. Slang, profanity, and clichés are frequently used without due regard to context, simply because they represent more or less fixed verbal habits. The peculiar characteristic of habits of any kind is that they tend to occur regardless of circumstances. That is why they are sometimes maladjustive. Responses, verbal responses included, are adjustive to the extent that they are conditional and so involve adequate evaluation of the particular conditions under which they are made.

Formal rigidity, then, exercises the maladjustive influence that tends to result from any highly unconditional, or highly conditioned, response. It is seen as the making of very similar reactions to widely different situations. It is a verbal expression of identification, and so, in a world of process, it represents and fosters mis-evaluation.

The scientific studies referred to previously and discussed in the Appendix, have indicated that formal rigidity tends to be greater in the language of younger children than in that of older children and young adults, greater in the language of children of low intelligence than of children who measure high in intelligence, and greater in the language of persons suffering from schizophrenia, a grave "mental" disease, than in the language of university freshmen who were presumably normal. In these studies rigidity was measured in terms of vocabulary diversity or flexibility. I have called the measure the type-token ratio (TTR), the ratio of different words (types) to total words (tokens). If, for example, in writing one hundred words, an individual uses fifty-seven different words, his TTR would be .57. Various forms of the TTR, as well as a number of related measures, have been developed and applied to the study of language, and these measures represent in certain respects a precise statement of an individual's verbal, particularly *formal*, rigidity. When the broad semantic significance of such rigidity is appreciated, the sense of the TTR and related measures becomes clear.

So far as everyday observation and general adjustment are concerned, however, such precise measures are neither possible nor essential. Without the use of technical research methods one can develop a rather sharp sense of formal rigidity in one's own language and in the language of other people. The fiction found in many newsstand publications, the so-called pulps, some of the women's magazines, etc., and radio soap operas, can be particularly well appreciated from this point of view. In general, the stories fail to represent adequately either the world of general experience or the author's individualistic evaluations of that world. Such fiction represents verbal rigidity in all its forms: content, formal, and evaluational. The plots, characters, action, situations, and "morals" are relatively standardized. In large measure too, the stories involve standardized words and phrases; it is on this basis, to a considerable extent, that the characters, who are not individuals but *types*, are recognizable as the gun moll, the detective, the poor working girl, the boss's son, etc. Such stories, then, constitute a sort of conventional and fictional map of the terrain of experience, and if one were to try to live by this map, real experience would indeed be fraught with shocks and disillusionments—as it is for the thousands who take "true stories" to be true stories. The value of what we call literary appreciation is to be found not in the drawing room over the teacups, but in the very practical ability to tell a reliable verbal map from a phony.

EVALUATIONAL RIGIDITY

Evaluational rigidity is closely related, as a rule, to the other two forms which we have discussed. It is exhibited most clearly by the chronic pessimists and the perennial pollyannas. Ned Sparks was Hollywood's version of one variety of this semantic peculiarity. A rather different type of evaluational rigidity is to be seen in the radio program in which Lionel Barrymore plays The Mayor of the Town who says, in effect, "Shucks, everything is going to turn out all right in the end. It always does." Another illustration of this is to be found in happy-ending stories and in melodrama, in which "virtue" always triumphs and the wages of "sin" is death. An elderly gentleman once said to me, "Dancing is not only evil, it is also a sin." And he said a great deal more than that, along the same evaluational groove. To some individuals the world is always going to the dogs, the younger generation is wicked and soft, civilization is doomed—and to others prosperity is just around the corner, the dove of peace is always laying eggs with double yolks, and this is the best of all possible worlds.

Such individuals indulge, of course, in unconscious projection to extraordinary degrees. What they express as evaluations of reality are merely projections of their own sour stomachs, or of their over-stimulated thyroids, as the case may be. These Pied Pipers of doom, or of the millennium, are misleading prophets, verbal map makers suffering from mild but persistent delirium. Habitually identifying inference with description and description with fact, they use language with a grand irresponsibility. Those people whom we call sentimentalists, for example, suffer from this semantic ailment of evaluational rigidity; they never quite learn to differentiate Santa Claus, the stork, and Mother Goose from the actualities of adult living. They weep at the movies, identifying Hollywood-manufactured lights and shadows with real life; they faint at the sight of wounded kittens, projecting their own stereotyped evaluations into the electro-colloidal phenomena in front of their eyes.

Evaluational rigidity is, indeed, a widespread disease in our culture. An appalling share of the remarks we make, presumably about the reality outside our skins, are remarks that refer, after all, to our own inner states. We form evaluational habits, so that our attitudes and sympathies become relatively fixed, and then we talk about the world through the verbal filters which represent these evaluational habits. Some individuals become all but incapable of a straightforward, accurate, descriptive account of anything. They moralize even in their most trivial conversation. They incessantly remind themselves, and all others within earshot, of the goodness, or the badness, of everything from sunsets to sardines. They develop a kind of semantic blindness; their eyes become so filled with words, so to speak, that they can no longer see what they look at. They end up living in a world of reappearing visions, semantic illusions, verbal mirages, an either-orish Never-Never

Land of Good and Bad, of Right and Wrong, of Love and Revulsion. Wracked with identity, they suffer from a semantic myopia which no glass spectacles can ever correct. It is rather more than merely interesting that, in all our concern with defects of vision, we have blandly assumed that we see with our eyes only, and have scarcely realized that our most serious defects of vision arise from the fact that we see not only with our eyes, but also, and more importantly, with our assumptions, beliefs, and attitudes. We see, as it were through verbal filters.

Maladjustments occur because of this, in that we tend to make and express highly similar evaluations of extremely different situations. This is to be seen with unusual clearness in what I have called *evaluative labeling*. This term is designed to emphasize our common tendency to evaluate individuals and situations according to the names we apply to them. After all, this is a way of saying that the way in which we classify something determines in large measure the way in which we react to it. We classify largely by naming. Having named something, we tend to evaluate it and so to react to it in terms of the name we have given it. We learn in our culture to evaluate names, or labels, or words, quite independently of the actualities to which they might be applied. This is a more specific way of saying that the levels of abstraction are potentially —and very often actually—independent.

So common is this tendency to evaluate names as names, that psychologists have been able to demonstrate that practically anyone, *in our culture*, reacts more or less profoundly to isolated words. Psychologists have developed an instrument which they call a psychogalvanometer, and they use it to record changes in electrical skin potential. Records taken by means of this instrument show that it is very common, even for so-called educated people, to undergo changes in electrical skin potential in response to hearing or reading isolated words such as *mother, blood, love, blue,* etc. A considerable change in electrical skin potential in response to such a word represents, after all, a rather profound organismic evaluation of the word.

This is a most remarkable illustration of reaction to a word as though it were the object, of identification of levels of abstraction. It is the more remarkable because it has been shown to be an almost universal form of such identification—in our culture. In fact, psychologists speak of it generally as "normal." They have actually drawn up tables of norms as to the amount of such organismic reaction to particular words! From an extensional point of view any such evaluation of words, as words—which is to say, of noises or ink marks—would appear to be pathological. In response to *mother,* for example, a thoroughly extensional person would react in some such fashion as this: "Mother? Which mother? Mother$_1$, mother$_2$, mother$_3$, etc.? Whom are you talking about, doing what, to whom, under what conditions, for what reasons, with what effects, etc.?" The word *mother,* as such, devoid of all context, is hardly more than a pattern of lines. To undergo a change in electrical skin potential in response to such a pattern of lines appears, indeed, queer. Nevertheless we show strong tendencies not only to evaluate isolated words, but to react with similar identifications to other varieties of symbols as well, such as pictures, flags, designs, etc.

It has been reported of a certain British colonial governor in Africa that he had been having great difficulty keeping the natives under control. One day, however, a friend visited him, sized up the situation, and made a suggestion. With the governor's consent he ordered from London a generous supply of large pictures of Queen Victoria. When they arrived he placed them on the walls in all the native huts. The governor's difficulties ended as if by magic; the natives became very subservient. Bewildered, the governor asked his friend, "Why on earth do these natives respond this way to a picture of Queen Victoria?" But his friend replied, "Picture of Queen Victoria? Oh, no. To these natives it isn't a picture of Queen Victoria. It *is* Queen Victoria!"

This, of course, could be true only of very primitive people. We consider ourselves much too civilized to behave that way. Perhaps a second look at ourselves would be interesting, even enlightening. In our own culture, a psychologist has reported a study in which he gave each of several college students an ice pick and a stack of photographs of faces. He instructed the students to pick the eyes out of the faces shown on the photographs. The students did so—until they came to a certain photograph. In each student's stack of pictures there was one of his own mother. None of the students would pick the eyes out of the picture of his own mother. They evaluated the "smear," the lights and shadows on the paper, quite as they would have evaluated their own real, live mothers. As though the study had been done in darkest Africa, to each of these college students it was not a picture of his mother—it *was* his mother.

Another and rather curious example of this sort of thing was turned up in a study by one of my students, Mrs. Naomi Berwick. It was her assignment to investigate a certain aspect of the evaluative behavior of stutterers. She began by asking each of several stutterers to tell her the name of the person to whom he would find it most difficult to speak. Then she had each stutterer read a passage five times at one sitting, and she marked each stuttered word. Now, it happens to be a well-established fact that when stutterers read the same passage over and over they stutter less and less in the reading of it; and in five consecutive readings, as in Mrs. Berwick's study, a very substantial reduction in stuttering takes place. So, having achieved in the case of each stutterer a very considerable decrease in amount of stuttering, Mrs. Berwick was ready to proceed to the main part of her study.

Without the stutterers' knowledge, she had some time previously obtained front-view photographs of the persons named by the stutterers as individuals to whom they would find it very difficult to speak. Immediately after the fifth reading in each case, she suddenly placed before the stutterer the photograph of the "hard" listener, and then she called for a sixth reading of the passage, the stutterer to read to the photograph. The amount of stuttering increased markedly, becoming now approximately as great as it had been during the very first reading. We see here a definite and quite profound change in behavior in response to a mere photograph. To the stutterers, as to the African natives and the college students, it was not a picture of a person, it *was* a person. Neuro-semantically the photograph, or symbol, of a human being had been identified with the real live human being whom it merely represented.

Anyone could, from his own experience and observation, easily add to the above many instances of similar identification. If you doubt it, call the next ten persons you meet a certain name, which is well known—and the very fact that it had best not be printed here is further evidence of the common tendency in our culture to identify words with what they are unreflectively taken to stand for. Surely no observing adult in our society has any least doubt of the overwhelming potency of our common verbal taboos, our tendency to evaluate words or labels as though they were in and of themselves as real as what they are assumed to label. It is almost a matter of destiny, for example, for a child to become labeled as a "stutterer," or as "awkward," or "lazy," or "stupid," or "delinquent."

A particularly clear case in my experience was that of a young lady, a university student, who required clinical attention partly because she appeared to be extremely awkward. Her hands appeared to be so lacking in dexterity that one might easily have suspected a condition of partial paralysis. She wrote poorly. She dropped things. She seemingly couldn't dance; in fact, she walked with such a shuffling and tottering gait that it was a wonder she remained, for all practical purposes, upright. Her motor incoordination gave every appearance of being quite genuine. After some time had passed, however, a particularly significant bit of case-history information came to light. It was learned that two years previously, while attending a fashionable girls' school, she had received recognition as the outstanding horseback rider in the school. Now, one might very well doubt that a genuinely awkward person could ride a horse with extraordinary grace and skill. A more searching investigation was made accordingly, and it was established that somehow, at about the age of four years, she had come to be regarded by her family as "awkward." She was told repeatedly that she was "awkward." Her cousins and her uncles and her aunts told each other that she was "awkward." The label stuck.

She adopted it. She told herself she was "awkward." But she had liked horses, and that had led to the giveaway.

The problem was attacked, then, as one in which evaluative labeling had been the determining factor. A few of the relevant principles of general semantics were explained simply to her. An extensional attack on her self-evaluations was carried out. As her evaluations changed, specific alterations in behavior became possible. Within approximately two months she was dancing very well and playing a respectable game of tennis, and the uncanny shuffle and totter had gone out of her walk. She was no longer awkward; in any basic physical sense she never had been. But for nearly twenty years she had been literally a semantogenic cripple.

Evaluational rigidity, as seen in the language behavior of the parents of this girl, and subsequently in her own language behavior, appears, then, to arise largely out of the tendency to evaluate labels as though they were reality. Evaluational rigidity would appear to be an extremely common, and scarcely recognized, form of semantic disease with which our society is riddled. It is even reasonable to assume that it serves to render futile—and worse than futile— many of our efforts to deal with maladjustment. That is to say, in attempting to aid maladjusted people, as in psychological clinics and psychiatric hospitals, we customarily label them in various ways. An individual shows certain behavior and we give it a name: *schizophrenia, hysteria, behavior problem,* or perhaps that red-eyed verbal monster, *constitutionally psychopathic personality.* From a semantic point of view, such horrendous labeling merely adds pine knots to the fire we are trying to put out. If we help anybody, after branding him with such names, we would seem to help him only in the face of the great odds we have created with our own diagnostic words. Would you find it particularly reassuring to be labeled a "constitutionally psychopathic personality"? Or would you feel as though you had been kicked in the teeth while trying to get to your feet? After all, we don't have to throw anchors like that to the people who are calling for life belts. This is not to say that diagnosis is unimportant. It is very important. It is fundamental to successful therapy. It is much too important to be rendered ineffective, or even detrimental, by a disregard of the semantic factors involved in it.

The whole problem of diagnosis, in medicine, psychiatry, psychology, and in everyday situations, represents a semantic swampland that we have hardly begun to explore. Blithely we go our accustomed way, separating our fellow men into the sheep and the goats, apparently never dreaming that if we call a child or a man a goat, and call him that officially and frequently, we are quite likely to have a goat on our hands. A rose by some other name can smell to high heaven. People can be made deathly sick by symbols. They can be driven to wild distraction and to the most disastrous behavior by words, particularly when those words refer to their deeply personal concerns and disturb their self-evaluations. There are many cases in which a diagnostic label may sicken the patient quite as much as it may enlighten—or confuse—the physician. It is this fact, very significantly, that we are talking about when we speak of treating the patient as well as the disease. Insofar as a diagnosis represents and fosters evaluational rigidity in the person who applies the diagnostic label and in the one to whom it is applied, it aggravates the condition which it names.

The Fifth Freedom

Over- and under-verbalization and rigidity in language behavior, then, not only are indicators of maladjustment, but also foster and intensify maladjustment. The language of people in quandaries constitutes in large measure the very stuff their quandaries are made of. It may be said that the science of human behavior is now at a stage comparable to that period in medical history before physicians had learned about bacteria and antiseptic methods. We have not yet learned very much about "verbal bacteria" and we have yet to accept generally such methods as are available for sterilizing our semantic swabs and scalpels, so to speak. We insist upon a kind of freedom of speech that is far more dangerous than the public drinking cup and the old family bath towel could ever have been. The names we call one another and the evaluations we make of them lead all too often to consequences that can be gauged only in the tragic units of fear and hate, of poverty and crime, of racial and class discrimination, and the other unlovely items in the long catalogue of human misdirection.

There is, however, a very challenging source of hope in the promise of what we might call linguistic antisepsis and semantic sanitation. The plague of misevaluation may yet be quelled quite as definitely as the black plague and the red scourge have been conquered by the microbe hunters. A civilization of science is by no means an impossibility; it is probably closer at hand than we suspect. And a civilization of science depends upon a scientific attitude toward language—a consciousness of abstracting, the semantic counterpart of Lister's antiseptics and Pasteur's antitoxins. With a scientific attitude toward language, toward symbolisms of whatever kind, we stand to gain a fifth freedom, making other freedoms possible—we stand to gain a freedom from confusion.

LANGUAGE AS TECHNIQUE

MAN HAS BEEN CALLED THE TALKING ANIMAL. MAN IS not the same as an animal, of course, precisely because he does talk. Animals have their problems and their tragedies, but man seems to be the only creature who can talk himself into difficulties that would not otherwise exist. When man developed an elaborate brain cortex he not only stood upright and thereby created for himself the problems of hernia and indigestion—problems which women have complicated for themselves by getting up on high heels—but he also, figuratively speaking, got his feet clear off the ground and exhibited a remarkable facility at plucking difficulties out of thin air. Indeed, it was a long leap from the jungle home of the chimpanzee to our modern civilization—and apparently we didn't quite make it.

We seem not to realize very clearly as yet what it means to be a symbol-using class of life. We still take our language pretty much for granted. Most of us stare rather blankly at the suggestion that the way we talk determines to an important degree the way we live. Such a suggestion implies clearly that our language should be changed; and being relatively unconscious of our language, and quite unaware of its structure, we are disposed to feel rather helpless about the possibility of changing it. Our common attitude seems to be that the language we have is the only language there is, and that only a crackpot would seriously suggest doing anything about it. Besides, it's *our* language. It is part of us; and, and as we see it, to criticize our language is to criticize us, and we don't like that. One of my university teachers once declared with unforgettable frankness, "If you attack one of my ideas I will defend myself just as I would if you tried to cut off one of my hands."

Moreover, most of us feel vaguely but intensely that there is something about our language that is to be cherished, fondly preserved, and passed on carefully to our children. Most parents, with hardly a flicker of reflection, see to it that their children are told over and over again the same fairy tales and nursery rhymes which they themselves learned by heart when they were young. The heritage of our literature—of Shakespeare, Mother Goose, the Bible, Dante, Shelley, Tennyson, Longfellow, etc.—is jealously preserved. The question as to whether the heritage of our literature should or should not be preserved is practically never raised by most people, and when it is raised for them it is commonly resented and dismissed with profound disdain. Fundamentally, the point is not only that we find it very difficult to imagine how our language might be changed, but also that we tend to reject rather violently the question as to whether it should be changed at all. It follows, of course, that insofar as our language reflects and fosters our maladjustments, individually and as a society, we tend to preserve and to cultivate our maladjustments.

Before we can change our language it is essential that we develop a certain kind of attitude toward it—the attitude that language is to be viewed as a form of behavior and that, like other behavior, it is to be evaluated as *technique*. As we have said before, we evaluate a technique by asking what it is designed to do, how well it does it, and with what consequences. A technique is a way of doing something, and language may be viewed and evaluated as a technique for accomplishing personality adjustment. In the last chapter we attempted to regard it and evaluate it from that point of view, and we shall continue to do so in the present chapter. In doing this, it is necessary to bring out the various respects in which language behavior may be observed, for as we learn to observe it we become more effectively conscious of it and more aware of its *alterable* features. In the last chapter we discussed verbal output and verbal rigidity; in the following pages we shall consider certain other important aspects of language behavior which are related particularly to its self-reflexiveness.

DEAD-LEVEL ABSTRACTING

We have already said a great deal about the self-reflexiveness of the process of abstracting. Language behavior can be viewed significantly with reference to this self-reflexiveness. In adequate language behavior there is a tendency to progress from description to higher levels of abstraction by clear and orderly stages, and to return to description and to non-verbal demonstration as the needs of evaluation and communication require. This can be appreciated particularly well by considering two varieties of inadequate language behavior, two forms of what we may refer to as *dead-level abstracting*.

LOW-LEVEL ABSTRACTING

The first of these is to be observed as persistent low-level abstracting, as seen in language that is monotonously descriptive. Probably all of us know certain people who seem able to talk on and on without ever drawing any very general conclusions. For example, there is the back-fence chatter that is made up of he said and then I said and then she said and I said and then he said, far into the afternoon, ending with, "Well, that's *just* what I told him!" Letters describing vacation trips frequently illustrate this sort of language, detailing places seen, times of arrival and departure, the foods eaten and the prices paid, whether the beds were hard or soft, etc. We tend to take our verbal habits with us wherever we go, and to preserve them remarkably against the threats of beautiful scenery or historic events. As has been suggested previously, we see through a veil of words. A traveler who can report what he actually looks at, and not merely what he sees, is rare and wonderful.

Another example of dead-level abstracting of low order may be selected from a number of examples that were unearthed by Dr.

Mary Mann in her study of the written language of patients suffering from schizophrenia. The following was written by a woman, 23 years old, who was instructed to write the story of her life. The passage reproduced here constitutes the first typewritten page of her story. It is of interest that most of the paragraphs were repeated word for word, and even error for error several times in later portions of her manuscript. Thus, she not only failed to rise appreciably above the levels of description and enumeration, but she repeated herself over and over again. It is worth noting that she had been a student at two eastern universities, and that at the age of eleven years she had scored an I.Q. of 136 (very superior) on the Stanford-Binet intelligence test.

I was born in a small town, ———, ——— which was very interesting. My sister and I were very happy playing, with dolls, blocks, and wagons. We never tired of watching grandfather milk the cows. We went to the store for grandparents buying candy etc. We had playmates which, we had much fun with.

We liked to go with our parents and cousins on picnics.

We later moved to ———, where we went to kindergarten, and grade school, my sister and I went to school, played piano, went to parties, and took care of our rabbits. We liked to watch our mother make cake, mash potatoes and cook we liked.

We also, lived on another street and went to another school where we played school.

I had a music teacher who was very nice and we played duets together many times. We went to ——— school where we had a series of books. We had pens, eversharp pencils, etc.

We also had some queer little cards with letters on them which we spelled with.

We some times had our dolls and played with doll buggies, etc. Made candy etc. We had a swing which afforded us much pleasure. Also took car rides in the Buick sedan.

We lived in ———, and went to school. Our folks were very kind to us and we always played and went to church. We took piano lessons, gym lessons and also dancing lessons. We went ice skating, roller skating, and we were always interested in our books.

We went to grade school and high school, and were very proud of our grades. We made candy, and had fun with company. Parties, etc. picnics out at the park. We had a King's Daughter's Circle. . . . We had a president, vice president, secretary, and treasurer.

The semantic significance of the language behavior represented above lies in the fact that it indicates and reinforces a general blocking of the abstracting process. It is language that gets nowhere. It leads to only very limited conclusions; as a matter of fact, it rather appears that no conclusions at all are reached. "Facts" are enumerated, but they are not well related to one another. It is as though one were to recite the *World Almanac*.

There are so-called *idio-savants* who clearly illustrate what is here being discussed—they can do rapid calculations, repeat long series of boxcar numbers, possibly give the populations of all the principal cities of the world, recite long passages from literature, and perform many other verbal feats that are of vaudeville interest. In that sense they are "savants"; in other respects they are mediocre or even woefully lacking in common judgment—hence the term *idio-savant*. It is of grave social significance that *some* of our radio quiz programs, or question-and-answer programs, are so popular. After all, they involve in large measure the idio-savant type of language behavior. Their popularity indicates how widespread is the tendency to substitute elementalistic bits of "knowledge" for integrated evaluation or judgment. Perhaps these quiz programs are so popular because what they represent is so familiar to us— we took part in something very much like them almost every day for years in grade school, high school, and even in college.

HIGH-LEVEL ABSTRACTING

Another variety of dead-level abstracting involves mainly the higher orders of abstraction. It is represented by the language behavior seen in delusions, so-called wishful thinking, certain systems of "philosopy," creeds, etc. It is characterized especially by vagueness, ambiguity, even utter meaninglessness. Simply by saving various circulars, brochures, free copies of "new thought" magazines, etc., that come to one through the mails or that are left on one's doorstep, it is possible to accumulate in a short time quite a sizable file of illustrative material. Much more, of course, is to be found on library shelves, on newsstands, and in radio programs. Everyday conversation, classroom lectures, political speeches, commencement addresses, and various kinds of group forums and round-table discussions provide a further abundant source of words cut loose from their moorings. In fact, as one becomes keenly aware of this sort of linguistic rash, the search for a fair face becomes long and far-ranging. The lantern used by Diogenes to find an honest man would hardly prove large enough for the task of seeking out a person whose discourse was unfailingly clear, valid, and significant.

The most serious forms of this sort of language behavior are to be found in patients suffering from grave "mental" illnesses. In their delusions and their reports of hallucinations they show how utterly disjointed the process of abstracting can become. At times their words bear no symbolic relation whatever to the non-verbal levels. This is seen most strikingly, perhaps, in the strange condition which psychiatrists refer to as "split personality," which is generally regarded as a basic feature of schizophrenia, or dementia praecox. In fact, the term *schizophrenia* is derived from the fundamental consideration given to this *schism* within the personality. Most psychiatrists speak of it as a split between "the intellect" and "the emotions." The patient exhibits an almost chronic poker face, a "dead-pan" or "dead-fish" expression. He seems usually to show no affective reactions, to experience little or none of the grief, affection, joy, etc., which are felt and expressed by normal people. But it would appear to be very difficult to understand this phenomenon as a schism between "the emotions" and "the intellect"; these terms are used as though they were mutually independent, even when applied to normal human reactions, and thus they imply that even a normal personality is essentially "split."

The so-called split personality of the schizophrenic can probably best be represented as a split, a lack of any effective relationship, between the verbal and non-verbal levels of abstraction. The patient can say without apparent feeling that his mother has just been run over by a truck, because for him it is a verbal "mother" and a verbal "truck," and in a basic sense he is not talking about anything real at all. He lives in a world of words which he so completely indentifies with—or mistakes for—reality that reality, as others know it, hardly exists for him. The question as to whether his statements are true or clear simply doesn't arise, so far as he is concerned, because he takes it for granted that his statements are absolutely true and entirely meaningful—they are sufficient for him. He has reversed the process of abstracting: words come first, and if the facts do not correspond to the words, so much the worse for the facts. In a deeper sense, he appears to act as though his words *were* facts. If you do not understand what he says he is likely to become angry or disgusted with you, if he does not ignore you entirely; if you disagree with his statements, he is likely to distrust you. For him the map *is* the territory, and any question as to how well the map *represents* the territory is simply irrelevant and "unthinkable." This explains to a considerable degree why such patients cannot be argued out of their delusions.

There is a certain uncanniness about the delusional language of schizophrenics. Psychiatrists commonly assert that they find it almost impossible to develop a "feeling for" schizophrenics, to "get inside their skins," to have any sympathetic understanding of their condition. They are so utterly impervious to what commonly passes for rationality that attempts to discuss their problems with them seem futile. They are linguistically irresponsible. In the common sense of the term, their talk does sound crazy. One of them, in conversing with me one time, was inquiring about some friends. This part of his conversation seemed more or less rational, although his tone of voice and general manner betrayed a diffidence, a lack of the normal interest in information about friends and associates. Some chance word used in talking to him served to change his focus of attention quite completely, and suddenly he began a long discussion of the influence of the sun's rays on intelligence and character, with the same tone of voice and diffident manner, and with apparently no regard whatever for the meaningfulness or validity of his remarks. He seemed not to consider that his listener might have a point of view different from his own. Superficially he listened to questions and comments, but his talk proceeded with no relevance to them. Seemingly what was said to him made no impression at all.

In such "crazy" language behavior these things stand out: (1) an "emotional flatness," an unresponsive, poker-faced air of detachment; (2) a grotesque confusion of sense and nonsense, essentially the same tone of voice, facial expression, and general manner being employed in making sensible remarks as in uttering the purest gibberish; (3) an apparent lack of self-criticism, a striking failure to show any glimmer of curiosity about whether the listener understands or agrees; and (4) a general confusion or identification of levels of abstraction, as though all levels were one and the same, there being no apparent differentiation between higher and lower orders of inference and between inference and description. In this sense, such language gives the effect of high-order dead-level abstracting.

The maladjustive significance of words gone wild, as seen in the language of schizophrenia, lies mainly in the fact that assumptions and beliefs go unchecked. They are not tested against non-verbal observation and experience, because they are identified, in value, with observation and experience. If the map *is* the territory, there is no question as to whether it corresponds in structure to the territory, and there is no possibility, therefore, of using the structure of the territory as a guide in revising the map. The map may be revised from time to time, but without reference to any territory. The orientation of the schizophrenic appears to be, in the main, not two-valued, but *one-valued*. That is, he seems to evaluate all levels of abstraction as the same, as one. And he appears not to recognize that there might be even two sides to a question; there is only one side, his own. It is not that he views his own assertions as right and all others as wrong; for him there simply are no other assertions except his own. One might suppose that a dog has no sense of right and wrong, for example, but only a sense of what *is*— a sense of is-ness, as it were, simply a one-valued orientation. A similar orientation appears to be represented by schizophrenic language. Hence, the incredible verbal irresponsibility of schizophrenics, and their baffling unresponsiveness to reality or to statements about reality. They appear to have carried identification to such lengths that they make scarcely any differentiations at all as between levels of abstraction.

The point to be emphasized is that schizophrenia merely represents an extreme degree of something which, in lesser degrees and in certain forms, is well-nigh universal in our culture. As has been pointed out, our common subject-predicate language implies a relatively static world of absolutes, generally two-valued, and it is more or less conducive to identification. These features of our language are most in evidence in the more advanced stages of maladjustment, and are least conspicuous in the language of science as general method. Schizophrenia happens to be probably the most grave form of personality maladjustment in our society, and the language of schizophrenia is for that reason particularly instructive. That is why it has been discussed at some length, but the impression is not to be left that those of us who are not schizophrenic exhibit a completely different form of language behavior. Leave the radio turned on for one whole day, and any such impression will be clearly dispelled.

DULL AND INTERESTING LANGUAGE

Dead-level abstracting is not to be regarded as falling into two sharply distinct categories, high-level and low-level. These are merely extremes. The basic term here is not *high* or *low*, but *dead*. That is to say, what is fundamentally important is the fact that the abstracting carried on is restricted as to the number of levels which it involves. If this sounds a bit technical, it can be put rather simply by referring to what we have all experienced in listening to what we call "dull" speakers and "interesting" speakers.

How does a speaker manage to sound "dull"? If you try to recall the dullest speakers you have heard, it is quite likely that you will find that they tended strongly to pitch everything they said at about the same level of abstraction. In general, speakers are dull because either they seldom rise above the level of detailed description, and so leave one with an undirected feeling of "So what?" or they seldom descend to the level of description, and consequently leave one with the disappointment that comes from having got nothing when presumably something had been promised. In either case one feels frustrated. The low-level speaker frustrates you because he leaves you with no directions as to what to do with the basketful of information he has given you. The high-level speaker frustrates you because he simply doesn't tell you what he is talking about, and so you don't know what it is he wants you to do, while at the same time he seems quite determined that you know or do something. Being thus frustrated, and being further blocked because the rules of courtesy (or of attendance at class lectures) require that one remain quietly seated until the speaker has finished, there is little for one to do but daydream, doodle, or simply fall asleep. When we experience such reactions, we refer to them obliquely by saying that the speaker was dull.

And how does a speaker manage to sound "interesting"? It is a common notion that a speaker is interesting if he talks about something in which the listener is already interested. Teachers of public speaking tend to put great stress on the importance of "choosing the subject," so that it will be well suited to the audience. Now, a moment's reflection will serve readily to remind you of the many dull speeches you have heard on subjects in which you were definitely interested; in fact, many of those dull speeches dealt with matters in which you were so deeply interested that you had put yourself to great inconvenience in order to go to hear them. And you have heard many interesting speeches, no doubt, on subjects in which you had had no previous interest at all, on subjects, in fact, of which you had not even heard before the speaker informed you of them. No, the secret of being an interesting speaker does not lie very largely in choosing interesting subjects. In a sense, there are no interesting *subjects*. It is the *experience of reacting* to practically any subject that can be more or less interesting, or dull. If, therefore, there is any "secret" to being an interesting speaker, it lies, in the main, in the manner of directing the listener's reaction to the subject.

If you will observe carefully the speakers you find to be interesting, you are very likely to find that they play, as it were, up and down the levels of abstraction quite as a harpist plays up and down the strings of her harp. There is a fairly systematic order about it, but there is variability as well. A harpist who lingers too long on one string offends our ear; just so, the speaker who remains too long on the same general level of abstraction offends our evaluative processes—no matter what his subject may be.

The story is told of the man who played the bass viol. But he didn't play it the way other people play a bass viol. His bass viol had only one string, and he kept his finger always in the same place while he bowed that one string. In this way he played long, long, day after day—until his wife became exasperated, gentle soul though she was. "John," she said, "why don't you play the bass viol the way other people do? Haven't you noticed that they have many strings on their bass viols, and they move their fingers up and down all the time when they play?"

"Sure they do," said John, as he went on bowing. "They're looking for the place. I've found it."

Shades of a few Senators, and perhaps the man across the hall!

Technical reports in scientific journals make very dry reading for most people—even for most scientists—because they are so heavily loaded with detail, not infrequently to the third and fourth decimal place, and the conclusions, if any are stated, are usually so carefully restricted to the specific data of the particular investigation reported that "So what?" is left almost entirely unanswered in any terms that the majority of readers would regard as vital. The authors start before the reader is ready, and they stop just when he is getting all set to ask some questions.

This is true except for the theoretical articles which are pitched on very high levels of abstraction, and are very dry indeed to most people, because they are so lacking in descriptive detail and cannot be understood at all, unless one is already thoroughly familiar with the other articles that are so dull because they are cluttered up with too much detail. The trouble with the writers who publish in technical journals is that they do not write for the public, not even for the reading public, not even for the "intelligent" reading public; they write only for each other. And each, as writer, tends to overestimate wildly the tolerance of the other, as reader, for semantic monotony. It is my carefully considered opinion that very few of the articles published in technical journals are ever read, even by scientists, with interest or with great care, except by the authors themselves and some of their very close friends and associates—and the authors' students, of course.

A particularly striking bit of evidence for the above statement was recently recounted by one of my friends. In 1931 he was engaged in research on certain reactions of infants, and he wanted to look up the report of a study that had been published in a German scientific journal in 1891. He went to the library in the university where he was doing his research, and there he found the complete volume of the journal for the year 1891. It had been in the library for forty years—in a university noted for scientific research and graduate studies in the particular field to which this specific journal was devoted, a university in which all candidates for the Ph.D. degree are required to have a reading knowledge of French and German—and here was this German scientific journal, a complete year's volume of it, and its pages, after forty years, were still uncut! To top it off, after my friend had kept the volume for three or four weeks he received a notice from the librarian informing him that it was overdue, and would he please return it!

Scientific articles and books are not dull, however, merely because of the subjects with which they deal. There are some publications on sex, even, written by experimental psychologists and biologists, compared with which a railway timetable would be very exciting reading. Many people who are passionately fond of flowers would find the technical treatises of botanists impressively lacking in fascination. Scientists study and write about people and the world in which they live, and those are the subjects of the most interesting books we have. The reasons for the unpopularity of technical journals are not to be found in their tables of contents so much as in the degree to which the writers restrict their generalizations and the extensional scope of their statements, or in the impression they sometimes give of floating about on magic carpets of inference.

By writing as they do, such technical authors frequently do achieve remarkable thoroughness and accuracy concerning the tiny islands of reality which they explore. Occasionally, then, a Newton, a Russell, or an Einstein can pull together a number of these very reliable but extremely limited conclusions and abstract from them a single conclusion of considerable scope and importance. In this way science does advance. But very few so-called scientists appear to understand the process. Most laboratory workers are so "data-bound," so engrossed in the reading of their respective dials and meters, so disdainful of any statements that do not contain such words as *gram* and *millimeter,* that their outlook on life narrows to the size of a small peephole.

After all, the human value of laboratory science lies not so much in the specific bits of data and the narrowly restricted laws or relationships which it discloses. Its human value lies for the most part in two other directions: first, in the method it represents, and the possibility of generalizing this method and of applying it widely outside the laboratory; second, in the broad implications, the very general conclusions, that are to be drawn from viewing not one but several specific laboratory experiments as related to one another. The inadequacy of most scientific writers is to be seen in the fact that each reports his own little investigation as a separate unit, and, of course, from his one little investigation no very general conclusions can be drawn. Of necessity, therefore, his work remains of slight importance until and unless someone else views his particular study in relation to a problem broader and more pervasive than the one with which he was concerned.

Einstein has never performed a laboratory experiment; that may well be a major part of the reason for his tremendous scientific achievements. Having never glued his eyes, so to speak, to any specific meter, he has been almost completely free to concern himself with many different meter readings, many different investigations and sets of data, and to see how widely scattered observations might be brought together in significant relationships. He works from the levels of observation and description to the higher levels of inference, arriving at conclusions that not only are well-based extensionally, but are also extremely general and therefore of widespread human importance. And then, from this vantage ground, he is able to formulate questions that serve to change our established habits of observation, and so lead to new knowledge. He represents science, as contrasted with mere technology. He represents science as general method, as contrasted with the sciences, such as the narrowly specialized aspects of physics, chemistry, psychology, etc. In that sense, he avoids the elementalism that suffuses the separate technologies and narrow fields of specialization. He represents the language of science at its evaluative best. He avoids the dead-level abstracting of both the fact-bound describer and the irresponsible generalizer. He plays upon a wide range of abstraction levels, and he plays upon them systematically, symphonically.

THE RANGE AND ORDER OF ABSTRACTING

There are, then, two basic considerations in viewing language with respect to self-reflexiveness. First, there is the matter of the range of abstraction levels that one's language involves. For purposes of evaluation its range should not be unduly restricted. If one talks or writes too much on the lower, more descriptive levels, or too much on the higher, more inferential levels, two unfortunate consequences are likely: (1) one's established, highly general assumptions remain largely unchecked and unrevised, and (2) from one's own experience no very general conclusions are drawn. The general result takes the form of rigidity or non-adaptability in one's evaluative reactions.

Second, there is the matter of the order of abstracting. In the interests of evaluation, lower-order abstractions should lead to abstractions of higher order, and the resulting higher-order inferences should be continually checked and corrected against lower-order observation and description. Any excessive slowing down or blocking of this process is potentially or actually maladjustive. In fact, such a semantic blockage amounts to a reversal of the abstracting process. That is, an untested assumption has the effect of keeping one from abstracting in the order of observation to description to inference. It is as though one were to proceed from inference to fact, in the pathological sense that one identifies inference with fact; one takes the inference to be fact, and in this way distorts reality. This is the mechanism of delusion—a reversal of the order of abstracting, involving semantic blockage.

KNOWING THE QUESTIONS

The personal and social importance of these matters is to be seen with unusual clearness in the ways in which we ask questions. There is first of all the matter of how many questions we ask. People differ greatly in this respect. There are some individuals who practically never ask a question. It seems not to occur to them that their information may be incomplete. Moreover, they usually show little if any hesitancy in answering the questions asked by others, or in offering opinions concerning whatever is being discussed. They sometimes exhibit a sort of verbal brilliance, but they exhibit also, and more importantly, a remarkable lack of self-criticism. Alfred Binet, the creator of the modern intelligence test, stressed the significance of self-criticism in his attempts to define intelligence. The extent and the effectiveness of one's self-critical tendencies are to be seen particularly in the questions one asks, especially the questions one asks concerning the validity and the significance of one's own beliefs and attitudes.

Even more important than the number of questions one asks is the nature of the questions. The direction and the extent of one's personal development in a general sense are determined in large measure by the kinds of questions with which one is mainly concerned. There are questions that tend to make us learn rapidly and well, and there are other questions that tend to lead us into ever-deepening confusion and maladjustment.

If ever there may be a truly significant reform of education, no small part of it will lie in teaching children not how to give old answers, but how to formulate new questions. It is indeed likely that nothing else is more basic in the educative process than the relative emphasis given to the techniques of inquiry. Leading educational authorities of today, like those of centuries past, regard the school as a place where children learn tools (reading, writing, and arithmetic) with which to learn content, skills, and attitudes. In other words, from the schools, children are supposed to acquire truth, efficiency, and propriety, so that they may earn their livings inoffensively, while preserving without unseemly reflectiveness the customs and beliefs of their culture. In this traditional design for education there is scant emphasis placed on the techniques of inquiry and evaluation. In brief, children are not taught how to ask questions effectively; rather, they are taught to give approved answers, which they often do not understand, to questions which they would not usually be asked anyway outside the classroom. That sort of education could very easily be improved.

What we speak of here, in simple terms, as the asking of questions actually constitutes the more substantial part of science as method. What a scientist does that makes of him a scientist is to formulate new questions, or to revise old questions, in such ways that they can be answered on the basis of systematic observation. His assistants can make the observations. His main task, as scientist, is to frame the questions in such ways that the observations will be worth making—will be reliable and relevant to the broadest possible human concerns.

This last point is very important. For example, the biologists who study rats are not really devoted to the ideal of developing bigger and better rats. When a laboratory worker becomes interested in the rats, as such, he is a fit subject for investigation himself. The biologists are concerned with broad human problems, such as those concerning physical growth, health, and disease. They study rats instead of people simply because the questions in which they are interested can be answered more quickly, if not always more accurately, in terms of their observations of rats. It takes longer to investigate the life processes of human beings, and it is more difficult to control the conditions under which the observations might be made.

Likewise the experimental psychologists who study people are not really interested in the particular few individuals on whom they make their observations. They are interested in the general implications of the facts which they observe. They are concerned with behavior, with love, laughter, and learning, not as it is exhibited by Elmer Jones, but as it is *represented* by Elmer Jones. If he were unique *in all practical respects* there would be no point in studying him. What would be true of him would not hold for anyone else. And it must also be stressed that if he were identical *in all respects* with everyone else, there would be no need of studying him. It would not be possible to learn anything new from investigating his behavior. In fact, if we were all identical it would not be possible to learn anything new at all, and it is not conceivable that it would occur to anyone to attempt it. The reason we have human problems is that as a psycho-social individual no one is utterly unique, and the reason we can profitably study ourselves as individuals is that no one is completely identical with anyone else. Neither are you a law unto yourself, nor are you the measure of all things. What the scientist sets out to determine are the differences that make a difference, in order that he may discover the similarities that may be abstracted in the form of general laws. That is why he occupies himself so painstakingly with individual facts, and that is why he ends up, when successful, with such sweepingly general theories.

What does a scientist do with a theory? Memorize it? Defend it? Form a cult around it? By no means. He uses it for a very specific purpose. *He uses it as a source of questions*, new questions that have never before been asked by anyone. And he uses the questions to direct himself and others to new observations that have never before been made by anyone. In this way he gains new knowledge, new answers, new theories that have never before been imagined by anyone. And from the new theories come more questions, and thus new answers, in a never-ending process. Science is a perpetual frontier. That is why it appeals to the young—when they understand it. That is why a civilization of science is practically a foregone conclusion. Young man, go west—and the West will take you with her.

To be scientific, then, is, in a fundamental sense, to ask questions —fresh, meaningful, clear, answerable questions. It is to ask these questions, moreover, out of a clear consciousness of one's abstractions, one's assumptions. The fact of the matter is that our beliefs *automatically become questions* the moment we realize that they are beliefs instead of facts. When we say, "Criminal behavior is hereditary," and assume that we have stated a first-order fact, no question arises as to the statement itself. But when we say, "Criminal behavior is hereditary," and realize that we have stated a hypothesis, a mere belief, it is actually as if we had said, "Is criminal behavior hereditary?" It is more than that. What our statement implies, since it is not absolute and final, is this: "Under what conditions does criminal behavior occur?" And if we are sufficiently conscious of abstracting, we quite automatically go on to ask, "To what, first of all, do the terms *criminal behavior* and *heredity* refer?" In short, simply to acquire the attitude that our inferences *are inferences* is to pull the stops of our abstracting processes, so to speak, so that inquiry leads freely to new conclusions and new conclusions lead ever to new inquiries. Our theories then become important because of the questions they embody and imply, and our questions become important because of the new theories to which they lead us. It is when a theory, an inference, or a conclusion, is identified with fact that no new questions arise, and the abstracting process becomes securely blocked.

HATTIE₁ AND HATTIE₂

Now, this consciousness of abstracting, this realization that our assumptions are assumptions—and that they are *ours* and may not be universally accepted, or valid—this tends to provoke us not merely to ask questions, but to ask meaningful, answerable questions. The reason for this is quite simple. To be aware that our beliefs are abstractions is to be aware that they were abstracted by us from some lower-order abstractions, and these in turn from abstractions of still lower order, etc. Eventually, then, we are brought back to reality, to the non-verbal levels of experience and observation. And so it is with experience and observation that our higher-order abstractions, our beliefs and assumptions, must check. We tend to ask, therefore, whether they do check. We tend quite automatically to put our questions in such form that they must and can be answered by direct reference to experience and observation. In that sense they are meaningful and answerable. At the same time, the answers to them tend to have very general implications on high levels of abstraction.

Suppose we take a very commonplace example, which has been chosen deliberately for the very reason that it is commonplace. Hattie Jones meets a friend, Sarah Smith, on the street and says hello to her. Sarah Smith does not turn to look at her, nor does she answer her greeting. Now, Hattie Jones does not operate extensionally. She promptly tells herself that Sarah Smith is mad at her. For Hattie Jones this is no mere hypothesis. It is a fact. She may, for a fleeting moment, and from time to time for the next several days, ask herself a question, but it won't get her anywhere. It won't get her anywhere because her question is this: *"Why is Sarah mad at me?"* It won't get her anywhere (except into trouble) for two reasons. One is that she doesn't know, in an extensional sense, what she means by *why*. The other reason it won't help her is that she is seeking to explain a "fact" that is actually nothing but a private inference. Every answer she gives herself, therefore, will only make her confusion more wonderful. She may end up with quite elaborate delusions about Sarah Smith, and ruin a friendship forever. Such consequences are not uncommon in everyday life.

This is only part of the story, however. In fact, what we have sketched may not even occur. That is, Hattie's statement that Sarah is mad at her may not lead her to ask any questions at all. It may catapult her into action immediately. She may stop the next acquaintance she meets and spout her fury, relating all manner of bitter and uncomplimentary words about Sarah Smith. Perhaps she will not ask her to her next dinner party, and will give her a cold shoulder at the next club meeting. One consequence will lead to another until Solomon in all his wisdom would be unable to restore what had once been a beautiful friendship.

But now let us imagine a different Hattie Jones, a Hattie Jones who is conscious of her abstracting processes, conscious of projection, extensional. When Sarah Smith does not turn to look at her and does not return her greeting, she jumps to no hasty conclusions and she is not overcome with certain and absolute convictions. She does not go completely blank, either. She rather quickly realizes that there may be any number of possible explanations of Sarah's behavior. That being so, there is no one explanation that she can depend upon with absolute certainty. Maybe Sarah had been deeply engrossed in trying to remember her shopping list. Possibly her garter had just broken and she was too fully concerned about that to notice anything else for the moment. Who knows, perhaps she had just been told that her house was on fire, that her mother had died, that her little son had fractured his skull. Possibly she was just daydreaming. And maybe Sarah was peeved at her about something. Maybe, but how could Hattie be sure? She could recall no good reason for such a turn of events. Oh well, these are not explanations, Hattie tells herself, they are merely questions—and there is only one way to answer them. She will wait. If anything has happened the news of it will get to her one way or another. Besides, she will soon see Sarah again, and then she will find out—at least, she will see whether Sarah is mad at her.

So, in a calm "I-don't-know-let's-wait-and-see" attitude, she goes her way, creating no trouble for herself. Three days later she finds herself at Mrs. Simpson's tea. There is Sarah. She comes over to Hattie and begins chatting in her usual jovial manner. Possibly Hattie has forgotten all about the street incident. If she hasn't, she may casually say, during the course of the conversation, that Sarah does seem to be getting absent-minded—a sign of age, you know.

"What do you mean?"

"Why, the other day I met you downtown and called out a lilting 'hello' and you came marching right past me, eyes front, like the Spirit of '76, and didn't even so much as nod to me."

"No foolin'?"

And in another moment one more gently falling leaf from the tree of life has settled gracefully on to the pool of history, leaving nothing more than a brief and pretty ripple.

Our imaginary, but representative, Hatties and Sarahs may, of course, offend the sensitivities of academic professors who fancy themselves profound. We need not, however, be impressed by that. The point is that when a scientific, extensional orientation is taken outside the laboratory, it is applied, for the most part, in such commonplace situations as the one in which our extensional Hattie so easily and gracefully applied it. To sum it up by saying that Hattie showed herself to be a smart and sensible person does not tell *you* what to do in meeting similar situations. To say, however, that she exhibited an extensional orientation, a consciousness of abstracting, is to imply a general and practical method which you, as well as Hattie, might learn and cultivate.

It is to be noted carefully that $Hattie_1$ (intensional Hattie) stated assumptions as though they were facts, and reacted accordingly, with little delay, to the map inside her head as though it were the territory outside her skin. She was apparently unconscious of her own projections. It is this sort of thing that we refer to as identification of the word with the object, or as the confusion of levels of abstraction. $Hattie_2$ (extensional Hattie) stated assumptions as assumptions so that they automatically functioned as questions to be answered on the basis of appropriate observation or factual report. Automatically, therefore, her reactions were delayed until the indicated observations or information could be obtained. She did not have to repress any anger, or muster up any will power, or call upon some mysterious reserve of virtue. She merely waited because there was nothing to react to until she met Sarah again at Mrs. Simpson's tea.

It is also to be carefully noted that $Hattie_1$ did ask a question, but it was a confusing question, and she made the mistake of answering it out of thin air, which is about the only way it could have been answered, and so added to her stupidity, confusion, maladjustment, or whatever you want to call it. The questions asked by $Hattie_2$, on the other hand, were meaningful and answerable, and so had a calming and orienting effect, because the information needed to answer them was fairly well implied and obtainable.

NON-SENSE QUESTIONS

There are certain words which tend to make for confusing, unanswerable questions. These words can be used harmlessly, even helpfully, by people who are conscious of the abstracting processes involved in their use, but they are not ordinarily used in such an insightful manner. Among these words are (there are many others): *why, should* or *ought, right* and *wrong,* and sometimes *how* and *cause.*

Maladjusted people tend to occupy themselves very much with such questions as *"Why* did this have to happen to me?" *"Why* does everybody hate me?" *"Why* was *I* born?" *"Should* I get married?" *"Should* a woman smoke?" "Is it *right* to make a lot of money?" "Am I doing *wrong* if I don't pray every day?" *"How* can I be popular?" *"How* can I be a *good* wife?" "What *causes* fear?" etc. Also they frequently are concerned with such questions as "What is the unpardonable sin?" "What is the meaning of life?" "Am I a failure?" and other such *is* questions in which there are one or more hopelessly vague terms.

Such questions contain *unlimited* terms. That is to say, the terms *why, should, cause, is,* etc., are used in such a way that one cannot recognize the limits of their meaning. Therefore, one is unable to know whether any particular answer is relevant or valid. Another way to put it is this: The terms are unlimited in the sense that the levels of abstraction on which they are used, and on which an answer is to be made, are in no way indicated. The terms are multiordinal (can be used on any level of abstraction) and they have no general meaning, because their meanings depend on the level of abstraction on which they are used.

For example, when a person asks, "Why was I born?" no answer is possible for the simple reason that there is no way of knowing what would constitute the answer required. The person might be asking, for instance, "Out of all the possible unions of spermatozoa and ova that might have occurred, what accounted for the occurrence of the one union from which I resulted?" If that is what he is asking, there would seem to be no answer possible, no observations that one might make in order to answer the question. It is simply non-sense. But perhaps the person wasn't asking that at all. Maybe he was asking, "For what purpose was I brought into the world? What am I supposed to do, now that I'm here?" Again, if that is what he is asking, one certainly has no way of knowing what particular observations might provide the desired answer. As it stands, the question is meaningless. That is, in fact, how a scientific person would answer it, and with that answer he would be peacefully content.

Now it is just possible that our friend in asking, "Why was I born?" is merely asking us to tell him the names of some standard textbooks on embryology, obstetrics, and anatomy. If so, we can easily answer his question. But the chances are that if he realized that he wanted that answer he wouldn't have asked his question so indirectly. Maladjusted people either don't ask for such readily available information, or else don't realize that such information is what they want. If they did, they wouldn't be maladjusted in the first place.

People in quandaries are peculiar not only because they persist in asking themselves such vague and unanswerable questions, but also because they don't realize that their questions are unanswerable. In fact, they don't seem to realize that their maladjustment is in any way related to their persistence in asking, and in trying to answer, such questions. They seem quite puzzled by the suggestion that their questions need rewording. They don't want to reword them. They want answers, absolute, now-and-forever, correct answers. And so they remain maladjusted, pursuing verbal will-o'-the-wisps with ever-increasing tension and despair.

Answers can be very relaxing. Answers are what we all want. Insofar as we get them we tend to be happy, or at least relieved. Even bad news is usually more satisfying than none at all. One prominent surgeon reports that practically all patients would rather be told frankly that they have an incurable disease, or that they have only six months to live, than to be kept in suspense. Nothing can be more demoralizing than a prolonged and futile search for keenly desired answers. Procrustes at his fiendish worst devised no more agonizing torture than that of striving interminably for answers that never come. And this is, in large measure, the torture from which maladjusted people suffer.

It is an unnecessary torture. It comes about as the result of a semantic trick. It can be avoided by the simple means of not asking—or of not trying to answer—unanswerable questions. Whenever one asks a question, one has then to question the question by asking, "What sort of observations, or reported observations, would serve to answer it?" If that cannot be answered, then nothing has been asked. There is no question to be answered. To illustrate this in terms of an old poser, you can find out how many angels can stand on the head of a pin simply by producing the angels and the pin—and if that is asking too much, nothing at all was asked in the first place.

What practically all maladjusted people need is not answers to their old questions, but new questions. It has been said that any fool knows all the answers. This statement can be improved a bit by saying that only a fool knows the answers to questions that only a fool would ask. The language of maladjustment is most clearly characterized by great looping verbal circles, spoken or thought, that revolve around questions which, failing to direct and organize observation, serve only to generate tension and conflict and the misery that accompanies prolonged confusion.

THE STRUCTURE OF CONFUSION

It is to be noticed that the persistent questions of maladjusted people tend to be vague and unanswerable for the reason that they involve language that is elementalistic, absolutistic, and two-valued. People in quandaries wonder, for example, whether their difficulties are "physical" or "mental," "material" or "of the spirit." They say that "the spirit is willing but the flesh is weak," or vice versa. They talk as if world problems were "economic" or not "economic," "political" or not "political." Their proposed solutions to problems are equally elementalistic. For example, they contend, often with great vigor, that "the love of money is the root of all evil," or that "we must return to religion," or that everything will be solved by some pension system or a particular tax plan. The Prohibition Amendment to our federal Constitution was an example of this sort of elementalistic orientation operating on a national scale. Disarmament, as attempted after World War I, without due consideration of the many relevant factors, was an example of elementalism on a world-wide scale. Many people are suspicious of panaceas, but not very many seem to know clearly why they are. The trouble with panaceas is to be found in the *structural assumptions* underlying them, structural assumptions which can be well summarized in such terms as *elementalism, absolutism, either-orishness*, etc.

Maladjusted and incompetent people reveal such underlying assumptions, of which they are evidently unaware but on which they nevertheless appear to act, when, for instance, they pin their hopes on a liver pill, or Vitamin B, or an eighteen-day diet, or a slogan such as "The customer is always right" or "Keep smiling." In other words, they seem to assume that some one thing accounts for everything (elementalism), that there is always one and only one right answer and that all other answers are wrong (either-orishness), and that *the* right answer is completely right, now and forever and without exception (absolutism). Such people give their answers in such terms because it is in such terms that they ask their questions. The terminology, or structure, of the question sets the terminology, or structure, of the answer. Questions formulated in elementalistic, absolutistic, two-valued terms yield answers formulated in like terms. And such answers lead to action that is confusing, inefficient, and progressively maladjustive.

In Brief

The verbal ineptitude of people in quandaries is to be observed, then, in extremes of verbal output; in content, formal and evaluational rigidity; in dead-level abstracting; and in the elementalism, the absolutism, and the either-orishness of the structure of the language they employ. It is to be observed, too, in the meaningless and so misdirective character of many of the questions which they persistently ask—or which they unreflectively attempt to answer.

With a fair amount of practice one can become reasonably skilled in observing these characteristics of language behavior in oneself and in others. The ability to recognize them gives one a measure of control over them, and a degree of insight into the basic mechanisms of adequate evaluation. It enables one to recognize a fool—and to avoid being one—a bit more readily than would otherwise be possible. It renders one more fully aware of what is involved in knowing how to read or listen, to speak or write. What is involved in these activities determines nothing less than the extent and the limitations of personal development and of social change.

THE MAJOR MALADJUSTMENTS

$\mathcal{I}$N FAIRLY LARGE MEASURE THE PROCESS OF GROWING UP is a matter of finding out that the first fifteen years were the hardest —because we didn't know that they were really the easiest. In other words, you never quite achieve a proper sense of proportion about a pimple until you have had a boil. The point of all this, so far as the study of personality is concerned, is that a clear appreciation of sanity, and of the common varieties of distress, is hardly possible without some acquaintance with the details of insanity. For most of us insanity, like Carlyle's genius, is impossible until it occurs. We seem unable to predict it. Its full-blown appearance, even in our intimate acquaintances, is practically always an occasion for sheer astonishment.

The main value of a study of the more severe forms of nervous and "mental" disease lies in the fact that it serves in a rather striking way the general purposes of a microscope. Ordinary lapses of memory, for example, are quite subtle, fleeting, and difficult to observe; but essentially the same phenomena, when seen in a well-developed case of amnesia, become very clear, at least with respect to certain outstanding features. We are all familiar with the common experience of feeling blue, but we scarcely realize what it involves until we have examined with some care a case or two of profound melancholia. There is hardly anyone who does not harbor a few strange beliefs, but their significance tends to escape us until we have encountered some of the stark delusions that lend to the psychopathic ward its slightly unnerving atmosphere.

In the present chapter, then, we shall look at our common confusions and inefficiencies through the "microscope" of psychopathology. We shall attempt to enlarge and clarify the picture of personality maladjustment which we have been scrutinizing by discussing certain major disorders encountered in "mental" hospitals. It is to be stressed, however, that we are in no sense "playing doctor." The treatment of these grave disorders is the concern of the medical profession, and this is to be emphasized without equivocation. Legal considerations make it all but mandatory and the welfare both of the patient and of society requires that only well-trained medical practitioners undertake the treatment of the nervous and "mental" disorders that we are presently to review. It is our purpose simply to have a look at some of the extreme forms of human maladjustment in order to sharpen our ability to observe —and to counteract—our own misdirected behavior.

GENERAL CLASSIFICATION

Psychiatrists and psychologists who make it their business to observe and evaluate human behavior have achieved a fair degree of agreement with respect to many of their observations. They do not always agree, by any means, in what they say about these observations; they do not always agree as to their theories. But they do not argue seriously, or very long in any instance, about what they see people doing. Those who reject Freud's theories admire nonetheless his astuteness as an observer; those who challenge the explanations of behavior advanced by Pavlov and his more modern followers show little hesitancy in accepting most of their data. It has even been possible for the members of the American Psychiatric Association to agree upon a standard classification of "mental" and nervous disorders, and the majority of psychiatrists report their observations in terms of this classification. True, they argue, sometimes heatedly, as to just how a particular case is to be classified or diagnosed, nor do they always agree, of course, as to how the observed disorders are to be explained or treated, once they have been classified. The followers of Freud, of Kraepelin, and of Adolf Meyer would hardly argue as to whether a particular patient insists that he is Napoleon, although they probably would argue vigorously about why he does and what had best be done about it.

We shall not reproduce here the American Psychiatric Associations's classification of "mental" and nervous disorders; it may be found in almost any textbook of psychiatry or abnormal psychology. Besides, it would take us too far afield. It is enough for our purposes to say that in this classification the major disorders are divided, most fundamentally, into the *psychoses* and the *psychoneuroses*. An attempt is also made to differentiate those which involve organic pathology from those which do not. We shall be concerned mainly with those which do not.

In general, the difference between a psychosis and a psychoneurosis is one of degree or complexity. In practice it is not always easy to differentiate the two, just as it is not always easy to tell the difference between a "normal" and an "abnormal" individual. Many, though by no means all, psychoneurotics are able to function reasonably well aside from their specific disabilities. A person may have an intense, uncontrollable fear of elevators or of trains, or he may be disabled from time to time by neurotic headaches, and yet continue to carry on as an outstanding author, actor, or business executive. A person with hysterical blindness may be ill in no other respect and may be a charming and astute conversationalist under most circumstances. Psychotics, on the other hand, are usually more completely disabled by their disorders. Their maladjustments tend to be quite generalized as to their symptoms and effects. An individual who is convinced that he is the victim of a nation-wide plot, or who persistently hears voices telling him to put his children in the basement furnace because it is a holy altar, is likely to be rather generally incapacitated from any ordinary social point of view.

The Psychoneuroses

The American Psychiatric Association classification lists three types of psychoneuroses and provides for any others that might conceivably be found. These three types are called *hysteria, neurasthenia,* and *psychasthenia*. It is to be recognized, of course, that under each of these headings further classifications can be made. All hysterics are not alike, and individual cases can be differentiated and classified from many points of view. In the final analysis, it is always an individual who develops a disorder, and he is still an individual after he has developed it.

Hysteria

In general, and very briefly, the chief symptoms of hysteria are various physical complaints for which no organic causes can be found. The hysteric is a person of whom it might be said that something gives him "a pain in the neck." The individual may be paralyzed in some part, or be unable to see or hear, or he may have a loss of sensation on certain parts of his body surface. He may suffer a drastic loss of appetite and refuse to eat. Or the main symptom may be that of amnesia, or loss of memory; the individual may even forget his own name, where he lives, what he does for a living, etc., or he may be under the impression that he is somebody else.

It is peculiarly interesting that these disabilities tend to come on suddenly and without apparent cause—from a medical point of view—and to go away, if they do, quite as suddenly and "mysteriously." More accurately, it is not that they go away completely, but that the symptoms change. For example, a patient may suddenly recover the use of a paralyzed leg, only to develop a paralyzed arm or suffer a loss of voice a week later. As many psychiatrists have pointed out, these are the cases who leave their crutches and recover their sight, as if by miracles, at shrines and temples—but their recoveries are by no means always complete or permanent, a point that popular magazine writers do not always make clear. Many of the so-called "shell-shock" cases, or war neuroses, are hysterical. In these cases the hysterical paralysis, blindness, or whatever it may be, frequently occurs far from any field of battle; it is not always the shock from actual shells that brings on the difficulties. In World War I many "shell-shocked" soldiers never left American shores, and not a few recovered after the Armistice was signed. Again in World War II, neurotic reactions have been found to occur far from any theaters of action, as well as under the stress of combat duty.

Nevertheless, hysterics are not malingerers in any ordinary sense. They do not consciously affect illness or incapacity in order to get out of disagreeable situations, or to avoid responsibilities and dangers. So far as they can honestly report, they simply and definitely cannot see, or hear, or move their legs, or whatnot. They may even complain, with evidently genuine sincerity, about their inability to follow their regiment, or to go through with the wedding, or whatever else it may be that their disability prevents them from doing. Students, for example, sometimes "cannot" write examinations; they try hard, and for all they know they earnestly and desperately want to write. In one of my classes there was once a young lady who suffered from a thoroughly incapacitating cramping of the right hand whenever in an examination she was required to write numbers. Such difficulties are essentially hysterical. The maladjustments that we call hysterical range in severity all the way from very occasional and minor disabilities to apparently permanent and constant incapacities of major proportions.

So far as the observable behavior of hysteria is concerned there is little to argue about. There are individuals who do present the kinds of reactions and symptoms sketched above. Whether or not they are to be called hysterical in a particular case is, of course, frequently debatable; from individual to individual the reactions vary in complexity, severity, persistence, apparent precipitating conditions, etc. It is the behavior, or symptoms, however, that concern us; whether they are called hysteria or something else—what name is to be applied—is not the major issue. Not that the art of medical diagnosis is of no significance; but what is important for our present purposes is that we recognize *as behavior* these disabling reactions, made usually under conditions of threat or danger and without apparent organic cause—and that we recognize them not only in severe hospital cases, but particularly in the milder forms in which they are to be observed outside the hospitals in our associates and in ourselves.

The hospital cases are instructive, as we have suggested, in the sense that a microscope is instructive. What is happening in a soldier who suddenly becomes blind shortly before his regiment is to sail is rather more obvious than what is happening in a mother who begins to have "fainting spells" two weeks before her only daughter's marriage. The soldier's case is more clear-cut in most respects, as to motivation and symptoms and possibly as to treatment. It is not so evident that there is anything "psychological" about what the mother is doing; the motivation is not clear, particularly if she expresses happiness about her daughter's marriage; her symptoms are somewhat vague, and the question as to the kind of treatment she requires may not be answered until after countless visits to physicians and clinics, and it may never be answered. Doctors' waiting rooms, according to their own testimony, are frequented by such mysteriously ailing women—and men, and even children. To say that they are all entirely psychoneurotic is probably to abuse an otherwise useful term, but to understand their symptoms *as behavior* is to add considerably to our understanding of certain rather common forms of "unsanity."

NEURASTHENIA

In neurasthenia, another type of psychoneurosis, we see in clear form the ravages of well-developed, "in-grown" boredom. The neurasthenic is characteristically weary, without enthusiasm, sad, inclined to react emotionally if pressed, generally buffaloed by the demands of ordinary living. Basically he appears to be overwhelmed by a deep sense of inferiority. He is likely to be annoyed, or at least fussed and disturbed, by criticism or advice. He may, or may not, complain of various physical symptoms for which no clear organic causes can be discovered. These alleged symptoms, if there are any, may seem consistent with his general weariness, the whole impression that he gives of just not being up to the general business of living.

We see in these more or less vague physical complaints of the neurasthenic, as compared with the rather more definite neurotic ailments of the hysteric, an instance of the difficulty of clearly differentiating in all cases between one form of psychoneurosis and another. Patients are as a rule predominantly hysterical, or predominantly neurasthenic, rather than clearly and exclusively one or the other. Moreover, in actual cases it is by no means always easy to differentiate these psychoneuroses from certain psychoses. It is sometimes quite difficult to decide whether a particular weary, distracted, possibly deluded, withdrawing individual is to be properly classified as neurasthenic or schizophrenic. In real life the symptoms are usually not as neatly arranged as they are in textbooks.

PSYCHASTHENIA

In the third type of psychoneurosis, psychasthenia, the main symptoms are obsessions, compulsions, and phobias. The obsessions are exaggerated, and often distressing, forms of recurring thoughts, or imagery, or doubts and fears. The individual may be frequently overwhelmed by the belief that he is being followed or that he is going blind. Such obsessions appear to be extreme forms of what is more normally experienced as worry, or as the persistent and agitated "mental mulling" that one undergoes during spells of insomnia. When these perseverating thoughts carry over into action the result is seen as compulsive behavior. For example, one case in my experience complained of a very serious loss of sleep. Every night, after going to bed, he would get up several times to go downstairs and make sure the lights were out, the doors were locked, the windows closed, etc. He felt an overpowering compulsion to do these things not just once, but some nights many times, keeping a nervous vigilance far into the small hours of the morning.

Some people show such relatively innocent compulsive tendencies as those of stepping on all the cracks in the sidewalk, or on none of them, of always keeping in step with their companions, or of invariably spitting into a river when viewing it from a bridge railing. A craving to play solitaire, or to put nickles into slot machines and pull the handle, approaches compulsion-like proportions in some cases. A student once consulted me because he had run up a debt of $350 in less than three months by playing slot machines, a debt that was for him enormous, and a source of agitated anxiety. In psychasthenia rather more serious and more strongly motivated compulsions than these, however, are to be seen. The classic form is that of hand-washing; the individual compulsively washes his hands every little while. Akin to this was the compulsion of a lady I once knew who meticulously refrained from touching stair railings for fear, so she said, of catching syphilis.

The phobias, or strong and more or less uncontrollable fears, of psychasthenics are probably quite familiar to the general public. The Sunday supplements and popular magazines frequently carry stories about phobias, especially those of famous people. It has almost become fashionable to lay claim to some such strange complaint as claustrophobia (fear of closed places), or agoraphobia (fear of open places), etc. There seems to be no limit to the things people can be afraid of. Some writer once listed the five great D's of fear: fears of death, doctors, dogs, demons, and darkness. A psychiatrist once told me of a case he was handling in which the number of phobias was so great that he spoke of the individual as suffering from "phobophobia." Common minor forms of phobia-like reactions are to be seen in the fears that some women have of mice, or the fears of snakes and of lightning that are so widespread. Stagefright is another very common type of reaction that for thousands of people comes very near to being a phobia.

In psychasthenics these common fears are extreme, or they are seen in unusual forms. Korzybski once had occasion to investigate the case of a man who had a strange fear of golf balls. I was once consulted by a man who had pronounced phobic reactions to situations in which he had to eat with other people. Another gentleman expressed marked and agitated concern over his "slips of the tongue," as when, for example, he would say "gotfor" instead of "forgot." He was a school teacher and was to all appearances fast approaching a "nervous breakdown" because of this peculiar anxiety. Some psychiatrists prefer to put these phobias and related anxiety states in a special category which they usually call "anxiety neuroses" because they represent such striking and definite reaction tendencies. Other psychiatrists, however, consider them as part of the general picture of psychasthenia.

Here again we see a reason for difficulty in diagnosis. The obsessions, compulsions, and phobias of psychasthenics are not always easy to distinguish from the delusions, stereotyped behavior, and depressed or agitated states of the various psychoses. Moreover, psychasthenic compulsions look in some cases quite like the irresponsible impulsiveness of patients diagnosed as "constitutionally psychopathic personalities." But, while there might be disagreement or doubt as to how an individual should be diagnosed or classified, there is usually no great doubt as to how his behavior is to be described. We will end up with a generally better understanding of maladjustment if we concentrate on gaining a fair knowledge of the actual behavior involved, and do not allow ourselves to be drawn into distracting controversies as to precisely how the behavior is to be classified.

THE PSYCHOSES

The American Psychiatric Association classification recognizes four main types of functional psychosis: *schizophrenia* (dementia praecox), *paranoia, manic-depressive psychosis,* and *involutional psychosis.* They are called functional because it has not been determined that they are due to organic pathology. Granted that there is some controversy on this point, the clearly prevailing opinion is that these disorders are not to be adequately accounted for on the basis of diseased or injured bodily tissue. At any rate, we are again mainly interested in the behavior exhibited by cases which represent the psychoses.

SCHIZOPHRENIA—SIMPLE TYPE

Schizophrenia is the most common of the psychoses. Twenty per cent or more of the beds in "mental" hospitals are occupied by schizophrenics. One is strongly tempted to regard this disease as peculiarly representative of the more important disintegrative forces within our culture. While its main symptoms are obviously extreme in form and intensity, there is, nevertheless, a disturbing similarity between them and corresponding behavior which, in milder forms, is very common indeed outside the hospitals.

In discussing dead-level abstracting in Chapter XII we touched on certain of the basic symptoms of schizophrenia. We referred to the lack of emotional tone, the "dead-pan" expression, and the verbal irresponsibility. This latter appears to be somehow crucial. It represents apparently a rather thoroughgoing lack of any consciousness of abstracting. Levels of abstraction are simply not differentiated. Psychiatrists agree quite well in reporting this sort of confusion as characteristic of schizophrenia. These patients somehow do not "think" well. The late Dr. William A. White has stated this by saying, in effect, that when they do use "abstract" language they appear to use it "concretely." In a somewhat similar vein, Dr. Kurt Goldstein has said that the difference between schizophrenic patients and normal individuals lies in the capacity for abstract behavior. So far as I can surmise, what Goldstein and White refer to is something that would be described, in terms of general semantics, as a relatively thoroughgoing identification, on the part of the schizophrenic, of the levels of abstraction. "Concrete" behavior appears to be, in its verbal aspects, a matter of using language on the relatively low levels of enumeration, labeling, or description. We saw an example of this in the passage of schizophrenic writing quoted from the study by Dr. Mann in the preceding chapter.

An example of what schizophrenics sometimes do when they appear to be attempting to write on higher levels of abstraction is to be seen in the following excerpt from material written by another of Dr. Mann's cases. This was a man 27 years old, who had developed schizophrenia while attending a law college. He had been, according to the hospital records, a "good average" student. What follows constitutes the first page, as typed, of what he wrote when instructed to write the story of his life.

In my easy moments as I gazed upon life I recollect those descriptive articles which compromise the outlay or possessions of a child from seven to eleven months such as those colored and carrying a significance and those which didn't.

Those fleeting moments are a collection which form a definite panorama for passive and active body and mind organization later.

Then come friends, babies of the same age, including my immediate sister, later by seven years another sister was born. These also carried a form of depictiveness, which helps to frame later instructions, such as through the church, city, school and state.

No special happenings, but just lived the ordinary life of an adult, rather including the early to later states. Have a high school diploma, college degree, and in the advanced stage of law work.

In particular, life has connoted much and is similar to that often found by the theatre goer after having reviewed a series of movies.

Life, in conclusion, carries many rigid and rough exteriors, mine factunately runs thru a gentle, mild and interesting vein. Its inclusion as pertaining and attachable to my person gives it no new inset or reestablishing being as free flowering as the mighty mississippi and as comparable as I should judge law.

In a survey of my life I think that sexual or bodily virtues have more or less been interfered with, which does not allow the necessary mentality to cope with the health and vigor of the writer,

Father, has often emphasized, the elementary aims, such as concentration, and the opposite deposition of subject of life as viewed personally by me, that is, being alive.

The brain, especially if one (the reader) has taken physiology, if very moved to sometimes interupt the nerves, that I should think would be the best moment to view life, as bluntly stated from a humanitarian stand point, and then in rereading this paper as to my Life, I would conclude that much is found in the dictionaries, and the different translations of languages the way a person feels, his senses and also probably a mass of inevitable conclusions.

A few paragraphs farther on, he wrote this:

Life, on the opposite pattern is very ericel, for it is very pictorial, and sometimes verges upon self inflection or repression with an accompaniement.

Take the word *life* for instance and take the word *law* both start out with letters, *l*, and of conventional numbers and size with the consequential effort of many other classifications which benumb the mind such as medicinial ether is also able to. I having paused for reflection cannot image the security which such momentum holds.

Just what is to be said of this in terms of "concrete" and "abstract" (as Goldstein and White use these words) I am not at all sure. We would, however, probably have little hesitation in referring to the above language as disorganized, vague, and relatively meaningless. Incidentally, in the word *ericel* it demonstrates an instance of one of the symptoms of schizophrenia that is mentioned in almost all textbooks—namely, neologisms, or coined words. Also, we can say, by inference, that this language reflects practically no consciousness of abstracting. If the patient was aware of a difference between inference and description, he gave almost no evidence of such awareness. This is probably what White refers to as the schizophrenic's use of "abstract" language as though it were "concrete." However that may be, it can hardly be missed that this patient was to all appearances identifying the different levels of abstraction. So far as one can judge, there is no evidence that he was aware that there might be such levels. From his point of view, so far as one can tell, there are just words, and words are words, description and inference are all one. And the almost utter uselessness of his statements as any sort of guide to reality may with some justification be taken as evidence that, for him, words and reality are all one, too. One can hardly imagine that he had asked himself, in writing the above statements, "What do I mean?" and "How do I know?" Such questions rarely, if ever, occur to a person who has no consciousness of abstracting and who therefore scarcely recognizes the value of relating language to reality.

Among their other main symptoms, schizophrenics tend to be relatively unsociable, or seclusive. They often give a history of having been withdrawing and shy and secretive during childhood and adolescence. A rather striking illustration of this was afforded by a fairly close acquaintance of mine who developed schizophrenia. Over a period of several years I had assumed that this individual was an orphan, and was quite startled upon being visited by the young man's parents and brothers and sisters soon after he had been committed to a hospital. He had never mentioned them, or given any hint of their existence, during a great many hours of conversation spread over a period of three or four years. Moreover, all during this time, as it came out, he had been very religious in the orthodox sense and had attended church regularly;

in the hospital he tended to have delusions that he was Christ. But he had never talked about his religious views, and I had supposed that he had no religious convictions of any kind. Schizophrenics are not only hard to get to know after they become full-blown schizophrenics, but they are also generally hard to "get next to" even before they become hospital cases.

Closely related to this seclusiveness is another outstanding symptom, a tendency to daydream and to indulge in well-developed fantasies. In the advanced stages of the disorder this tendency is seen in the delusions and hallucinations that give to schizophrenia such a large part of its bizarre character. Everybody, of course, daydreams more or less; it is a matter of how *daydreaming* is defined. In schizophrenia it is something more than the whimsical, wistful, or petulant sort of imagery and silent speech that we all experience from time to time and that we recognize as daydreaming. To the schizophrenic it is quite real. In fact, in the advanced stages of the disorder, a schizophrenic's fantasies are apparently as real to him as is anything else. Even his spoken language is in many respects largely expressive of fantasy. A delusion, in a sense, is simply a daydream taken seriously and acted upon as though it were positive fact, and delusions make up one of the fundamental types of schizophrenic behavior.

Children show something roughly analogous to this in the difficulty they sometimes have in distinguishing fact from fancy. At times when they seem to be pretending, one cannot be certain that they are. A six-year-old boy, for example, failed to show up for dinner one evening and was discovered perched on a branch in a tree in the back yard. His mother stood on the ground near the tree and called to him, but he looked dreamily past her as though he didn't see her at all. Convinced finally that he was not going to descend soon, the family went ahead with dinner. The next day at lunch the father casually asked the little boy (who had come down from the tree in time to go to bed the night before), "Well, did you have a good time last evening pretending you were a bird?" And the child, quite put out by this, replied with some vigor, "Pretending I was a bird? I *was* a bird!"

Some psychiatrists, among them the late Dr. White, have advanced the view that schizophrenia represents a "regression psychosis," in the sense that the schizophrenic adult literally reverts to childlike behavior. Such a view has in recent years been rather widely discredited, however. As Dr. Norman Cameron has expressed it, the schizophrenic does not go back to an earlier stage of behavior, he develops simply a different pattern of behavior. The child may have difficulty, or so it seems at times, in telling the difference between fact and fancy, but the crucial point is that he is developing the ability to tell the difference, while the schizophrenic has lost this ability. It is somewhat like the difference between the forgetfulness of a five-year-old boy and the absent-mindedness of his seventy-five-year old grandfather. The two phenomena may look more or less alike, but they certainly have vastly different implications.

There is a great deal of interest in the content of schizophrenic delusions, but their chief importance, so far as we are concerned, lies not so much in what they are about as in their structure and in the patient's attitude toward them. In content they tend to be either self-accusative and persecutory (other people are "out to get him") or self-glorifying and grandiose (he is Napoleon or Christ, or in some other sense very great and powerful). In structure, delusions are fairly well represented by the diagram on page 139. They might be called "semantic cancers"; they are like malignant growths in the realm of belief. They may start from a bit of actual experience, an observation or two, which are caught up, as it were, in a dizzy whirl of intensionalization. Fed into a preformed set of assumptions, the few facts mushroom into an elaborate body of belief. In some cases it is difficult to see that the body of belief ever did have even a slight basis in fact or experience.

In any event, a delusion, once formed, appears as an elaborate verbal superstructure that floats, as it were, without factual support. We can express the matter in two ways that are actually almost equivalent. We can say that a delusion is unrelated to reality, and so goes unchecked by data or experience. Or we can say that a delusion is a belief that is identified with reality—a map regarded as a territory. It is revealing that some patients, when asked how they have developed their beliefs, reply simply that they are not beliefs, they are facts. A delusion, in such a sense, represents a reversal of the process of abstracting, in that the verbal levels are evaluated as being more basic than the non-verbal levels, or as being the same in value or importance. Such a reversal of the process of abstracting may be regarded as the fundamental mechanism of delusion.

This is seen even more strikingly in hallucinations. The schizophrenic who sits in a corner of the ward "talking back" to the voices he hears would seem to have progressed a stage beyond mere delusion. It is in hallucination that we see, in its most bald and astonishing forms, the mechanism we have called unconscious projection. To see the little men who aren't there and to talk to them, or run away from them, or plot against them, is to show unmistakably a confusion of inference not merely with description, but with reality. So thoroughgoing is this confusion that reality, in the ordinary sense, ceases to have any significant effect on the patient's evaluations. It is almost as though the world outside his skin had ceased to exist for him. The non-verbal levels of abstraction, as we know them, have, for him, been split off from the verbal levels, as we know them—in that he no longer differentiates the one from the other but deals exclusively, or nearly so, with words as though they were facts. In this sense, the delusions and hallucinations of schizophrenics express vividly a particularly free and uncontrolled identification of the levels of abstraction. This would appear to be about as fundamental a statement of the matter as one might make.

Another prominent symptom of schizophrenia is variously referred to as self-centeredness or egocentricity, infantilism, a strong tendency toward self-reference, etc. In common terms, schizophrenics tend to be extraordinarily selfish. In a sense, of course, we are all "selfish." Again, it is largely a matter of definition, and of differentiation—there is selfishness$_1$, selfishness$_2$, etc. Most of us most of the time, perhaps, are selfish in ways that have some social value, while the selfishness of schizophrenics tends to have no value to anyone else, and to constitute a social menace.

The psychiatrist, Dr. John Dorsey, once remarked that in growing up normally we pass through three stages which we represent, respectively, by saying, "Please help me," "I can take care of myself," and "Please let me help you." When we help others we are being as selfish, probably, as we are when we demand that others help us. Philanthropy is as satisfying—sometimes much more so, no doubt—to the philanthropist as it is to those who receive its benefits. We do not object to this, however, so long as somebody does receive benefits. We do object to philanthropists who regard the educators and scientists to whom they give money as though they were their own employees. We object because such philanthropists are saying, in effect, "Help me," instead of "Let me help society." We do not like gifts that enslave us. This may be true because of our own selfishness, and it may be our own selfishness that also prompts us to dislike those who let us help them but who return nothing, not even "gratitude" or "honor," to us.

So it is that we do not value the kind of selfishness exhibited by schizophrenics. There is nothing in it for us, for society—nothing, that is, but expense and discomfort and concern. We will tolerate, even respect, very considerable egotism on the part of a concert violinist or a shrewd business executive, because we enjoy fine music or we like to be paid 10 per cent dividends. But an egotist who bales no hay, so to speak, is regarded simply as a dead weight from the standpoint of society.

Now, the schizophrenic's egocentricity, like his emotional flatness, appears to be simply a consequence, an expression, of his basic out-of-touchness with reality. His self-centered concerns have no social value because social reality means so little to him. It is not an effective source of his evaluations and decisions, nor does he check those evaluations and decisions against their social effects. He has withdrawn to such an extent into his private world of words that he is scarcely to be regarded any longer as a social being. He has broken off relations with the world. It might almost be said that he has actually "gone blank." There is no longer an effective connection, for him, between the verbal and non-verbal levels of abstraction. Since he identifies verbal and non-verbal levels, and so operates as though on one level only, what happens on the non-verbal levels, as we know them, "makes no difference" to him on the verbal levels. It is in this dimension that his personality is "split." Therefore, to a large degree, what happens *to* him makes no impression *on* him.

The schizophrenic may be no more selfish than the rest of us, but he is less sociable, less responsive to the effects that his selfishness has on others—he simply leaves others out of account in evaluating what is important to him. This is what a baby does too, and this suggests why we speak of the schizophrenic as being infantile. There is a difference, of course, and we should never overlook it: the baby may be counted on soon to pay some attention to us. For the schizophrenic the outlook is less hopeful—at least from our point of view. Perhaps that should be added with some emphasis, because we cannot be sure how the patient looks at it. Professor E. B. Guthrie has even gone so far as to say that it is not the schizophrenic, it is his family, that suffers from schizophrenia!

It is also to be observed that in schizophrenia there is to be seen something that we might call rigidity of personality structure. This too appears to be a function of the patient's generalized semantic blockage, his identification of the levels of abstraction. Normally we avoid extreme rigidity simply because we remain more or less responsive to reality, and as reality changes so do we. It is precisely by losing this responsiveness that we become "set in our ways" and "narrow-minded." It is by ignoring the shifting demands of our surroundings that we develop rigid interests and systems of habit and routine. It is by ignoring the changes that go on around us that we maintain, fixed and unvarying, our political, religious, and social attitudes. This unresponsiveness, which most of us develop in some degree as we grow up in our culture, the schizophrenic develops to such a degree that his words and actions often seem utterly irrelevant to his surroundings. He may sit for hours moving his hands in what appears to be a senseless stereotyped manner. His delusions may become fixed and systematic and be almost completely unaffected by what he sees or is told, or by anything that happens to him or around him. Rigidity in behavior and a narrow range of interests, even in relatively normal degrees, are danger signals. In the degree to which they are seen in schizophrenia they represent very grave derangement.

Finally, it is not to be missed that many of these symptoms express, or at least suggest, a certain kind of feeling tone. We have noted the schizophrenic's emotional flatness, his "dead-fish" manner, but we must not be too literal about this. As a general statement it is quite all right, provided we are aware of its limitations. Insofar as the schizophrenic does show emotional reactions, there are three main statements to be made about them. The first is that they tend to be irrelevant to the immediate situation, as this situation is viewed by others, at least. When others would be shocked, grieved, or delighted, the schizophrenic is rather likely to show no such reactions. He may seem at such times to be profoundly indifferent, or to be preoccupied with something else. Moreover, when others can see no occasion for it, the schizophrenic may exhibit sadness or, perhaps a kind of uncanny contentment, or some other emotional response, such as inappropriate silliness.

The second statement to be made in this connection is that in many instances and in various ways the schizophrenic's reactions appear to express, or at least suggest, "bad feeling," ill will, hatred. These patients are sometimes quite sensitive, resentful, irritable, aggressive. Particularly in their delusions and in their depressions there would seem to be a strong undercurrent of hate. Their case histories often give abundant evidence of the sorts of experience and social relationships from which hatreds are likely to develop. The frustrations which many of these patients have undergone appear to have been most baffling and injurious. Schizophrenics more or less characteristically give histories of difficulty in getting along with others, feelings of distrust, resentment, and contempt toward others. But such feelings may have been expressed rarely, under great pressure, if at all. They have smoldered. These patients show, in dramatic and tragic ways, the human significance of hate. It is significant, not only in the devastation of its direct effects, but also in the fact that it consumes enormous amounts of "energy." Not only is one's "supply of energy" limited, but also there are only so many hours in a day and only so many years in a lifetime; the "energy" and time that one devotes to hating are lost forever so far as constructive activity is concerned. One of the major lessons of schizophrenia is that hatred is to be viewed as a particularly pathological form of behavior.

The third observation to be made concerning the emotional reactions of schizophrenics is that a considerable measure of their feeling tone is that of depression. They are a sad lot, generally speaking. This is not always true, of course, nor is it always clearly evident when it is true; but close investigation reveals in most cases a fairly dark-blue background, so to speak. Deep feelings of unworthiness, of inferiority, of guilt, shame, disappointment, self-rejection, sadness—these are common symptoms, and forerunners, of schizophrenia. Not infrequently they are mingled with strong fears and a sense of catastrophic foreboding. Hospital attendants keep a sharp eye out for suicidal tendencies in these patients.

In the careful observation of schizophrenia we find much, indeed, to sharpen our ability to judge human behavior. From such study we can hardly avoid the conclusion, for example, that deep and persistent depression, the sad expression of a chronic heavy heart, is a cardinal sign of semantic ill health. Happiness, hope, good will, a fairly good opinion of oneself, and a sense of humor are not merely the means to popularity, they are basic to health itself in the full sense of the word. What one notices above everything else in a psychopathic ward is a sort of lifelessness, a depressing lack of ordinary good cheer. Viewed in this light, schizophrenia may be regarded as that which appears when the capacity for friendship has been utterly lost. After one has grasped the terrible significance of this fact, one appreciates in a new and deeper sense the sounds of happy laughter and the warmth of artless affection.

SUMMARY OF SIMPLE SCHIZOPHRENIA

In summary, so-called simple schizophrenia is characterized by:
1. A profound lack of consciousness of abstracting, as shown in

2. Thoroughgoing identification of the levels of abstraction, and

3. Unconscious projection.

The chief consequences of these basic symptoms are the following:

1. Emotional apathy as a general rule. When emotional reactions are exhibited they are likely to be irrelevant to the situation in which they occur, and to indicate fundamental feeling tones of hatred and depression; there is a grossly impaired capacity for friendship.

2. Delusions.

3. Hallucinations.

4. Egocentricity.

5. A rigid and generally infantile personality structure.

Special Types of Schizophrenia

Four types of schizophrenia are customarily recognized: *simple* (which is in general what we have been discussing), *hebephrenic, catatonic,* and *paranoid.* By and large, all are characterized by the basic symptoms we have been describing; they differ mainly in the particular ways in which the various symptoms are expressed, or in the relative emphasis given to one or another of them.

In hebephrenic schizophrenia, for example, the distinguishing characteristic is what one would usually call "silliness." Joking, chuckling, giggling, etc., may occur when there is no apparent reason for them; they are likely to appear very inappropriate to an ordinary observer. The hebephrenic may seem not merely silly, but also lewd and careless about his person. He may disregard the accepted proprieties regarding toilet habits, etc. The psychoanalysts, emphasizing "sex" as they do, tend to make a great deal of this fact in their theoretical discussions of these patients. There are possible interpretations other than the sexual, however. One psychiatrist has expressed the view—with which many other psychiatrists would doubtless agree—that the schizophrenic handles his bodily excretions and exhibits other such behavior not because of some sexual perversion or regression, but simply because he is "absent-minded," so to speak. He does these things in more or less the same vacuous manner in which a normal person doodles while waiting for a phone call. A general semanticist would be inclined to regard this silly, lewd, and improper conduct quite as he would regard much of the rest of schizophrenic behavior, such as the apathy and the delusions. That is to say, he would regard it as one type of expression of the schizophrenic's detachment from reality which results from his identification of the levels of abstraction.

The distinguishing feature of catatonic schizophrenia is very striking, indeed. The classical form of the symptom is usually called *cerea flexibilitas*—waxy flexibility. These curious patients will hold a posture, even what appears to be an awkward one, for hours at a time. You can place an arm of such a patient in almost any particular position and for some time thereafter, it will stay that way. Sometimes, having assumed a posture, the patient may become quite rigid, and it is difficult then to move his arms or legs. One is tempted to say of these cases that they are "scared stiff," or "bored stiff," perhaps, although this is not to be taken too literally.

In view of this profound immobility, it is quite astonishing that on occasion these patients show very vigorous and sudden reactions. In this connection, Korzybski relates an experience he had one time in a "mental" hospital in which he was doing some investigations. He was introduced by the attending physician one day to a catatonic patient who happened to be a Lithuanian. As a Lithuanian he had been indoctrinated with a deep hatred of the Polish people. For years he had been in a state of catatonic stupor, immobile, indifferent, unresponsive, with only a few brief lucid intervals. Upon being introduced to Korzybski, however, he immediately sprang at him and seized him by the throat. A considerable struggle ensued. The attending physician had made the grievous mistake of introducing Korzybski as "the noted *Polish* scientist"!

We see in this incident a dramatic example of undelayed reaction, which is integrally associated with identification and allness. Such an incident is very instructive. It represents in extremely pathological form a kind of behavior that, in lesser degrees, is very common in our culture. We have discussed it many times in the course of this book. I once knew a student, a brilliant research worker, who, upon receiving his Ph.D. degree, was employed by a large corporation—but only after he had agreed to take the necessary legal steps to change his name! This is the same wolf in slightly less shabby clothing. Speaking of shabby, we may be reminded that in Japan skin color does not have the social importance that it has in our own part of the world. Instead, the Japanese are very sensitive to the amount of hair on the face; the more hair the lower the caste, or, at least, the greater the social handicap. This is another form of expression of the sort of identification that underlies our own racial and class discriminations—and that motivated the catatonic's savage, undelayed leap at "the noted *Polish* scientist." As we remarked once before in this book, there are in a sense no crazy people; there are only crazy ways of behaving.

As to paranoid schizophrenia, there is considerable controversy as to whether a genuine or valid distinction may be made between this and paranoia. The latter is generally recognized as a type of psychosis different from schizophrenia. What seems to be the situation is that there are a number of borderline cases who are paranoid but who also appear to be schizophrenic. If we consider them as belonging in the general category of schizophrenia, they differ from other schizophrenics mainly in the fact that their delusions are paranoid in character. This is to say that they express a pathological suspiciousness of other people. Insofar as these cases are schizophrenic we have already discussed them; insofar as they are paranoid we shall discuss them presently.

In Bold Relief

In the schizophrenias, more than in any other type of major disorder, we see in bold relief the kinds of inadequate evaluation and inefficient behavior which, in their milder forms, make our own lives rather less pleasant and fruitful than they undoubtedly could be. What, in discussing the behavior of more ordinary folk, we called overintensionalization, is seen in schizophrenia as stark delusion. What we have called unconditionality is to be observed in these hospital patients as pathological rigidity of behavior, as general unresponsiveness and lack of emotional tone, or as persistent hatred or depression. Hypertonicity, or excessive tension, and the conflicts that go with it are to be compared and contrasted with the catatonic stupor seen in these gravely disordered cases. And we have noted in the Lithuanian catatonic referred to above what undelayed signal reactions can be like in highly developed form. The ordinary varieties of allness, which we daily express in our somewhat too dogmatic and premature conclusions, flower, in schizophrenia, into what seems to be an all-out identification of abstraction levels, an utter confusion of fact and fancy. Maslow and Mittelmann in their *Principles of Abnormal Psychology* actually tell of a case who would sometimes write the word *beefsteak* on bits of paper and then eat the paper! Unconscious projection runs riot in the schizophrenic's "voices" and visual hallucinations. And so it goes throughout a long list of semantic inadequacies that, in less bizarre forms, are so common in the reactions of so-called normal people. In schizophrenia the law of identity and the general orientation that it fosters and implies come to life grotesquely in the Frankenstein of civilization.

PARANOIA

The other psychoses, *paranoia, manic-depressive psychosis,* and *involutional psychosis,* are characterized fundamentally, and in varying degrees from case to case, by the same types of symptoms that are basic to schizophrenia. As we noted earlier, quoting Korzybski, identification may be regarded as a generalized symptom underlying all varieties of "mental" and nervous disease. There would appear to be marked confusion of the levels of abstraction, and reversal of the process of abstracting, in all of the psychoses. In general, we might say that schizophrenics are "well-rounded," more *generally* affected; the other psychotics are the "specialists" in this bizarre business of human misfiring.

In paranoia the chief symptom is extreme suspiciousness expressed in delusions. There appears to be, as a rule, a background of seclusiveness, egocentricity, secretiveness, and profound feelings of inferiority amounting to a sense of guilt. The basic mechanism in these cases would seem to be that of unconscious projection of this sense of guilt or self-depreciation into others. That is to say, the individual assumes that other people regard him as he regards himself. He accuses himself of misdeeds, shameful attitudes and conduct, or general unworthiness, and then, by projection, he creates for himself a world in which other people accuse him of the same things. Self-reflexively this develops to the stage where he imagines that these other people are plotting to take action against him. He has delusions that they are spreading scandalous rumors about him, or that they mean to deprive him of his property or to kill him by poisoning his food or in some other way.

Once such a delusion has become thoroughly detached from the lower levels of abstraction it tends to become more and more systematized and elaborate. Frequently, in the course of this process, which is more or less "unconscious" of course, a most interesting turn of events takes place. The delusion changes from one of persecution to one of grandeur. It is as though the paranoiac were to say to himself, "Why are all these people conspiring against *me?* Why are they trying to kill *me?* Why, of course. Now, I see why. It is because of my great power, my great wealth. Naturally, then, I would have many enemies. Every great figure of history has had to contend with enemies, just as I have to contend with them. I, too, am great." And perhaps he will add, "I am Napoleon. That is why they are conspiring to kill me. They fear me. Naturally, they would, because I am the Emperor Napoleon."

As so many psychiatrists have observed, there is, generally speaking, nothing illogical about the paranoiac. If you accept the assumptions that he accepts, you will have to agree that most of his remarks, and you will grant that most of his actions, follow quite logically, indeed, from those assumptions. Logic, as such, is no guarantee of sanity. Logic merely guarantees consistency, and, with logic, one can be consistently paranoid just as well as one can be consistently Presbyterian or consistently Republican. This helps to explain why you cannot argue a paranoiac out of his delusions. By arguing you stimulate him to "reason," and by "reasoning" he makes his delusions the more wonderful. Paranoiacs quite often exhibit a verbal brilliance, and thus they illustrate dramatically the danger involved in verbal brilliance, as such, wherever it may be found. An abnormally high I.Q., potentially a great asset, may sometimes be cause for alarm. There is an old saying that it takes brains to go crazy. It does require very considerable verbal brilliance to develop the more intricate delusions that are found in some cases of paranoia—not everyone could "think up those things."

MANIC-DEPRESSIVE PSYCHOSIS

The peculiar feature of manic-depressive psychosis is its so-called circularity, as the name implies. In classical cases of the circular type, the behavior shifts back and forth from profound depression to extreme excitability and lack of restraint. There are a great many cases, however, in which this circularity is not present. In some the persistent feature is depression, and these cases are called *manic-depressive depressed*. In others the main characteristic is extreme excitability, the so-called manic state, and these cases are called *manic-depressive manic*.

Considering both phases of manic-depressive psychosis, we find in varying degrees most of the symptoms of schizophrenia. As a matter of fact, cases in which depression is the persistent and predominant symptom are often very hard to distinguish from schizophrenic patients, in whom also states of depression are sometimes very pronounced. The depressed cases may even approach outright catatonia in their stuporous immobility. In some cases they will not even eat and have to be tube-fed. They are secretive and uncommunicative. They tend to be utterly unsociable and withdrawing. Quite characteristically they are sad beyond words, languishing in a heavy swelter of remorse. To attempts to rouse them they respond generally with irritability or stupor. In some cases fairly well-developed delusions are found, usually self-accusatory for the most part. In others, the heavy pall of pessimism, regret, and sorrow under which they suffer has not taken the definite form of organized delusion. They strike one as being all but completely beaten, defeated, evaluationally exhausted.

In its manic phase this psychosis is one of the most striking in the whole catalogue of insanity. Compared to a classical manic case, the ordinary circus clown is a wallflower. The manic state represents a long-sustained, fitful, and highly variegated series of explosions of human energy. Tragic as they are, manics are on occasion incredibly comic, particularly in their incessant verbalizing in a sort of random uninhibited fashion, in response to practically anything and everything that occurs around them. The brakes are off the tongue and the result is sometimes a verbal hash far beyond the wildest accomplishments of double-talk virtuosos.

Occasionally, a glimmer of sense shines through this verbal cloudburst. One summer J occupied an office in a psychopathic hospital directly across a court from the women's ward. One of the manic patients on this ward came frequently to one of the windows and shouted with great abandon, "What's the matter with the world outside? Bring in the wood!" After the lady had shouted her raucous message two or three hundred times over a period of several weeks, I began to take it more or less seriously. I never did figure out the significance of "Bring in the wood!" but her question, "What's the matter with the world outside?" came to sound like a lingering trace, and perhaps a very strong trace, of sanity.

Some of these patients exhibit a happy-go-lucky, shallow sort of sociability. Occasionally one might tag at your heels for hours, keeping up a generally senseless chatter, friendly in somewhat the same way that a frisky, barking puppy is friendly. In some cases there is a dangerous aggressiveness, showing itself in impulsive and vicious attacks upon attendants, physicians, or other patients. These are the patients who are sometimes placed in padded cells, or wrapped securely in wet sheets. They are a definite source of danger to others, and to themselves.

Distractability is possibly the most noticeable feature of manic behavior. The attention shifts quickly, fitfully, continuously. In walking along a corridor a manic might touch all the window sills, smell of any flowers that are standing about, walk around—or go out of his way to step on—various floor markings, keeping up all the while a continual patter loosely pertaining to the people passing

him, the view through the windows, occasionally breaking into irrelevant ditties or rhymes, and filling in with random remarks,
some of which might pass for "wisecracks" at a cocktail bar. Toned
down 500 per cent, and with reasonable coherence, he might be
regarded as "pretty sharp."

Another outstanding feature in some cases is stereotypy—that is,
a tendency to persist in fixed patterns of behavior. Certain actions
or remarks may recur over and over again, as in the case of the
lady mentioned above who shouted the same thing from the same
window hundreds of times throughout most of a summer. As a rule,
however, these stereotyped reactions are not obviously related to
the rest of the patient's behavior. In general, the manic gives the
impression of disorganization on a grand scale. His specialty is
flamboyant and vigorous incoherence.

In both the depressed and manic stages there is a marked disorientation. The patient may not be able to realize where he is, or
to tell the season. He may not even know what year it is. Even the
manic who, in a superficial way, appears to be overly responsive
to his surroundings is, in a deeper sense, almost wholly oblivious
to them. As in schizophrenia, so in this psychosis, there appears to
be a thoroughgoing identification of the levels of abstraction, an
utter confusion of sense and nonsense, of inference and description,
of fact and supposition. Evaluations are not checked against observation and experience, because, as it would seem, no effective
differentiation is made between observation and belief, between
experience and make-believe.

INVOLUTIONAL MELANCHOLIA

Involutional psychosis usually comes fairly late in life, and by
some authorities it is associated with the menopause, or so-called
"change of life," or at least with definite decline in the vigor of
sexual functioning. Other authorities do not place particular emphasis on the sexual factor, but are inclined to relate the disorder
to general loss of vitality and hope. We shall limit our remarks to
the form of this psychosis known as involutional melancholia. Involutional melancholia involves, as the name might be taken to

imply, a "turning in upon itself" of profound melancholy, a self-reflexive sadness. It tends to occur at that time of life when the future becomes insignificant in comparison with the past. It might be regarded as the reaction of a pathologically poor loser, coming into the last half of the ninth inning, so to speak, with the score still standing at no hits, no runs, and fourteen errors, and with the game about to be called anyway because of darkness.

Associated with this deep depression there is likely to be a more or less general deterioration of intelligence in the ordinary sense. The simplest decisions appear to be overwhelmingly difficult, loss of memory is sometimes profound, and there is a general state that can well be indicated as elaborate befuddlement. Not infrequently the feeling tone is marked by a subdued undercurrent of bitterness. Unreasonable fears sometimes complicate the picture. Suicidal tendencies are not uncommon. The wringing of hands, the drooping postures, and the sorrowful and remorseful mumbling imply that the patient's outlook is confined to vistas of doom.

Again, as in the other psychoses, the process of abstracting appears to be hopelessly blocked. Reality is distorted incredibly and thoroughly identified with grotesque inference and supposition. The patients appear to be utterly impervious to facts or to statements about facts. For them the normal relation between language and reality seems to have been blotted out, with a resulting flurry of windblown words, darkened in this case by ominous low-hanging clouds of doom and hopelessness.

CONSTITUTIONALLY PSYCHOPATHIC PERSONALITY

Finally, we come to that exasperatingly fascinating character, the constitutionally psychopathic personality. He is the Peck's Bad Boy of the lunatic fringe. In almost every hamlet in the land there is someone who is known among his neighbors as "the town character." Recall the "town character" best known to you, and you will recall an individual who probably represents in his way what is generally meant by psychopathic personality. A particularly engaging account of this problem has been presented by Dr. Hervey Cleckley in his book, *The Mask of Sanity*. It is of special interest that Dr. Cleckley summarizes his views concerning this disorder by referring to it as *semantic dementia.*

What Dr. Cleckley means by this term can best be appreciated by reference to the outstanding symptoms exhibited by so-called psychopathic personalities. Perhaps the word that most deftly represents these symptoms is *impulsiveness.* It is not, however, the utter lack of restraint of the manic that is exhibited by these cases. They are somewhat remindful of the psychoneurotics in that, aside from their "episodes" or special weaknesses, they tend to be, at least apparently, more or less competent and generally normal. Among the cases presented by Dr. Cleckley there are some rather substantial individuals, including one rather noted psychiatrist, director of a hospital. Among those I have known is an editorial worker, sufficiently capable to be forgiven by his employer for his occasional interludes of utter incompetence—interludes actually of total absence from his job.

Psychopaths, as they are often called, are also somewhat remindful, at least in some cases, of the patients suffering from hebephrenic schizophrenia. That is, they sometimes show a strong trace of silliness, or at least hail-fellow-well-met superficiality, under conditions that would seem to call for quite serious, even solemn, behavior. There is a certain attitude of not caring whether school keeps or not, shown in some instances, for example, by leaving a job some noon to go to lunch and just never coming back, not because of any clear grievance but apparently from sheer whimsy. The point is clarified somewhat by the story about the fellow who, when asked by the judge why he had thrown the brick through the window, replied, "I really don't know, Judge—it just seemed to be the thing to do at the time."

This here-we-go-gathering-nuts-in-May disposition expresses itself in a most baffling display of unconcern for the generally accepted responsibilities of maturity. There is a fringe of behavior that lies almost outside the law and almost inside the realm of "mental" disease, and it is along this shady "straight and narrow" that the psychopath staggers through his dizzy career. Veering in one direction, he lands in jail; reeling in another direction, he winds up, usually for a brief stay, in a "mental" hospital. With luck, or money, or influential friends, however, he may suffer only the pained and exasperated censure of his family and a few intimate associates. To the pleadings and urgings of these patient but baffled counselors, he is rather more than likely, after each escapade, to respond with apparently fervent and evidently sincere resolutions to stay on the wagon, to go straight, to turn over a new leaf. He makes up with his wife, makes a clean breast of it all to his distressed parents, apologizes all around, and for a few days, or weeks, or even months, he holds a steady job, saves a little money perhaps, goes to church on Sundays, and drinks nothing more perilous than lemonade. And then, one day, by way of a fourth highball, a fist fight, a contiguous blonde, or a bit of bad arithmetic on his check stubs, he slides with an uncanny sense of indirection back into his old groove just off the vague edge of decorum. In one of the more useful words of our common speech, he is just not dependable.

Some of these psychopaths have very evident, sometimes outstanding, ability along certain lines. The part of the "great" actor played by Monte Woolley in *Life Begins at Eight-Thirty* illustrated, in certain respects, this strange mixture of brilliance and unreliability. The reader can doubtless call to mind a number of psychopaths, or near psychopaths, among the more newsworthy personalities of the theater, the world of sports, or political life. It would be an indiscretion, of course, to mention them by name in this book. The legends of the California gold rush and the Klondike boom are, in part—and a particularly fascinating part—a story of overstimulated psychopaths whose exploits, under the influence of gold dust, had an unusual attention-getting value. These hybrids of genius and incompetence are so striking because they promise so much that is noble—and come through with such a distracting abundance of futility.

Not all psychopaths, however, are streaked with genius. Some of them can scarcely be distinguished from the feeble-minded. They are noticeable chiefly because their dullness and inadequate judgment have such a high nuisance value for society. They are stupid people with bad habits. There are individuals of generally low intelligence who are, nevertheless, conscientious and dependable on their particular level of competence, and who exhibit consistent honesty and propriety in their social reactions. What distinguishes the dull-witted psychopath is mainly a lack of normal restraint, showing in combativeness, petty dishonesties, sexual irregularities, or perhaps a tendency to carry drinking to the stage of stupor. Among those intriguingly planless wanderers, those cockleburs of the travel world, the hoboes, psychopathic personalities are to be found in an instructive and fascinating variety. Each year at harvest time during my boyhood in the Kansas wheatlands, life was enlivened no end by an influx of these seasonal strangers, with their legends of the road, their tall tales of brawls in faraway dives, their sentimental yearnings for homes and mothers they had not seen for years. Always they were going home "this time," as soon as they were paid, but as soon as they were paid one somehow never doubted that they would find themselves soon in other dives or dice games, or that they would simply lose their money from sheer carelessness, or even give it away. Their homing instinct never quite got them through.

The general picture of psychopathic personality is that of a lack of normal inhibitions, an episodic or pervasive immaturity, an unreliability and shallowness. This last point is somehow crucial. This shallowness of feeling has been stressed by Cleckley; it is this which he seems to bring into main focus in speaking of the disorder as semantic dementia—a deficiency in ordinary judgment and common sense in matters of personal development and social relationships. The psychopath's evaluations tend to be infantile and superficial. He acts in ways that betray a disregard of consequences; and to the consequences themselves, however unfortunate, he reacts with an outward show of remorse beneath which can be sensed a shrug of the shoulders, so to speak. He *seems* to know better, he *seems* to care about the sorrow he causes, he *seems* to make genuine resolves and efforts to mend his ways—but he is not what he seems. Dr. Cleckley sharply summarizes this inconsistency, this façade of maturity which almost conceals the infantile character within, by referring to it in the title of his book as *The*

Mask of Sanity. During his lucid intervals, and even, to some degree, in the midst of his strange interludes, the psychopath exhibits a social grace that is hardly part of him, a knowledge of common sense that he does not understand, a facility with words that mean little to him, form without substance. As with beauty that is skin-deep, so it is with the psychopath's seemingly good judgment and social sense, which are only word-deep.

The general impression which one gets from all this does suggest the term *semantic dementia;* what is suggested is a sort of evaluational imbecility, a lack of deep feeling and integrated convictions. It is somewhat remindful of the story about the horse who ran smack into the side of the barn with a resounding crash, not because he was blind but because "he just didn't give a damn." The psychopath seems incapable of discriminating between one impulse or action and another in terms of their respective consequences. He seems unable to tell the difference between a genuine feeling of sympathy, or affection, or respect, and a phony outward show of such feeling. The words of love, good will, and cooperation just don't mean as much to him as they do to the general run of people, although he may be able to use them, like a skilled actor, to create the illusion of sincerity. For him the levels of abstraction are not utterly identified, but they are only vaguely discriminated. The process of abstracting is not completely blocked, but it stalls or reverses itself under rather slight pressure—it is not dependable.

SEXUAL MALADJUSTMENT

There is left to consider a type of symptom that is to be found in some form in all of the major personality disorders—sexual maladjustment. It is not regarded, as a rule, as a separate disorder, in and of itself. Just as delusions or compulsions, as such, are viewed as symptoms rather than as disorders, so sexual maladjustments are viewed ordinarily as symptoms, and they may be part of the general pattern of practically any type of disorder.

Of sex, in cases of personality maladjustment, there is likely to be too little or too much, or what there is is likely to be misdirected. In other words, these cases tend to react, where sex is concerned, with aversion, fear, or excessive prudishness, with irresponsible promiscuity, or with some sort of perversion.

Probably the most common form of sexual maladjustment, so far as the general run of people is concerned, is simple prudishness. The subject of sex is not merely avoided but elaborately shunned, not out of indifference but because of attitudes of shame and fear acquired in early childhood from parents whose understanding of the matter was definitely prescientific, to say the least. In its extreme forms this more or less simple prudishness becomes clearly abnormal aversion, strong fear of sexual experience or even of sexual discussion, and a generalized inability to derive any satisfaction whatever from this sphere of human experience. Frigidity and impotence are the ultimate consequences—ultimately disastrous for the race and potentially tragic for the individual and his mate.

In our society, for better or for worse, the only conditions under which sexual relations are accepted as being entirely normal are those involved in monogamous marriage. It is fundamentally in consideration of this fact, therefore, that any particular type of sexual behavior is evaluated in our culture. For us, that sex education, or training, is best which makes for successful monogamous marriage. This has not always been true, and even today it is not true for all parts of the world, but it is the rule generally in western civilization and it holds for practically all sections of the United States. And sexual maladjustment is to be understood particularly well in relation to this basic fact of our social tradition. The simple rule is that we tend to regard as maladjustment any form of sexual behavior that does not tend to conform to the accepted moral code, according to which the sex act may properly occur only between legally married partners, and according to which, moreover, sexual compatibility and pleasure, and the having of children, are understood to be part and parcel of a normal marriage relationship.

Now obviously frigidity and impotence, any seriously diminished capacity for sexual pleasure, strong fears of pregnancy, aversion to children, or general prudishness make successful marriage unlikely or even utterly impossible. For various reasons arising out of our generally unfortunate sex education, most people seem to assume that divorce and unhappy marriages are almost always due to unfaithfulness on the part of husband or wife, or both. As a matter of fact, marriages are more frequently wrecked, directly or indirectly, by prudishness—by the inability to enjoy sexual activity and its normal biological consequences. The results of this are to be seen in divorce, or strained relationships fraught with tension and general misery, childless homes or unwanted and therefore unhappy children—and, in many cases, unfaithfulness.

In the psychoses and psychoneuroses a great variety of sexual maladjustments are to be found, but among the most conspicuous is that of abnormal aversion to sex. In schizophrenia, for example, there tends to be a pronounced reduction in sexual drive. Some of the delusions, especially those of a religious character—which are fairly common—appear to represent abnormal resolutions of strong sexual conflicts involving a generalized classification of anything sexual as "sin" or "evil." Certainly one of the most prominent features of the major "mental" and nervous disorders is the lack of mature healthy sexual impulses. Patients in psychopathic hospitals are often conspicuously lacking in what has come to be known in the common speech as sex appeal. Generally speaking, they simply are not lovable.

Promiscuity is found in adolescents and adults who are assumed by most people, perhaps, to be "oversexed." Perhaps they are—in a superficial sense. In a more fundamental sense, however, they appear to be "undersexed." That is to say, they are for the most part quite lacking in mature sexual drive. Their desires have nothing to do with pregnancy and the having of children. They fear or even loathe these normal consequences of the sex act. Their desires are quite completely limited to the excitement of strong sensations; they desire only to be sensually stimulated. For them the sex act is scarcely anything more than mutual masturbation. Promiscuity is truly an expression of sexual immaturity. It is to this extent a symptom of infantilism. It is suggestive, in fact, of psychopathic personality as above described.

Sexual perversions occur in an almost incredible variety of forms.

It would take a very large book indeed to describe them all. For our purposes it is sufficient to point out that among the more common varieties there are two that are outstanding. These are masturbation and homosexuality. In our culture masturbation is very common. The more reliable investigations would seem to indicate that about half of the female population and well over that proportion of the male population indulge in the practice more or less, particularly during the adolescent years. There is a tendency on the part of some authorities to take the view that masturbation is harmless, at least physiologically, provided it is not practiced "excessively" and provided the individual does not worry about it. Viewed, however, as a semantic reaction—and it would certainly seem impossible to regard it as an exclusively physiological act, whatever that might be—masturbation would appear to be, at best, a fundamentally unnatural form of behavior. This is not to endorse the unfortunate teachings of certain misguided moralists that its results are inevitably tragic. Far from it. Such teachings are clearly more dangerous than is masturbation itself. The point is— and it would seem to be obvious enough—that masturbation is a far cry from normally mature sexual relations, regardless of how common it may be especially among adolescents *in our culture*. Semantically it is on a par with irresponsible promiscuity. If it does not give rise to a sense of guilt, fear, or anxiety it may have no lasting or serious effects, but this is certainly not to say that it constitutes fundamentally normal behavior.

Homosexuality is, as a rule, considerably more serious in its consequences. Homosexuals tend to find it very difficult to adjust to the normal marriage relationship—unless they have undergone a reasonably successful program of clinical treatment, or are extremely fortunate in the choice of a marriage partner. Many of them, of course, never get married at all. There are many kinds of homosexual practice, but essentially it is a matter of mutual sexual stimulation by two persons of the same sex. In a sense it is a relatively elaborate form of masturbation, a form of behavior that is even more immature than promiscuity. Its harmful consequences are both direct and indirect. Directly, it tends to make for habits and attitudes that preclude the possibility of normal marriage and the taking on of mature family responsibilities. Indirectly, it tends to make for the kinds of self-evaluation that are not conducive to happiness and efficiency. In common language, homosexuals tend to lose their self-respect, because of the very powerful taboos with which society confronts them, and also because of their failure to achieve what even they usually recognize as sexual maturity.

It is possible that there are some individuals who are so constituted physically that homosexuality is somehow natural for them. It is possible, that is, that there are so-called true homosexuals. It is very probable, however, that the great majority of persons who practice homosexuality are quite capable of normal sexual relationships. In fact, it is likely that most of them are essentially similar to persons who masturbate more or less habitually. To put it a bit too simply, perhaps, they have solved their sexual conflicts by means of a particular compromise which allows them some form of sexual expression but does not involve the risk of pregnancy or the violation of the moral code which forbids heterosexual relations outside the conditions of marriage.

All sexual perversions are, in fact, compromises in this sense. They are not always worked out very consciously or deliberately, of course, but they serve the purpose of compromise, nevertheless, and this is probably a large part of the reason why they are so common and why they persist as patterns of habit. It is to be fully appreciated that since our moral codes do not condone pre-marital or extra-marital sex relations they tend to produce conflict in some degree almost universally among unmarried persons—and unsatisfactorily married persons—with normally healthy sex drives. These sexual conflicts constitute one of the most conspicuous features of our culture, and the only solutions possible, in view of our moral codes, are marriage or some sort of compromise. Even utter celibacy is a compromise solution, unless one assumes that the sex drive is somehow destroyed, and if the individual remains in reasonably good health there would appear to be no grounds for any such assumption.

It is a great source of maladjustment in vigorous, young unmarried individuals that they are somehow taught that for them there is, outside marriage, some sort of entirely satisfactory solution to their sexual conflicts. The average age of marriage has been rising steadily for some time. Economic uncertainties and the increasingly long periods of general and professional education make it presumably necessary for more and more young people to postpone marriage well beyond the time when they are emotionally prepared for it. These young people ask for advice, a way out of the sexual dilemma in which they find themselves, and there are a great number of puritanical and prudish elders who tell them that they have no problem. They do have a most distressing problem, and the only solution society sanctions is the very solution they cannot have, except after long waiting, because of the way society is constituted.

The least that can be done for these young people can be put into three general statements. First, their parents, teachers, clergymen, physicians, and other responsible elders can be realistic enough and honest enough to tell them that there just isn't any solution for them, other than marriage, that will be completely satisfactory. Any other solution is, at best, a compromise, and any compromise in such matters involves certain disadvantages, to say the least. Second, so long as we prefer to preserve the moral codes which make such conflicts and dilemmas necessary for unmarried persons, there would seem to be special need for a general understanding and appreciation of the occasionally unfortunate, or at least irregular, compromises that do occur. So long as we persist in a policy of frustrating the strong natural drives of young people, we would seem to be under some obligation to respond to their reactions to that frustration with something more enlightened and effective than intolerance and condemnation. Third, if this is granted, it might well be expected of us that we undertake with some vigor to carry out such social and economic changes as would make the frustration less often necessary or more tolerable. If we do not know what such changes might be, the least we can do is to encourage or undertake the necessary investigations, with the scientific bargain that whatever the results of such investigations may be we will act on the basis of them to achieve the kind of society in which sexual maladjustment may be the exception rather than the rule.

SUMMARY: SYMPTOMS OF MAJOR MALADJUSTMENTS

Throughout this recital of the symptoms of the major forms of human misdirection, a fundamental pitch, so to speak, and several prominent harmonics have been detectable. A simple listing of the main symptoms will help to sharpen the outline of the general picture of demoralization. (The more basic symptoms, at least from my point of view and in the light of general semantics, are the first three listed.)

1. *Lack of consciousness of abstracting,* with consequent
2. Identification of levels of abstraction, of inference with description, of description with non-verbal observation and experience, etc.
3. Unconscious projection, as seen most obviously in delusions, hallucinations, and hysterical ailments.
4. Allness, as shown in excessive certainty and overvaluation of words as such.
5. Undelayed reaction, impulsiveness, overreaction, etc.— most clearly shown in the manic state, in the obsessions, compulsions, and phobias of psychasthenia, and in the shallow impulsiveness of psychopathic personalities.
6. Rigidity—an absolutistic, elementalistic, two-valued, even one-valued, orientation, as exhibited so clearly in the rigidity and unresponsiveness of the schizophrenic, and in the fixed and systematic delusions of the paranoiac.
7. Infantilism, egocentricity, socially useless or harmful selfishness—an incapacity for friendship and affection, an exaggerated self-defensiveness.
8. Ill will, bitterness, hostility, as seen particularly in some manics and paranoiacs.
9. Depression, feelings of inferiority and unworthiness, guilt

feelings, and self-accusation, so prominent in involutional melancholia, the depressed phase of manic-depressive psychosis, in many cases of schizophrenia, and, to a lesser degree, in neurasthenia.

10. Sexual maladjustment, of which there are three main types: excessive prudishness and lack of mature sexual feelings; promiscuity; and perversions, the most common of which are masturbation and homosexuality.

HOWEVER AND THEREFORE

Two points are to be stressed in relation to these ten symptoms. The first is that, as seen in the major psychoses and psychoneuroses, they are exaggerated beyond the degrees in which they are seen in our more common difficulties and confusions. In their less extreme forms, however, they are the marks of ordinary maladjustment. The question as to whether a particular individual at a particular time presents a major or a minor personality disorder is often very difficult to answer—because, after all, the differences among "sanity," "unsanity," and "insanity" are matters of degree. The difference between ordinary suspiciousness and paranoia is not to be drawn with a fine line. What we all know as "feeling low"—discouragement, sadness, grief, regret, ennui—merges in its more serious stages into pathological depression. Under certain circumstances, practically all of us behave in some measure like constitutionally psychopathic personalities. In short, as we have said, we have been looking, as it were, through a microscope, viewing under magnification the inefficiencies, the miseries, the misdirected impulses, the confusions that make "the average man" something less than a paragon of wisdom and serenity. We have been looking at ourselves in a semantic hall of mirrors, discovering how we would behave if we were a little more depressed, a bit more deluded, rather more impulsive, beset with more intense fears or regrets, drawn taut with greater anxieties than the ones we have. It is to be hoped that the experience has been more enlightening than frightening.

And that leads us to the second point to be emphasized with regard to the above ten symptoms: they are to be understood. It is not a mark of maturity to be depressed by them, to wonder at them with feelings of personal anxiety, or to shun any constructive consideration of them. An understanding of the behaviors we have been reviewing is one of the surest safeguards of our own semantic health.

It is most pertinent to consider the ten major symptoms listed above as symptoms of the various aspects and types of grave demoralization. They high-light the more serious consequences of prolonged or excessive frustration and the deepening sense of failure and desperation which it tends to generate. But, as we have previously considered, this frustration is not necessarily, not even to an important degree, due to actual adversity, to real enemies, or obstacles, or misfortunes. Real and tangible opposition, or clear and understandable misfortune, may anger a man or temporarily discourage him, but they will rarely drive him mad. The sort of frustration that propels a man to wild distraction or to deep depression arises in the main from persistent and pervasive misevaluations. Viewed objectively, the experiences and circumstances which appear as the apparent "causes" of major personality deterioration are not as a rule extraordinary, but the evaluations made of them are outstandingly confused or extreme. In the language of ordinary common sense, it is not what happens to you, it is how you take it, that matters. Our folk wisdom is well expressed in the common belief that there is something fundamentally sound about the individual who can "take it."

To put it too simply, but with clear focus on a sizable grain of truth, the person who can't "take it," whose frustrations become utterly demoralizing, is one who has in a basic sense been "spoiled." He is a person who has learned somehow to expect too much, to expect it with too great certainty, and to value it much too highly. To him the game is not worth playing, at least according to the rules, if he can't win—and he has so set the stage for himself, so placed his goals, that he can't win. His goals are so vaguely defined—in terms of "success," "happiness," "wealth," "moral purity," or whatnot—that he could have no way of knowing whether or not he had achieved them, and so he assumes that he has not. Or his goals are recognizable but are set so high that achievement of them is out of the question. Yet they are so highly valued, their achievement is so essential to his self-respect, that the frustration he experiences in failing to realize his goals is simply more than he can endure without losing his poise, his "grip," his fundamental sense of realism. He is, in common terms, a poor loser—because of the way he evaluates that which he assumes he has lost. His career is spent on a dizzy roller coaster that carries him from idealism to frustration to demoralization—and what we have been viewing in this chapter are the final stages of his unregaling journey.

Finally, it is to be heavily emphasized that this chapter constitutes almost the briefest possible summary of the major "mental" and nervous disorders. Moreover, it is the present writer's summary and, although the attempt has been made to limit it for the most part to descriptions of types of behavior, it is to be expected that others will not always agree with the statements presented. As was stated at the beginning of this chapter, there is in this field a very great deal of controversy even when there is substantial agreement with respect to observation and description. This fact must be clearly recognized in considering as brief a summary as this, in which a tremendous amount of detail is necessarily left out; and it is particularly appropriate, therefore, to invoke the old and wise word of caution: "I say what I say, I do not say what I do not say."

It has been said and it is to be repeated for emphasis that our interest in these major disorders is not primarily an interest in the disorders themselves. Rather, some knowledge of them is of value to us mainly because they represent in bold relief, and so serve to illustrate with unusual clearness, certain principles and mechanisms that are basic in our own less spectacular confusions and difficulties. Just as we cannot be sure that we talk sense unless we know how we might talk nonsense, so we cannot be sure of our own sanity unless we understand how we might behave without it. The crucial point is that if we know what conditions and what kinds of training to provide in order to make a child become schizophrenic, we can be trusted, as parents and teachers and responsible adults generally, to build a saner world and to train our children to live more sanely in it. There is an old saying that anything is easy if you know how; we can make it more meaningful by adding that, in large measure, knowing how is a matter of knowing how not to.

Chapter ~~~~~~~~~~~~~~~ XIV

OUR COMMON MALADJUSTMENTS

THE GRAVE DISORDERS THAT WE HAVE BEEN VIEWING in the last chapter are not usually seen outside the "mental" hospitals. Some knowledge of them, however, helps us to appreciate a great deal of the behavior exhibited by our acquaintances—and ourselves. It is doubtful, indeed, that in our culture any person goes through childhood and grows up without experiencing in some degree what we nowadays speak of so glibly as personality maladjustment. With the advent of modern psychiatry, and especially child psychology, it has been made to appear that growing up is a very hazardous venture. Whole books are written about the special problems of the only child, or of the youngest child, or the oldest—and no doubt there are problems peculiar to the second child in a family of four, or the third child in a family of five. There are difficulties that particularly characterize the orphan, the child of divorced parents, the dull child, the boy or girl who is exceptionally bright, the child who lives on a farm, the child who lives in a city. In short, there is apparently no set of circumstances under which a child may grow up that is not potentially maladjustive. Either side of the tracks, so to speak, has its disadvantages.

As a matter of fact, anyone would be hard put to define the normal child, or the normal adult. Authors who attempt to do so tend to end up stating their definitions in negative terms; that is, they tend to define the normal in terms of the absence of various abnormalities. You are normal if only you are not abnormal. But by the time *abnormality* is defined, you are left with the disturbing suspicion that there is no one, including yourself, from whom abnormality is entirely absent.

The Meanings of Normal

It serves to clarify the matter somewhat to realize that there are many ways of defining normal behavior or personality. As commonly used, *normal* is defined in statistical, medical, social, and legal terms. The term can also be used in an engineering sense. A word about each of these meanings of *normal* will no doubt be helpful.

From a *statistical* point of view, we regard the average as normal. Normal intelligence, for example, is defined by psychologists as an I.Q. of 100—or as one from 90 to 110—because, by definition, 100 is the average I.Q. as determined by such a test as the Stanford-Binet. The average American family has "slightly less than" three children, and so it is normal, statistically, for parents to have two or three children. There is a normal height, weight, age of marriage, income, amount of schooling, length of life, etc., in a statistical sense. Just so, with regard to personality, however it may be defined in terms of behavior, there is a kind of normality to be seen in the behavior, the moods, the attitudes of the so-called average person. If you are much happier than the average individual, or much more depressed, then, statistically, you are not normal. This is, of course, a rather superficial way to define the normal. It represents essentially an acceptance of the status quo. It discourages one from trying to find out why the "average" person behaves as he does, or from trying to get him to behave differently, because it idealizes the average person. It does not imply that individual differences are as important as they often turn out to be, but it does imply that genius is as abnormal as imbecility. It says, in effect, that fifty million Frenchmen can't be wrong. From some points of view they certainly can be.

In a *medical* sense, you are normal if you are not sick, generally speaking. The medically normal individual has a postnasal drip, perhaps, is rather susceptible to common colds, has a certain amount of dandruff, does not possess a highly satisfactory set of teeth, tends to be short of breath and to tire rather easily, but still he is not bed-ridden and he is able to hold down a job with sufficient competence to stay on the pay roll. From the standpoint of a busy physician he is not in need of intensive medical care, he can pass an ordinary life insurance examination, he can probably qualify for military service, at least of a limited sort, etc. Medically, then, in a practical sense he is normal—but he may not be "strong" and he may die of "heart failure" before it would seem that he should. So far as per-sonality is concerned, you are normal for all practical purposes, from a medical point of view, if a psychiatrist disposes of you with a few words of advice, because his waiting room is filled with other persons who need him worse than you do. When all is said and done, whether or not you are normal medically depends on how many doctors there are. If there were enough doctors most of us would be "sick"—that is, the physicians would have time to attend to our minor flaws and inefficiencies, and they would be interested in do-ing so. Your normality, from a medical point of view, is relative— to the demands placed upon you, the degree of discomfort and incapacity you will tolerate, and the availability of medical service.

Socially, whatever is approved by enough people, or by suffi-ciently influential people, is normal. The socially normal person gos-sips more or less, abuses his wife moderately, spanks his children occasionally, tells a lie now and then, loses his temper sometimes, smokes more and works less than his minister and his banker con-sider proper, and is more selfish, irritable, confused, and unin-formed than Harry Emerson Fosdick and Robert Maynard Hutch-ins think he should be. But he is not sufficiently different in these respects from most of his fellows to attract undue attention to him-self. Generally speaking, it is the very unusual or conspicuous per-son, the individual with a high nuisance value, the person whose views and habits and interests are distractingly out of line with those of the group—it is such a person who is socially abnormal. In any society there are certain mores, conventions, and proprieties; and it is normal, in the eyes of the society, for the individual to con-form to them. Your dress, speech, manner of eating, your ways of spending money and time, your house furnishings, the books you read, the candidates you support, the company you keep determine in large part whether you are socially normal. Social normality is measured, after all, against the criterion of group approval. It tends to parallel statistical normality, but it does not necessarily do so. The Marx brothers, or Fiorello LaGuardia, for example, are not statistically normal, but socially they are.

In a *legal* sense, the permissible or the not forbidden is normal. Someone has said that in Paris what is not permitted is forbidden, but in Berlin what is not forbidden is permitted. In any case, whatever is legal is normal in the eyes of the law, however unusual it may be or however much it may offend the public taste. Once war is declared, for example, it becomes normal indeed from a legal point of view to indulge in the killing of certain human beings; in fact, refusal to do so is, in a sense, "against the law." On the other hand, certain activities that are socially approved in large measure and that are within the range of statistical normality may be, for a time at least, illegal. This was essentially true of drinking in the United States during the prohibition era. While it is true in a rough sense that the laws tend to correspond to accepted social standards —to be what we agree to make them—yet our legal codes reflect conspicuously the forces of tradition and of vested interests. They do not express perfectly the so-called popular will, or the attitudes of all minority groups, so that there is some discrepancy between the legally normal and the statistically as well as the socially normal.

As was mentioned above, the term *normal* can also be used in an *engineering* sense, and it is in such a sense that it tends to be used in general semantics. Consider, for example, the attitude of a skilled mechanic toward your car. He does not measure its performance against that of "the average car," or against the dictates of social approval, or against minimum legal requirements. Nor does he take the medical point of view that if your car runs reasonably well it is normal. Rather, he examines your car, its driver, and the conditions under which it is used, and then he says, in effect, "It is constructed in such and such a way, its driver possesses such and such a degree of skill, it is used on paved roads, and is stored in a dry garage. Very well, it should, accordingly, start easily, accelerate and brake according to standard, do eighty miles an hour, go twenty miles on a gallon of gas, etc. If it isn't doing these things it isn't performing normally." Its performance is to be judged by the engineering standards that apply to it.

On human levels, from an engineering point of view, the average is too much to expect of some individuals under some conditions, too little to expect of other individuals under other conditions. Moreover, what is socially approved, medically required or condoned, and legally permitted may be unreasonable or inefficient with respect to a particular person, with his specific potentialities and opportunities, or lack of them. Such a person as Helen Keller, for example, is statistically and medically wanting, socially limited, and legally restricted, but highly normal or efficient from the standpoint of the engineer who considers what she has to work with and the conditions under which she has to work. A society matron with a college degree who does no particularly useful work, collects match books, and patronizes palm readers is, by virtue of these facts, statistically, socially, medically, and legally within the normal range, but from an engineering point of view she is functioning far below what could reasonably be expected of her. The engineer is interested in the relation between your demonstrated and your potential efficiency. If you make average grades when you could top the class, you are not normal, and if you top the class and work yourself into a nervous breakdown doing it you are not normal, either. If you are twenty pounds overweight, the doctor may pass you but the engineer won't. If you believe in astrology, the judge will not object but the engineer will. And it doesn't matter how many other people there are like you. From an engineering point of view fifty million Frenchmen can be dead wrong.

From the engineering point of view of general semantics, identification of words with facts, of inference with description, may be carried on within the law, outside the hospital, in the best families, and by practically everybody—but it constitutes gross human inefficiency nevertheless, and is, in this sense, pathological. The general semanticist, like the engineer, considers the discrepancy between potential and actual performance. If you "know better" you should do better—from an engineering-semantics point of view. To do less than your potential best is justified only when you can't help it—which means that it is justified quite often, but not as frequently as it would seem to occur.

With regard to the treatment of personality maladjustments, these different definitions of *normal* take on a great deal of significance. The definition adopted sets the scope of the problems to be treated and the objectives to be sought. If the normal is defined statistically, any maladjustments that lie within the average range will go untreated and nothing more than average behavior will be encouraged. A good deal of "adjustment to maladjustment" will result. There will be a strong tendency to maintain the status quo of the population as a whole—to keep the drainpipe of civilization in good repair but not to be overly concerned with what comes through it. With such a policy the energies of teachers, clergymen, psychiatrists, psychologists, and social workers are devoted more to the rehabilitation—or custodial care—of personalities already damaged or wrecked than to the raising of the general average degree of adjustment. They are concerned with water that has already come through the dikes, not with the dikes through which it continues to come. Essentially the same remarks apply to policies based on social, medical, or legal definitions of the normal. After all, not to be disapproved, not to be sick, and not to be put in jail are rather negative goals, from which rather than toward which one might intelligently work.

A more positive policy is suggested by our public health programs, which have been affected more or less by an engineering attitude. In public health work we have not been motivated entirely by a desire to see everyone enjoy average health. In large part we have attempted to remove or control the sources of disease and to raise the health average of the whole nation, even of the entire world. We have not accepted the infant mortality rate or the average length of life, as found at any given date, as a standard to be maintained. We have striven consistently to lower mortality rates, to lengthen the life span, to eliminate epidemics, to make the average person more and more healthy. By improving the physical condition of the people and the conditions under which they live, we have attempted to reduce the discrepancy between the statistical average and the potential maximum of public health. We still have far to go, but past accomplishments make encouraging and exciting the further possibilities. In fact, we cannot easily underestimate the importance of maximum public health as a goal around which sweeping social reforms might be oriented. If only we were to undertake more deliberately and systematically than we have so far to improve the health of every citizen, we would undoubtedly create in the process a culture far more adequate, by human standards, than anything yet known or dreamed.

In the prevention and treatment of personality disorders a policy somewhat like that underlying our public health programs is called for—from an engineering-semantics point of view. By focusing attention on potential rather than average adjustment we can avoid projecting into the future the miseries and half measures of the past. By diverting our major concern from the drainpipe of civilization to the wellsprings of sanity, we may hope to change the average man from the frustrated, tense victim of confusion that he tends to be into the clear-eyed, cooperative, creative creature that he seems capable of becoming. We have too long taken ourselves for granted, placed our trust in spirits, fate, and chance, and mistaken for human nature what have been merely the fruits of human misdirection. While waiting for a Moses to lead us into the promised land, we have forgotten how to walk. Under the illusion that what we see is reality, we have neglected to consider how it might be changed. We have mistaken habit for wisdom. What was good enough for father is not good enough for us, for the simple reason that it wasn't good enough for father, either. If we can do better, then, from an engineering, a semantic, a time-binding point of view, we should. Undoubtedly we can.

MALADJUSTIVE TENDENCIES

With this brief orientation to the problem of normality, we may more effectively consider those respects in which we—that is, most of us—fail to measure up to reasonable engineering standards of normal personality adjustment. We have considered the general pattern of our common maladjustments, the IFD sequence, in the opening chapter, and in the last three chapters we have examined some of our ordinary language inadequacies and the symptoms of the major psychoses and psychoneuroses. We shall now attempt a classification of those "minor" difficulties which are found—and they are found in considerable abundance—outside the psychopathic hospitals among college students, housewives, businessmen, farmers, and people generally. They are the problems that come to the attention of child-welfare workers, school psychologists, clinical psychologists, and other lay workers who minister to the needs of individuals who are in trouble, but not to a degree that requires confinement in a hospital. This classification will be made largely in terms of what we shall call behavior *tendencies*. Any classification of this kind must necessarily be arbitrary. Its purpose is to call attention to some of the more important differences among specific maladjustments, and to make discussion of them more convenient. Anyone who has read the preceding sections of this book will realize that the following classification is presented from a non-elementalistic and relativistic point of view. Realizing this, the reader will not be disturbed or confused by the fact that the classes or categories overlap to a very considerable degree. They are categories not primarily of people but of behavior, and their chief purpose is to focus attention on certain features of behavior, without in any sense implying that the particular categories presented are the only possible ones or that they will invariably be the most useful ones. They are useful for our present purposes, however, and that is their chief recommendation.

ANXIETY TENDENCIES

Worries, fears, and forebodings of various kinds make up a considerable share of our common personality maladjustments. In more primitive cultures there are in the main two kinds of fear: fear of the supernatural and fear of real and impending dangers, such as storms, disease, wild animals, and human enemies. In our own culture, too, there are these kinds of fear, but there is also, and rather more importantly, what we might best call evaluative fear. This is to say, it is not so much facts of actual experience that torment us; it is to a greater degree the evaluations we make of these facts, and the hobgoblins we create out of thin air.

As we have said, we too have fears of the supernatural. A rather common anxiety, particularly among children and infantile adults, is that concerned with the notion of "the unpardonable sin." In some families and communities hell-fire and damnation still strike un-hygienic terror into the hearts of children and immature grownups. The lively image of an angry god disturbs the equanimity of many a person in the more backward regions of the civilized world, and a considerable amount of futile behavior is motivated by an attitude of fearful appeasement toward the "great spirit." In some individuals this anxiety takes the form of a vague distrust of "luck" or "fate." There are great numbers of people who feel that somehow there are external forces, undefinable and unpredictable, in the face of which the only possible attitude is one of fear, dread, and timorous hope. Life for such people is in no small part a more or less continual effort to avoid the evils they "know" and the sins that may be. Like their primitive brothers, they fear abstractions they cannot define in the quieting terms of extensional realities.

Modern religions tend, of course, to depend less on thunder and more on rain, as it were, to be concerned less with providing harps for the deceased and more with insuring social welfare for the living. Religions so concerned with the real conditions that make for poverty, crime, and ill will, and that are oriented to the tangible possibility of making a better social order here and now—or as soon as possible—tend to exert a positively adjustive influence. It is the older religions of the more primitive caste, whose main preoccupation was with sin because their main objective was salvation, that yielded—and still yield—a considerable by-product of desperation and fear. If this sort of fear is less conspicuous among ourselves than it is in less developed societies, it is because our religions to a greater degree focus the attention of the churchgoer on those realities which do not inspire fear so much as they stimulate chagrin and positive social action.

Again, as we have said, we also experience fear of real danger, although scientific enlightenment has made a considerable proportion of such dangers less disquieting for us than they are for primitive peoples. To one who can make a rational explanation of them, lightning and smallpox are strikingly different from what they are to one for whom they are distressingly mysterious. Child specialists still spend a deal of time, of course, allaying fears of dogs, darkness, lightning, and other natural phenomena. By and large, however, these are childhood bogies. Among adults, aside from the phobias seen in the psychoneuroses, there are few anxieties of this type other than those concerned with pain, disease, and death, and a rather universal "respect" for snakes, fire, and high water.

It is the evaluative fears that are most prominent in the general run of people. For the most part these center around anxieties concerning self-evaluation, social status, and economic security. Self-respect, a good reputation, and a sufficiency of the world's goods would be placed high in the scale of values of most people. Failure to achieve or to maintain these values places the ordinary individual under a well-nigh intolerable strain. This is especially true in our American culture, with its highly competitive aspects and the premium it places on personal achievement, popularity, and wealth. Because these goals are so indefinitely defined for most individuals, and yet are so desperately cherished, the pursuit of them generates a degree of apprehensiveness that leads often to states of frustration, worry, and loss of self-assurance.

Most people are vaguely afraid of strangers, of the boss, of what the neighbors will say. They are afraid of the wolf at or near the door, the wolf that creeps closer as old age approaches. They show, as a rule, not a wild, agitated fear, but a steady, pervasive anxiety from which they find it difficult to relax. This anxiety tends to condition their moods, their judgment, their state of tension, their general outlook on life. It tends to make them self-defensive, resentful, ill at ease. It is no small part of the price we pay for our particular brand of civilization. We may understand it best as an anxiety *tendency*—a tendency to approach with a mild but unsettling fear each new person, each new situation, each new day. Once we have developed the tendency, we find a seemingly endless variety of things of which to be afraid. And when at last we come to be afraid because we know we are afraid—when we come to have a fear of fear—we have moved self-reflexively into a stage of maladjustment that lies very near the unlovely domains of psychopathology.

WITHDRAWING TENDENCIES

Closely allied to fear, and expressive of it, is what we commonly call shyness, a tendency to avoid or to withdraw from certain situations or activities. We recognize quite readily that underlying and motivating these avoidance and withdrawing reactions are those self-evaluations that we know as feelings of inferiority. Studies that have been made by many psychologists have shown that feelings of inferiority are admitted by about three out of every four individuals, at least at the age levels of high school and college. The so-called inferiority complex is so common, in fact, that there would seem to be little need to discuss it; practically everyone knows about it from personal experience.

It is well to remind ourselves, however, of certain basic features of this form of maladjustment. In the first place, it represents obviously a disorder of self-evaluation, and its evaluative character is to be stressed. Even persons who, by reasonable objective standards, are very successful can and frequently do suffer from feelings of inferiority. Such feelings are by no means to be taken as evidence of "real" inadequacy. In fact, it is not uncommonly the very persons who have become accustomed to high levels of performance, outstanding achievement, and positions of great authority who suffer most keenly from loss of self-regard when, by circumstance or age, they are forced to relinquish some measure of their status. They tend to feel that they are "slipping," that they have overreached themselves, that they are no longer useful or of any importance. In a competitive society most people come to feel that if they are to avoid the stigma of failure they must continually improve their positions. To lose, though only by a narrow margin, to relinquish status, even at the age of sixty-five or seventy, are disturbing experiences to most men.

In large part this would appear to be due to our essentially two-valued orientation, in terms of which we recognize only the two alternatives of "success" and "failure." We can hardly have persistent feelings of inferiority unless we recognize only two classes of people, the inferior and the superior. It is scarcely possible for us to indulge in self-abasement unless we are convinced that we must either be right or be wrong. People with inferiority complexes tend to live in a world of black and white, so to speak, blind to all the intermediate grays. It is possible, after all, to arrange one's frame of reference in such a way that one does not feel inferior. It is a matter of defining the race in which one runs. I once had a student who came frequently for clinical conferences because he tended to feel inferior to his professors! The self-assurance of thousands of high school girls is shaken because they compare their appearance and degree of sophistication with that of reigning movie stars. Children tend to feel inferior more or less, simply because they are children in a world of grownups, to whom, from many points of view, they are inferior. What they need desperately to learn is that they need not judge themselves by adult standards.

In terms of a two-valued orientation we are all out of step but Jim. That is, only one man can be the richest, for example, and all the rest of us are poorer than he is. Only one man can hold the record for the high jump, and all the rest of us are inferior to him. In an organization only one man can be president, and all the rest of us must feel inferior to that one man. We are all out of step but Jim.

The inferiority complex is, therefore, practically a universal phenomenon in a two-valued culture, and that is what ours tends to be. It would be practically unheard of, on the other hand, in a culture in which the predominating orientation were infinite-valued. In such a culture, "inferior" and "superior" would be recognized as relative terms, and always the question would be asked automatically, "Inferior (or superior) to whom, in what respect, when, under what conditions, and from whose point of view?" And because that question would always be asked, it would hardly be possible for anyone to come by the conviction that he was "inferior"— inferior to everybody else, in all respects, all the time, under all conditions, and from all points of view. It is this amazing conviction from which many people in our society tend to suffer. True, only the most gravely afflicted generalize the feeling as absolutely as is here implied. Most of us feel that we have some redeeming features. But within particular areas of experience, frequently very extensive areas, we generalize our feelings of inferiority without respect to extensional details.

The practical significance of such generalized feelings of inferiority is that they are expressed, as a rule, in withdrawing *tendencies*. That is to say, feeling inferior to other people, we tend to avoid them, to withdraw from competition—or cooperation—with them. We limit our associations, shut ourselves off from social contacts, deprive ourselves of experiences from which we would be likely to gain much that we lose by withdrawing from them. Having called the grapes sour, we miss out on the rich red wine they would have yielded up to us. A shy child is not, from an engineering-semantics point of view, a normal child. A withdrawing seclusive adult is not a normal adult. Sociability is a sign of semantic good health—and a means to enriching experiences. Most people cannot live alone and like it. Those who do are very likely to be running away from something much more important than that toward which they seem to be headed. It is not so much that they are retreating into themselves as it is that they are escaping from themselves—from their own self-evaluations, their feelings of inferiority. But they run in verbal squirrel cages, and they never really get away from the demoralizing abstractions from which they shrink.

AGGRESSIVE TENDENCIES

Some individuals, however, do not react to frustration and failure, to self-evaluations of inferiority, by withdrawing from the field, so to speak. They react, rather, with exaggerated aggressiveness. The relation between frustration and aggression has been considered in systematic detail by Professors Dollard, Doob, Miller, Mowrer, and Sears, a group of Yale psychologists, in their book, *Frustration and Aggression*. It has been dealt with by other writers also, and it is generally accepted that one of the more common reactions to thwarting and failure, in our society at least, is that of more or less agitated aggressiveness. Among adults, however, it does not usually take the form of open, frank, physical attack. It is more often to be observed as verbal criticism, backbiting, argumentativeness, faint praise, opposition to election candidates, to committee actions, etc.

In our culture the amount of human energy that is drained off, as it were, into these tangents of attack and ill will is gravely appalling. It represents a stupendous waste of our human resources. The mechanisms by which aggression operates are therefore of fundamental importance, since it is only by an effective understanding of these mechanisms that its ravaging effects may be diminished. We are speaking, of course, of aggressiveness that is inefficient and maladjustive, that involves and fosters misevaluation. There is a sense in which aggressiveness is normal and desirable; in some forms and at certain times it has survival value to a high degree. The advantages, the downright necessity, of spunk, gumption, the ability to override obstacles, are too well understood to require any elaborate discussion. But it is to be equally well understood that aggressiveness can be ill advised, detrimental in its effects, motivated in ways that render it maladjustive. It is to be clearly recognized that it is this sort of aggressive behavior that we are discussing. It is the mechanisms underlying this kind of behavior that we are interested in understanding.

From such a point of view, then, it is to be clearly appreciated, first of all, that all frustrations do not lead to aggression. As Professor Maslow and other psychologists have pointed out, there is a crucial difference between the frustrations that threaten one's status and those that do not. To be thwarted in love is not at all the same as to lose a tennis match that is being played merely for recreation. It is the sort of thwarting and failure that disturbs one's

self-evaluations that are likely to be reacted to by a show of aggression. Moreover, a sufficient amount of such failure tends to result,
at last, in noticeable degrees of discouragement and depression.
Even the most hardy individuals lose some of their fight, in time,
if their fighting proves to be of no avail. Aggression, like any other
technique, tends to be abandoned when it doesn't pay. It would
appear that we have so much of it in our culture because quite often
it does pay, or seems to at least. We reward it, at least in many of
its forms and in many situations. In one way and another we spend
a tremendous amount of hush money—very often the mule that
kicks the hardest gets the hay. Quite early many children learn that
threats delivered by means of loud yells are not always ineffective.

A point of great significance, then, is the fact that aggressiveness
is in large measure a form of learned behavior. This means that it
is not something to be taken for granted as a fixed item in human
nature. It is learned, as most other behavior is learned, simply to
the extent that it gets results—and *to the extent that the individual
recognizes no more effective means whereby he might obtain the
same or more desirable results*. It is this latter consideration that
is crucial, from a general semantics point of view. For there are
more effective means than maladjustive aggression to get more desirable results than it produces.

The outstanding mechanism underlying aggressive reactions to
frustration would appear to be that of unconscious projection. A
curious illustration of this is provided by an incident that occurred
some time ago in a traffic jam in downtown Chicago. It all started—
and grew progressively and rapidly worse—when a rather old car,
small and of a well-known make, stalled at one of the world's busiest
street intersections. As the din from automobile horns, starting with
a few scattered sirens, rose steadily toward a thoroughly unnerving
crescendo, a little man, intent but distracted, emerged from the
stalled machine with a crank clutched in his hand. He made his way
to the front of his car, where a mounted policeman frowned im-
perially upon him; and as the crowd of bystanders along the curbs
grew to incredible proportions the little man cranked and cranked,
fitfully, desperately, fruitlessly. Finally, after one last frantic

whirling of the crank, the little man straightened up, stepped back, and to the accompaniment of the pulsating blast of thousands of sirens and with one of the largest galleries before which anyone ever performed, he flung the crank with all his strength against the radiator and stalked off through the crowd.

Not every frustrated person "abandons ship" in such a dramatic fashion, but there are countless acts of aggression that are like this one in the fundamental respect that they involve unconscious projection. After all, just what was it at which the little man hurled the crank with such conclusive vengeance? It was the tormenting reflection of his own evaluations of the car. He would get even with it! It couldn't do that to him! So convincing was his demonstration that it is with some little effort that we come to and realize that the car itself was really innocent of any motives. Anything about it at which the crank was hurled was quite obviously projected into it by the frustrated little gentleman.

It is by no means apparent that aggression as a response to frustration would be as common as it is in our culture if we were effectively trained from childhood to be conscious of projection— of to-me-ness. It is precisely this consciousness of our projection mechanisms that enables us to see that very often, if not always, there are other and more effective means whereby we may obtain the same or more desirable results than those we achieve by means of aggression. Without such consciousness we make war against will-o'-the-wisps, shadow box with little men who aren't there, and leave untouched the real sources of our frustration. Evaluations— misevaluations usually—misplaced by projection outside ourselves, become great red herrings leading us away on violent crusades from which we return exhausted and, as a rule, with bruised and empty hands. Hurling cranks at radiators starts no motors—and smashes good radiators—and by the same token hurling invectives and fists at persons whose intolerable characteristics exist, after all, in our own heads—this sort of attack, arising out of "mistaken identity," creates more human problems than it solves.

It constitutes, nonetheless, one of the more common forms of mal-adjusted behavior in our society—partly because it sometimes pays, or seems to, partly because something like it, aggression in its more "intelligent" forms, appears at times to be necessary, but mainly because we are not for the most part effectively trained to be conscious of projection. If we were, we would as a rule, without having to be reminded to "count to ten," delay our name-calling and crank-throwing long enough to realize that they are misdirected—that the pink elephants we were about to chase away are really cavorting *behind* our eyes and are not really stampeding us at all.

Unconscious projection, harnessed to aggressive tendencies, sometimes has the effect of propelling the individual toward outright paranoia. As a matter of fact, there would appear to be a touch of paranoia in almost every outburst of aggression; paranoid tendencies, like any others, vary in degree from mild to severe. What distinguishes the person with well-developed paranoid tendencies is the attitude that even when other persons are not thwarting him, nevertheless they intend to. The mote of suspiciousness is practically always in his eye. If our little man in the traffic jam had been not merely aggressive but also highly paranoid, he would have been quite convinced that someone had deliberately arranged for his car to stall right where it did and that all the people who gathered round had been tipped off beforehand. He probably would have felt as he walked away from the scene that he was "escaping." Things don't just happen to a paranoiac; he fancies himself a victim of planned circumstances, or a fugitive from them.

The person with paranoid tendencies is inclined to approach individuals and situations with his guards up and with a chip on his shoulder, so to speak. He does not wait to be attacked before assuming a posture of counterattack. He carries about with him a chronic attitude of self-defensiveness which he expresses in undelayed tensions, overt reactions, and verbal assaults. It may be said that he has a very low frustration tolerance; it takes less to frustrate him because he is more inclined than most people are to expect frustration. In the competitive struggle he has become convinced that no one is on his side. All are against him. He projects this inference to the world about him, and then sees in all he looks upon the unnerving reflection of what he projects.

There would appear to be, then, a rather close relation between aggressive reactions and paranoid patterns of evaluation. The merely aggressive person simply fights back when frustrated, but if he "frustrates" easily and very often he will tend to become *set* to fight back, to look for frustrations, to assume that other people intend to block and oppose him. He tends to acquire the "mad-dog philosophy" that life is a matter of biting or being kicked. Many so-called behavior-problem children, for example, give one the impression that they have been beaten or thwarted once too often, and so have concluded early in life, and too literally, that the best defense is a good offense. It takes a tremendous amount of reassuring to break down their conviction that the world is against them.

Maladjustive aggression, therefore, not only involves unconscious projection, but as the evaluations that are projected become more and more *generalized* there is a tendency for the aggressiveness to assume the character of paranoia. The combination of unconscious projection and identification (undue generalization) is potentially a very dangerous one, and it goes far toward explaining a great deal of delinquency, crime, and "mental" disease—as well as many of the more disheartening social frictions, incompatibilities, and the general unfriendliness that make life for all of us rather less pleasant and fruitful than it might well be.

Schizoid Tendencies

One of the most serious, and least recognized, aspects of common maladjustment is to be seen in what might be called schizoid tendencies. In the preceding chapter we discussed schizophrenia in some detail, and we suggested that it appeared to be in many ways representative of certain common adjustment difficulties peculiar to our general culture. The fact that it is one of the most prevalent of the "mental" diseases lends some degree of credence to this view. What is even more convincing, however, is the fact that a very considerable share of the symptoms presented by persons with relatively minor problems appear to be essentially schizoid in character.

For example, as was pointed out in the opening chapter of this book, maladjusted people tend to be "idealists." They are perfectionists. Both their standards and the tenacity with which they cling to them appear to be crucial. Their standards, or ideals, are of interest in the present connection in two very important respects: they are highly intensional and they involve a great deal of self-reference. The tenacity with which they cling to these ideals is important in the practical sense that it tends to make for a highly routinized manner of living and a pronounced rigidity of personality structure.

The ideals of the maladjusted are highly intensional in the sense that they are arrived at, or adopted, without any considerable weighing of experience. In the final analysis they are for the most part simply accepted naïvely from books and from parents, teachers, and other "authorities." This becomes particularly clear when such persons are called upon to defend their ideals. There is, in one form or another, a good deal of the "Mother knows best" attitude in their defenses. Sprinkled throughout their arguments are such remarks as: "My father always used to say . . ." "When I was a little girl my mother told me many times . . ." "It says in the Bible . . ." "In school I was taught . . ." "I have a very high regard for Professor So-and-so and he thinks . . ." etc. Only in the most limited ways, if at all, have they undertaken any extensional evaluation of their adopted beliefs, attitudes, and goals. They have seldom compared their notions and their standards with those of other people, so far as their personal effects and social value are concerned. In fact, they exhibit in general the provincial unreflective attitude that people with other ideals and ways of living are somehow queer, uncivilized, or just "wrong." It all adds up to the general statement that such maladjusted persons are naïve. They really don't know why they live the way they do, or why they cherish the goals for which they so doggedly strive. They are like "good" little boys and girls doing with a kind of sprightly dumbness what they have been told to do.

To choose an obvious illustration, a schoolteacher who once consulted me because she "never seemed able to get all her work done" told in considerable detail about her practice of making out daily and weekly schedules for herself. Even her time for recreation was rationed. Spare-time intervals down to ten-minute periods were accounted for in her neat designs for living. Life for her was a veritable succession of deadlines. And—inquiry revealed what was to be predicted: she insisted on keeping the top of her desk cleared.

When asked why she wanted to plan her time so carefully and why she wanted nothing on her desktop, she said simply that people should be orderly, they shouldn't waste time, they shouldn't leave stuff lying out on their desks. Why not? Well, it just wasn't right. It apparently had never occurred to her to evaluate these standards in terms of their effects on the people—such as herself—who try to maintain them. They were simply the right standards to live by, right in an absolute, utterly intensional sense. She was living by a definition of "the good life," and it had not entered her head that her difficulties might be due to the definition. It was as though, in designing her life, she had simply left reality out of account. The schizoid tendency was quite obvious.

It was obvious also in relation to the self-centered character of her goals. They were goals *for her* in a peculiarly limited sense. She wanted *her* life to be neat and orderly, she wanted things to go smoothly for *her*. She was not scheduling her time in order to have two evenings a week free to do volunteer work at the local hospital, or in order to find time to care adequately for her children (she had no children, and in the course of the interviews it came out that she was not very fond of children). She did not seem, consciously at least, to value her neatness because it might make her a better schoolteacher, but she had thought that it would favorably impress the superintendent. She wanted to impress him; and that fact motivated, in part, not only her time-scheduling and desk-clearing, but also her neatness of dress and her punctuality in attending teachers' meetings and other such functions. In fact, so far as could be ascertained, she was attending the university summer session and working toward an advanced degree simply in order to please the superintendent and, in general, to get *herself* ahead. There was no convincing evidence that she looked upon her graduate study and the expected Master's degree as a preparation or means to more effective public service on her part. Her goals were conspicuously egocentric. Her feelings, her comfort, her security in having other people approve of her—these were, in a deeper sense, her real goals. Her neatness and exaggerated orderliness were merely means to these ends. She was at the relatively infantile if-you'll-be-good-to-me-I'll-be-a-good-girl-so-you'll-go-on-being-good-to-me stage of personality development. Her superficial efficiency and outward co-operativeness were primarily symptoms of profound selfishness.

She had clung to her intensional, self-centered ideals for many years. In fact, they appeared to have been well rooted in her early childhood, and she came to the clinic with no intention of giving them up. She apparently saw no relation whatever between them and her basic unhappiness, her feelings of being harassed, her steadily decreasing enthusiasm for her work, her associates, her future. It is significant that her main complaint was that she "never seemed able to get all her work done." There are doubtless millions of people in our culture who complain that they can never get all their work done. Why should they want to? What is it they are going to do when they get all their work done? What are they going to do when they have their desks all cleared? When they have their time all scheduled, their habits all formed, their beliefs all settled, their papers neatly filed—then what? The fact appears to be that they are not really getting ready to go anywhere or to do anything. They are trying to make the world stay put, to stop the hands of the clock, to shut out all disturbing stimuli—to get away from reality, from work and unfinished tasks, from people and the demands they make upon them, from responsibility and censure. They are apparently trying to slip away into a private inner world of words that always mean the same things, of days all like the same ideal tomorrows, of evenings with the same book before the same fire that never goes out, where *yes* never means *maybe* and two times two are always four—the Big Rock Candy Mountain of schizophrenia.

It is not that the millions of people who fit this general pattern in some degree are schizophrenic. What is to be recognized is the schizoid *tendency*. The schoolteacher mentioned above was not suffering from schizophrenia, but the essential features of her maladjustment suggested quite definitely, though in minor degree, this particular type of disorder. One such person is of no great social consequence, but millions of such individuals lend to society a distinctive over-all character that is not altogether reassuring. What one notices particularly about this schizoid type of orientation is its discomforting and incapacitating effects: the seemingly unaccountable fatigue, boredom, and irritability, the ennui and discontent that drive people in droves to gang-buster movies, murder mysteries, the funny papers, bubble dances, and turtle derbies, and all the other means of semantic thumb-sucking which our society so abundantly supplies—to meet the demand which it so profusely creates. And beneath these obvious symptoms one finds, if one investigates, the overintensionalized, absolute, self-centered ideals pursued according to a rigid routine, with fixed patterns of interest, attitude, and belief, which form the basic structure of the schizoid orientation.

ORDER₁ AND ORDER₂

The impression is not to be left that orderliness, as such, is maladjustive. Efficient habits and routines, directed to significant purposes, clearly understood, and modified easily and effectively in response to changing circumstances, are very different in their effects from the highly intensional, misdirected rigidity that we have been discussing. It is routine followed out essentially for its own sake, or in relation to largely unevaluated and self-centered goals, that is maladjustive. This is particularly true if the goals are difficult to achieve, as such goals usually are, and if they are not richly satisfying when achieved. And self-centered goals do not as a rule yield deep or lasting satisfactions. People who pursue them tend to become increasingly discontented, to suffer, sometimes deeply, from the growing realization that they are devoting their lives to nonessentials. The "mess of pottage" they bargain for gives to their lives a pervasive quality of disappointment. In the end they react predominantly with resentment, or with apathy, a generally lowered interest in living, and a tendency, not always conscious of course, to seek ways of escape from the demands—and so also the opportunities—with which life confronts them.

Order in an extensional sense, on the other hand, is utterly basic to adequate adjustment. It sometimes appears to have a rather higgledy-piggledy character, however. If there is any difficulty in understanding this, it is probably due to the fact that *order* has more than one meaning. It is a multiordinal term. Extensionally, order is a matter of space-time relationships—of what, where, when, in what relations to what. Living an orderly life, extensionally, consists in coordinating effectively the structure of one's beliefs, feelings, and actions with the structure of reality. When one's pattern of attitudes and belief and one's routine of action no longer fit well the extensional circumstances in which they are made to function, there may be a high degree of intensional order, but extensionally there is disorder. Conversely, the process character of reality requires ordinarily such a degree and rate of continual readjusting that an extensionally well-ordered life may appear quite disordered or inconsistent from a thoroughly intensional point of view.

The next time you are told by a long-absent friend that "you are still the same old Wilford!" you might with considerable justification wonder whether you have been complimented—or diagnosed. "The same old Wilford" is likely to be in some need of semantic repair if "the times have changed"—and they usually have.

INFANTILE TENDENCIES

In some degree the anxiety, withdrawing, aggressive, and schizoid tendencies we have been discussing are essentially infantile. What we have said about them, however, does not serve to cover adequately the matter of infantilism or immaturity. It is a common and generally sound belief that the early years of life are very important in determining the character of later development. What is not so widely recognized is the obvious implication that, because of this, later development tends to fall rather short of full maturity. The attitudes, beliefs, habits, the general orientation, acquired in early childhood do tend to persist into adult life, and insofar as they do, they give to the adult personality an infantile caste. In very large measure what a psychiatrist, or a clinical psychologist, does for a maladjusted person is to bring him up to date, so to speak, to help him to "act his age." In this sense a psychiatrist serves as a sort of semantic catalyzer hastening the process of personality development.

The problem is in some degree clarified by a simple story about a physician who one time experienced a momentary perplexity in attempting to open a door. As a small boy about four years old, he had frequently eaten with his father in the physicians' dining room of the hospital where his father was a staff surgeon. His father had then assumed a position elsewhere, and eventually the boy, grown to manhood, graduated from a medical school and became a doctor in his own right. When thirty years old or so, he had occasion to return to the hospital where his father had worked when he was a small boy, and once again he had lunch in the physicians' dining room. It was a pleasant experience, but when, after the meal was finished, he came to open the door leading out of the dining room an unaccountable tenseness and uncertainty came over him. One of the other physicians promptly opened the door, however, and they went out into a corridor. But the young doctor was curious. He excused himself and went back to the dining-room door to see whether he could find out why he had been so strangely confused upon trying to open it. And as he reached down to turn the knob, the explanation became suddenly clear. Reaching down, he was reminded that he had not reached for that doorknob since he was four years old— and when he was four years old he had always reached *up* to turn the doorknob.

Most maladjusted persons are still reaching up to turn the doorknob, so to speak. Having grown to adulthood so far as age is concerned, they are still tending to react as they learned to react when they were children. They have to be taught to reach down instead of up to open the door, as it were. After all, personality reeducation is called *re*education advisedly. It is to be noted very particularly that in personality reeducation a great deal of time is usually spent in delving back into the childhood of the person being *re*educated. Writers on the subject do not always make it pointedly clear why this is done. The chief value of doing it is to make clear that the childhood experiences were *childhood* experiences. In general, the value of a critical reexamination of one's life history lies in the fact that it helps one to recognize that certain experiences *are matters of history*. It helps one to differentiate what is past from what is present, and so to appreciate the crucial fact that certain childish evaluations and reactions are, in present circumstances, neither appropriate nor necessary. The young doctor in the story above solved his "problem" by realizing that he no longer should or needed to reach up in order to open the door. In briefest summary, that is the way, in effect, that most of our adjustment problems come to be solved, if they are solved at all.

What we have to say about infantilism, then, is in the main simply this: Practically all of our maladjustments, of whatever kind, are in some degree infantile in the sense that they involve, directly or indirectly, evaluational and reaction tendencies that have persisted since early childhood.

Among the reasons for this fact, there are two of outstanding importance. The first is that much of what is learned early in life tends to be learned well, particularly if it involves crucial emotional experiences. The second is that, in most cases, the early beginnings of maladjustment arise out of family relationships, and part of the reason why they persist is that these family relationships continue to operate, sometimes all through life.

These two facts are not entirely unrelated. One of the main reasons why certain reactions learned in the first years of childhood tend to be well learned is that they are reactions which involve the deep and complex emotions peculiar to the family situation. It is to be considered that those aspects of behavior which we ordinarily regard as basic to a person's character, or disposition, are made up, for the most part, of his predominant degrees and patterns of tension, his likes and dislikes, his characteristic moods or feelings, his fears, his hates and loves and the conflicts involving them. It is precisely such aspects of behavior that largely determine a person's individuality and make him recognizable from one time to another as a distinct personality. They go far, therefore, to set the limits and the pattern of the individual's personality development. Now, it is especially these aspects of behavior that tend to be learned well during the first few years of life. And they are learned in the home as a result of more or less emotionally colored family experiences. Thus, they become associated with specific persons and situations that tend to recur and to be reacted to over and over again during the years of greatest growth and development. So it is that a person's early personality pattern tends to become firmly established by the time he reaches adulthood—and so it is that his adult personality tends to reflect an infantile quality.

Special note is to be made of the heavily emotional character of these reaction patterns that are so well learned in early childhood. To say that they are heavily emotional is to imply chiefly that they are predominantly non-verbal, involving for the most part direct organismic evaluations in terms of "pleasure" and "pain." During the first year of life a child shows relatively little language behavior, and what he does show is quite crude, expressing for the most part states of satisfaction and discomfort. Not until the age of two or three years does the language of "the normal child" become significant as language in the ordinary sense, and serve to any considerable degree the purposes of external reference. Usually when even a two-year-old says "Ball" or "Car," it is the tone of voice and the accompanying gestures and facial expressions, rather than the words themselves, that indicate what is being expressed; and what is being expressed is for the most part an attitude toward, rather than information about, whatever is being referred to. Moreover, the attitudes expressed are essentially two-valued. The child either approaches or avoids, accepts or rejects, caresses or attacks the stimuli with which he is confronted. The scheme of classification with which he deals with sounds, sights, smells, tastes, pressures, temperatures, and internal sensations provides simply for two kinds of evaluation, positive and negative.

In terms of the functioning of the nervous system, these early reactions of the child are predominantly thalamic. For purposes of making clear the point of this statement, we may consider the brain as being comprised of two major areas or regions, the cortex and the thalamus. For all practical purposes it may be said that incoming nervous impulses pass through the thalamus before reaching the cortex, and that outgoing impulses pass through the thalamus after leaving the cortex. Moreover, there are direct connections whereby incoming impulses may be relayed out at the thalamic level before reaching the cortex.

Generally speaking, the language functions and voluntary actions are controlled through or by the cortex, whereas direct, non-verbal, involuntary reactions to stimulation are mediated predominantly by the thalamus. Essentially the cortex exercises the functions of (a) delay of reactions, (b) differentiation, and so evaluation, of stimuli, and (c) regulation of the thalamic and other lower levels of the nervous system. Now, language—which is to say, symbolization generally—develops as the cortex develops, and in turn it provides the means, in large measure, for the cortical functions of delay, differentiation and evaluation, and regulation. It provides the basis of effective consciousness and of the voluntary control of behavior. The crucial fact is that a child's cortex is not fully developed at birth and does not fully mature, so far as is known, until late adolescence, or around the age of eighteen years in most individuals. Brain weight increases more or less rapidly until the age of eight years or so, and then only gradually until at about the eighteenth year the limit of growth is practically reached. Language development follows a roughly corresponding course, and studies of "mental" growth, as determined by means of standard intelligence tests, reveal also a generally parallel curve.

These facts are of fundamental importance in relation to the persistence of infantile modes of behavior. The point is that what is learned non-verbally, by means of direct experience on a predominantly thalamic level, tends to be learned more thoroughly and with more lasting effects than what is learned on a merely verbal level. This is especially true if what is learned thalamically involves pronounced satisfaction or discomfort, and is frequently repeated. The infant or young child, having an incompletely developed cortex and scarcely any language, is a relatively thalamic creature whose evaluations are expressed by direct action for the most part, rather than in verbal form. Even such verbal behavior as he does exhibit tends to be quite reflexive, involuntarily expressive rather than consciously communicative and directive. These direct reactions are expressive mainly of positive or negative feelings, and because they occur repeatedly and have immediate and felt consequences, they tend to become firmly established modes of behavior. Moreover, as has been mentioned, they become associated with individuals and situations which tend to remain in the child's environment, and so to call forth from the child, as he grows older, more or less consistent types of reaction.

By the time the child's cortex has matured and his language has become relatively elaborate, his basic modes of behavior have been well set, and because they have been established largely on the thalamic or involuntary level they are not particularly susceptible to modification by cortical and direct linguistic influences. You can't talk to the thalamus, so to speak—which means that it is difficult to talk a person into giving up the attitudes and evaluations he learned early in life. It is difficult for essentially the same reason that it is impossible to talk a fish into behaving in ways to which it is not accustomed. Language means nothing to a fish and it means little to a child, simply because the language functions are not performed by the thalamus. Strong positive and negative evaluations, expressed more or less involuntarily in states of tension and in other patterns of essentially reflex action, are not easily brought under conscious control by verbal means.

This does not imply, however, that language is useless in dealing with the infantile reactions of adults, but that language can be used most effectively in two ways in dealing with such reactions. First, it can be used for the purpose of directing the individual into the kinds of firsthand experience that will enable him to re-evaluate and to unlearn, thalamically, the infantile reactions. Mere discussion that does not lead to action is of little effect. For example, there is little point in merely telling an individual to relax; but by telling him precisely how to relax—and preferably by showing him how and by getting him to do it—it is possible often and to a large extent to reduce his infantile, self-defensive tensions. Again, you can hardly tell an adult to stop stuttering and expect him to stop, but you can tell him to perform certain kinds of speech in certain ways under certain conditions, and thus direct him into experiences from which he can learn thalamically to speak with decreased fear and tension. In general, what has been learned thalamically, especially in early childhood, must be unlearned thalamically—that is, by direct experience—for the most part. You will scarcely affect your own infantile behavior by reading a book, for example, unless it stimulates you to appropriate direct action. The young doctor a few pages back, who was confused in attempting to open the door, resolved his confusion and tension by actually going back and manipulating the doorknob, instead of merely "thinking" about it or spinning vague theories. The "thinking" he did do was effective because it led him to take action appropriately.

The second main purpose which language can serve in the reeducation of infantile reactions is that of bringing about insight or consciousness concerning the reactions and their mode of development. If you have a fear of lightning, a plausible explanation of how you acquired it and why you have maintained it will help you to eliminate it, provided it enables you to realize that the causes of it are no longer present, or to see what positive action might be taken to remove the causes. What will help you most of all, however, is an understanding not merely of your fear of lightning or of fear in general, but of the fundamental processes of evaluation. It is a generalized consciousness of abstracting that will go furthest to counteract infantile reactions of whatever kind, to prevent further misevaluations, and to promote general maturity. In other words, the kind of language that is most effective for purposes of personality reeducation is that language which can be used adequately for talking about language. It is this that provides for self-corrective evaluation of evaluations, the basic mechanism of maturity.

Immaturity, or infantilism, is to be recognized, as has been said, in practically any form of personality maladjustment, but it can be described particularly well in terms of certain of its aspects. In the first place, it is characterized by a relative lack of adaptability. This is simply another way of calling attention to the obvious fact that infantile reactions develop in infancy or early childhood and persist into adult life. It is their very persistence that constitutes a lack of adaptability, since insofar as old reactions are maintained new ones are not developed. The individual continues to reach up to open the door, as it were, long after he should reach down. This is a way of saying that he fails to differentiate new situations from old ones, and to differentiate himself at age twenty from himself at age three.

For the normal adult the melody of childhood may linger on, but the song has ended; he does not permit the memory of early fears and affections to determine unduly his present conduct. He views his childhood as history, and he recognizes that evaluations and reactions adequate for him as an adult were neither necessary nor even possible at the age of four. Growing up and achieving maturity are for the individual what the process of time-binding is for the race. It is a matter of starting each new day not where yesterday began but where it ended. La Rochefoucauld once remarked that we differ mostly from ourselves. By doing so judiciously we become mature adults.

The reactions that persist into later years and give to the adult an infantile character may be described by such terms as *superficial, irresponsible, impulsive, naïve, selfish, two-valued,* and they reflect an exaggerated dependence on others, a lack of adequate self-sufficiency. The infantile individual may not seem always to *respect* authority, but he takes it into account to an excessive degree. For him, authority is to be obeyed in a childlike manner, or to be attacked or resisted in an equally childlike manner. He acts, in large measure, simply to avoid punishment or to win praise and affection. The "model" child, the "clinging-vine" wife, the "senselessly" misbehaving schoolboy illustrate by their conduct an unhealthy dependence on others whose authority they take for granted—and with whom they feel themselves to be in actual or potential conflict. The bully or the delinquent is out not to reform society, but only to rebel against it. He is not constructive or creative in socially significant ways, simply because he is so completely oriented to authority as such. He courts it, escapes it, or beats it down if it seems possible or desirable to do so. By courting it he wins affection; by escaping it he avoids punishment; by flaunting it he wins the praise of others who would like to flaunt it too, and he senses something that, by his standards, feels like self-sufficiency.

As seen in the case of a single immature individual, this authoritarian orientation may not seem to present an overly grave problem. Viewed, however, as a pervasive aspect of a whole society, determining in ways that are crucial the life patterns of millions of individuals, it hardly inspires an attitude of nonchalance. There is something incongruous about a democracy, for example, in which children are trained to behave in certain ways on the basis of the explanation that their parents and teachers will like them if they do and will punish them if they don't. There might be nothing incongruous about it if the children were merely instructed to behave naturally. As George Devereux has remarked, however, there are no "natural" ways of doing 95 per cent of the things we do; practically all of our conduct is socially determined. There is nothing necessarily maladjustive about this. In fact, it would appear to be inevitable that most of our behavior is socially determined. What is potentially maladjustive is the manner in which we are motivated to behave in the particular ways that society approves and demands. If the motive is simply a respect for or a fear of authority, in the absence of any incisive evaluation of the authority, the prescribed attitudes and habits may be established but they are not likely to be always exercised judiciously and constructively, or to be modified effectively as circumstances vary.

This exaggerated dependence on authority, or deference to it, arises out of and encourages a disinclination to accept responsibility, even for one's own conduct. In the absence of a mature sense of responsibility, evaluations are likely to be offhand and superficial, and to be based primarily on considerations of personal comfort or selfish advantage. Action tends to be impulsive, undertaken more or less unreflectively and without adequate regard for its consequences. The general impression created by the infantile person is that, so far as his understanding of himself is concerned, he is remarkably naïve. He seems quite unaware of his motives, or of the specific nature of his conflicts, or of the reasons for the course of his development. He tends to take himself quite completely for granted, as though no explanation of his behavior were possible. His vocational aims are likely to be undefined, or else fantastic. Any attempts he may make to express his "philosophy of life" are likely to be halting and meager. In our common speech, he just isn't wise to himself. In all of these important respects he acts quite like a child.

From a practical point of view, these infantile modes of reaction are important because they are so common. They are to be found in some measure in practically every form of maladjustment, and in mild degrees, at least, they would seem to be not entirely absent from the personalities of most people. For these reasons personality reeducation is in large part a matter of getting the individual to grow up, to exchange childish attitudes, beliefs, and habits for mature methods of evaluation and modes of reaction. The well-adjusted person is one who "acts his age" and is adequate to the responsibilities and opportunities with which he is confronted and which he himself helps to create. Reduced to its simplest terms, maturity lies in reacting adequately to the *differences* between today and yesterday.

SPECIAL DISABILITIES

The maladjustments we have been discussing frequently give rise to, or are in some measure due to, various deficiencies or disabilities. As a matter of fact, most children and adults who are in some way maladjusted seek clinical service not as often for their basic maladjustments as for their physical complaints, or their difficulties in school and work or in specific social situations. The result is that vocational guidance workers, educational counselors, and physicians are very often called upon to deal with complaints or disabilities that are actually symptoms of underlying personality disorders.

In the psychoneuroses particularly, and to some extent in the other "mental" and nervous disorders also, various physical complaints and disabilities are conspicuous symptoms. In the maladjustments of the common run of people this type of symptom is also present. One of the most ordinary forms in which it occurs is that of weariness, a tendency to tire readily, not only from hard physical labor but also and particularly from activities that involve relatively little muscular exertion. Some individuals are kept in a nearly chronic state of exhaustion by the mere business of living—of personal care, of getting up every morning, doing each day a familiar routine job, and keeping up a small number of social relationships. Clear-eyed, hard-working, zestful, outgoing persons by no means make up the majority of the general population. One lady, writing in a popular magazine a few years ago, described her own ingenious system for combating ennui by saying that she took one hour off every day, one day every week, one week every month and one month every year. In other words, she "rested" a little over five months out of every twelve. But what most people need are not long vacations, more sleep, or less work. Very few of the maladjusted persons whom I have known clinically would have benefited very much from "shorter hours and more pay"—at least, not from shorter hours. Most of them have seemed to need longer hours and more pep.

There was one time a student in one of my classes who almost invariably fell asleep during the lectures. (It was reassuring to learn that he fell asleep in practically all his other classes, too!) Finally, on his own initiative, he asked for help, and it turned out that he was getting from eight to ten hours' sleep every night, and that the physicians he had consulted had been unable to discover any organic causes for his perennial drowsiness. His condition was not entirely unaccountable, however. He had rather pleasant daydreams but no definite vocational or other plans for his future. He had come out of the Ozark Mountains to attend the university at the instigation of a famous uncle, whose aspirations for him were in most particulars beyond his ready comprehension. He was reacting to the university somewhat as most young boys react to a piano lesson on a warm spring day. But his loyalty to his uncle and the rules of the university required him to attend class lectures, and, without being particularly conscious of the processes involved, he simply resolved his conflict by dozing off and so shutting out the distracting stimuli to which his professors subjected him. Since he didn't understand what was happening to him, he began to worry about his pronounced sleepiness, suspecting that it signified some strange malady. It was only after receiving medical assurance to the contrary that it occurred to him to consult a psychologist.

In his lack of insight this student typified the great majority of people who complain of ailments and disabilities which are due primarily to maladjustments of one sort or another. Most people take their semantogenic headaches, fatigue, digestive disturbances, etc., to physicians, and they honestly believe that what they need is a capsule, a diet, or an operation. They follow a good general policy, of course, in going to a physician. Upon receiving medical assurance of their physical soundness, however, they tend to be simply bewildered or discouraged. They lack the elementary self-understanding that would prompt them to consult a psychologist or psychiatrist. Given even this rudimentary self-awareness, they might not have any such "physical" complaints in the first place, or at least they would have them less often and in less severe forms.

Among those psychologists who are followers of the late Alfred Adler there is a tendency to assume that the maladjusted person is inclined to make use of those specific weaknesses that are most "available" to him. One person will react to a situation that threatens him with failure by "losing" his voice, because he is subject to frequent attacks of laryngitis; another person will react to a similar situation with a "stomach upset," because he is more susceptible to digestive disturbances than to any other form of incapacity. While there is a certain plausibility about this theory, it would hardly appear to provide a sufficient explanation in most cases. If one is faced with a singing performance that is an occasion for anxiety, there is some degree of "logic" in suffering a loss of voice, whether or not one is subject to frequent attacks of laryngitis. If one dreads the prospect of attending a formal dinner which will be attended by certain persons one does not want to see, a rather direct escape is afforded by a "stomach upset," even though one may have a "cast-iron" constitution. The number of weaknesses "available" to most of us is probably great enough to provide a plausible disability for almost any occasion. And we can be direct about it, "using" a sore throat to avoid a speaking engagement, or we can be subtle and discover that we have an ailing back. All this is by no means meant to imply that all such semantogenic ailments are produced at will and with full awareness of the motives and relationships involved. They range all the way from those that are frankly deliberate to others that are utterly unconscious, through all the intermediate degrees of awareness and innocence. They may be temporary to suit a particular emergency, or more or less permanent, serving as a sort of season ticket, as it were, to a box seat, with pop and hot dogs, where one can watch the game without risking one's own knuckles.

This general interpretation of supposedly physical complaints must not be carried too far, of course. There are still bacteria in the world; and a great many aches, pains, and states of fatigue have little or nothing to do with personality maladjustments. People with personalities as normal as any one might see get sick now and then. What a psychologist might take to be a neurotic backache is not infrequently diagnosed correctly by an oral surgeon as an infected tooth. Some stomach ulcers are not brought on by worry, and some headaches are due to eyestrain. While recognizing that maladjusted persons sometimes "seek" security and solace through essentially neurotic disabilities—and, in addition, "get the most out of" any real illnesses or fractured bones that come their way—it would be gross nonsense to contend that even with respect to maladjusted persons all ailments are neurotic or "mental." A casual reading of certain books and magazines devoted to "psychology" would indicate that this warning with regard to the obvious is by no means unnecessary. The notion of semantogenic disabilities, valid as it is in some instances, is certainly not to be applied indiscriminately. In any case, it is nothing more than a working hypothesis until it is well tested; the fact that it proves in many cases to be a hypothesis that works means only that it is to be considered as a possible explanation of ailments and incapacities that do not seem to be due to organic causes.

With regard to personality maladjustments arising from actual physical handicaps there is probably less possibility of abusing a sound theory. Discriminating students of the deaf, the blind, the crippled, stutterers, children who cannot read, people with diseased hearts or tuberculosis or some other genuine disability, agree in the general statement that in some measure the majority of such handicapped persons tend to develop attitudes and social reactions that reflect the influence of their handicaps. The so-called psychology of the handicapped is in large measure the psychology of frustration and insecurity. To most people it makes a great difference to be handicapped in any serious degree in the exercise of activities for which they have strong natural tendencies or on which society places a high premium. Those who seem to have achieved serenity in spite of grave handicaps will usually be found, on close scrutiny, to have done two things. First, they have got around their disabilities somehow, have compensated for them, have found really significant outlets for their more important drives and interests—and they have probably achieved some measure of material security. Second, they have cultivated effectively a scale of values consistent with their particular potentialities and limitations. They have not called the grapes sour—they have really learned to like apples.

Handicapped individuals who have not succeeded in these respects are rather more than likely to feel frustrated, to fear for their security and their social status, and to feel inferior to more sound and healthy folk. After all, they live in the same competitive society in which their fellows also live, and they feel themselves to be at a disadvantage in it. How they react to the frustrations they experience, whether with timorousness, self-pity, aggression, or in some other way, depends largely on their training. Their daydreams, their interests, the kinds of people they like and the ones they dislike, the attempts they make to achieve approval and to earn a living, their moods and aspirations and dreads are all more or less colored by the particular kinds of disabilities with which they have to contend. With the memories of yesterday they anticipate tomorrow, and as the memories are patterned so is the future regarded.

What the handicapped person needs, if he is to achieve an adequate personality, are abilities with which to gain some measure of security and status in spite of his incapacities, and a sense of proportion enabling him to recognize his liabilities in a proper relation to his assets. A lame boy who can sell the horses he carves from wood and who enjoys watching a football game is neither remarkable nor pathetic—except to an onlooker who doesn't have his point of view. He is no more pathetic than the thousands of sound, sturdy boys who never make the varsity team, and he is no more remarkable than any other person who can also carve wood or repair radios or do anything else for which he happens to have the necessary ability. The astonishment with which many individuals regard a one-armed lawyer or a stuttering novelist recalls one of the more droll remarks of Artemus Ward: "I knew a man out in Oregon one time who didn't have a tooth in his head, not a tooth in his head—and yet that man could play the bass drum better'n any man I ever saw."

The only lame boys who are pathetic are the ones who have not learned to walk as well as they can, and who have been taught to envy anyone who can walk better than they do. They are the ones who do not realize how many things can be done with imperfect legs, or without legs at all. They are those who have somehow acquired the preposterous notion that if they can't dance or win a foot race they are of no use in the world. Most so-called handicapped people are not really handicapped; they are just different. By taking account wisely of the difference that the difference makes, most of them would undoubtedly discover that in any fundamental sense it makes very little difference indeed. As Ralph Waldo Emerson's squirrel said to the mountain, "If I cannot carry forests on my back, neither can you crack a nut." Are you handicapped if you are relatively ignorant of the geography of Uruguay, if you are unschooled in algebra, or cannot name the muscles in your back? You are, from somebody's point of view. Who isn't handicapped—from somebody's point of view? It's the point of view that matters.

The poet Heine wrote some of his finest work during his last

years when he was a relatively helpless invalid, paralyzed throughout most of his body. Earl Carlson, a severe spastic paralytic, won
his way through medical school after his parents had died and left
him alone and without money; and in spite of a grotesque deformity
he became one of the world's greatest medical authorities on the
very incapacity by which he refused to be handicapped. The story
of the deaf, blind, mute Helen Keller, who became a public lecturer, cannot be told too often; as one of the most inspiring personalities of all time, she compels one to reexamine whatever one
might have regarded as a handicap. One of my acquaintances is a
successful consulting psychologist, although he is blind. Even the
blight of "insanity" itself was turned into a tremendous source of
social benefit by Clifford Beers, who emerged from a "mental"
hospital to establish the National Committee for Mental Hygiene
and to instigate some of the most significant social and medical reforms that have ever been accomplished. On the university faculty
of which I am a member there are five stutterers and at least four
professors who formerly stuttered. A successful lawyer of my acquaintance is armless. A great professor of anatomy under whom
I studied illustrated his lectures by extraordinary blackboard drawings done with colored chalk, although he was color blind—and
during the closing period of his brilliant career he delivered his lectures from a wheel chair. Just what is a handicap?

The people whom we call handicapped had better be called exceptional. It is a less inferential term. The individual who is exceptional by virtue of a specific disability or an unusual physical
characteristic may or may not develop a maladjusted personality.
If he does, it is likely to be due to the frustration and insecurity
which his exceptional condition involves—but, for all practical purposes, it involves frustration and insecurity only to the extent that
he does not learn to evaluate it extensionally in ways that enable
him to exploit his remaining abilities and to achieve status by means
of them. There are exceptions to this general rule, of course. Diseases and injuries are sometimes all but completely ravaging in their
effects; "mental" subnormality, senility, and various psychoses
frequently reduce their victims to almost utter incompetence; and

some individuals afflicted in less severe forms lack the resources necessary for effective compensation. The fact remains, nonetheless, as George D. Stoddard has so aptly pointed out, that we can very often make a silk purse out of what we *thought* was a sow's ear.

Not All

A relatively complete catalogue of common maladjustments would amount to an incredibly voluminous and disheartening encyclopedia. Enough has been recited in the preceding pages to give a fair indication of the variety and scope of those confusions and inefficiencies that make the world we live in so unconsolingly representative of us who live in it. What has so far been said is doubtless sufficient to emphasize the widespread need for a reevaluation of the general way of life, the essentially prescientific culture to which, as individuals and as a society, we have become accustomed. What was "good enough for father" appears to have been none too good. A judicious exercise of the processes of time-binding should serve to cast us up on a much higher level of human adequacy than we have so far achieved. It is not only later than we think, but we have also not progressed as far as we imagine.

Tomorrow, however, is a long day.

$\mathcal{C}$hapter ～～～～～～～～～～～ XV

AND SO, FORTH

$\mathcal{T}$HE RECITAL OF WOES AND WORRIES FROM WHICH WE have just emerged carries one message of consolation that is clear and definite: each of us can say, "I am not alone." Misery not only loves company—it has company.

How common are these maladjustments? This question cannot be answered precisely, of course. The census taker does not ask you whether you have an inferiority complex, and the Gallup poll has not yet been turned to the purpose of a national counting of up-turned and twisted noses. Ordinary observation of one's friends and associates, and of oneself, of newspaper headlines and what comes over the radio would lead one to conclude that everybody—including oneself—is not altogether wise and happy. And this conclusion appears to stand up quite well, to take on some rather disquieting aspects, in fact, on the basis of such systematic surveys as have been made.

THE PREVALENCE OF MALADJUSTMENT

In his 1938 book, *Modern Society and Mental Disease,* Dr. Carney Landis reports that "mental" hospital records show 1 out of every 200 American adults to be institutionalized. On the basis of U. S. Army reports, state hospital records, and surveys made by the Metropolitan Life Insurance Company, Dr. Landis estimates that 1 out of every 10 adult males can be expected to be incapacitated at some time because of "mental" illness.

Dr. Stanley Cobb of Harvard University, in his recent book, *Borderlands of Psychiatry,* says that there are in this country about 600,000 hospital patients with "mental" illnesses, not counting the institutionalized feeble-minded, who number about 100,000. This is in agreement with the statement by Dr. Landis that 1 out of every 200 American adults is institutionalized. In addition, Dr. Cobb estimates on the basis of surveys and hospital admission and discharge records that there are from 600,000 to 2,500,000 "mentally" ill persons outside the hospitals, besides 2,500,000 feeble-minded. Beyond these, according to various investigations which he cites, Dr. Cobb indicates that there are probably 6,000,000 individuals, to be found in what he calls the borderlands of psychiatry, suffering from psychoneuroses, epilepsy, alcoholism, certain speech disorders, and various types of impairment of the nervous system. These figures total somewhere between 7,000,000 and 9,000,000, not counting the feeble-minded. Moreover, Dr. Cobb does not include in his estimates certain types of speech and reading disabilities, and it is not clear that he includes all of the maladjustments that fall under the headings of delinquency and "behavior problems." Published surveys indicate that anywhere from 2,000,000 to 5,000,000 children and adults have such disorders, and they are disorders that tend to be due to, or to create, personal maladjustment. These various figures, then, taken altogether, come fairly close to the over-all 10 per cent estimate of Dr. Landis. None of these figures, of course, covers such common and sometimes grave problems as those of divorce, and the host of essentially unnamed and generally unclassified miseries of unwanted children and unhappily married adults. There is, besides, a vast army of sufferers from unclear or guarded dreads and regrets, transient or persistent, that sift unnoticed through the nets of surveys and physicians' reports.

About the best summary statement one can make is that roughly 1 out of every 10 persons in the United States undergoes at some time in his life a relatively serious personality derangement. For every such person there are several who experience less severe forms of maladjustment; the number depends on how *maladjust-*

ment is defined. On any realistic basis, it is doubtless larger than any chamber of commerce would care to admit. In order to appreciate what the above statistics mean, the next time you walk along the street check off every tenth person you meet. In a brief walk of three or four blocks tally up the number of men and women who on this basis should be either coming from or going to a psychiatric clinic. Incidentally, as you make your silent survey it will be of particular interest, and not a little disturbing, to notice how difficult it is to tell which 10 out of every 100 individuals appear to be the most likely candidates.

Social Reform and Individual Responsibility

Viewed extensionally, any thoroughgoing attack on this widespread problem of personality maladjustment must necessarily involve a considerable transformation of the society in which we, as individuals, live. There is a basic contradiction, at least from an engineering-semantics point of view, in speaking of a well-adjusted slum dweller. The world we make for ourselves determines in the main the kinds of misery we find in it.

What we call social reform, however, reduces to the behavior of individual human beings responding to specific situations. It is to be considered, for example, that although a few dust-bowl farmers can be moved to better lands against their own wills, or at least in spite of their indifference, and a few slums can be cleared without any very loud cheering by the tenants directly concerned, even such undertakings can be carried out only on the personal initiative of some individuals—and such undertakings by themselves leave much, indeed, unsolved. From an individual point of view, it is poor policy to wait for personal adjustment to come about by virtue of the decisions of someone in Washington, or by virtue of that vague depersonalized abstraction known as "cultural evolution." Any brilliant decisions made in Washington, or New York, or Yale University are all to the good, of course, and will make easier the attempts of many individuals to deal with their own particular difficulties. The professional social planners are to be encouraged to enrich the lives of as many of us as they possiby can, but probably when they have done their best the statistics of maladjustment will still be challenging. Moreover, the more adequately individuals learn to make their own semantic repairs, as it were, the more is society made ready to receive the benefits that professional social planning can bring.

In the last analysis, it is by the efforts of individual human beings to improve their own lives that any substantial and lasting social progress is achieved. Certainly, so far as any particular individual is concerned, adjustment is to be accomplished to a high degree only if he assumes the responsibility for its accomplishment himself. This is not to advocate personal isolationism by any means. Personal adjustment is necessarily social adjustment and cannot be achieved in isolation. In assuming responsibility for his own welfare, the individual does not shut himself off from the assistance that his fellows can give him. On the contrary, it is necessary for him to cooperate with them, and to make effective use of any facilities for personal development that society provides.

THE PROMISE OF SCIENCE AS METHOD

What does our society provide that is outstandingly useful to the individual who is seeking personal adjustment? From a general semantics point of view, the chief answer to this question is quite clear: Our society provides the means and the opportunity to cultivate a scientific orientation toward the issues, the problems, the situations to which the individual must adjust or relate himself. Alongside the traditional authoritarian institutions and customs that are still so prominent in our culture, there exist great centers of scientific research and training: large organizations, governmental agencies, etc., devoted to experimental and generally extensional attacks on a great variety of problems; a vast literature, a little of which even seeps into the daily press, that is scientific in character, conveying relatively reliable information and interpretation; a large number of hospitals, clinics, and educational centers in which one can obtain intensive treatment for personal maladjustments and training in their prevention; and a steadily increasing number of individuals among one's neighbors and associates whose outlook and approach to life problems are fundamentally scientific.

After all, personal adjustment is basically a matter of problem-solving. The one clearly effective method of problem-solving that the race has so far developed is the scientific method. It is effective with regard to personal problems no less than it is with regard to those problems which we do not usually look upon as personal. Our society provides us with this method, and with the opportunity to apply it—and the more we apply it the more we increase the opportunity to do so.

The scientific or extensional approach to personal problems, described in some such terms as have been used in this book, is so straightforward that one may well wonder why it is not universally taught to children and used by adults as a matter of course. One might wonder, in fact, just what people do about their problems when they do not use such an approach in dealing with them. It is not that one has much difficulty in seeing the effects of their muddling—the effects are to be seen in the symptoms of their maladjustments. But just how do they muddle? Precisely what do they do that gets them into trouble and messes up their lives? Perhaps the best way to ask the question is this: Just what would you train a child to do in order to insure that he turn out to be an inefficient, confused, and demoralized adult?

One can answer this question at great length by writing an elaborate handbook and manual of stupidity, or one can answer it quite briefly and to the point, which is what we shall try to do. In order to insure that a child will become a maladjusted adult, he should be trained to confuse the levels of abstraction. So trained, he will indulge persistently in unconscious projection; he will overgeneralize as a matter of course; his reactions will tend to be unconditional, stereotyped, and undelayed; he will be relatively tense, resentful, and self-defensive in general; he will fail frequently to differentiate sufficiently between past and present, between one situation, person, or experience and another, and so will react similarly and thus inappropriately on quite different occasions. Being untrained in evaluation, he will tend to accept whatever is presented to him with sufficient show of authority—the authority of age, precedence, popularity, or financial prestige—and so he will be prey to unscrupulous advertisers, self-interested journalists, and institutionalized mountebankery of various kinds. He will attempt to solve his problems, of which he will have a great number, not by trying to state them clearly and by taking personal responsibility for obtaining reliable factual answers to his own well-hewn questions—but by trusting in a childish way the pills, platitudes, and divers prescriptions of anyone whom he has been trained to regard as an authority. So doing, he will flounder and then confuse himself all the more by laying the blame for his misfortune more or less indiscriminately on everything from bad love and poor luck to allergy and Allah— everything except his own unconscious identifications. Give a child by such means a misleading map of the terrain of experience, teach him to confuse the map with the territory, and you will not have long to wait for frustration and demoralization to overtake him and make of his life an instructive example of how not to administer the human heritage.

But why, then, is not a forthright extensional approach to personal problems universally taught to children? Again the answer could be an encyclopedia of misdirection or it could be fairly short and pat. The latter is harder to give, but we shall attempt it. I teach a course in general semantics to students who have had from two to six years of college and university training, in addition to at least twelve years of elementary and high school education. One might suppose that in the course of so much schooling, to say nothing of their home training and informal learning, someone would have taught them how to apply easily and consistently such simple and obvious principles as are set forth in this book. With few exceptions —and mostly partial exceptions at that—it would seem that no one has. What is in this book may, or may not, be more or less familiar to certain psychologists and scientists of various kinds, but it appears to be definitely unfamiliar in any full and effective sense to the vast majority of even university upperclassmen and graduate students, so far as I have been able to judge on the basis of several years of experience in the actual teaching of general semantics. If the material is significantly familiar to the general public, it is not always clearly apparent in the details of public policy and private conduct.

The answer, then, appears to be relatively simple: Teachers and parents teach children what they know about, and they seem not to know much about extensional procedures for handling personal problems. They just haven't been exposed to a systematic and detailed account of the process of abstracting, or to deliberate training in evaluation and extensionalization. This concise answer to the question is to be extended, of course, by adding that teachers and parents—people generally—have been traditionally trained both inadvertently and deliberately to identify the levels of abstraction, to rely more heavily on vested authority than on their own evaluative processes, and so to use methods that do not always work very well in dealing with personal problems. It hardly takes a professional detective to recognize the significance of all the X's that mark all the spots where individual maladjustments reflect the beliefs and customs of the culture in which the individual lives. There is not only method in our madness, but there is also learning in our method. Learning implies teaching, and when learned misevaluations and inefficiencies are widespread one must conclude that they are widely taught.

This would appear to be the simple answer to why forthright extensional methods of personal adjustment are not commonly practiced. It is like accounting for the fact that the Romans did not use our system of numerical notation, which is so much more efficient than theirs was: They didn't use our system because they didn't know about it—and because they didn't know about it they took pride in the one they did have and taught their children to use it. In short, a scientific approach to personal problems is not widely used because it is not widely taught, and it is not widely taught simply because those who are in a position to teach it have not been made well acquainted with it.

We tend to forget how new our civilization is, even in its more crudely developed aspects, and how unfamiliar to most people are the newer scientific approaches to problems of human behavior. It seems unlikely that any creatures bearing significant resemblance to modern men existed even thirty thousand years ago. In fact, there still live on this earth great numbers of men who resemble a present-day physicist or experimental psychologist only in certain gross biological ways. The population of this planet is an incredible mixture of practically all the cultural strains that have ever existed, ranging all the way from certain tribes that anthropologists refer to as Stone Age people up to such groups as the American Association for the Advancement of Science. Within one and the same individual, not infrequently one can discover beliefs and attitudes characteristic of almost every discernible period of our recorded history. There is probably not a single living human being whose orientation to life is exclusively scientific in the modern sense. There are indeed many New Yorkers and Londoners of our own day who are fundamentally less modern than was Aristotle, or Homer, or Archimedes. Few of us certainly have yet caught up with Galileo or Francis Bacon.

A scientific approach to personal problems is, then, by all means new and, by ordinary standards, even revolutionary. The first psychological laboratory was established by the German, Wilhelm Wundt, at Leipzig, less than seventy years ago. Many of the pioneers in psychology, the scientific study of behavior, are still living as this is being written, and none of them has been long dead. A large proportion of the scientific investigations of human personality have been made in the last twenty-five years, and there are certain aspects of maladjustment, particularly those involving language behavior, on which scarcely any research has been done even yet. It is to be said, in fact, that the application of scientific method to the more intimately personal aspects of behavior is only now beginning to get under way.

In view of all this, it is to be realized that there is something almost bold in the proposition that the method of science not only provides a means of investigating personality, but also represents in itself the pattern of behavior that constitutes normal personality.

That is the fundamental proposition of this book, and of general semantics. *The method of science is the method of sanity.*

OUR MAJOR PROBLEM

Between the behavior that we call insane and the behavior that we call scientific there are differences that are utterly crucial for what they indicate about the behavior that we call sane. To be effectively conscious of those differences is a basic responsibility of every university president, every school superintendent, every teacher and parent, every public official, every person who occupies a position of influence. It is, in fact, essential, for many practical purposes, to any individual at all. It is a cardinal purpose of this book to make these differences reasonably clear.

The basic aim of science applied to problems of personal behavior is to bring about personal behavior that is itself scientific. But, as has been indicated, science is so new in the world that few among us are quite certain of what it involves. We speak glibly of our time as the scientific age, but we muddle through it—or endeavor to—in largely prescientific ways. We have managed to apply scientific techniques to our material environments and to our industrial facilities with Aladdin-like effects, but we have managed to do this without getting ourselves caught in the wonder-working rollers of those same scientific techniques. As Lewis Mumford has so sharply put it, man himself does not mirror the perfection of his instruments. The reason would appear to be simple: man has shied away from turning upon himself the very methods by which he has perfected his instruments.

It is a critical consequence of this uneven development that the social structure which science tends to produce is in our own day only half formed. The physical transformation has been in considerable measure achieved. We can now send our words from New York to Bombay in a twinkling—but they are still in the main the words of an old and naïve era. We can drive our cars eighty miles an hour along four-lane magic carpets—to play the pinball machines. We can sail the stratosphere on wings of wizardry—to bomb an industry, or even a kindergarten, into oblivion. The society that science can build is only half constructed, and for lack of coordination we appear now in many respects to be tearing it down by our frantic but lopsided efforts to bring it to completion.

Prescientific men can neither build nor maintain a scientific culture. Man, the toolmaker, has still to fashion the tools for his own reworking, lest he use the tools he has already made for the witless purpose of his own undoing. So long as men use science to solve only their material problems, by their very successes they create problems of higher order and of more grave significance: the mightier the battleship, the more desperate the need to remove the motives for its use. In no other fact is our predicament as a world culture more starkly dramatized than in the frenzy with which we employ science to manufacture weapons with which to preserve—not to eliminate but actually to preserve—the prescientific customs and institutions to which science is so inevitably opposed. We wage war fervently in order to defend, so we proclaim, the very culture that is warlike in its deeply cherished traditions. We staunchly preserve and persistently nourish our nationalistic and other group loyalties in ways that serve to disunite the peoples of the earth. And we use the *techniques* of science to achieve these ends which are inimical to the time-binding implications and practical possibilities of the general *method* of science. We are working at cross-purposes with impressive vigor. Not only does the left hand not know what the right is doing; it is undoing it.

This discordance in the structure of our culture is no impersonal academic affair. Its effective manifestation is to be seen in the millions of discordant personalities of bristling or fatigued individual human beings. The conclusion of comprehensive surveys is, as we have seen, that one out of ten Americans spends some part of life suffering from a "mental" disorder—and for every person who is frankly and gravely imbalanced, there are two or three others who are not far from it. While medical science and public health practices have been increasing the average span of life, much less has been done to render our longer lives less miserable or more fruitful than were the briefer earthly careers of our forebears. The microscopic bacteria of our physical environments have been combated with remarkable effectiveness, while the "verbal bacteria" of our semantic environments have gone for the most part unsuspected. They have, in fact, flourished in their enriched media of high-speed communication. The spume of the back-fence gossip, the bully, and the bigot can now be sprayed daily over entire continents. We can and do make two neuroses thrive where one languished before.

The explanation of all this hardly lies in our stupidity. The mathematician Thompson once said, in a gesture of encouragement to his students, that what one fool can do another can. In order to encourage ourselves toward the remaking of our society, we can extend Professor Thompson's wisdom by pointing out that what a "fool" has achieved in one direction he can achieve in another also. After all, our foolishness is rather definitely specialized; it is limited to certain of our activities only. We are not stupid in any general or fundamental sense. In those areas in which we have applied the method of science we have made tremendous progress. To quibble over that is to twist the meaning of *progress* into a veritable semantic pretzel. And the intelligence that has created this progress can produce progress of other kinds as well.

It is not by applying the *method* of science that we have wrought destruction. We have done that by applying the *results* of science in the very areas of our experience where we have failed to apply the *method*. The scientific method that has raised communication from the level of the jungle drum and the town crier to the pinnacle of modern radio has in itself done no least iota of harm. It has been the failure to apply that same method to improve the semantic reactions of those who use modern radio that has intensified the waste and misfortune which those reactions involve. The scientific method that has produced atomic bombs is in no sense responsible for the tragedy in their wake. The tragedy of atomic bombs is due to the fact that we have not used the method of science for changing the ways which men have so long employed to settle their disputes. It is simply that with atomic bombs those traditional and cherished customs are far more deadly than they were with muzzle-loaders. We have erred not in refining the scientific method, but in failing to use it on us who use it.

AND SO FORTH

It is the distinctive contribution of general semantics that it formulates the *method* of science in a way that makes reasonably clear the possibilities of its application to our personal and social problems. It presents this method, in fact, as a design for living in the everyday sense of the word. It attempts to cut through the bewildering overgrowth of elaborate theory and technicality, and so to reveal the heartening simplicity of the few notions, principles, and techniques that make up the fundamentals of science.

It is undoubtedly true that even young children can learn these fundamentals quite as easily as they now learn various prescientific beliefs and customs that would appear to be much more complicated. This is, indeed, an encouraging possibility and one not to be cast aside with an undelayed gesture of incredulity. A society goes forward, if it does, on the restless feet of its little children. The world they "get inside their heads" is in large measure the world in which they and their own children must live. The worlds that we of the present generation carry about inside our heads are not to be passed on from father to son lightly and without sober reflection. The essential humanity of our children lies in their time-binding possibilities, and the least we can do for them is to do nothing to them that will block their time-binding endeavors. Heavy hangs over the head of any father who prescribes a belief for his own son —without providing him, also, with a method for revising it.

What can be wisely prescribed is *method*, the most effective method known to us for making evaluations and for solving problems. That method, if one is to judge by demonstrated results, would appear to be the method of science; and, in saying this, heavy emphasis is to be placed on the language of science, for this is the better part of the method. It is this that gives to science its pervasive social significance and its warmly human values. As we watch the process of "getting the world inside one's head," we are forcefully impressed by the strange mechanism through which it is accomplished. It is done in the main with symbols. As it impresses itself upon the individual, language plays a double role. On the one hand, it tends to mold the structure of the culture in which the individual is to find his opportunities and limitations. On the other hand, it is the chief medium whereby the individual interiorizes that culture structure, and so acquires a personality that reflects, for better or for worse, the society in which he lives. He is indeed deluded who does not know how very much he is a child of symbol.

The emphasis given here to the importance of training young children in extensional methods of inquiry and evaluation is not meant to imply that the adult population of the world is to be viewed as water gone over the dam. The tricks that an old dog can learn can make him young again. Adult learning is, of course, fraught with the difficulties of unlearning well-established and elaborate patterns of belief and conduct. The difficulties, however, are not utterly insurmountable. Unlearning of the kind with which we are here concerned is largely a matter of giving up one's self-defensiveness, and a clear consciousness of abstracting tends to make this altogether possible. Once the blockages involved in self-defensiveness are removed, learning in adult years would seem to be essentially like learning during childhood, and scarcely more difficult. Not only is this possibility to be seriously weighed with reference to its promise for older persons, but its social importance is also to be stressed: if children are to be trained, adults must train them. The adult individual can hardly fulfill his social responsibilities by remaining set in his ways, particularly if they were also the ways of his forbears. Socially considered, the old dog who learns no new tricks is a dead weight.

In the practical and urgent terms of personal adjustment and social progress, these remarks become significant only to the extent that each of us interprets and applies them to advantage. Throughout this book we have discussed directly and indirectly the difficulties that we tend to have in living with ourselves and with one another. We have considered some of the ways that are available to us for dealing with these difficulties, and for preventing them. The matter of application of the principles and methods that have been presented must of necessity depend upon personal decision. In the meantime the need for decision persists in ever-varied forms.

The future from which we can never escape swiftly becomes the past which we can never recapture. In this relentless transformation, the realism of our hopes insures the treasure of our remembrances. As we remember so we aspire, or despair, and so we mature as we change creatively with changing circumstance, or we disintegrate as we resist the changes we cannot forestall. Because history does not repeat itself, we invite disheartening chagrin by striving to preserve that which has become history. It is the clear admonition of experience that we can only become what we could have been by declining to be what we have become.

In order to make of these urgent words more than an earnest admonition, the chapters that follow have been written in an effort to show at least some of the practical ways of moving ahead toward the exciting prospect of what we might have been. The meaning of this book, as of any other, is to be found in those who read it, in what they feel and say and do because of it. In the hope that this meaning may be enriched, the book's concluding chapters have been designed to lead the reader, if he will, out of the world of words and some distance at least into the realms of decision and of action

PART V

Applications

$\mathcal{C}hapter$ 〰〰〰〰〰〰〰〰 **XVI**

IN OTHER PEOPLE'S QUANDARIES

$\mathcal{O}$N WORKING WITH PERSONALITY CASES, I AM SOMEWHAT like the surgeon who remembers his own appendectomy each time he enters the operating room. Some day I hope to write "The Memoirs of a White Rat." As a severe stutterer, with the adjustment problems that go with stuttering, I have been examined, diagnosed, tested and treated, checked up on, drilled, observed and charted; I have been psychoanalyzed and hypnotized; I have written my autobiography and changed my handedness. In the laboratory my reflexes have been checked, my eye movements have been photographed, my breathing has been recorded on yards and yards of smoked paper; my blood has been analyzed, my blood pressure measured, my pulse palpated, and I have been hyperventilated; my phi phenomena have been examined and so has my chronaxie; I have sat in cold water while my tremors were recorded; I have taken sodium amytal and hashish and described the resulting sensations to a laboratory stenographer; I have sat for electrocardiograms, audiograms, and electroencephalograms; my intelligence has been estimated, my body build classified, my voice recorded, my basal metabolic rate determined, my emotions rated, my nerve impulses graphed; and I have been asked whether I liked my mother better than my father and whether I find it hard to get rid of a salesman. I have talked with pebbles in my mouth, with my teeth together, while breathing with the diaphragm and in time to a metronome. I have relaxed, gone on and off diets, sung the scale and stuttered on purpose. Somehow in the course of all this I received the B.A., M.A., and Ph.D. degrees and came to be known as a speech pathologist, a clinical psychologist, and a general semanticist. Having specialized in my own defects, I found that other people came to me with theirs. Talking to them, I have been my own most attentive listener, and I have gradually acquired a point of view. In this chapter I shall try to present it.

The work which I have done with personality adjustment cases has been carried on in the University of Iowa Psychological and Speech Clinic, sponsored by the Departments of Speech, Psychology, and Child Welfare, and operated in cooperation primarily with the University Hospitals, College of Medicine, Department of Student Health, College of Dentistry, College of Education, and the State Department of Social Welfare. Advantage has been taken, therefore, of the services of psychiatrists, neurologists, and other medical specialists, as well as psychologists, social workers, and educators. Constant association with a variety of professional specialists has influenced me to take precautions, to refer complicated cases to others better qualified to handle them, and to consider any particular case from varied points of view.

I have worked mainly with two types of cases: speech defectives whose personality difficulties have centered largely around their speech handicaps, and university students whose adjustment problems have come to light in the course of their efforts to get along in the classroom and on the campus. Some of these students have been referred to me by their department heads or their instructors; others have come of their own accord. The majority have been enrolled in my own classes; courses in speech pathology, clinical psychology, and general semantics tend to stimulate many students to seek help from the instructor for problems which either they have not previously recognized, or for which they have supposed no definite help was available. Generally speaking, the cases have involved what would ordinarily be called minor maladjustments. Their more common patterns have been described in Chapter I and in Chapter XIV.

Having been trained in clinical and abnormal psychology before I undertook the study of general semantics, I have applied this newer discipline in accordance with the background which I brought to it. The discussion that follows is to be evaluated in view of this fact. I shall try to indicate the more important ways in which general semantics may be applied to personality case work of the kind with which I am acquainted. The discussion will be presented under the headings of Examination, Diagnosis, and Treatment. I shall use the terms *case* and *student* interchangeably, not only because most of my cases have been students, but also because in the sort of personality reeducation with which I am familiar the case is much more a student than a patient.

EXAMINATION

It is usually true that when a person first comes to a clinic because of some adjustment difficulty he wants, above everything else, to get something off his chest. He wants to talk. He may not be ready to "tell all," he may not know quite how to say what he has to say, but at least he does not come just to read the magazines on the waiting-room table. No unnecessary obstacles should be put in his way. He should not be stopped by a receptionist who is clearly more interested in the clinic's filing system than she is in his anxieties. Certainly no clinician who has ever been a case himself would begin by putting the distraught individual through the cold inquisition of a standardized case history interview, or by giving him a test. To one who has come hoping to get something off his chest, it can be a frustrating and discouraging ordeal to be put through a test or a routine set of questions by an examiner who seems to regard him as a potential entry in a statistical table. He wants a listener. Tests can come later, and so can questions about birthplace, amount of schooling, and ages of brothers and sisters. It is enough for the data sheet to see to it that he does not get away the first time without leaving his name and telephone number. (Because I work with speech defectives as well as adjustment cases, perhaps I should make clear that I am speaking now about the examination of individuals whose problems are primarily those of adjustment. The examination of speech cases ordinarily follows a fairly definite routine and may be much more impersonal.)

Until the case seems to have talked himself out, the most important thing a clinician can do for him is to listen, and to encourage him by a helpful question now and then to say some more. A major share of the clinician's art is the art of listening. It is a rare art. Most people, especially parents and teachers, practice at giving advice, and that is why they are such poor listeners—and that is why they so often make matters worse instead of better whenever they try to help others. In order to be a good listener, one must have overcome the tendency to burst into speech in response to everything one sees or hears. Trying to tell your troubles to some people is all but hopeless for the simple reason that the moment you start to talk they do too, and you end up having to listen to *their* woes, unable to squeeze a word in edgewise and wondering how to get away in time for dinner.

Once you begin to observe people from this point of view, it is astonishing how seldom you meet a person who listens patiently and attentively, and who asks questions as if he were really listening and not as though he were watching for an opening to take over the conversation. It seems true of the great majority of people that when they are not talking to others they are talking to themselves. Abstracting on the silent level is a skill they have never heard of, or if they have they have not cultivated it. It is precisely this skill that a clinician must develop to a high degree.

This is sometimes stated obliquely by saying that a clinician must not be prejudiced, or express moral judgments of the story that the case tells. Authors who state it this way usually support the statement by pointing out that any show of prejudice or moral judgment will discourage the case from talking freely. This is sound, of course, but there is an even more basic consideration: it is simply that one cannot indulge in moralistic signal reactions and listen effectively at the same time. Before one can give an individual any very helpful suggestions, one simply has to hear him out.

There is more to the art of listening, however, than merely keeping still and expressing no moral judgments. A good listener is one who seems alive. Many standard textbooks on clinical psychology stress so much the importance of being impersonal and "unemotional" that those who study these textbooks tend to develop chronic poker faces. One of the advantages of being a case before you become a clinician is that it helps you to understand how exasperating it is to try to talk confidentially to a "post," to a person who is so utterly impersonal, noncommittal, and "unemotional" that you lose all interest in continuing. After all, one cannot talk very long if no definable response is forthcoming from the listener. A clinical case must be assured that the man behind the desk is interested in what he has to tell him, and that he is not being bored to death. A poker face is sometimes a valuable asset in clinical work, but its value depends on the way in which it is turned on and off. When it becomes frozen, it places a fatal damper on the verbal impulses of the case.

One of the reasons why a chronic poker face is disastrous in this kind of work is that most cases are more or less depressed, worried, and grim. Hardly anything else does them quite as much good as an occasional good big smile. Certainly anyone who has worked any length of time with maladjusted people has been struck with the fact that they do not laugh easily. For them "life is real, life is earnest," and all too often they act as if the grave were its goal. There is no clinical sense in meeting their lack of spontaneity with an equal lack of spontaneity. If there is any place that needs an atmosphere of hope and chins-up cheer it is a place where people go for personality reeducation.

In other words, a clinician must have a way of listening with his face and eyes, so to speak. Keeping discreetly quiet, he must nevertheless be alert and responsive. It is his main task, especially at first, to respond to the student in such a way that he will talk as freely as possible, and with less and less restraint as he continues. This is true not only because the clinician needs as much information as he can get, but also because there is some degree of curative value in talk itself. Telling one's troubles to a listener who is interested but not critical, sympathetic but not maudlin, can be extremely relaxing and reassuring.

In order to get the student to talk sufficiently it is sometimes necessary to ask questions. They should not be difficult or embarrassing questions. "What happened then?" or "How did you feel about that?" or "Tell me a little more about that" is representative of the sort of questions and comments that tend to lead to continued talking. The questions should follow naturally from the student's own statements, and should seem reasonable to him. Sometimes a case will be so inhibited that a great deal of encouragement is needed to get him to talk. There are two more or less effective ways to give this encouragement. One is to discuss his problem, so far as you can determine what it is, giving him general information that will help him to understand it, making it clear that if he could tell you a little more you would be able to be more helpful. The other way is to be reminded of your own or other people's difficulties that are similar to his, and then to tell him at some length about these other problems in which he is interested because they are like his own and toward which he can be somewhat "objective" because he is not directly involved in them. Misery loves company—and profits from it, provided it serves to demonstrate that one's own misery is neither unique, mysterious, not utterly unacceptable in the eyes of other people. It is simply a matter of helping the case to see that what he considers shameful or foolish is old stuff to you. By taking the initiative in discussing matters that he considers unmentionable, you can usually lead the student by degrees to open up and talk frankly about his own troubles.

In connection with interviewing of this kind, especially in the early stages, there is the practical question of note-taking. Most people talk a little more freely, until their confidence has been gained, if the clinician does not take down what they say. Some cases, however, seem to assume that notes will and should be made. The main thing, of course, is that the case be entirely assured that anything he says will be treated confidentially and if this requires that no notes be taken, then paper and pencil should be put aside. The clinician can summarize what he remembers of the interview after the case has gone. After a few conferences there will probably be no objection to the recording of even rather detailed notes.

After one or two conferences, if things have gone reasonably well and a good working relationship has been established, it is helpful in many cases—and it is always time-saving—to have the student write up some of the more important aspects of his problem. These written statements can be put to good use in later conferences. Whenever it seems likely that considerable time will be needed to work out the problem, the clinician may ask for a written autobiography. For most students this is a genuinely interesting assignment. The autobiography need not be discouragingly long and detailed. The ones I have obtained have ranged in length for the most part from 1000 to 10,000 words, with the average around 5000. The life story should be written as fast as possible and without revision. It should ordinarily follow a simple chronological order, beginning wth a brief statement of family background, such information about birth and infancy as the student has available, and going on then to the earliest memories and proceeding year by year up to the time of writing.

There are many advantages in such an autobiography. It puts into written form a great deal of information about the case that might not otherwise be obtained at all. It gives the student an opportunity to review his problem in a more or less organized fashion. It can be done outside conference hours and so saves the clinician considerable time. It can be used as a basis for fruitful discussion of the problem. In using the autobiography usually the first thing to be done is to ask the case to fill in the gaps. In writing his life story he may have skipped from the eighth to the twelfth year, for example. Asking him to fill in this period may bring to light important facts that he has repressed. Such information may make other parts of the story, as written, much more meaningful. In any event, it throws considerable light on the case to compare what he has included in his written account with what he has left out of it. Having filled in the gaps with reasonable care, the clinician can then go over the autobiography with the student, tracing the development of important attitudes and behavior tendencies, considering how the student might have handled crucial situations differently and with different consequences, laying a groundwork of insight and perspective for a positive program of reeducation.

After retraining, most students are entirely willing to allow their autobiographies to be read by other cases, or even to be published in some instances, at least in discreetly disguised form. This makes it possible to accumulate a library or file of autobiographies which can be used for clinical purposes. (An autobiography, or any other material given in confidence by a student, is never to be passed on, or read by others, without his full permission.) In some cases much can be gained by having a student compare his own life story with the stories that have been written by others. Many cases assume either that their own problems are unique, that no one else suffers as they do, or that their experiences are universal, that everyone else has the same difficulties they have. The reading of several autobiographies helps to correct both of these misconceptions.

In addition to information obtained in interviews and through written statements, various kinds of data should be secured in some cases from other persons and by means of tests and special examinations. Because the relationship between clinician and student is a confidential one, however, it is not advisable to seek information from the student's parents, teachers, employers or friends without his definite permission and approval. In fact it is usually best to have him obtain such information himself whenever he can do it effectively. If he cannot do this without endangering his relationships with the other persons involved, there is usually serious question as to whether the clinician should attempt it either. One would want to be quite certain that the information sought is definitely essential. If it is, it should be obtained without arousing anyone's unjustified curiosity. Educational administrators do not seem always to appreciate the importance of professional ethics in such matters, and insist on systems of filing, reporting, and staff discussion that make it all but impossible for the clinician to maintain a properly confidential relationship with the case. There are times when the last person on earth to be questioned or informed about a student's adjustment difficulties would be his department head, or his dean. The situation in which I have worked has been all but ideal in this respect, and I feel that the value of this cannot possibly be overemphasized. Actually, it has seldom been necessary in the personality case work that I have done to go beyond the information furnished by the student himself, and when it has been necessary it has been possible to do so without betraying important confidences.

Tests and special examinations can usually be made available, of course, without placing the student at a personal disadvantage. Even so, there are disadvantages in a mere routine or unreflective use of tests, or in the unnecessary referral of a student to special clinics. From some textbooks one might gain the impression that certain tests are to be given to every case that is examined, or that a particular case history outline is to be used in interviewing everyone, or that every student who cannot get along with his roommate is to be seen by a psychiatrist, a neurologist, a psychometrist, and a social worker before any reeducational work is done with him. Such a policy obviously represents an intensional orientation and violates even the most elementary horse sense. There is no point in giving a test except for a definite reason. Just so there is no apparent sense in referring a student to a specialist unless you can tell the specialist just what information about the student you want him to give you. This was brought home to me very effectively one time several years ago when I referred a stutterer to a neurologist "on general principles" and got back a report which read in full: "Diagnosis—stuttering."

Generally speaking, there are four kinds of tests that have proved to be of some value, or that have seemed to me worth trying, in working with common adjustment cases: tests of intelligence, vocational aptitudes, scholastic achievement, and "personality." It is by no means necessary to give an intelligence test to every case of personality maladjustment, particularly when one is dealing with university students, but such tests are useful in certain cases. They are useful especially for evaluating the suitability of a student's goals and for appraising the reasons for scholastic difficulties. As was pointed out in Chapter I, the ideals or goals for which many students strive are more or less beyond their easy reach, and some-times it is important to be able to evaluate their goals in relation to their intelligence. It is practically never a question of determining whether or not a student is feeble-minded; you don't often need a test to determine that. But the test score may be a means of keeping a potentially first-rate salesman, for example, from becoming an incompetent lawyer. In other instances, it helps to find out whether a student is failing his courses because he lacks ability or for some other reason. Occasionally one also can make some use of a test score in determining whether a student's confusion in discussing his problem is due primarily to a low level of intelligence or to various semantic blockages. In the clinic with which I am associated, the intelligence tests most often used are the Stanford-Binet and Wechsler-Bellevue. In some cases the Otis Self-Administering Test of Mental Ability is satisfactory.

A vocational guidance bureau is available for the cases with whom I work, and the service it renders is quite often of great prac-tical value. A considerable proportion of maladjusted students either have vaguely defined vocational goals or else are straining to achieve professional levels for which they do not appear to have the necessary abilities. In a number of cases the vocational guidance bureau, as a result of its tests of aptitude and interest, has been able to give recommendations that have played a large part in bringing about more rational vocational planning and generally improved adjustment.

A service of similar value is provided by the rather comprehen-sive examination program for entering students. The program in-cludes a battery of tests covering the major subject-matter areas and the basic skills in reading, speech, writing, and mathematics. The data provided by these tests are of considerable value in evalu-ating the adjustment problems of certain students who are enrolled for courses for which they are not well fitted, or who are suffering from special handicaps for which they need remedial instruction, or who are simply not equipped for college work. The tests are equally useful in working with students who are shown to be capable of good university work but who lack proper motivation, or who are unable to utilize their abilities because of personal maladjustments.

There are many so-called personality tests. About all I can say of them conscientiously is that in my own experience they have not proved to be as fruitful as the other procedures discussed. However, many other clinicians speak highly of them. Those like the Bernreuter Personality Inventory, which can be easily scored by totaling the number of "maladjusted" responses to the questions contained in the test, yield a score which cannot always be interpreted very meaningfully without interviewing the person whose score it is. And if the person is properly interviewed, it often turns out that little or nothing additional is gained by giving him the test. Doubtless such tests have their uses, especially in surveying large groups for purposes of screening out the individuals who might seem to require special study. In individual case work, however, their value seems to be quite limited so far as I can judge.

Of the other personality tests, probably the projective type, particularly the Rorschach, is the most widely used. The test consists of ten ink blots, some of which are colored, and as each one is shown to the subject he is asked to tell what he sees in it. People see different things; some say the blots or parts of them look like animals, while others report human figures, various kinds of objects, etc. In some responses color is emphasized, in others form or shape. Some subjects notice small details, others do not, emphasizing, instead, the blot as a whole. Certain responses are more commonly given than others, and unusual responses are noted by the examiner. The test is scored and interpreted in various ways. Several hundred articles have been published in psychological journals about this test, and some of the authors make impressive claims as to their ability to "predict" an individual's "personality" from the test responses and with no other information about him. Other writers dispute such claims.

After all, such a test provides a means of observing a person's "unconscious" projections—provided, of course, that he does not know too much about the test. A general semanticist, or any thor-

oughly extensional person, if I may with some degree of justification judge by my own experience, would as a rule, I suppose, if
shown an ink blot, say that it resembles an ink blot. I have been
told that this would be an "abnormal" reponse. To refuse to "see
things" in the ink blots is, I understand, to behave in a pathological
manner. From a general semantics point of view, this is of considerable interest, and the problem appears to be very complex.
In the meantime, if one is given to indulging in unconscious projections, the Rorschach test probably reveals something about their
nature, and possibly their significance, particularly in the hands of
a skilled and wise examiner.

It is not to be missed of course, that unconscious projection can
be readily observed in a great variety of ways. It is by no means
limited to one's responses to ink blots. One of the important applications of general semantics to personality case work lies in the
relatively continuous observation of unconscious projection, particularly in language behavior. Most maladjusted persons show
some degree of unconscious projection in almost every remark they
make. Whether they show it in unusually significant ways when they
talk about ink blots is, I should judge, a clearly empirical question.
That they do exhibit it in significant ways when they talk about
themselves, or other people, or their surroundings, is hardly debatable. Certainly the principle of the Rorschach test appears to be
sound. It is the principle, however, the systematic observation of
projection, as well as the Rorschach test, as such, that is (to me)
to be emphasized.

There are, of course, many other types of tests, laboratory procedures, and observational techniques that can be used in studying
personality. Many of them are described in the books listed at the
end of this chapter. It is the purpose of this discussion not to
describe a comprehensive technology of personality investigation,
but only to indicate the procedures which I have found to be most
practical and useful in dealing with the types of cases I have known.
Actually, so far as such cases are concerned, the techniques so far
mentioned, taken all together, make up a rather ideal procedure.
It is seldom, indeed, that they would all be used in working with

a particular case. The extensional details of the case determine which ones are to be employed. The general principle is to make the examination and treatment no more complex or severe than the ailment—to leave the water at least no muddier than it was to begin with. Any technique is to be employed only for a clear purpose, only if there is a specific need for it.

A number of cases come for only one or two conferences, and for these, elaborate examination procedures are out of the question. There are many adjustment problems, at least among university students and speech clinic cases, that are for all practical purposes temporary: a crucial course examination to be hurdled, a disappointing love affair to be thought through, a death in the family to be accepted, a financial difficulty to be corrected or adjusted to, quarrels with roommates to be ironed out, vocational plans to be clarified, fairly definite adjustments to be made to some aspect of the campus social life, etc. With respect to such problems, the clinical job is little more than that of getting a reasonably adequate individual "over the hump." The clinician needs simply to have from the student a statement of the problem in its main essentials, in order that he may supply him with information that will make it clear what practical steps can be taken immediately to make the situation manageable. It is impressive how many adjustment difficulties of this temporary nature can be solved with a little relevant information that for some reason the student has never happened to run across.

An extensional point of view sharpens one's awareness of the little things that so often underlie seemingly big problems. The immediate causes of blue moods, worries, and animosities are frequently insignificant almost beyond belief. The clinical importance of this may be expressed by pointing out that one would not ordinarily shoot ducks with a howitzer. General semantics tends to make one concentrate to an unusual degree on the facts of the case, which means that it tends to make one reduce clinical procedures to a horse-sense minimum. At the same time, it also tends to make for necessary thoroughness. No available techniques are rejected on general principles, but any particular technique is evaluated in functional relationship to the actual facts of each specific case. Techniques are not "good" or "bad"; their purposes are specialized. This is to say that judgment has to be exercised, rather than rules of thumb, in their use and interpretation.

Finally, it is to be made clear that any clinician is properly obligated to refrain from trying to treat certain cases. It is for all practical purposes true that a case which is so complicated as to require a more extensive examination than has been described above is one that is appropriately to be referred to a psychiatrist. One of the ways in which a clinician discharges his responsibilities most effectively is that of not going beyond a first or second interview with any case whose maladjustment is of a grade of severity, or of a type, that he is not equipped to handle. Any responsible and trustworthy clinician works in cooperation with professional specialists who can do certain things better than he can, with whom he consults freely, and to whom he refers cases who can be served more safely and adequately by them.

DIAGNOSIS

In the preceding section on Examination, nothing has been said about a case history outline, because such an outline is used most significantly in summarizing a case for purposes of diagnosis. One keeps a case-history outline in mind while compiling information about an individual, but the information will be obtained more effectively if one follows not the prepared outline, but the leads that arise in the course of case conferences. Usually, before summarizing the case there will be a few loose ends of data to be obtained by direct questioning. In the course of my own experience I have gradually developed the following outline, which serves simply as a guide, to be condensed, elaborated, changed, and in general adapted to the facts and needs of any particular case.

OUTLINE FOR SUMMARIZING A PERSONALITY ADJUSTMENT CASE

I. Statement of the problem *as of now*, in terms of specific *alterable* features of
A. Behavior
1. Overt (predominantly non-verbal): readily observed behavior, and

also such reactions as shown in states of tension, pulse rate, etc., that are not outwardly obvious

2. Evaluative (predominantly verbal)

a. Outstanding specific evaluations (ideals or goals, attitudes, assumptions, beliefs, conflicts, fears, resentments, disappointments, etc.)

b. General methods of evaluating

(1) Intensional (orientation on basis of statements or suggestions of others who represent for the case the authority of age, prestige, "public opinion," tradition, etc.)

(a) Main individuals, books, organizations, or institutions representing such authority for the case

(b) Conflicting authorities

(2) Extensional (orientation on basis of direct experience, experience of others well reported and reasonably checked, authority of science broadly considered—as in Chapters II to IV— as against authority of age, precedence, etc.)

(a) Main specific experiences and sources of information taken into account by the case

B. Stimulating and limiting conditions

1. External to the person (semantic environment)

a. Home, school, neighborhood, specific groups and individuals, opportunities for earning money, working conditions, etc.

2. Internal

a. Characteristic evaluative reactions importantly related to those directly involved in the problem and which are described under A-2 above

b. Intelligence, fund of information, educational background, vocational preparation, specific skills or lack of them, etc.

c. Physiological and organic factors (health, vitality, specific physical handicaps and assets, etc.)

II. Data *relatable* to the problem as of now

A. History of the present problem

1. *Description* of the problem at its onset

2. Time and specific conditions of onset

3. Main alterations in problem as it has developed, and times and conditions of these alterations

4. Extent to which previously aggravating factors are operating *now*

B. Family background (*insofar as it can be related to problem as of now*)

1. Biological (physical characteristics of the family)

2. Semantic (roughly, social or symbolic): ideals, goals, beliefs, assumptions, attitudes, evaluative methods characteristic of the family

     3. Socio-economic background of the family
  C. Personal development of the case
     1. Birth and early development, diseases, etc.
     2. Educational experiences, formal and informal
     3. Experience record (work, hobbies, friendships, group memberships, travel, etc.)
  D. The case's own judgment as to the relation of all this (under II) to his present problem
III. Plan of retraining
  A. Specific alterations (in behavior or in stimulating and limiting conditions) to be attempted, in what order, and by means of what specific procedures
IV. Prognosis
  A. Alterations to be expected and how soon
  B. Alterations not likely to be achieved, with reasons

Sections I and II of this outline define for practical purposes the term *diagnosis* as it is here used. The major purpose of the diagnosis, as indicated by sections III and IV of the outline, is to provide a basis for a program of reeducation, and an estimate of the probable success of such a program.

Diagnosis is not viewed here as mere labeling. From a general semantics point of view, the less labeling in the usual sense the better. Not calling a person psychoneurotic, not classifying him as psychopathic, not labeling him as an introvert, gives that person less to live down. The point is that such labels, *as commonly interpreted,* discourage a case and unnerve him more than they enlighten and relieve him. Of course, after a student has had the opportunity to gain a reasonable understanding of himself and to acquire a set of semantic shock absorbers, so to speak, he can stand being called practically anything. After he has developed a fairly effective consciousness of abstracting, and the sense of humor that goes with it, "names can never hurt him." But to tell a worried, depressed individual that he is a psychopathic personality, or that his score on a personality test indicates a high degree of neuroticism, is scarcely different (to him) from telling him, in a less professional vernacular, that he is not acceptable. Any schoolboy knows that. Some day no doubt psychologists and psychiatrists will understand it, too. Some of them understand it now.

The quickest way to find out that a rose by some other name can take on a peculiar odor is to be the rose. I discovered this unforgettably, while I was still a student, the first time I spoke to an audience of speech teachers and speech correctionists. The chairman asked me to say a few words just after the main speaker, a psychiatrist, had concluded his remarks. And what the psychiatrist had elaborately told the audience was that stutterers were psychoneurotic. At that time—and particularly at that moment—I was a very severe stutterer. I tried to save the day, such as it was, by pointing out that if stutterers sometimes appeared, to some persons, to be neurotic, at least part of the reason was to be found in such speeches as the one we had just heard. After the kettle has been painted black, very few people can see their faces in it.

After all, we learned once that it was not mere quibbling over words to contend that a person should not be called a witch. We are learning the same lesson as we come to appreciate more and more clearly that calling a man a Negro is different from calling him a nigger. We are gradually becoming less naïve about our language. It is easier than it used to be for most of us to realize that words often help to create what they name. You can see how this works if you persist long enough in calling a child awkward, or stupid, or nervous. It should not be impossible for clinicians to learn that labeling a case with a derogatory, discouraging, fearful, socially handicapping name is one way, sometimes an appallingly effective way, to deepen and prolong his maladjustment.

This is not to say that a person should not be told the truth about himself, so far as anyone knows the truth; but nothing is gained by dressing the truth up like a scarecrow. The truth can be overstated. One way to overstate it is to express it by means of diagnostic labels that counteract their possibly enlightening effects by paralyzing the individual with dread and shame and unjustified convictions of inferiority and defectiveness. Most students simply do not understand what you are talking about when you call them neurotic—except that you are in some measure dooming them to lives of incompetence and ostracism. To insist, "But they *are* neurotic!" is simply to miss the point that matters most to them. It matters most to any responsible clinician, too. The elementary semantics involved in this has already been discussed under the heading of Evaluative Labeling in Chapter XII.

The outline given above indicates that personal maladjustment is to be diagnosed *descriptively*, in terms of behavior and the conditions that give rise to it or that limit it. The question is not "What type *is* the person?" or "What traits does he *have?*" or "What is *the* name of his maladjustment?" The important question is, "What does he do, in response to what, where, when, with what effects?" And in answering this question the emphasis is to be put on those features of the behavior, and of its conditions, that are alterable. The individual's problem is to be solved by bringing about changes in his behavior, or in the conditions under which it occurs. It is the chief purpose of the diagnosis to indicate what these changes may be. If labels are used at all, they should be used only to the extent that they help in achieving this purpose, to enable the individual to behave more adequately, or to change constructively the conditions under which he lives.

Some relevant descriptions of maladjusted behavior have been given in Chapter XIV; descriptions of more grave forms of maladjustment have been given in Chapter XIII. Symptoms of maladjustment have been described, throughout the book, in terms of various kinds of violations of the principles of general semantics: identifications, allness reactions, undelayed signal reactions, self-defensive tensions, unconditionality of response, semantic blockages, unrealistic goals, maladjustive language structure, etc. These need not be repeated here. It is sufficient simply to point out what is clearly indicated in the above outline: that maladjustment reduces to verbal and non-verbal aspects of *behavior*. As such it is to be understood with reference to the environments in which it occurs, and the developmental background and present capacities of the individual.

Before leaving the matter of diagnosis, a word should be said about the general notion of "cause." What "causes" a sense of inferiority? What "causes" stuttering? In many textbooks there is a tendency to answer such questions by listing several factors that might possibly produce a particular disorder. Lists of this kind tend to breed case-history outlines, and the indiscriminate use of such outlines sometimes leads to more or less meaningless statements of "cause." In summarizing a case the "cause" of maladjustment is sometimes stated by listing willy-nilly all the diseases the person has had, the falls and frights, change of schools, etc. Now by any reasonable standards the fact that a case had mumps at the age of four has no place in a statement of the "cause" of his maladjustment *unless its relationship to the maladjustment can be indicated*. In the outline given above, section II is headed "Data *relatable* to the problem as of now." If a case-history fact cannot be related to the present problem it has no place in the summarization of the case. Working with the notion of cause from this point of view sharpens one's sense of discrimination, clarifies diagnostic statements, and reduces waste motion in interviewing and in retraining.

Generally speaking, there are two ways in which a childhood experience, or any fact in a student's past, can be related to his present problem. First, it may involve a set of conditions that are still operating. A person's childhood attitudes toward his father may still be important because his father is still living and the attitudes are therefore being renewed or kept alive from one day to the next. Second, conditions may have changed radically but the student is identifying the present with the past, reacting, as it were, to a father who died ten years ago, or evaluating each new social situation as though it were like the one in which he was intensely embarrassed at the age of six. The clinician needs to know, then, the nature of the past situation or experience with which the case is identifying present situations or experiences. Unless the past is still living, so to speak, in the student's identifications, or unless factors that were once important are still operating, one should be very cautious and clear in stating that a past fact is a "cause" of a present difficulty.

The term *identifications* in the preceding sentence is not to be translated as *memories* or *associations*. Memories do not necessarily involve identifications. Moreover, to associate one fact or experience with another is not to identify them. Memories and associations are not necessarily maladjustive. On the contrary, they can be extremely adjustive in their effects. In order to associate two facts or experiences one has to recognize them as different from each other. To identify them is to act as if they were not different. Thus, an association contains the germ, at least, of adequate evaluation. And reliable memories, evaluated as memories, are a safeguard against identification. These distinctions are fundamental in the evaluation of case-history facts as "causes" of maladjustments.

Finally it is to be recognized that the outline presented here as a guide in diagnosing and summarizing a case is to be adapted to any student with which one works. In some cases it would need to be elaborated quite fully; additions might be required. In others, the problem will be so slight, or the time for dealing with it so short, that the outline in its entirety will prove to be much too inclusive. An extensional approach to the case will determine the actual use to be made of the outline.

TREATMENT

In section III of the summarization outline it is indicated that the plan of retraining is to be stated in terms of "specific alterations (in behavior or in stimulating and limiting conditions) to be attempted, in what order, and by means of what specific procedures." Everything that is done by way of examination and diagnosis is deliberately pointed toward such a plan of retraining. Thus, the maladjustment is investigated and diagnosed in terms of behavior and the conditions under which it occurs, with emphasis on the alterable features of both.

Since there are many kinds of alterations that may be attempted, one needs some sort of system or basis for planning a retraining program. The possible alterations need to be grouped somehow if one is to keep from becoming confused. One needs a scheme for making important relationships reasonably clear. Such a scheme or system should grow out of actual experience with cases. The attempts which I have made to organize my own clinical work have resulted in the gradual development of a practical formulation

which can best be presented by means of a diagram, like that in
Fig. 14. (This diagram was developed from the original form designed by Dr. Hartwell Scarbrough.)

In this diagram four general groups of factors are represented,
and each is shown as interrelated with all the others. The alterations that might be attempted in any case of personality retraining
can be considered in terms of these four factors. We may regard
the four factors as four general kinds of observations that can be

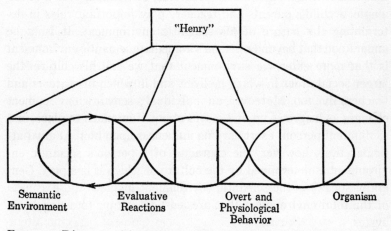

FIG. 14. Diagram of interrelationships among groups of factors to be
taken into account in personality retraining.

made of "Henry"—that is, of any individual. Or for certain purposes we may regard them as four ways of talking about "Henry"
—four special languages, as it were. The point of including "Henry"
in the diagram is to emphasize that any one factor or point of view
represented is partial and incomplete, and that all four, at least,
are required for anything resembling a relatively full account of a
case. It is not enough to describe a person merely in anatomical or
organic terms, or only in terms of physiology and overt behavior,
or of his evaluative reactions (attitudes, etc.), or of the semantic
influences that play upon him. Something important can be said
as a rule, but an adequate account cannot be given in any one of

these limited languages. All four of them are needed to talk meaningfully about "Henry." Moreover, they are all interrelated: what might be said in terms of one of them depends upon what there is to say in terms of the others. A few words about each will perhaps be helpful in showing how such a scheme can be put to practical use.

By *semantic environment* is meant the individual's environment of attitudes, beliefs, assumptions, values, ideals, standards, customs, knowledge, interests, conventions, institutions, etc. For example, a child's parents and teachers play important roles in determining the nature of his semantic environment. It is to be understood that beyond a person's immediate semantic environment is that more extensive environment that we call his culture, the larger social order in which he lives, and in which his parents and teachers live too. Moreover, an individual's semantic environment changes as he grows up and moves about from place to place, and as different persons exert varying influences upon him. At any particular time, however, the character of a person's semantic environment is determined by the culture of which it is a part. Generally speaking, the semantic environment includes those aspects of the total environment that are least important to a dog or an oyster.

In the case history outline given in the preceding section, factors of semantic environment are covered mainly in the following items:

I. A. 2. b.
      (1) (a) and (b)
      (2) (a)
  B. 1. a.
II. A. 2., 3., and 4.
  B. 2. and 3.
  C. 2. and 3.

Evaluative reactions include the individual's own attitudes, beliefs, assumptions, values, ideals, etc. Taken altogether, they may be regarded as that part of his semantic environment which the individual has interiorized, or adopted. They make up what are sometimes referred to as the psychological aspects of behavior, but calling them evaluative reactions tends to stress what is most important about them, at least from a general semantics point of view. For practical purposes, evaluative reactions may be regarded as predominantly verbal. At least, they are to be observed largely in the individual's language behavior.

In the case history outline, evaluative reactions are included under:

I. A. 2.
B. 2. a and b.

II. A. 1. and 3.
C. 2. and 3.
D.

Under the heading of *overt and physiological behavior* we include generally what the person does—his predominantly nonverbal behavior. We include, as overt behavior, his activities in the way of work or recreation; his characteristic posture, manner of walking and moving about; his mannerisms, gestures, facial expressions, voice quality; his laughter or lack of it; his avoidance of certain social situations, etc. As physiological behavior we include such things as states of tension, important characteristics of pulse rate and heart action, glandular functions, digestive disturbances, headaches, illnesses, etc.

The outline covers these items under:

I. A. 1.
B. 2. c.

II. A. (possibly)
C. 1.

By *organism* is meant not a static unchanging organic structure, but the relatively invariant relationships involved in the processes of growth and deterioration. In the living organism there is no fine line between "physiology" and "anatomy." Roughly speaking, by physiological behavior we mean those bodily changes that can be observed from moment to moment; by the organism we mean those bodily characteristics which change so slowly that from one day, or week, or month, to the next they seem to remain constant.

Factors under this heading are included in the outline under:

I. B. c.

II. A. (possibly)
B. 1.
C. 1.

In the next chapter the specific problem of stuttering will be discussed from a clinical point of view in terms of these four factors. In this way the practical application of what is represented by the above diagram will be made more evident. In the present chapter discussion will be limited to more general considerations.

There are several points to be made with respect to the diagram. These points may best be made, perhaps, by discussing some of the important differences between this way of formulating personality adjustment problems and the main traditional ways of formulating them. For practical purposes, we may say that there are three other formulations to be contrasted with this one. They may be represented in the following ways:

A. Organism > Behavior. Behavior is caused by the organism. It is, according to this view, simply an expression of the constitutional or hereditary characteristics of the person. This formula provides for only a one-way relationship: the organism affects behavior, but behavior does not affect the organism. In other words, Henry gets his sociability from his father's side of the family, his thrift he inherits from his mother, but Henry's own experiences have no causal significance. Or your organism determines how gracefully you dance, but dancing a great deal and with good instruction will not affect your organism, according to this theory. This is the oldest theory of behavior that we have. It was essentially the theory advanced by Aristotle. It is Popeye's point of view: "I yam what I yam." It is widely held, even today. Perhaps most people still "explain" their own behavior and that of their associates by saying in one way or another that it is due to "human nature." In other words, according to this theory, people behave as they do because they were "born that way." An appalling number of the cases with whom I have worked have expressed in all seriousness the view that their maladjustments were "inherited," or were at least due to "something physical."

Such a theory reduces personality reeducation to whatever might be accomplished by surgery, pills, and the careful selection of one's grandparents. In terms of it, about all the clinician can do is to advise the maladjusted individual to make the best of the bad bargain that his parents made with Fate, and to be glad it wasn't worse. The theory may not be utterly false, but it is false enough to be almost utterly impractical. This is a good thing to remember the next time you hear some "hardheaded, practical" sage proclaiming through his spacious nose the ancient "wisdom" that you can't change human nature.

In our diagram the influences of the organism on behavior are provided for, but with two important conditions. The first is that the organism is regarded as a changing and changeable factor. The other is that the relationship between the organism and the other factors included in the diagram is not a one-way affair. The organism not only affects but is also affected by the other factors.

B. Environment > Organism > Behavior. This is a more modern theory of behavior, but it retains in large measure the flaws of the older. It is, in fact, the same as the older theory, with one exception. This is that another factor has been added, but it has been added in such a way that it doesn't make a great deal of difference. For hundreds of years it has been suspected by some observers that a satisfactory explanation of human behavior cannot be given in terms of the organism alone. John Locke, Rousseau, and many others in more recent times have given clear expression to this conviction, and have emphasized more or less the influence of a person's environment upon his development. By most of those who voiced this view, however, and by most laymen today who subscribe to it, it is assumed apparently that the influence of environment is very greatly limited. After all, so the theory seems to go, the organism does determine behavior, and the organism can be modified only to a slight degree by environmental forces. Success in spite of "bad" surroundings and failure in spite of "good" ones are to be accounted for by the easy verbalism that blood will tell.

Two other points are to be noted about this theory. One is that it involves, as does the older one, only a one-way relationship: the environment can in some measure affect the organism, the organism determines behavior, but what an individual does, the experiences he has, the training he receives, etc., do not react back on the other factors. This feature of the theory makes it most unsatisfactory, of course, as a basis for personality reeducation. The other point to be noted is that most people who talk in terms of this theory seem not to be very clear on what they mean by environment. One might well get the impression from many writers that, insofar as environment is defined, its most important aspects are to be found in disease bacteria, unsanitary conditions, smoke-laden air, unsightly slums, outmoded plumbing, and the like. Such things are important, of course. So far as personality adjustment is concerned, however, semantic aspects of environment appear to be even more important. As a matter of fact, sanitation, adequate housing, etc., are simply the effects of semantic forces prevalent in a community or in a culture. In turn, these effects have a desirable semantic influence, but the point is that this interrelationship between human behavior and human environments is not well indicated by this theory. One of the basic reasons for this defect of the theory would seem to be that the term *environment* is not adequately defined.

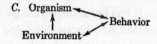

This is a still more modern theory. In one form or another it is held by most psychologists and psychiatrists, who differ among themselves chiefly in the relative emphasis which they give to the various factors and relationships involved in the theory, or in the way in which they define the various factors. With the work of Freud, Pavlov, Thorndike, Lewin, Hull, Adolf Meyer, and other psychologists during the past fifty years or so, and especially in more recent years, there has come a growing realization that the older theories of behavior were exceedingly undeveloped. Considerable advances have been made, and are constantly being made, in clarifying the basic terms used in describing and explaining behavior, and in organizing our knowledge about it. Along with these advances has gone an increased effectiveness of clinical methods of dealing with personality problems. A detailed discussion of these advances, except as they are treated elsewhere in this book, would carry us far afield, however. It is enough for our present purposes to indicate, as we have done at the head of this paragraph, the essential features of a type of theory which may be regarded as intermediate between the older ways of looking at behavior and the formulation diagramed a few pages back (Fig. 14).

(Throughout this discussion I have used the word *theory* loosely and with considerable reluctance. I have used it mainly to avoid awkward forms of expression. The four schemes presented might better be regarded as patterns or forms—skeleton structures—for molding or constructing a great variety of specific theories. They differ in the number of factors each involves, and the way in which the factors are assumed to be related. They differ also in the way in which the factors are defined.)

In applying the point of view that has been diagramed to personality case work, the program of retraining is planned with reference to the alterations that might be attempted with respect to each of the four factors represented in the diagram. The following discussion—as well as that concerning the treatment of stuttering in the next chapter—will follow this pattern.

Semantic Environment. Children with behavior problems are sometimes dealt with by removing them from their own homes and placing them in foster homes, or in special schools or institutions. This is an extreme example of a change of semantic environment. Residential schools and institutions for the crippled, blind, deaf, gravely maladjusted, etc., are brick-and-steel evidence that we do in some measure understand the importance of semantic environment—or at least environment—in relation to behavior. Brick-and-steel—because sometimes the way in which such schools and institutions are run indicates a profound lack of appreciation of semantic factors. In some instances, however, these factors are taken into account quite effectively in institutional and school policy.

Other evidence of our recognition of the importance of semantic environment is to be seen in our system of public schools, trade schools, colleges and universities, hospitals, clinics, housing projects, art galleries, concert halls, theaters, libraries, publications, radio broadcasting facilities, etc. They may not always be used "in the public interest," but the very fact that we jealously maintain them testifies to the importance we place on controlling somehow the semantic influences that affect our lives.

In personality reeducation of the sort we are discussing, the changes in semantic environment that turn out to be practical tend to fall into the two main groups. First, there are those that can be brought about by making available to the case the best that his environment has to offer. That is to say, some direction can be given to the semantic influences playing upon the person by referring him appropriately to clinics, vocational counselors, and the like; by getting him enrolled in schools or in specific courses suited to his needs; by acquainting him with organizations in which he can find opportunities for self-development and socially useful activity; by introducing him to books, magazines, music, art, etc., from which he may benefit; by placing him in contact with individuals whose influence on him would be beneficial; by helping him find satisfying employment, recreational facilities, social activities, leisure-time interests, etc. It is a matter not of changing the environment, as such, but of bringing the case more effectively into contact with certain of its aspects. This is a very important part of personality reeducation in many of the cases of the general type with which I am familiar. It amounts to setting up the opportunities that make reeducation possible.

The other main type of change in semantic environment consists in the reeducation of the persons who are associated in important ways with the case. In discussing examination procedures we have already emphasized the importance of professional ethics—of not violating confidences—in discussing a case with other people.

Aside from the fact that a child's parents and teachers might be consulted and advised without the child's knowledge, the clinician should not discuss matters that are confidential, or enlist the co-operation of other persons, without the knowledge and permission of the case. One must be particularly conscientious in this respect in dealing with husbands and wives.

In connection with examination procedures it was pointed out that it is usually preferable to have the case himself speak to any outside persons who need to be consulted. This is even more important in the retraining phase of the program, because everything possible should be done to help the student develop more self-sufficiency, more ability to deal with his own problems. Only for good reason should the clinician speak for the student in enlisting the cooperation of friends, fraternity brothers, instructors, employers, parents, etc. The student should speak for himself, and thereby cultivate his self-assurance by taking responsibility as much as possible for his social adjustments. Becoming a mature person is in no small part a matter of learning by direct experience that you can in a measure create your own semantic environment and control the attitudes and reactions of other people toward you. The student should be given ample opportunity to learn this—and leading him around by the hand unnecessarily and making him feel that he cannot very well get along without you will go far to keep him from learning it.

There are, however, two things that a clinician can do for the student without weakening his self-reliance. The first is to give technical information, which he cannot be expected to convey as well as it must sometimes be conveyed, to his parents, teachers, or other persons who should have it. This is particularly necessary when the adjustment problem is complicated by some special handicap, such as a hearing loss, speech defect, or some crippling condition. In such a case the clinician has the responsibility of seeing to it that the people most concerned, those who exert the greatest influence on the student, understand as clearly as possible the nature and significance of the special handicap and how it may best be dealt with. There are usually advantages, moreover, in having the student himself sit in on the conferences with parents and others, so that he too may profit from the explanations given and feel the atmosphere of interest and cooperation that is ordinarily present in such conferences.

In the second place, the clinician can arrange classes or group meetings for many types of students. So-called group therapy has become fairly common in work with personal adjustment cases. In some forms, such as the psychodrama technique of Moreno, it is quite elaborate. In a way that is less spectacular perhaps, but at least equally effective so far as I can judge, group therapy has been developed by Professor Bryng Bryngelson in his course in speech hygiene at the University of Minnesota. A few words about this course will help to clarify what is meant by group therapy. In Professor Bryngelson's course there are usually from twenty-five to thirty students, and their chief reason for being there is that they have various kinds of adjustment problems. During the first nine or ten meetings of the class Professor Bryngelson lectures about personality, gives the students a language for talking effectively about their difficulties, and creates the atmosphere of scientific honesty which is so essential in this type of group work. Then Professor Bryngelson tells his own life story, discussing himself and his personal problems frankly and adequately.

This sets the stage for the students' participation in the course. They begin to volunteer to tell their own stories. Before they do this they have written their autobiographies, but these have been submitted confidentially to the instructor. Now each tells the group what he has written, usually elaborating it in considerable detail. By the time three or four have done this, the rest are ready to follow, and over a period of several years no student has ever refused to participate. A few have overcome their reluctance to speak only with great difficulty, but even they have come through eventually.

One of the interesting features of the course is that in talking about themselves before the class, the students speak for part of the time before a full-length mirror, describing themselves as frankly and accurately as they can, commenting on any blemishes or defects and discussing their feelings about them and the part which they have played in their maladjustments.

After a student has talked about himself, told his life story, and discussed his adjustment difficulties, the other members of the group ask questions, make comments, offer suggestions—and finally take their turn on the platform. The instructor stays in the background for the most part, but is present to answer questions, offer constructive criticisms, provide encouragement, and in general stimulate group morale.

In such a situation the members of the group get to know one another unusually well. Many of them make their first close and satisfying friendships during the course. Incidentally, at the last meeting of the class each year there is a banquet attended by former students as well as those who are just completing the course. This is no pink tea, "And how do you do" affair. It is not a "testimonial dinner." It has most of the features of a family reunion —except the jealousies, resentments, and restraints. It is a meeting of people who are not afraid of hurting each other's feelings, a meeting in which the toes that are stepped on have no corns on them. This annual get-together, the class meetings, the personal associations among members of the group, all serve to reinforce, and to make extensional in various ways, the reevaluations and adjustments learned through the more formal aspects of the course. This sort of group therapy, then, is more than just a timesaving device, a way of giving thirty persons what would otherwise be given only to one in the same period of time. What each of the thirty gets is rather more than could be given to him alone and in isolation from the group. Group therapy provides an on-the-spot opportunity to put to practical social use the adjustment principles being learned. This means that it provides for learning by doing. Moreover, for each student the learning is intensified through direct observation of—and active participation in—the adjustment processes of the other members of the group.

In the work which I have done (aside from some exploratory work with the psychodrama technique) the group therapy principle has been used to some degree in two ways. In the first place,

I have attempted to conduct my classes in clinical psychology, and particularly in general semantics, so as to provide a limited measure of group therapy effect. The word *limited* needs some emphasis, for whether with justification or not I have exercised considerable restraint out of deference to what I judge to be the social realities of a state university. (Professor Bryngelson works with adult evening classes, which are semantically rather different from those made up of regular university students living under ordinary campus conditions.) For the most part, students enroll for these courses for academic as well as, or rather than, personal reasons. The classes are relatively large. All of which apparently adds up to the fact that the opportunities for thoroughgoing group therapy in such courses are decidedly limited.

There are some opportunities, however, and they are exploited as far as possible. The students are given information about maladjustment in terms which they can rather easily relate to their own experiences and those of their acquaintances. Since they are given this information while they are sitting together in the same room, a certain amount of "group feeling" and mutual understanding is built up. In some measure each student comes to realize that the lectures and readings are about him—and his classmates. The effect of this carries over more or less into the bull sessions and conversations outside class hours, in which some degree of group therapy spontaneously takes place.

This effect is reinforced by the discussion of specific cases in class lectures. While this discussion is sufficiently discreet from the point of view of professional ethics, nevertheless it can be made effectively pointed. It is the old technique of giving a person insight into his own maladjustments by telling him about some other individual who closely resembles him. Doing this in a group situation seems usually to heighten its effect. Moreover, by discussing judiciously but with frankness his own adjustment problems, the instructor can demonstrate more or less effectively an aspect of adjustment which some of the students can put to their own uses under conditions which they find to be suitable. In some instances class discussions provoke rather significant self-evaluations which of course intensify the group therapy effects.

The second way in which I have been able, under university conditions, to provide some measure of group therapy has been limited almost entirely to work with stutterers. For several years the practice has been followed of holding two or three group meetings each week during the school year for stutterers attending the speech clinic. These meetings are used for several purposes, including speaking practice, demonstration of remedial techniques, etc. One of the purposes is that of personality reeducation, and in the relatively small group, in which the members share more or less the same adjustment problems, it is possible to use a group therapy approach rather more than in the larger classes referred to above. The approach involves mainly lectures specifically concerned with the adjustment problems of stutterers, abundantly illustrated with examples drawn from the personal experiences of the students and of the instructor; discussion by the stutterers themselves of their day-to-day problems in meeting particular speech situations, of their own attitudes and behavior tendencies, of their "successes" and "failures" in carrying out their retraining programs.

One interesting feature of these group meetings is the "heckle session" in which one stutterer speaks while the others heckle him by doing such things as trying to get him to change the subject, questioning him about what he is saying or about other things, kidding him, and telling him—sometimes quite frankly—what they consider his strong and weak points to be. The heckle session is quite beneficial to most students in helping them reduce signal reactions and develop poise "under fire."

Another technique that has been found to be of value is the "group interview." One stutterer takes the platform and the other members of the group ask him questions. The questions asked are more or less personal and are designed to give the stutterer an opportunity to bring his problems out into the open by means of the answers he gives. There is a strict rule, however, that allows him to decline to answer any question that he does not feel free or ready to discuss, and he knows he will not be criticized in any way for taking refuge in this rule. Because such a rule is enforced, the speaker is under the obligation to be as frank as possible in the answers he does give. In actual practice there is a tendency for the questioners to exercise more restraint than the one being interviewed, so that very few questions go unanswered. One of the advantages of this technique is that it can be pitched at any desired level of frankness and intimacy, and so can be easily adapted to the person being interviewed. It is especially useful in the first meetings of a group, because it allows the members of the group to become acquainted with each other's problems gradually. As the interviews are continued from meeting to meeting, the group members get to know each other better and better and the problems discussed become more and more significant. Ultimately a very considerable group therapy effect can be brought about.

Doubtless this sort of group work could be done as well with students who have problems other than stuttering. A group should probably contain at least six and not more than thirty, preferably twenty or less. In the work with stutterers it has been found that the group meetings are a valuable supplement to the individual conferences, and no doubt this would ordinarily prove true in working with many other types of cases also.

As has been said then, changes in semantic environment reduce largely to those that can be brought about by making available to the student those opportunities for readjustment that his environment has to offer, and by informing and attempting to alter the attitudes of those persons with whom the student is more or less closely associated. So far as possible, the student himself should undertake to reeducate and inform his associates in ways that will further his adjustment to them, but the clinician can do at least two things in this connection. He can provide the student's parents, teachers, and other close associates with technical information and explanations. He can provide, so far as may be practical, group therapy.

This summarizes in large measure what can be done in altering the semantic environment, at least in the type of personality reedu-

cation which is here being considered. To be added to this is mainly
the suggestion that the case be encouraged to get acquainted with
other people, to be responsive to the friendly approaches of others,
to form friendships. This does not mean that he should be made
into a jolly, shoulder-patting extrovert, or a professional joiner of
clubs, or a chronic leader of community singing; but there are advantages in eliminating, or reducing, the student's identifications
and semantic blockages in evaluating other people and in reacting
to them. And in order to do this it is definitely helpful, in some
respects essential, that he not avoid the company of other people,
that he take some initiative, in fact, in getting to know them and
in getting them to know himself better. It is simply a matter of being
extensional in evaluating one's semantic environment and in responding to it.

From the clinician's point of view, two more points need some
emphasis. One is that he, the clinician, is an extremely important,
in some ways the most important, factor in the student's semantic
environment. Whether or not he tries to be or wants to be, he is a
living example, in the eyes of the case, of personal adjustment.
This simple fact makes some clinicians seem quite incongruous.
When the discrepancy between what the clinician preaches and
what he himself practices is sufficiently great, what he preaches is
likely to be quite ineffectual. The general everyday behavior of
the clinician tends to determine his effectiveness as much as or
more than the way he lectures or his manner of conducting an
interview. The sanity that is expected of him is sometimes a strain,
especially in view of the fact that his own semantic environment is
by no means always conducive to the good sense that seems to be
required of him. For such reasons, it is to be sufficiently appreciated
that the clinician has need himself of the adjustment that he tries
to help others acquire.

The other point is that the clinician, if he is to make his left hand
support what his right is doing, has the responsibility of taking an
active interest in those community and cultural changes that hold
some degree of promise for bringing about more adequate conditions for human living. He has the responsibility, for example, of

doing what he can to reduce racial prejudice, class conflicts, signal reactions toward "the handicapped," and other evidences of semantic blockage that make homes, schools, and communities maladjustive in their effects. Legislation, socio-economic programs, educational reforms, publications, and organizations designed to make it possible for individuals to live with themselves and with each other more fruitfully than they otherwise could, deserve the support of any clinician who is more than a five-dollar-an-hour nosey body. To return to a phrase used before in this book, a clinician is obligated by the logic of his interests to do more than merely busy himself at the drainpipe of civilization. Writing in the journal *Ethics* (Vol. 54, 1943, pp. 14–28), Professor S. A. Nock has crystallized the issue in these words: ". . . consider how many people there are who live impeccable lives and devote honorably won fortunes to the alleviation of human suffering and who have yet passionately upheld an anachronistic scheme of society that makes such human suffering inevitable." Any clinician who permits himself to be included in the vast company indicted by Professor Nock runs the absurd risk of having his total effort produce a net loss from a broad social point of view.

Evaluative Reactions.   Personal maladjustments tend to become ingrown. That is, the maladjusted individual becomes, as a rule,

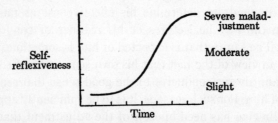

FIG. 15. Schematic representation of the self-reflexive character of personal maladjustment: the maladjusted person's tendency to respond less and less to external realities and more and more on the basis of his own misevaluations.

more and more difficult to help as time goes on. His attitudes become more firmly established, his behavior patterns more rigidly set. His effect on himself becomes increasingly detrimental. In other words, nothing fails like failure: maladjustment is self-reflexive. (See Fig. 15.)

To put it simply, changes made in a person's semantic environment are effective in producing changes in adjustment to the extent that the person responds to them. A practical test of the severity of the individual's maladjustment lies precisely in the degree to which he does respond to such environmental changes. Mild cases are, in an important sense, those for whom it is sufficient to alter relevant conditions: to supply needed information, to bring about a change of attitude or policy on the part of persons whose influence on the individual is important, to provide vocational guidance, and to effect other changes of the kinds discussed in the preceding section. Severe cases are those who persist in their disabling misevaluations and corresponding behavior difficulties in spite of such changes in semantic environment. The major maladjustments described in Chapter XIII are illustrative. Such cases would ordinarily be referred to a psychiatrist.

Between these extremes there is a large group who can benefit significantly from environmental alterations provided they are given suitable retraining in the basic processes of evaluation. It is this group, together with the milder cases already mentioned, that concern us here. The milder cases too, of course, stand to gain from evaluational retraining. It is this sort of retraining that we shall now discuss, and we can do this most effectively in terms of a diagram (Fig. 16).

We are particularly concerned in this section with the levels of general orientation and specific evaluations, as represented by M-1 and A-1, and M-2, and A-2, in Fig. 16. What Fig. 16 is designed to indicate can be summarized briefly in this way: Maladjustive behavior in its specific forms (particular overt reactions, tensions, and other physiological conditions) may be viewed as the expression of specific evaluations (attitudes, assumptions, beliefs, ideals, etc.). But these specific evaluations in turn are determined by the individual's general orientation (basic language structure, evaluational methods, etc.). Likewise, adjustive reactions (A-3) follow from adjustive evaluations (A–2), which in turn follow from an adjustive general orientation (A–1).

Now, one of the important things that this diagram is designed to show is the fact that personality retraining methods can be classified for practical purposes in terms of the levels and relationships represented by the lines *z, x,* and *a.* Consider, for example, how much effort is expended by parents and teachers in the attempt, usually futile and frustrating, to change maladjustive behavior (M–3) into adjustive behavior (A–3) directly and by fiat, so to speak, without regard to the evaluations and general orientation responsible for the behavior. This sort of retraining is represented

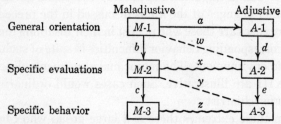

FIG. 16.   Schematic diagram of levels of maladjustive and adjustive reaction and the relationships among them. (Modified from Korzybski and Kendig, "Foreword," in *A Theory of Meaning Analyzed,* by Pollock, Spaulding, and Read. General Semantics Monographs, III. Chicago: Institute of General Semantics, 1942.)

by the wavy line *z.* It is generally ineffective for the simple reason, indicated by the broken line *y,* that adjustive behavior (A–3) does not tend to follow from misevaluations (M–2). It is responsible for a tremendous amount of the turmoil and ill will, distrust and desperation, that transform little red schoolhouses into torture chambers and give the lie to "home sweet home." The wavy line *z* stands for the nagging, whipping, scolding, the standing of children in corners, the orders to be obeyed without question, unexplained punishments and rewards, the do-as-I-say-and-don't-talk-back dog-training indulged in by authoritarian elders, supervisors, and "advisers" who make "man's inhumanity to man" tragically more than a literary quotation. Animal trainers apparently find this method indispensable. It appears to have little value in the home, school, or clinic.

Another method, rather more enlightened, is represented by the wavy line *x:* the attempt to change behavior by changing the *specific* attitudes, assumptions, motives, goals, etc., responsible for the behavior. This would appear to be the most commonly used type of personality retraining in modern clinics, and something like it is to be found in relatively enlightened homes and progressive schools. It is as effective as it sometimes is because, as shown by the line *e,* adjustive evaluations tend to be expressed in adjustive reactions. It is as ineffective as it rather frequently seems to be because, as shown by the broken line *w,* a maladjustive general orientation—largely disregarded in this type of training—does not tend to produce adjustive evaluations. One of the most common complaints of parents, teachers, and clinicians is: "I've told him and told him, I've explained over and over again how his attitudes are wrong, his motives are at fault, he's irresponsible, he doesn't think things through—I've told him and told him—and nothing happens. Sometimes I think what he needs is some good old-fashioned discipline!"

Instead of reverting to "good old-fashioned discipline," however (which is represented by wavy line *z*), we can progress to the method of retraining indicated by line *a.* It is in this method and on this level that general semantics most distinctively operates. Consciousness of abstracting, the main objective of general semantics, includes an effective awareness of the relationships between behavior, specific evaluations, and general orientation. Training in general semantics affects chiefly the factors of language structure, the mechanisms of projection and of evaluation generally. The methods of personality retraining which follow from the principles of general semantics are designed, in terms of Fig. 16, to bring about:

1. A clear statement of maladjustment, in any particular case, in terms of specific behavior (M–3). A recognition of changes to be made in this behavior in order to make it more adequate (A–3).

2. An understanding of the maladjustive evaluations (M–2) that

tend to give rise to this behavior. A recognition of changes to be made in these evaluations in order to make them more adjustive (A-2).

3. An appreciation of the general orientation (M-1), particularly in terms of language structure and the process of abstracting, underlying specific misevaluations. Cultivation of a more adequate orientation (A-1) that will make more fully possible the revised evaluations (A-2) needed for more adjustive behavior (A-3).

The particular techniques employed are clearly directed to these objectives. In this section we are concerned chiefly with those which are designed to bring about changes from M-1 to A-1, and so from M-2 to A-2. The techniques described in Chapter X, the extensional devices, delayed reaction, and semantic relaxation, are of particular interest. Actually of course, these techniques may be practiced on the behavior level (A-3), as we shall see in the next section, but in the present connection it is important to emphasize that they serve to demonstrate and reinforce the principles upon which they are based. It is also to be stressed that without a knowledge of these principles, one's practice of the techniques is likely to be merely a matter of going through motions that mean little and change one's adjustment slightly if at all. Consequently the extensional devices, delayed reaction, and semantic relaxation are to be used, first of all, to demonstrate general principles; and this use of them is to be supplemented by sufficient discussion of the bases and implications of the principles. The sort of discussion meant here is of the type presented in this book in Chapters II through IX, particularly V through IX. It covers the essentials of scientific orientation (A-1) as contrasted with prescientific orientation (M-1), and so of the premises of non-identity, non-allness, and self-reflexiveness; the process of abstracting, and the principles of probability, conditionality, and symbol reaction.

This may tend to sound as though personality reeducation were a very "intellectual" and complicated matter. Properly adapted to the individual, it may be as simple or as thoroughgoing as circumstances require, or allow. As has already been indicated, many adjustment problems are so simple or so temporary that, from a practical point of view, it is hardly sensible in dealing with them to go beyond suggesting a few changes in behavior and attitude, and helping to alter conditions in such a way as to make these suggestions useful. Sometimes a little reading material—such as Chapter I of this book—can be recommended in order to make the suggestions more meaningful. In some cases a course in personality adjustment or general semantics will prove beneficial. In fact, there are a large number of cases who can best be handled in such a course, supplemented by a few individual conferences. One of the reasons for writing this book has been to provide a text that might help to make courses in general semantics, or the psychology of adjustment, useful in this connection, and to provide substantial reading material for use in individual case work.

Cases differ in the amount of general semantics instruction they need and the amount they can grasp and use effectively. To some individuals general semantics must be presented slowly and in very simple terms, not only because they are lacking in intelligence or have serious semantic blockages, but also because it may prove to be more or less upsetting to them. To have certain beliefs and attitudes seriously challenged, or to become too suddenly aware of certain identifications, can be rather disturbing. For this reason any responsible clinician will be constantly on the alert for any disquieting effects of his instruction. He will give reassurances and allow ample time for readjustments as circumstances require. Instruction must be adapted to the individual, not only as to kind but also as to amount and rate. This holds, of course, whether the clinician is a general semanticist or not.

Changing a student's evaluations is rarely achieved by arguing with him. Since many students—and many clinicians, too—are inclined to argue, however, it is essential to know that there are in general two ways to deal with an argument. One way is to get into it. This is not good clinical technique. The other way is to analyze it. By doing this skillfully one can lead the case to examine his own attitudes, beliefs, goals, etc., and to understand them more fully. One can give him a language for talking about his own language—for evaluating his own evaluations. This is done by acquainting him with at least the following:

1. One-valued, two-valued, multi-valued, and infinite-valued language structures. The difference between either-or statements of evaluation and evaluations made in terms of degrees of difference, as on a continuum or graduated scale. Thus, not "success" or "failure," but degrees of difference between expectation and achievement.

2. Certainty versus probability. Absolute versus relative evaluations. The principle that what is observed is a joint product of the observer and the observed, that what is known represents a relationship between the knower and the knowable. The mechanisms of projection. To-me-ness. Subject-predicate statements versus (a) statements of conscious projection and (b) behavioral, actional, and conditional statements of structural relationship in terms of space-time order. The extensional sense of quotes and hyphens.

3. Orientation in terms of process differences versus constancy identity. The extensional sense of indexes, dates, and *etcetera*'s. The mechanisms of identification and allness. Symbol reaction versus signal reaction.

4. Intensional versus extensional orientation. The extensional and operational basis of the vagueness-clarity continuum. Meaningless questions and statements. Non-verbal and verbal levels of abstraction. Silent abstracting (see Assignment No. 12, Semantic Exercises). The role of inferential data (highest inference levels and submicroscopic level) in the process of abstracting. The essentials of problem formulation and scientific method. An everyday working understanding of what is meant by the experimental or extensional checking of attitudes, assumptions, and beliefs. Dead-level abstracting. Self-reflexiveness. Time-binding. Adjustment as adjustments.

5. The relation of personality structure to culture structure and semantic environment. The role of language structure in this relationship. The relationships involving semantic environment, evaluative reactions, overt behavior and physiological conditions, and

the organism (Fig. 14). Relationships among the levels of behavior, evaluations, and general orientation (Fig. 16).

These fundamentals are to be presented not "in the abstract" but so far as possible, in direct relation to the student's own behavior, evaluations, and basic orientation. They are to be presented in such a way as to provide him with a language for talking about *his* language, a basis for evaluating *his* evaluations, a means of understanding *his* maladjustive reactions. They should add up to an adjustive general orientation for him, pointing the way to adjustive attitudes and reactions meaningful in relation to his own particular needs and situations. That is why, in the section on Examination, emphasis was placed on the importance of relevant detail concerning the alterable features of the student's behavior, history, and present circumstances.

In terms of practical procedure, then, a student's specific attitudes, beliefs, etc., are not to be disputed. Rather they are to be discussed in terms of the fundamentals summarized above. The student is to be trained to recognize the degree to which his evaluations are two-valued, involve identification, unconscious projection, lead to signal reactions, etc. In such terms he can learn to see the possibility of changes in his basic orientation—and so in his specific attitudes, assumptions, etc., and in his reactions to particular situations. In this way personality reeducation can be made to proceed, as shown in Fig. 16, from M–1 to A–1 to A–2 to A–3. This sort of reeducation tends to make not only for the permanent elimination of specific maladjustments, but also for a *generalization* of the adjustive process. Not only are present difficulties dealt with, but possible future troubles are to an important degree forestalled.

In the next chapter some of the specific misevaluations of stutterers are discussed and certain of the basic factors related to them are indicated. Statements made there will serve to illustrate, in terms of practical details, a semantic approach to the evaluative aspects of maladjustment. Further clarification will.be provided in the section that follows immediately.

Overt Behavior and Physiological Conditions. Many of the statements that might be made here have already been made in Chapter X. The devices and techniques described there were classified under three headings: the extensional devices (indexes, dates, *etcetera*'s, quotes, hyphens, and special terms), delayed reaction, and semantic relaxation. These provide some of the more practical ways of applying the general semantics principles in actual situations and from moment to moment in daily life. There are, in addition to these three, a variety of other techniques of effecting changes in behavior, of which two are particularly important. One is that of deliberately testing specific assumptions by making definite *observations* of one's own behavior—or the behavior of others—and of its consequences under stated conditions. The stutterer who insists that other people laugh at him, for example, can profitably be set to work collecting tally marks—actually counting the number of people who do and who do not laugh at him. In the bargain he will have to define *laugh* and *at him,* and this in itself will be very advantageous. The other technique is that of deliberately trying out ways of behaving that would seem to express adequate evaluations. In *Winnie the Pooh,* Rabbit is met one day by Pooh Bear who says, "Hallo, Rabbit, is that you?" and Rabbit replies, "Let's pretend it isn't and see what happens." That expresses the general idea. Let's pretend we like spinach and see what happens. Let's pretend the next "damyankee" we meet is not a "damyankee" and see what comes of it. Let's pretend the boss is not our sworn enemy and see if it makes any difference. In other words, let's figure out as best we can how a well-adjusted person would behave and then, as an experiment, let's behave that way and carefully observe the consequences. That is, let's don't just sit around and talk about adjustment. Let's try it.

The important point, of course, is to apply these techniques— rather, to train the case to apply them—in the most effective ways to the problems created by his own particular identifications, semantic blockages, signal reactions, etc. First of all, the student needs to understand the general principles upon which the techniques are based. Using the techniques, even though awkwardly at first, will help him, of course, to gain a better understanding of the principles. Evaluations and basic orientation are altered when behavior is changed, and vice versa. This means that the clinician does not give the case a "full" explanation of the principles and a new set of attitudes before having him do anything about actually changing his behavior. It also means, however, that he does not instruct the case to change his behavior before he has given him any understanding of the techniques to be used. If he does, the case will simply go through motions to little or no purpose. Teaching a person the technique of semantic relaxation without first teaching him at least a little general semantics is actually all but impossible, and may even be worse than useless. Likewise, talking very long about semantic relaxation or the extensional devices, for example, without actually trying them out can be equally futile.

As soon as the student feels that he has some understanding of a technique, and sees in some degree how he may use it to change his own maladjustive behavior, he should try to use it. He will probably be awkward in using it, and will come back and report various difficulties. Then there needs to be more talk about the principles underlying the technique, but the point of this talk is to enable the student to try again. Gradually in this way a measure of readjustment can be brought about. It is a matter of *training*, and in effective training the practice and discussion, the doing and the talking, go hand in hand, each making the other more meaningful and fruitful. Personality reeducation is somewhat like good football coaching: the chalk talks lead to practice and scrimmage, which indicate a need for more chalk talks, which lead to more practice and scrimmage, etc.

Some examples of experimental observation, directed alterations of behavior, and applications of the techniques described in Chapter X are provided in the Semantic Exercises which follow Chapter XVIII. Other illustrations are in the chapter that follows this one. In personality case work a purpose of the examination and diagnosis is to indicate specific changes in behavior that would be beneficial. A purpose of the changes made in semantic environment and in the student's evaluative reactions is to make these behavior changes possible and likely. The behavior changes themselves can be helped along by having the student make certain observations that will aid him in revising his maladjustive attitudes and assumptions; by having him deliberately alter his behavior in specific ways and in particular situations, noting the consequences; by showing him how to use the extensional devices generally and for his specific purposes; by training him in making delayed, evaluative, symbol reactions; and by encouraging him in the use of semantic relaxation so far as this may seem advisable.

Organism. If the student has some diseased condition or seems to be lacking energy, it is the clinician's responsibility to see to it that he receives proper medical attention. The relationship between organic states, physiological conditions, and evaluative reactions is close and complex. Articles published in the journal *Psychosomatic Medicine*—perhaps the most relevant publication—make this sufficiently clear. So far as personality reeducation is concerned, there would appear to be three statements to be made in this connection:

1. An individual needs a certain amount of energy, he needs to "feel good," in order to carry out an effective program of personality retraining. Run-down and fatigued, he tends to revert to old patterns of behavior. For this reason it is important to see to it that he receives necessary medical service and observes adequate rules of physical hygiene—proper practices with respect to eating, sleeping, exercising, working, and relaxing.

2. The clinician who is not an M.D. has the obligation of not pretending to be one, of not "playing doctor." In case of doubt as to the physical condition of a student, he should obtain a physician's judgment and advice.

3. A student's evaluations of—or theories about—his physical constitution and hereditary background are sometimes important in relation to his personality adjustment. If this is so in a particular case, due attention should be given to it and helpful reevaluations should be brought about to the degree that the facts appear to warrant them. Reliable facts about one's heredity should be taken into account whenever they make any difference, but unfounded wor-

ries or delusions about one's genes should be treated as symptoms of maladjustment. Judged by reasonable scientific standards, most of us know next to nothing about our heredity, and any notions we have about it had best be put to the what-do-you-mean? and how-do-you-know? tests before we base any serious decisions on them. Our grandfathers endowed us not only with limitations but also with potentialities; if we keep sufficiently busy trying to make the most of the potentialities we usually don't notice the limitations very much.

Suggestions for Further Study

If you are interested in doing something about your own adjustment problems, you should consider doing some of the assignments in the Semantic Exercises, especially Nos. 2 and 3, although many of the others may also prove to be of value. If you judge yourself to be very seriously maladjusted you would be well advised to consult a psychiatrist or a reputable psychologist. If you are uncertain about where to go for help, you might best write to your nearest large university, addressing the head of the psychology department or the dean of the medical school. This may sound like alarming advice. It is not meant to be at all. Actually, the number of people who would profit from psychiatric or psychological service is greater by far than the number who seek or receive it.

Most of those who read this book, however, will probably not feel a need to consult a psychiatrist. Many will nonetheless want to do further reading about personality retraining, and for them a list of books and articles is presented below. In most of them further bibliographies will be found. No attempt has been made to make the list exhaustive. On the contrary, it contains very few references: mainly those which I have found, probably for personal reasons, to be particularly stimulating or informative. Some of the references have been included because they describe points of view or methods which appear to be worth careful study but which have not been discussed in this chapter. Other references will be found in the bibliography at the end of the book.

SUPPLEMENTARY READINGS

BRYNGELSON, BRYNG. "The Interpretative Symbol," *Quarterly Journal of Speech*, 1938, *24*, 569–573.

HERTZ, M. R. "Rorschach: Twenty Years After," *Psychological Bulletin*, 1942, *39*, 529–572.

HORNEY, K. *The Neurotic Personality of Our Time*. New York: W. W. Norton & Company, Inc., 1937.

LOUTTIT, C. M. *Clinical Psychology*. New York: Harper & Brothers, 1936.

MASLOW, A. H., and MITTELMANN, B. *Principles of Abnormal Psychology: The Dynamics of Psychic Illness*. New York; Harper & Brothers, 1941.

MORENO, J. L. "Who Shall Survive?" *Nervous and Mental Disease Monographs*, 1934, No. 58.

Psychosomatic Medicine (journal). Published quarterly with the sponsorship of the Committee on Problems of Neurotic Behavior, Division of Anthropology and Psychology, National Research Council, Washington, D. C.

ROGERS, C. R. *Counseling and Psychotherapy*. Boston: Houghton Mifflin Company, 1942.

SHAFFER, L. R. *The Psychology of Adjustment*. Boston: Houghton Mifflin Company, 1936.

SHAW, C. (ed.). *The Jack-Roller: A Delinquent Boy's Own Story*. Chicago: University of Chicago Press, 1930.

STRECKER, E. A., and EBAUGH, F. G. *Practical Clinical Psychiatry*. Section on Psychopathological Problems of Childhood, by Leo Kanner. Philadelphia: The Blakiston Company, 1940.

SUPER, D. "The Bernreuter Personality Inventory: A Review of Research," *Psychological Bulletin*, 1942, *39*, 94–125.

TRAVIS, L. E., and BARUCH, D. W. *Personal Problems of Everyday Life: Practical Aspects of Mental Hygiene*. New York: D. Appleton-Century Company, Inc., 1941.

THE INDIANS HAVE NO WORD FOR IT

THE PROBLEM OF STUTTERING

AN EXAMPLE OF A GENERAL SEMANTICS APPROACH TO A particular type of adjustment problem is presented in this chapter. The problem is that which centers around one of mankind's most baffling and peculiar disorders: stuttering. (It is sometimes called stammering; we may consider the two terms as synonyms.) That is to say, it is baffling and peculiar from our traditional points of view; from a semantic point of view it appears somewhat less strange and unaccountable. The history of man's attempts to deal with the disorder, and the explanations that have been made of it, are quite as fascinating as the disorder itself. The story of stuttering is, in miniature, a burlesque history of human "thought." Aristotle's theory that stuttering was due to a defective organism, specifically a defect of the tongue, remained relatively dominant for over two thousand years. Even as recently as the middle of the last century, the disorder was treated, at least by certain French surgeons, by cutting pieces out of the stutterer's tongue. Needless to say, particularly since this was in the days before anesthetics and modern antiseptics, many stutterers were "cured" by this method—permanently! In one of the minor but intriguing eddies of the rising river of Heraclitus, scientific workers have finally cast off the spell of verbal authority and have got around to looking carefully at stutterers' tongues, and at other relevant facts, with the humane result that surgeons now put their knives to more appropriate uses on other types of patients.

Somewhat less than one per cent of the population stutters; there are roughly a million stutterers in this country. Moses was apparently a stutterer. So were Charles Darwin and Charles Lamb. According to published reports and more or less common knowledge there are many present-day celebrities who belong, in this respect, in the company of Moses and Darwin and Lamb. Among them, of course, are the present King of England, Somerset Maugham, Jane Froman, and any number of comparable, if in some instances less newsworthy, individuals. But stuttering is a plague of the common man as well. On the average, the intelligence of stutterers is the same as that of other people. In fact, one of the most perplexing characteristics of stutterers—from traditional points of view— is their normality: stutterers are people who stutter; otherwise, stutterers are people.

The discussion that follows is based on what I have been able to learn during some twenty years of experimental and clinical study of the problem. Use is made of general semantics to the extent and in ways that seem to be indicated by clinical and research findings.

STUTTERING AND SEMANTIC ENVIRONMENT

William Nuttall, an English stutterer, writing in the journal *Psyche,* in 1937, said in effect, that whoever finds a cure for stuttering will have found a cure for all the ills of society. We should not permit his possible exaggeration to distract us from the peculiarly fundamental wisdom which he expressed. In a sense, what he said of stuttering might also be said of such other perplexing forms of behavior as thumb-sucking, or nervousness, worry, gossiping, etc. Mr. Nuttall elaborated his point by saying that he seldom if ever stuttered when alone (as is true of stutterers generally), but only when speaking to other people, so that whatever the causes of his disorder, they must lie in those other people quite as much as in himself. In his own way, Mr. Nuttall was pointing a finger in the direction of semantic environment—the environment of attitudes and evaluations, opinions and beliefs—as a source of his difficulties.

THE SEARCH FOR A STUTTERING INDIAN

The significance of semantic environment in relation to stuttering is further suggested by certain experiences that I have had in attempting to investigate stuttering among North American Indians. A few years ago one of my students, Miss Harriett Hayes, became a teacher on an Indian reservation in Idaho. She carried with her a set of detailed instructions for making a study of the stutterers among the Bannock and Shoshone Indians, with whom she was to work. At the end of the school year, however, she returned with the highly interesting information that *she had been unable to find any stuttering Indians*. Moreover, the superintendent of the school and the other teachers, many of whom had been in close association with Indians for as long as twenty-five years, had reported to Miss Hayes that they had never seen any stuttering Indians. Since then I have received reports, from unknown original sources, of one stuttering Indian in the State of Maine and two in the Rocky Mountain area. It has not been possible, however, to verify these reports. Over a twenty-five year period there have come to the University of Iowa Speech Clinic one half-breed Indian from South Dakota, who had lived almost entirely among white men, and one strange case of a full-blooded Indian, also from South Dakota, who had been educated in a mission school.

This latter case is of special interest, for the reason that he did not appear to be either a typical Indian or a typical stutterer. When brought to the Iowa clinic he was about twenty years old. For the previous two years he had apparently been unable to speak at all, and it was for this reason that he was referred to us by the head of the mission school. There was a history of the boy's having "stuttered" for an indefinite, but limited, period immediately before his "loss of voice." A neurological and general physical examination revealed nothing of importance. It took about a month to obtain from the boy, in written form, the highly significant information that he had regarded his earlier stuttering as "a sign from God," which he had interpreted to mean that God intended for him not to talk at all. His "loss of voice," therefore, had been his way of expressing his obedience to God's will. He was convinced, however, of his utter inability to speak, that God had sealed his lips.

This presented a neat problem from a speech-correction point of view. With childlike simplicity he had come to believe what he had been taught, and he had learned his lesson so well that it seemed both impractical and dangerous, particularly in view of the short time available, to attempt to undo the effects of his previous teachings. Dr. C. Esco Obermann, who was assigned to the case, finally hit upon an ingenious solution, however. He managed to convince the boy that he had misinterpreted "God's sign." Dr. Obermann reinterpreted the earlier stuttering as a test of faith, and asserted that God would be pleased only if the Indian lad would continue to speak and so to spread the gospel in spite of the stuttering. A day or so later the Indian boy came to Dr. Obermann in a state of high excitement. He could talk again! And he stuttered only slightly. Eventually arrangements were made for him to enter a monastery—which is probably not a practical solution for most stutterers!

(As it turned out, it was not a practical solution for this case either. Since the above was written, the young man showed up again, but I was able to see him for only a few moments. Apparently he had not remained long in the monastery; he had been working here and there as a laborer. He was stuttering only slightly and seemed in other respects also to be in about the same condition he was in when he left the clinic five years before.)

The point of the story is simply that this stuttering Indian was far from being representative either of Indians or of stutterers— and it is the only case of a full-blooded Indian stutterer of whom I have been able to obtain any verified direct or indirect knowledge. For all practical purposes, then, it may be said, so far as I am aware, that there are no stutterers among North American Indians living under conditions comparatively free from the white man's influence.

A year or so after Miss Hayes had made her preliminary study of the Indians in Idaho, I arranged with another of my students,

John Snidecor, who was then located in that region, to continue the investigation. Professor Snidecor was to make special note of two things: the language of the Indians, and their policies and standards concerning the care and training of their children. He made a thorough investigation, interviewing several hundred Indians. He was also granted permission to appear before the chiefs and members of the tribal councils.

He learned in the main two things. First, these Indians had *no word for stuttering* in their language. In fact, when he asked whether there were any stutterers in the tribes, he had to demonstrate stuttering for the chiefs and the council members before they could understand what he was talking about. They were intensely amused by his demonstrations. Second, their standards of child care and training appeared to be extraordinarily lax in comparison with our own. With respect to speech in particular, it seemed to be the case that every Indian child was regarded as a satisfactory or normal speaker, regardless of the manner in which he spoke. Speech defects were simply not recognized. The Indian children were not criticized or evaluated on the basis of their speech, no comments were made about it, no issue was made of it. In their semantic environments there appeared to be no speech anxieties or tensions for the Indian children to interiorize, to adopt as their own. This, together with the absence of a word for stuttering in the Indians' language, constitutes the only basis on which I can at this time suggest an explanation for the fact that there were no stutterers among these Indians.

A STUDY OF STUTTERING CHILDREN

One need not go to the North American Indians, however, in order to glimpse the importance of semantic environment in relation to stuttering. There is a very large group of persons belonging to the white race who apparently do not stutter, namely, very young children in our own culture. Through George D. Stoddard, then Director of the Iowa Child Welfare Research Station, I obtained funds in 1935 from the Laura Spelman-Rockefeller Foundation with which to conduct a study of the onset of stuttering. Up to that time it appeared to be more or less generally taken for granted that stuttering at its onset was essentially the same as stuttering in adults, that stuttering children were generally retarded or constitutionally defective, and that stuttering ordinarily begins as a result of illness, injury, shock, or some other more or less serious and dramatic event. From the research to be described it seemed quite impossible to support any of these commonly accepted views.[1]

In the first place, it was discovered that when the attempt is made to find stutterers shortly after they have begun to stutter, so that relatively detailed and accurate information might be secured, the cases obtained are practically all young children. Three out of four of the children investigated had begun to stutter at or before the age of three years and two months. However—and this is extremely important—all the children encountered in this study *had talked without stuttering for from six months to several years before the onset of stuttering.*

In this research 46 stuttering children were involved, and for each stuttering child investigation was made of a non-stuttering child of like age, sex, and intelligence level. Relatively thorough observations and case-history studies were made; two or more interviewers examined independently the case of each stuttering child, and in large measure the investigations were carried out in the homes of the children. On the average each stuttering child was kept under observation for a period of two and one-half years. Over a period of approximately five years I had the assistance of seventeen workers trained in speech pathology, chief among whom were Charles Van Riper, Dorothy Davis Tuthill, Hartwell Scarbrough, and Susan Dwyer. Professor Lee Edward Travis, then Director of the Iowa Speech Clinic, was at all times available for consultation.

Without going into elaborate detail, it is to be reported that:

1. *Practically every case of stuttering was originally diagnosed as such, not by a speech expert but by a layman—usually one, or both, of the child's parents.*

---

[1] A preliminary report of this investigation has been published. See W. Johnson, "A Study of the Onset and Development of Stuttering," *Journal of Speech Disorders,* 1942, 7, 251–257.

2. *What these laymen had diagnosed as stuttering was, by and large, indistinguishable from the hesitations and repetitions known to be characteristic of the normal speech of young children.* Under my direction investigations have been made of the fluency of children between the ages of two and six years. These studies have been done at the Iowa Child Welfare Research Station by Dorothy Davis Tuthill, George Egland, Margaret Branscom, Jeannette Hughes, and Eloise Tupper.[2] They have well established the fact that young children speak in such a manner that from 15 to 25 per cent of their words figure in some kind of repetition. The initial sound or syllable of the word is repeated, or the whole word is repeated or the word is part of a repeated phrase. Another way to summarize the data is to say that the average child was found to repeat, in some fashion, about 45 times per 1000 words. In addition, there are frequent hesitations other than repetitions.

These repetitions and hesitations are not accompanied by any apparent tension or anxiety on the part of the child. They seem to occur somewhat more frequently when the child is "talking over his head," when he lacks sufficient knowledge of what he is talking about, when the listener does not respond readily to what the child says, or his vocabulary does not contain the seemingly necessary words. Such conditions appear to occur often in the speaking experience of very young children. It is what you would experience if asked to speak for ten minutes about Einstein's theories or any other subject concerning which you lack both information and vocabulary. After all, it takes a child a few years to acquire the experience, the words and the language skills necessary for the smooth handling of ordinary conversation. Also, non-fluency seems to occur more frequently when the child is talking in the face of competition, as at the family table when others are talking a great deal and are paying slight attention to the child's own attempts at expression. There is a tendency for more non-fluency to occur under conditions

---

[2] D. Davis, "The Relation of Repetitions in the Speech of Young Children to Certain Measures of Language Maturity and Situational Factors," *Journal of Speech Disorders*, 1939, *4*, 303–318, and 1940, *5*, 238–246. The studies of Egland, Branscom, Hughes, and Tupper have not yet been published. They were all done as M.A. theses in the Iowa Child Welfare Research Station.

of shame, sense of guilt, etc., occasioned by parental scolding, rebuff, or disapproval, particularly when these serve to create negative evaluations by the child of his own speaking rights or ability. There is probably increased non-fluency, also, during "language spurts," as during the transition from the speaking of single words to the speaking of short sentences, or from the speaking of simple sentences to the use of complex sentences, or when the child is discontinuing the pronoun *me* in favor of *I*, etc.

There are doubtless other conditions that tend to increase hesitations and repetitions in the child's speech. The point is that these conditions are very common, and while they may occur more frequently in some environments than in others, they occur sufficiently often for all children so that the speech of early childhood is in general quite non-fluent. What is important is that the so-called stuttering children were found to have been apparently normal, even with respect to speech, at the time when someone, usually the parents, first regarded them as stutterers. And, as has been mentioned, they had all talked for considerable periods without being regarded as defective before they had come to be diagnosed as stutterers.

3. Stuttering at its onset was found, then, to be remarkably different from stuttering in the adult. Stuttering as a clinical problem, as a definite disorder, was found to occur not before being diagnosed, but *after being diagnosed*. In order to emphasize this finding, I have coined the term *diagnosogenic;* stuttering is a diagnosogenic disorder in the sense that the diagnosis of stuttering is one of the causes of the disorder. The evaluations made by the parents (usually) which they express, overtly or implicitly, by diagnosing their child's speech as "stuttering," or "defective," or "abnormal," are a very important part of the child's semantic environment. Insofar as the child interiorizes this aspect of his semantic environment, he too evaluates his speech as "defective," "difficult," "not acceptable," etc., and his manner of speaking is consequently made more hesitant, cautious, labored, and the like. In this way normal speech hesitations and repetitions are transformed

into the exaggerated pausing, effort, and reluctance to speak which are so conspicuous and frustrating in the speech of adult stutterers.

Thus we see certain interrelationships among the child's semantic environment, his own evaluations, and his overt behavior. *The more anxious the parents become, the more they hound the child to "go slowly," to "stop and start over," to "make up his mind," to "breathe more deeply," etc., the more fearful and disheartened the child becomes, and the more hesitantly, frantically, and laboriously he speaks—so that the parents, teachers, and others become more worried, appeal more insistently to the child to "talk better," with the result that the child's own evaluations become still more disturbed, and his outward speech behavior becomes more and more disordered.* It is a vicious spiral, and all the factors involved in it are closely interrelated.

4. The stuttering children were found not to be retarded in development. They were compared in several ways with the non-stuttering children who were also investigated. The stuttering children were not more retarded in speech, in walking, teething, and other common indexes of development. The only child who had suffered a definitely serious birth injury was a stutterer who was no longer stuttering at the close of the investigation. The stutterers had not had more diseases and injuries, and those they had had did not appear to have been related to the "onset of stuttering" (this term is now put in quotes because it appears to be misleading—it refers merely to the original *diagnosis of stuttering*).

With respect to handedness and changes in handedness, the two groups of children could not be differentiated. In fact, there were 14 non-stutterers as against 12 stutterers who had undergone some handedness change, and this difference between 14 and 12 is not significant. Moreover, conditions of handedness seemed not to be related to the degree of speech improvement achieved by the stuttering children during the course of the investigation.

In brief, no evidence was found that there *are* stutterers, in the sense that the stutterers investigated were a different kind of children, that they differed from the non-stutterers in any basic anatomical or physiological respects.

5. In this investigation of young stutterers it was found that practically all of the children, *after being diagnosed,* developed overt speech behavior that was in some degree unusual and of clinical importance. At the end of the study about three out of four had regained normal speech, so far as the parents, teachers, and investigators could judge. In general, this result was obtained by conveying to the parents and teachers essentially the explanation of stuttering that is here being presented. For all practical purposes the children were neither talked to about their speech nor given any instructions as to how they should speak. Moreover, nothing was done from a physiological point of view, except that general principles of physical hygiene were recommended, but in very few cases was there any unusual need for such a recommendation. Insofar as anything was done directly about the problem in any case, it was done entirely or mostly with reference to the semantic environment.

That is, an attempt was made to change the attitudes and policies—the evaluations—of the parents and teachers concerning the child as a person and as a speaker. An attempt was made to create a semantic environment for the child in which there would be a minimum of anxiety, tension, and disapproval for him to interiorize. In this way we undertook to produce in the child such evaluations of his own speech as would permit him to speak spontaneously, with pleasure, and with confidence, confidence not in his ability to speak perfectly but in his ability to speak acceptably. It was essential therefore, although it should be stressed that it was not possible in all cases, to get the parents and teachers to evaluate the child's speech and to react to it—*regardless of how he spoke*—in ways that would convince the child that his speech was approved. As the child appeared to sense that his speech was being thoroughly approved, his reluctance to speak, his exaggerated hesitancy and caution and effort in speaking all decreased. The eventual result tended to be speech that was free, spontaneous, a source of evident enjoyment to the child, and speech that was *normally* fluent—not perfectly fluent, for perfect fluency is as "abnormal," or unusual, as very severe stuttering.

In order to enable the child to speak with normal fluency, it was also necessary in some instances to bring about certain changes in the home or school. I have remarked that children—and this holds for adults as well—tend to speak more fluently under some conditions than under others. I am not now talking about stuttering. I am referring simply to the essentially effortless and apparently unconscious hesitations and repetitions in the normal speech of children and adults. Whenever a home or school was found in which there seemed to be an excess of conditions that tended to make for non-fluency, an attempt was made to reduce or eliminate these conditions.

In some cases, for example, the attempt was made to expand the child's vocabulary or to give him a wider range of experience. In other instances, the parents were urged to be more responsive to the child's remarks. On the whole, however, certain other considerations were of greater importance. It was rather commonly observed, for instance, that not only the standards of speech to which the child was being held were too high, but that also the parents were inclined to be perfectionists generally. For example, the child was being held to abnormally high standards with regard to table manners, cleanliness, toilet habits, and obedience; or certain words, innocent to the child but profane or vulgar to the parents, were vigorously, almost frighteningly, forbidden; the child was being constantly requested to be quiet or to sit still, etc.—the full list is truly impressive. (One sees here very vividly the difference between the semantic environments of Indian children and those of some of our own children.) Whenever such standards were discovered, an attempt was made to get the parents to adjust their ideals to the actual level of development and ability of the child. The effect of this was generally calming and appeared to be in some measure reflected in the child's speech.

Another measure that was found to be advisable and helpful in certain cases was that of bringing about a more affectionate and friendly relationship between the parents and their child. Their tendency to be critical and disapproving, as evidenced, for example, by their regarding his normally hesitant speech as defective, tended to make for generally strained relations and for apparent feelings of insecurity on the part of the child. Just as you might speak hesitantly in a situation in which you feel that you are not welcome and that what you say is not being well received, so a child tends to be less fluent when too much criticism and too little affection raise doubts for him as to whether his parents like him and will stand ready to give needed help and encouragement.

On one occasion in this study of young stutterers, I spent several hours with a stuttering boy's father, a conservative and very busy merchant who spent almost no time with his son. In the mornings the little fellow would tag at his father's heels, trying to visit with him as he bustled about the house and out the door, lost in a fog of business cares. The boy was non-fluent in his attempts to speak with the father, who scarcely listened, and seldom replied, to what the boy said. The father was not harsh to the boy; he just paid no attention to him, with the result that the child was frequently under considerable strain in his efforts to get an amount of attention and recognition that seemed altogether reasonable. Finally, I actually showed the father how to get down on his hands and knees and play with the boy. I got him to play catch with the child out in the yard, to take him riding with him, to read to him, and in other ways to be companionable. This was one of the cases in which the stuttering was very definitely eliminated.

In other cases it was a matter of getting the parents to use less severe methods of discipline, to refrain from scolding the child or making derogatory remarks about him in the presence of his friends, to play games with the child, or just to hold the youngster and cuddle him enough to establish some feeling of warmth and affection. Some parents are so doggedly set on making little ladies and gentlemen of their youngsters that they seldom look on them as little children.

In general, then, and in the respects indicated, the treatment of stuttering in young children is to be directed not toward the child, but toward the relevant evaluations—the attitudes, assumptions, beliefs, etc.—and the resulting policies and reactions, of the child's parents and teachers and the other persons who affect his own evaluations and reactions. It is a matter of changing the child's speech responses by changing the pertinent features of the conditions under which they occur.

Non-Fluency vs. Stuttering

In adults the problem is quite different, but in both children and adults certain general principles are fundamental. To begin with, *a clear distinction must be made between non-fluency and stuttering*. Most young children and many adults speak quite non-fluently, repeating frequently, pausing conspicuously, saying *ah* or *uh,* etc. They speak very differently from stutterers, however, who may be even quite fluent by ordinary standards but who exhibit considerable strain, embarrassment, and apprehensiveness with regard to such non-fluency as they do have. It is the stutterer's anxiety and strain, the fear and the effort with which he pauses or says *uh,* repeats sounds or prolongs them, that serve to distinguish him from the so-called normal speaker.

(It is also to be considered that stuttering, as the term is here being used and as it is ordinarily used among speech correction workers, is to be clearly differentiated from certain speech repetitions and blockings seen in some cases of psychoneurosis and of brain injury. Systematic research is needed in order to make this important differentiation obvious in detail, but clinical observations serve to indicate its fundamental aspects. For example, stutterers, in the standard sense of the term, can for all practical purposes talk without stuttering when speaking in time to rhythms, such as the beating of a metronome, the tapping by the stutterer of his own foot, the rhythmic flashing of lights, etc. Two stutterers can read together, with few and minor exceptions, without stuttering, even when they read different material. Also, they adapt to a reading passage, stuttering less and less with each successive reading of it; on the average this adaptation amounts roughly to nearly a 50 per cent reduction in stuttering in five successive readings of a passage. Now, so-called psychoneurotic "stutterers" and non-fluent brain injury cases do not show these phenomena, according to such clinical observations as I have been able to make. Outwardly, at least to an untrained ear, they may sound like stutterers, but basically the disorder they present appears to be markedly different from that of ordinary stutterers. To a trained ear this difference is apparent even on the basis of casual observation. We may expect significant further research in this connection in the not far distant future. In the meantime stuttering is not to be confused with other disorders that resemble it superficially.)

It is commonly supposed that what ails the stutterer is that he cannot speak fluently. The degree to which such misconceptions as this can come to be widely accepted is indeed fascinating. *The fact of the matter is that the stutterer cannot talk non-fluently.* He can speak fluently all right; so long as his speech is fluent, as it is 80 per cent or more of the time in the majority of cases, his speech cannot very well be distinguished from that of a normal speaker. To say that stutterers cannot talk fluently is to commit a fantastic misrepresentation of the facts. If they talked non-fluently as well as they talk fluently they could only be regarded as normal speakers. Their peculiarity lies in the fact that whenever they do hesitate or repeat they make a great show of fear and effort, instead of proceeding to stumble along calmly as normal speakers do.

In a fundamental sense, stuttering is not a speech defect at all, although excessive non-fluency might sometimes be so regarded. Stuttering is an evaluational disorder. It is what results when normal non-fluency is evaluated as something to be feared and avoided; it is, outwardly, what the stutterer does in an attempt to avoid non-fluency. On such a basis his reluctance to speak at all, his shyness, his excessive caution in speaking, his great effort to speak perfectly which shows up in his facial grimaces, bodily contortions, and strained vocalizations—all this, which is what we call stuttering, becomes understandable when viewed as avoidance reactions, reactions designed to avoid the non-fluency which the individual has learned to fear and dread and expect.

In the normal speaker non-fluency is simply a *response* occasioned by some external stimulus or, perhaps, by a lack of vocabulary or preparation. As a response, in this sense, non-fluency is, indeed, normal. For the stutterer, on the other hand, non-fluency has become a *stimulus* to which he reacts with anxiety and with an effort to avoid it and its supposed social consequences. Non-fluency as a response is hardly a problem; non-fluency as a stimulus is something else again. The child's repetitions of sounds, words, and phrases are of no consequence until they come to serve as a stimulus for his parents or teachers. When that happens, they tend to become for the child the same sort of stimulus they are for his parents and teachers, who, in large measure, create his semantic environment. As they react with worry and disapproval and with an effort to get the child not to repeat, so the child in time adopts their worry and disapproval of his own speech, and consequently he makes a great effort to talk without repeating. These attitudes and this effort are, in the main, what constitute stuttering. Simple hesitancy in speech is normal and harmless. But *to hesitate to hesitate* is relatively serious in its consequences.

It is these attitudes of fear and embarrassment, and this second-order hesitating to hesitate, these anxious exertions of effort to speak perfectly and without non-fluency—these are the symptoms of stuttering that stand out in the adult. They may be present in rather young children, of course, since in some semantic environments it does not take very long for the child's own evaluative behavior to become seriously affected. The essential point is that before the child has interiorized his semantic environment to a very considerable degree, the problem can be dealt with effectively for the most part by changing the semantic environment itself, without any direct attempt to change the child's own evaluative or overt behavior so far as his speech is concerned. Besides, a child's semantic environment tends to be fairly largely confined to the home and is created by very few individuals, so that it *can* be changed effectively in a great many cases.

TREATING STUTTERING IN ADULTS

In the case of older children and adults, on the other hand, a more direct attack on the problem is usually necessary. The individual's semantic environment extends eventually beyond the home or the school; it becomes too big to be easily manipulated. Besides (and this is more important) the individual has interiorized it. His non-fluency has become a stimulus not only for the people around him, but also for him. He reacts to it in his own right, so to speak. It is his own evaluations that now largely determine his overt behavior, and so those evaluations must be attacked directly. All the relevant factors are interrelated, however, and it is generally more effective to work on all of them than to limit attention to one only. Anything that can be done to change the semantic environment, to modify attitudes and policies in the home, school, neighborhood, or community, or to educate "public opinion" in the larger sense, helps to promote favorable changes in the individual's own evaluative behavior. Likewise, any changes that can be brought about more or less directly in the stutterer's manner of stuttering in order to make it more bearable, may make it easier for him to evaluate it differently. Moreover, a program of physical hygiene will sometimes help to keep the individual "feeling good," so that he will have the energy for an enthusiastic and sustained attempt to overcome his difficulties.

From this point of view, then, the problem of stuttering is not to be regarded elementalistically as being *either* "physical" or "mental," either "organic" or "emotional." It is neither "all in the mind" nor "all in the tongue." The approach throughout is non-elementalistic and relativistic. Nor is it to be missed that within this frame of reference no two stutterers are to be regarded as exactly alike. The specific procedures that appear to be most helpful in one case may not be helpful in another. We must go further and say that the specific measures that are advisable for a particular stutterer at one time, or in one situation, are not necessarily advisable at another time and under other circumstances. There is no single method of treating stuttering from the point of view here presented. Any particular stutterer is to be examined, evaluated, and treated extensionally with reference to the specific alterations advisable and feasible in his own case. It is even possible that for some stutterers the factor of physical constitution would be more important than any other, although in the general run of cases other factors would appear to be of definitely greater significance.

On the basis of this general statement, it is possible to discuss in more specific terms the treatment of stuttering in well-developed or adult cases:

Semantic Environment. As a general rule, it is advisable to see to it that the stutterer's family, teachers, employer, friends, and associates are made acquainted with the nature of his problem. An explanation, in simplified terms if necessary, along the lines presented here will often go far to weaken the taboo against nonfluency which the stutterer usually feels whenever he speaks at home, in school, or elsewhere.

For example, most people are inclined to praise a stutterer when he speaks fluently. The practical effect of this is to strengthen the stutterer's conviction that he should never speak non-fluently; as a consequence, he tends to become a bit more anxious and to exhibit more tension in his attempts to avoid non-fluency. In other words, he tends to stutter more severely when praised for speaking fluently. *It is better to praise the stutterer whenever he handles his nonfluency calmly and without undue strain.* This notion may sound odd to those who are unfamiliar with the problem, but there are very few parents, teachers, or other persons who will not do what they can to help a stutterer, once they see clearly what there is to do. In general, what there is to do is to adopt the attitude—and mean it— that the stutterer is under no obligation whatever to speak fluently, that, in fact, he is to be complimented for speaking non-fluently in an unworried, unhurried, effortless, and forthright manner.

It is also generally advisable to create in the stutterer's semantic environment the attitude that he is a worthy individual. He should be able to feel sure of his parents' affection and reasonable moral support without having to struggle for them. He should not be given reason to suppose that his teachers pity him, or look down on him as a person. His employer should make clear to him the respects in which his speech is and is not the basis for any criticisms of his work, and he should help him to see those aspects of his work in which his efficiency is not affected by his speech difficulty. It will pay the employer in the long run to follow such a policy, and it will help the stutterer considerably to achieve an adequate reevaluation of himself and of his speech.

It is well to encourage a stutterer to develop his talents along various lines, and to provide opportunities for him to do so. One of the marks of a healthful semantic environment is that it provides the individual with stimulation for possible self-development. It should not, however, stimulate him beyond the reasonable limits of his ability, for to do that is to invite failure, and nothing fails like failure. Experiences of success, on the other hand, are healthful in their effects. In order to experience successes, one's goals must be reasonably specific and recognizable, and they must be practically attainable. But there must be goals; one must be provided with something at which to shoot, so to speak, and with the opportunity to shoot at it. If a stutterer has athletic ability, or can serve as school cheerleader, or shows promise of becoming a writer or trombone player, then he should be provided with the necessary opportunities to experience success accordingly. It is definitely beneficial to have a good opinion of oneself—based on performance, properly evaluated. If a stutterer can have positive evaluations of himself as a person, he is correspondingly more likely to evaluate his speech non-fluency with less dread and trepidation. It is the difference between stuttering just after you have fanned out, and stuttering just after you have hit a home run with the bases loaded. Stuttering$_1$ is not stuttering$_2$!

Finally, it should be said that most stutterers should be encouraged to speak as much as possible. In this respect, however, parents and teachers need to be realistically alert. For a stutterer, speaking can be extremely grueling and demoralizing, and any stutterer varies considerably from time to time in his ability to "take it." In general, it is advisable for him to do most of his speaking, and as much speaking as he can, in such situations as he can manage with the greatest poise and satisfaction. But he should be encouraged and helped to extend the range of such situations. Most stutterers will benefit from speaking in those situations in which no premium is placed on fluency. As the stutterer loses his dread of non-fluency he speaks with less anxiety, and with less hesitation and strain—that is to say, with less stuttering. This general principle should guide the stutterer's parents and teachers in providing him with speaking experience.

So far as oral recitation in school is concerned, it is best for the teacher to discuss the matter frankly with the pupil, making clear to him that he may recite if he wants to, and that in doing so he need feel no obligation to talk perfectly. He may prefer to recite only when he volunteers to do so. It may be advisable to excuse him from the wear and tear of longer recitations, such as book reports. It may even be advisable to excuse him from all oral work, to arrange matters so that he need not even answer roll call. In such a case extra written work might well be assigned. In other cases, no special consideration whatever need be given so far as oral work is concerned. Every case must be handled on its own merits. There are no rules of thumb. The main thing is to see to it that the child does not become demoralized, and that he develops such evaluations of himself and his speech that he will want to speak and that he will enjoy speaking to the greatest possible degree.

One more point: As far as possible, the stutterer himself should undertake the task of changing his semantic environment. In this way the job will be done more thoroughly, and the stutterer will be developing a frankness about his own problem in talking about it to others, and he will be acquiring valuable experience in dealing directly with his elders and associates. "I, a stranger and afraid in a world I never made," in the words of the poet Housman, is not the theme song of an individual who takes upon himself as much as he can the responsibility for making his own semantic environment. It is of great adjustive value to learn that the evaluations which other people make of oneself, and the attitudes they have which affect one's own living, can in a measure be determined by one's own efforts. A stutterer, like anyone else, needs to learn that he is in large measure responsible for the manner in which others regard him and for the policies toward him which they adopt.

Evaluative Behavior. Evaluative behavior, as the term is here used, involves the forming and expression of attitudes, beliefs, wishes, likes and dislikes, assumptions, etc. We are not born with opinions or attitudes; rather, we are born into a semantic environment from which we derive them. The notion that repetitious speech is socially taboo is one of the features of many semantic environments in our culture. Whenever this taboo is highly developed, the child is put under considerable strain, since repetition is one of the prominent characteristics of speech in its early stages. The baby does not say, *Da,* but *Da, da, da.* This tendency to repeat continues into early childhood and even into the adult years to some extent. It is very significant, therefore, that such writers as Froeschels, Bluemel, and Van Riper have emphasized that "primary stuttering"—"stuttering" in its early stages—consists of simple repetition. It is very significant, that is, that they have called such repetition "primary *stuttering.*" We have seen that this sort of repetition is quite normal, especially during early childhood, and the fact that even speech experts would call it "stuttering" indicates the extent to which, in our society, speech repetition is tabooed, or disapproved.

Once a child has been called a stutterer, it is this taboo against non-fluency that is of particular importance in his semantic environment. The very fact that he is called a stutterer serves to strengthen the taboo. It is likely that if you have never been regarded as a stutterer, you can come nowhere near appreciating the uncanny, crushing power of the social disapproval of whatever is regarded as stuttering. It is probably one of the most frightening, perplexing, and demoralizing influences to be found in our culture. In this connection, it is of great interest that a similar condition is found to exist among certain primitive tribes. For instance, in his book, *Primitive Behavior,* Professor W. I. Thomas says, "Almost every Bantu man and woman is a fluent and sustained speaker, and Dr. Gordon Brown, who is working among one of the tribes, informs one that the most prevalent mental disturbance is in youths who realize that they are unable to become finished speakers."

Stuttering, in my opinion, is quite incomprehensible unless one takes this cultural factor of taboo into account. On the other hand, the behavior of stutterers appears to be quite understandable when viewed as their attempts to avoid non-fluency, and thus to avoid the consequences of the taboo against non-fluency. We have seen that what happens to bring about the stutterer's difficulty is that his parents or teachers confuse or identify his normal non-fluency with stuttering. To the child, then, non-fluency comes to be the *same* as stuttering. For him, the taboo against stuttering becomes generalized as a taboo against non-fluency. Out of this semantic confusion he develops the fearful effort, exaggerated hesitancy, etc., which we call well-developed stuttering. He develops this behavior as an attempt to avoid the non-fluency that was originally disapproved, but this stuttering behavior is disapproved also, and he is left in a disheartening quandary from which he can see no possibility of escaping.

Now most speech correctionists attack this problem (without stating the problem in these terms, however) by attempting to build up the stutterer's confidence in his ability to speak perfectly. In order to do this, they try to get the stutterer to speak while thoroughly relaxed, or to speak very slowly with a sort of drawl, or to speak in a monotone, or in time to some set rhythm, etc. The resulting speech, while usually free from "stuttering," is frequently more or less grotesque. Try going to a restaurant and ordering a meal with any one of these speech patterns, and you will get the point. If the parents of stutterers would adopt such speech patterns for themselves they would probably be less gullible in accepting the recommendations of those who advocate them. What such methods amount to is a powerful reinforcement of the taboo against stuttering with which the stutterer has been contending. What the so-called speech correctionist says, in effect, is this: *"Don't stutter. Whatever you do, don't stutter. You can even talk in this strange manner that I am suggesting, but don't stutter."*

If, for some odd reason, the stutterer is actually content to speak in the grotesque manner that is advocated, or if, by some miracle, he gains from the use of it a kind of abnormal confidence in an ability to speak perfectly, the results might be in a way satisfactory. But I have used such methods on myself and I have seen many other stutterers who have used them, and it would seem that the results are usually tragic. It is common knowledge that, except in rare instances, these artificial speech patterns tend to wear out; in time the individual stutters as much, or more, when he talks slowly or in a monotone, etc., as he ever did. When that happens, he is not back where he started from—he is far behind that point. He is again a stutterer, but the taboo against stuttering has been intensified by the "speech correction" he has had. His fear and desperation are now greater than before.

Simply by making a clear differentiation between stuttering and the normal non-fluency which it is designed to avoid, such unfortunate methods and the misunderstandings from which they arise may readily be eliminated. What the stutterer needs to learn is simply that he ceases to stutter to the extent that he permits non-fluency to occur. This does not make sense, of course, until a clear distinction is made between the effort to avoid non-fluency (which effort constitutes stuttering) and non-fluency. The stutterer suffers from a semantic confusion, which he has interiorized from his semantic environment. He *identifies* non-fluency and stuttering.

It helps the stutterer greatly to observe that so-called normal speakers are non-fluent. In the absence of systematic research on the speech fluency of adults, I can only report scattered observations of normal speakers, professional lecturers for the most part. Counting their repeated syllables, words, and phrases, their exaggerated hesitations, conspicuous pauses, their *uhs* and *ahs*, they tend to average from five to eight non-fluencies per minute in continuous, relatively extemporaneous speaking. For one famous lecturer, 540 non-fluencies were tabulated in slightly less than one hour. For another, 65 *ah*'s were counted in five minutes. So they go. This sort of thing is normal. Stutterers generally regard it as very unreasonable, as torture even, when first instructed to speak with this much non-fluency to be performed deliberately. To them it *is* stuttering. Nevertheless, when they do speak with such deliberate non-fluency, wholeheartedly, they loosen up very considerably, speak more smoothly, stutter much less. This of course is precisely what one would expect if one regards their stuttering behavior as an effort to avoid non-fluency.

So far as evaluative behavior is concerned, therefore, the stutterer needs to understand the taboo imposed by his semantic environment. He needs to understand the semantic confusion involved in this taboo as he has interiorized it. *He needs to differentiate stuttering from non-fluency, and to see stuttering as his attempts to avoid non-fluency.* Stated in so many words, this may sound rather simple. In practice it involves extraordinary difficulties. The indicated alterations in evaluative behavior have to be made in the face of powerful counteracting influences in the stutterer's semantic environment. It is usually very difficult to get the stutterer's parents, teachers, and associates to make similar changes in their own evaluations. As a rule they continue to praise him for speaking fluently, and to express or imply sympathy and anxiety when he does not speak fluently. Also, having learned to regard him as a stutterer, they quite automatically regard any non-fluency he may exhibit as stuttering—even though they give no heed to similar non-fluency in their own speech.

It must be realized, too, that for a stutterer to speak with repetitions, hesitations, etc., *on purpose,* is to reverse drastically long-established habits. He has been oriented for years, as a rule, to doing everything possible to keep from doing the very thing he is now being told to do. He is being asked to abandon evaluations which have come to seem natural to him. He is being asked to cultivate evaluations that strike him as contrary to common sense. Like so many other principles and practices that have been developed by modern scientific students of behavior, these too may appear to be very simple, but in our culture they are not easy to put into practice. Insofar as they are adequately applied, however, their value becomes evident.

Overt Behavior. A great deal of what might be said under this heading has already been indicated and implied. The main alterations to be made, so far as the stutterer's overt behavior is concerned, involve the deliberate performance of non-fluency, the sloughing off of certain mannerisms, grimaces, etc., and an increase in the amount of speaking and in the number of situations in which speaking is done. The primary objective of these behavior changes is to aid the stutterer in cultivating the evaluations that will lead to fearless, enjoyable, spontaneous speech—to speech of *normal* (not perfect) fluency.

In the usual case perhaps the steps to be taken would be of this order: First, it is sometimes necessary, or at least advisable, to convince the stutterer that he is capable of normal speech. This can be done by having him read in chorus with another person, even another stutterer. Strangely enough, as has been indicated, two stutterers are with rare exceptions able to read aloud together without difficulty. It is also helpful in some cases to have the stutterer read and talk when alone, or perhaps to his dog, since practically all stutterers can do this without stuttering. Such practices are helpful to the extent that they counteract any assumptions the stutterer may have as to his physical inability to speak.

Second, practically every adult stutterer exhibits certain mannerisms, or so-called associated movements, such as closing his eyes, turning his head, swinging his foot, etc., while stuttering. In some cases, these mannerisms are responsible for much of the social handicap. Moreover, they can frequently be eliminated; the stutterer can rather quickly learn from directed practice, preferably before a mirror, that he can stutter without doing some of these things. The value of eliminating such mannerisms lies in the fact that the social handicap is reduced, and the stutterer's notion that his stuttering is fixed and unalterable is weakened. One must be careful, however, not to carry this too far; one must see to it that the individual understands that he is not being instructed not to stutter at all. Such an instruction would tend to strengthen the taboo with which the stutterer has to contend, and would result in increased tension and discouragement.

Third, insofar as possible the stutterer should deliberately imitate his own stuttering. This should be done at first in front of a mirror with no one present but the teacher; or the stutterer can do it by himself provided he understands clearly what he is to do. Later, he should do it in speaking to other people. Having learned to imitate his own manner of stuttering, he should practice faking it without the effort and hurry that usually characterize it. He should do this at first while he is alone or with his teacher, and later in other situations. In doing this, the aim should be to make the stuttering entirely effortless, free from grimaces and fear—a forthright, unhurried, deliberate performance of what would otherwise be done under protest and with tension.

After considerable practice in this, the stutterer is ready for the fourth step, that of adopting a streamlined pattern of non-fluency. This is not to be confused with stuttering; for the non-fluency pattern is adopted and used *instead of* stuttering. Probably a simple repetition, like "tha-tha-tha-this," is most preferable, partly because it was just such behavior that was originally diagnosed as stuttering and needs therefore to be reevaluated as normal and acceptable. However, a simple, effortless prolongation of the first sounds of words will, in some cases, prove satisfactory, although considerable practice is required in prolonging the p and t. Also, care must be exercised lest the prolonging become a complete stoppage reaction, which would be merely another way of stuttering. Having adopted, say, a simple repetition pattern, such as "tha-tha-tha-this," the stutterer should practice it a great deal when alone, preferably before a mirror. If a dictaphone or, better, a mirrophone is available, it is helpful to record one's speech, using the new repetition pattern, and then listen to it over and over again, in order to become thoroughly accustomed to it, and to learn to do it as smoothly and effortlessly as possible.

Gradually, then, the stutterer should introduce this pattern of non-fluency into his everyday speech, trying it out first in the easier situations and then introducing it in more and more difficult situations. He should employ it whenever he would otherwise stutter and he should also feign it liberally in saying certain words on which he would not otherwise stutter. He will find that the more non-fluency he fakes the less he will experience a tendency to stutter. This follows because his stuttering constitutes his attempts to avoid non-fluency, and to the extent that he is set to perform it, he is not set to avoid it. As times goes on, the amount of feigning can be gradually reduced, since the tendency to try to avoid non-fluency (to stutter) will have been weakened, and eventually normal speech becomes possible.

What is accomplished by this means is that the individual ceases to be a stutterer and becomes instead, for a time, a rather non-fluent speaker. The unusual amount of repetition in his speech, provided it is performed wholeheartedly and without apparent effort, calls far less attention to itself than one might suppose, and is, for other reasons also, far less serious than the stuttering. One of the main reasons why it is less serious is that the repetition tends to decrease in amount with time. This is so because the voluntary repetition is performed in order to counteract the impulse to stutter (to avoid repetition or other non-fluency). But this impulse to stutter tends to become weaker and weaker, and to occur less and less frequently, as the strength of its motivation, which is the desire to avoid non-fluency, is decreased. As the inclination to stutter decreases, the need or occasion for voluntary repetition decreases correspondingly. Gradually, therefore, the individual's speech comes to be less and less non-fluent, and tends eventually to become quite smooth. Thus, the vicious spiral of stuttering leading to more stuttering as the individual develops a stronger and stronger set to avoid non-fluency —this vicious spiral is reversed, so that there is less and less stuttering as the individual develops a greater and greater tolerance for non-fluency. And as the threat and dread of stuttering decrease, the need for actually performing non-fluency decreases, and the individual speaks more and more smoothly.

Finally, it should be added that as the stutterer proceeds with this program he should be encouraged, even definitely assigned, to speak more and more and to enlarge the range of his speaking situations. As his evaluations of non-fluency change, he will exhibit less reluctance to speak, less of a tendency to avoid social contacts. This should be encouraged judiciously, remembering at all times that the main objective of all these measures is to help the individual to cultivate such positive evaluations of his speech as will enable him to speak without fear and tension, and with enjoyment and poise.

Physical Condition. On the basis of the more adequate scientific studies done to date, there seems to be little or no reason for supposing that stutterers as a class have any greater need for physical hygiene than do other people. As a population generally we are not, on the average, the answer to a wise physician's prayer. Fundamental lack of good health is indicated by most of us in the condition of our teeth, the relative ease with which we catch colds, our tendency to become fatigued readily, and in various other ways. Stutterers, then, are not to be compared with an ideal population of non-stutterers who enjoy perfect health. They compare very well, indeed, with non-stutterers as they actually are found to exist with respect to their physical condition.

What may be important, however, is the possible tendency for some individuals, at least, to lack enthusiasm and to become discouraged under conditions occasioned by excessive fatigue, loss of sleep, improper diet, lack of exercise, or disease. In order to carry out effectively the sort of corrective speech program outlined above, the stutterer needs as much energy, enthusiasm, and "good feeling" as possible. Once a stutterer has begun to change his speech behavior, the main thing with which he has to contend is the tendency to revert to old habitual ways of behaving whenever he feels tired and discouraged. From this point of view, good health is important for a stutterer.

It need only be said, in this connection, that for the most part physical hygiene involves adequate practices of eating, sleeping, exercising, working, and relaxing. Beyond that, anyone is to be advised to see a doctor, and to report back sufficiently often for him to check the effectiveness of his recommendations and to forestall any serious threats of disease. So far as stuttering is concerned, it is to be said simply that, although anatomical and basic physiological matters are usually of little importance, if they are shown to be of importance in a specific case they should be given proper attention.

STUTTERERS DIFFER—AND CHANGE

A great deal more could be said about stuttering. The impression is not to be left that the results of scientific studies of the problem have been fully covered. Several hundred investigations of stuttering have been made and a large number of publications on the subject are available. In order to summarize, and especially to evaluate this material, it would be necessary to write a very large book. In fact, in order to elaborate in detail the basis and the implications of the discussion that has been presented, it would be necessary to expand that discussion to the proportions of a volume of considerable size. The main purpose in writing this article has been to suggest one type of practical approach to the problem.[3]

In the actual carrying out of this approach, use is made of any specific techniques and of any particular manners of explanation and instruction that seem advisable in specific cases. Details of treatment depend upon the age and background of the individual, the nature and complexity of his semantic environment, the severity of the stuttering, the time available for conferences and instruction, etc. Not only are no two stutterers alike, but no one stutterer remains the same from time to time. The principles presented here, insofar as they are sound, are useful only as they are judiciously adapted to the individual and to his ever-changing state and circumstances.

[3] A concise statement of the point of view presented here is to be found in W. Johnson, "A Semantic Theory of Stuttering," in Eugene Hahn, *Stuttering: Significant Theories and Therapies*, Stanford University, Calif.: Stanford University Press, 1943.

THE URGENCY OF PARADISE

OTHER PROBLEMS, TOO

$\mathcal{A}$ LITTLE SEMANTIC SLUMMING WILL MAKE IT CLEAR that stuttering is by no means the only form that fear and tension take. It is only one of the many noises made by the square pegs of misevaluation as they rattle and bang about in the round holes of reality. It remains to be pointed out, therefore, that the essentials of what has been said in the last chapter may be applied generally to a considerable range of problems. Indeed, none of our troubles occurs in a semantic vacuum, and for an understanding of practically all of them it is necessary to look closely to the semantic environments in which they take place. Moreover, most of our difficulties involve, as stuttering does, evaluative reactions that are maladjustive. Again, like stuttering, practically all of our maladjustments show themselves in some sort of physiological changes and muscular tensions and movements, all of which take place in an organism. In other words, if stuttering has been in some measure explained in the preceding chapter, then a great deal of other behavior also is to be explained as well in more or less the same terms. Tendencies to become angry easily, or depressed, or flustered, or worried—or pointlessly gay—or "unaccountably" tired, even ill, are all more or less understandable in terms of the relationships among (a) semantic environment, (b) evaluative reactions, (c) physiological and overt behavior, and (d) the organism. Precisely because this is so, it would involve a good deal of fruitless repetition to discuss in detail each of the many problems that might be considered in the way in which we have dealt with stuttering.

It will be useful, however, to suggest that in trying to understand and do something about any specific adjustment problem, the following questions might profitably be used as a rough guide:

A. With respect to semantic environment
   1. What particular policies, attitudes, beliefs, customs, prejudices, standards, etc. are emphasized in your environment in ways that create difficulty for you?
   2. Who are the specific individuals, and what are the institutions, agencies, or situations through which these policies, etc., affect you in disturbing ways?
   3. Particularly, what kinds of strivings, what goals or ideals, does your semantic environment encourage, reward, or enforce—and what obstacles does it place in the way of their achievement so far as you are concerned? (See Chapter I.)
   4. In what specific respects, and by what procedures, can your semantic environment (as defined in these terms) be changed to your advantage?
B. With respect to evaluative reactions
   1. Which of your own beliefs, attitudes, ideals, conflicts, etc. play an important part in your problem?
   2. What important identifications, semantic blockages, allnesses, unconscious projections, etc., do these involve?
   3. What are the goals toward which you are striving, and in what ways are you frustrated, day by day or in long-time terms, in your attempts to achieve them? (See Chapter I.)
   4. In what respects, and by what procedures, might you increase your awareness of these factors, so as to state your problems more clearly in a way that will point up the practical possibilities of changing your evaluative reactions?
C. With respect to physiological and overt behavior
   1. In what important tensions, undelayed signal reactions, and other forms of behavior do you express your maladjustive beliefs, attitudes, ideals, frustrations, etc.?
   2. To what extent can you change these ways of behaving to advantage simply by experimentally trying out other ways of reacting?
   3. What desirable changes in your outward behavior would probably result from particular alterations in your evaluative reactions?
D. With respect to the organism
   1. What features of your physical make-up set specific limits to your evaluative reactions, or to your physiological and overt behavior?

2. To what extent, and by what procedures, can these features of your physical make-up be changed?

With these questions as a guide, a considerable number of personal problems can be rather clearly formulated, and practical ways of dealing with them can be worked out with prospects of worthwhile results. The case outline and the procedures described in Chapter XVI, together with the techniques discussed in Chapter X, are designed to be of help in this connection, of course. These simple guides and methods make up a considerable body of practical know-how.

After all, changes in personality in large part boil down to changes that are to be described in these terms. However, they are changes that do not usually occur very fast or to any great extent, at least in desired directions, unless they are deliberately planned and encouraged. The methods that have been described, particularly in Chapters X and XVI, can be helpful in bringing about such changes—but it is to be thoroughly recognized, of course, that *the only way to learn how to use these methods is to use them.* Merely knowing about them, or sitting around talking about them, does nothing to make you the Captain of your Fate. Knowing about the methods and talking about them are useful only if the knowing and the talking lead to effective doing. For those who feel that they do recognize this, but who yet are impressed by the mystifying character of the little word *how,* the exercises described following this chapter should prove, in some measure at least, to be helpful and encouraging, provided they are actually done. They should help one to get started, to take the first few faltering and utterly important steps out of the vapory world of words and into the vast, exciting reaches of actuality and action. Once started, the process of readjustment tends to lead steadily toward the discovery that a scientific, or extensional, way of living is fun as well as fruitful.

DISORDERS OF COMMUNICATION

Among the many, many other things left to write are a few words about what goes on, and what goes wrong, when Mr. A. talks to Mr. B. Throughout this book we have, of course, discussed from one angle and another the process of communication, and especially the 'language of maladjustment. There is something to be gained, however, by high-lighting the fact that what is common to the various aspects of communication, to speaking, writing, listening, and reading, is to be seen precisely in the process of abstracting. This means that the defects and inefficiencies that so often affect these language functions are to be understood to an important degree as disorders of abstracting.

For this reason a discussion of problems of communication will serve two important purposes. In the first place, it will indicate the nature of some of the most serious semantic difficulties we have, as individuals and as a society. In the second place, it will provide a particularly meaningful summary of the more important points discussed in this book. There will be practical value in such a summary, and it will be the more interesting because of the light it will throw on the process of communication, a process with which we are all vitally concerned day in and day out.

In many universities and colleges attempts are currently being made to develop courses in communication skills, which are intended to integrate the teaching that has traditionally been done separately in courses in English and speech. In some universities this general trend is taking the even more ambitious form of departments, or schools, or divisions of communication, bringing together the research and instructional programs in speech, radio, journalism, and allied areas. These stirrings of reform seem to be motivated by a growing realization that there must be some sort of fundamental relationship among the various language functions. In most instances, however, there appears to be some difficulty in working out practical means of coordinating the efforts of the various administrators and instructors concerned. The crucial fact would appear to be that the sort of integration being sought can only be cultivated *within* the individual teacher, not *among* several different teachers.

What is needed for the teaching of language—as distinguished from the specialized teaching of the writing of language, or the speaking or the reading of it, or the listening to language—is a generalized language for talking about language behavior. What is needed is a terminology that represents writing, speaking, reading, and listening as closely interrelated aspects of the basic process of communication itself. It is this sort of language about language, about *communication*, that general semantics provides.

A little simple analysis tends to bring this out rather clearly. There are certain questions that serve to reduce the problem of communication to practical terms. Just what is involved in communication and what are the various stages in the process? What functions take place at each stage? At what points do problems arise, and what kinds of errors or disorders tend to occur? Essential answers to these questions are given in the following outline. (It should be mentioned perhaps that the outline has not been prepared solely for teachers of communication skills. In the fascinating serial story of Mr. A talking to Mr. B, each of us plays the part of Mr. A or of Mr. B, and so the outline that follows should provide each of us with some clue to the frustrations and astonishments we not infrequently experience in talking to Mr. B or in listening to Mr. A.)

The skeleton plan of the analysis is shown in Fig. 17.

OUTLINE OF THE PROCESS OF COMMUNICATION:
STAGES, FUNCTIONS, AND POSSIBLE DISORDERS

Stage 1: An event, or happening. This might be anything that a person can hear, see, smell, taste, etc. It is a source of sensory stimulation. The point is that communication—like abstracting—begins fundamentally with some aspect of reality, something experienced as first-order fact. This does not mean that every statement we make is about first-hand experience, but ultimately any statement makes sense only if it can be related somehow to reality as observed or experienced by somebody.

Stage 2: Stimulation of observer: visual, auditory, chemical, mechanical (pressure), electrical, X-ray, etc.

  I. Functions
    A. Sensory reception
  II. Disorders
    A. Sensory defects or deficiencies
      1. Affecting sense modes of sight, hearing, smell, taste, touch, kinesthesis, etc.
      2. Special reactions to stimulation by electrical currents, X rays, chemical substances, foods, gases, etc.

1. An event occurs

2. which stimulates Mr. A through eyes, ears, or other sensory organs, and the resulting

3. nervous impulses travel to Mr. A's brain, and from there to his muscles and glands, producing tensions, preverbal "feelings," etc.

4. which Mr. A then begins to translate into words, according to his accustomed verbal patterns, and out of all the words he "thinks of"

5. he "selects," or abstracts, certain ones which he arranges in some fashion, and then

Mr. A speaks to Mr. B

by means of sound waves

and light waves

6. whose ears and eyes are stimulated by the sound waves and light waves, respectively, and the resulting

7. nervous impulses travel to Mr. B's brain, and from there to his muscles and glands, producing tensions, preverbal "feelings," etc.

8. which Mr. B then begins to translate into words, according to *his* accustomed verbal patterns, and out of all the words *he* "thinks of"

9. he "selects," or abstracts certain ones, which he arranges in some fashion and then

Etc. Mr. B speaks, or acts, accordingly, thereby stimulating Mr. A—or somebody else—and so the process of communication goes on, and on—with complications, as indicated in the outline in the accompanying text . . .

Fig. 17. Schematic stage-by-stage summary of what goes on when when Mr. A talks to Mr. B—the process of communication. The functions and possible disorders at each stage of the process are indicated more fully in the Outline of the Process of Communication, pages 471–476.

Stage 3: Organismic evaluations (preverbal "feelings")
I. Functions
    A. Transmission of nerve currents from eye, ear, and other sense organs to the spinal, thalamic, and cortical levels of the central nervous system
        1. Relay of nerve currents from spinal, thalamic, and cortical levels out to muscles and glands, with consequent bodily changes (muscular tensions, glandular reactions, etc.)
II. Disorders
    A. Impaired transmission because of damage to nerve tracts resulting from infections, tumors, hemorrhages, toxins, mechanical injuries, inherited defects, etc.
    B. Impaired transmission due to acquired or learned semantic blockages, as seen in inattentiveness, disinterest, stupor, prejudice, aversion to colors, etc., fear, fainting in response to certain odors, etc., excessive self-defensiveness and the like

Stage 4: Verbalization of organismic evaluations (putting feelings into words, roughly "thinking")
I. Functions
    A. Symbolic formulation (translation of "feelings," tensions, "hunches," impulses into words and other symbols)
II. Disorders
    A. Deficiency in vocabulary, in knowledge of grammar, and other aspects of language development
    B. Aphasias (disorders of language due to brain injury or disease)
        1. Faulty expression
        2. Faulty reception or comprehension
        3. Mixed, plus defects in verbal association, in naming, etc.
    C. Disorders due to generally intensional, prescientific orientation
        1. Identifications
        2. Semantic blockages
            a. Allness, inadequate conditionality, undelayed signal reactions
        3. Two-valued language structure
        4. Absolutistic orientation
            a. Elementalism, undue certainty
        5. Ventriloquizing: prescientific orientation to vested authority (see Chapter IV)
        6. Lack of consciousness of projection
        7. Rigidity of language structure (see Chapter XI)
            a. Content
            b. Formal
            c. Evaluational
        8. Dead-level abstracting (see Chapter XII)

    D. Deficiencies in knowledge concerning facts to be symbolized (lack of information, "ignorance")

        1. Lack of adequate understanding of the point of view of the listener or reader

Stage 5: Verbal and non-verbal expression of evaluations

  I Functions

    A. Speech

    B. Writing

    C. Use of special symbol systems, such as those of art, music, the dance, mathematics, special codes, etc.

    D. Auxiliary functions

        1. Gesture

        2. Posture

        3. Facial expression

        4. General bodily action

        5. Voice (pitch, loudness, quality, rate or timing)

        6. Background or setting, staging

          a. Use of music, banners, sound effects, color, lighting, clothes, special uniforms, etc.

        7. Special means of transmission

          a. Use of radio, television, movies, telephone, telegraphy, type-writing, speech recording, diagrams, pictures, methods of printing, etc.

  II. Disorders

    A. Speech and voice defects

        1. Articulation (sound omissions, as in *pay* for *play;* sound substitutions, as in *wun* for *run;* sound distortions, as a "whistling" *s,* or slighted, indistinct sounds)

          a. Chiefly due to faulty training, or lack of proper stimulation (no significant organic cause)

            (1) Foreign and regional dialects

          b. Chiefly due to organic conditions

            (1) Cleft palate

            (2) Faulty mouth structures, such as high and narrow hard palate, dental irregularities, large tongue, etc.

            (3) Cerebral palsy (spasticity, athetosis, ataxia, due to damaged nerve cells)

            (4) Aphasias

            (5) Paralyses

            (6) Hearing loss

          c. Chiefly due to "psychological" conditions

            (1) Mental deficiency

      (2) Common maladjustments, such as infantilism, shyness, withdrawing personality, etc. (see Chapter XIV)

      (3) Psychoneuroses and psychoses (see Chapter XIII)

  2. Fluency-anxiety problems

    a. Stuttering (see Chapter XVII)

    b. General non-fluency—repetitive, jerky, slow, irregular, labored speech

      (1) Chiefly due to faulty training

      (2) Associated with psychoneurosis, psychosis, mental deficiency

      (3) Associated with organic pathology, such as cerebral palsy, aphasia, paralysis, etc.

  3. Voice

    a. Pitch too high, too low, monotonous, patterned

    b. Loudness too high, too low, monotonous, patterned

    c Rate, or timing, too fast, too slow, monotonous, jerky, patterned

    d. Quality defects: hoarseness, harshness, nasality, etc.

      (1) All these may or may not be associated with organic pathology, hearing loss, maladjustment, or faulty training

  4. Word usage

    a. Mispronunciations

    b. Faulty grammar

    c. Inappropriate or ineffective word choice

  5. Lack of knowledge and skill in special means of transmission

    a. Radio, television, telephone, movies, speech recorders, etc.

B. Writing deficiencies

  1. Inadequate handwriting skill

    a. Due to faulty training

    b. Due to maladjustment

    c. Due to organic conditions, such as paralysis, etc.

  2. Misspellings, errors in punctuation, etc.

  3. Lack of skill in use of special means of writing, such as typewriting, or lack of facilities for printing, poor page layout, etc.

C. Lack of knowledge and skill in use of certain symbol systems, such as those of art, music, mathematics, etc.

  1. Lack of skill in organizing what is communicated according to the rules appropriate to the symbol system used, and according to the purposes of the particular communication being attempted

D. Lack of skill in use of background or setting, staging

E. Paralyses, crippling conditions, diseases, etc. interfering with expressive gesture, posture, and other bodily action
   1. Physical unattractiveness, or characteristics of shape and size, skin color, etc., which tend to call forth unfavorable reactions on the part of listeners (due often to signal reactions on the part of the listeners, of course)
F. Evaluational disorders
   1. Stage fright and other fears, antagonisms, undue awe of the listener, feelings of inferiority, unworthiness, etc.
G Defects in means and conditions of transmission
   1. Defects in means of transmission
      a. Radio static, unclear or inappropriate printing, etc.
   2. Interfering conditions
      a. Noise, poor lighting, distractions, etc.
Stage 6: First-order stimulation of listener or reader (or spectator) by the light waves and sound waves received from the speaker, or the light waves received from the printed page
   I. Functions
      A. Sensory reception
   II. Disorders
      A. Sensory deficiencies, particularly defective vision and hearing loss
Stage 7: Organismic evaluations (preverbal "feelings") of the listener or reader (see *Stage 3*)
Stage 8: Verbalization of organismic evaluations (putting feelings into words, roughly "thinking") by the listener or reader (see *Stage 4*)
Stage 9: Verbal and non-verbal expression of evaluations by the listener or reader: the speech and action of the listener or reader which constitute the observable effect of the communication (see *Stage 5*)
Etc.: The speech and action of the listener or reader—*Stage 9*—set up stimulation in other persons, and so the process of communication continues indefinitely, involving the stages, functions, and possible disorders summarized in this outline

The great extent to which the process of abstracting is basic to communication is indicated by this outline. In fact, communication is seen to be an attempt on the part of one person to convey some of the products of his own abstracting to another person. He does this usually by speaking or writing—that is, by producing sound waves or light waves, or both. The other person "receives" these sound waves or light waves and then proceeds to abstract from them evaluations of his own, which may or may not correspond to those which the speaker or writer intended to convey to him. Finally, he expresses these evaluations in words or deeds that may please or astonish the speaker or writer. In other words, communication consists of two processes of abstracting laid end to end, as it were.

What there is to be said, then, about communication is to be said in great part under these headings:

1. Sources of sensory stimulation, or "reality"—that is, the submicroscopic level of abstraction, as shown in Fig. 9, page 135. It is in such terms that we can describe what ultimately there is to talk or write about.

2. The sensations of the speaker or writer: the initial abstracting which he does on the macroscopic and (in some instances) the microscopic levels, as represented in Fig. 9. He can communicate only what he can "take in." If he is blind, for example, he will have no visual sensations to abstract and convey.

3. The preverbal abstracting by the speaker or writer of his sensations. He does this abstracting on the "silent" levels.

4. The verbal abstracting of the speaker or writer—how he puts into words his preverbal tensions, "hunches," etc. He does not, of course, overtly express all the words he "thinks of."

5. The speaking or writing, the words actually expressed. These are the abstracts that are "selected" to be communicated.

6. The light waves and sound waves produced in speaking or writing. We see and hear them as ink marks, bodily actions, and the kinds of sounds we call spoken words. What they "are" as physical events is to be represented ultimately on the submicroscopic level of abstracting. They can be observed, of course, on the microscopic and macroscopic levels. (Incidentally, it is in this connection that a great deal of research in communication has been done: through detailed analysis of voice waves by Professor Carl E. Seashore and others, through electronic research leading to more and more efficient means of sound wave transmission, through investigations in "visual education," and through studies of the perception of various kinds of type used in printing, etc.)

7. The sensations of the listener or reader: his initial abstracting, on the preverbal levels, of the light waves and sound waves.

8. The preverbal abstracting by the listener or reader of his sensations.

9. The verbal abstracting of the listener or reader—how he puts into words his preverbal tensions, "hunches," etc. He, like the speaker or writer, does not overtly express, or even seriously consider, all the words he "thinks of."

10. Finally, the verbal-level abstracting of the listener or reader as outwardly expressed by him in words or in action.

We see that the whole process of communication from beginning to end is to be described chiefly in terms of abstracting and its products. To be trained in communication, therefore, is to be trained primarily in abstracting. Whether you speak, write, read, or listen—or act, paint, or play a piano—is incidental. Whether you speak English, French, or Chinese is incidental. Whether you write prose, poetry, numbers, musical notes, or draw designs is incidental. Whether you listen to a newscast, a sermon, a poem, a weather forecast, or a lecture on atomic power is incidental. What is fundamental is that in all such activities you are abstracting and so evaluating symbols that are being or may be communicated. How well you do so will depend largely on how highly conscious you are of abstracting, how well you know and how skilfully you can apply the principles and techniques of abstracting. (Refer to Chapters V through X.)

The disorders of communication, as listed in the preceding outline, are all in some measure disorders of abstracting, or stand in some relationship to such disorders. Besides the defects in means and conditions of transmission (radio static, poor lighting, etc.) the disorders of communication are seen to fall rather definitely into three categories:

1. Disorders of abstracting, in the speaker and in the listener (or writer and reader)

2. Disorders of overt expression (speech defects and impaired bodily action due to paralyses, etc.)

3. Disorders of sensory reception (mainly visual deficiency and hearing loss)

Strictly speaking, disorders of overt expression, e.g., speech defects, and disorders of sensory reception, e.g., hearing deficiencies, are different from the evaluative disorders of abstracting such as are listed under *Stage 4* in the outline. But their practical effects, so far as communication is concerned, depend in no small part on how they are evaluated. You cannot give an adequate account of a speech defect except by describing the person who has it and the people who react to it. The *communicative* significance of stuttering, for example, does not as a rule lie in the fact that it renders speech unintelligible, because it seldom does. It lies rather in the fact that the listener evaluates it as important. Most of us pay considerable attention to hesitancies in speech, to foreign dialects and nasal twangs. We place a great deal of value on niceties of voice and diction and rhythm—or of grammar and spelling. We like our wisdom to come wrapped in Cellophane, as it were—with the result that, if it is wrapped in Cellophane, we accept a lot of nonsense, too, and we pass by no end of wisdom that comes in brown paper. A two-hundred-pound man who lisps can utter the most urgent truth, only to have it disregarded by listeners who permit their evaluative processes to be short-circuited by the inconsequential fact that the speaker produces a *th* where they are used to hearing an *s*. It is not that they are unable to understand what he says—if they listen to what he says. The trouble is that they listen to his lisping. His speech is actually less defective than their listening. As a matter of fact, if listeners did not evaluate his lisp as a defect it just wouldn't be one; it would have as a rule no *communicative* significance at all.

Similarly, a speaker whose complexion happens to be relatively dark, so that his listeners classify him—more or less irrelevantly—as a Negro, can speak great wisdom only to have it fall, quite often, on what actually amount to *deaf* ears. His skin color obviously could have no *communicative* significance were it not for the evaluative habits, the signal reactions, of the listeners who attach importance to it. Indeed, one of the particularly serious aspects of racial prejudice lies in the fact that it makes for such ineffective listening. Any kind of prejudice, racial or not, tends to result in a sort of functional deafness—"I'd never listen to that guy. He can't tell *me* anything!" In fact, it works both ways. The prejudiced individual not only refuses to listen; he also on occasion refuses to talk. It is when people get to the point where they won't speak to each other that communication breaks down completely, and the basic importance of evaluational disorders in relation to the process of communication becomes as plain as the up-turned nose on a long face. One of the most serious things about the Negro-White problem is that so many fair-skinned people are not on speaking terms with so many persons who have dark complexions. Until they learn to talk to each other, and especially to listen to each other, there will continue to be a Negro-White problem.

In like vein there is something extremely important to be said about dictatorial forms of government—about authoritarian policies anywhere: in the church, the army, the medical profession, the school, in industry, or in the home. The extravagantly disregarded soldier at Honolulu who reported to his lieutenant on the morning of December 7, 1941, that he detected approaching planes, only to be ignored, will live through history—for those who can read history—as a symbol of the inefficiency of communication in the sort of rigid structure found in authoritarian organization. To a general semanticist—to any scientifically oriented person—the "meaning" of Pearl Harbor is that freedom to speak is dangerous when it is separated from the obligation to listen. The value of democracy, with its *ideal* of free speech and "open-earedness," lies fundamentally in the provision it makes for efficient communication—for talking *back* as well as down. In a peculiarly basic sense, democracy consists in listening without semantic blockages. And this means the boss and the officer and the teacher as well as the worker, the private, and the pupil. One of the most astonishing sights to be seen all too often in our schools is a teacher of civics or political science conducting a class in "democratic government" with the pupils sitting in neat rows dutifully giving answers prescribed by the teacher and the book. A dictator can't teach democracy. It just can't be taught with a hickory stick any more than it can be taught with a bayonet. It can only be taught by a good listener.

The point of all this is that to a large extent the importance of speech defects, and of other characteristics of speakers (such as skin color or social status) is to be found in the evaluative reactions of those who listen, or refuse to listen, to them. The "correction" of speech defects has to be done in part through the reeducation of those who listen to them and *for* them. Just so, the solution of racial conflicts is hardly to be found in plastic surgery; it promises to be found largely in effective training in communication—as when the abstracting process of a person with a dark complexion, for example, is laid neatly end to end with the abstracting process of an individual with a pale complexion, to form one efficient process of communication. Whenever in the teaching of communication anything less than this sort of result is achieved, the verdict would seem to be that however much voice and diction, or spelling and punctuation, have been improved, communication has not been taught.

THE URGENCY OF PARADISE

Even before August 6, 1945, these considerations were of basic importance. Since that unforgettable day, when we arrived with bewildering suddenness in the Atomic Age, they have become urgent to the point of sheer desperation. The race against destruction has now become a sprint. Prejudices and other semantic blockages that gum up the communication process will evidently have to be dissolved if the great majority of us are to escape the fleeting and thoroughly unrewarding experience of sudden death. In the past when words failed, men resorted to communication by means of hot steel, but most of us never got in the way of it. The next time words fail, millions of us will die, having discovered a second or two beforehand, if at all, how extremely advantageous it would have been had we learned how to talk to other people and how to listen to them.

We cannot go back to the Middle Ages, or even to July, 1945, with atomic bombs in our hip pockets. There is nothing to which we can *return* that will insure our safety, to say nothing of our further personal and cultural enrichment. The scientific method that produced atomic power can lead only to vast devastation when joined with the traditional prescientific evaluating that converts this power into bombs. There is plainly nothing "good" or "bad" in atomic power itself. We can use it, however, to make a shambles or a paradise. There is clearly nothing destructive about the scientific method, as such. What is destructive is a prescientific way of living in the atomic world produced by science. It takes people who are scientific in dealing with the personal and social problems created or intensified by scientific achievements to survive in such a world. And these problems are in no small part those of language structure, of semantic reaction, of communication.

Whenever the stakes are precious, words must not fail us any more. The same scientific method by which we have made our means of destruction so utterly effective must be used to make our communication, and so our social organization, correspondingly efficient. In releasing the long-pent-up fury of the atom, we have created for ourselves the necessity of quickly becoming what we might have been, of designing and establishing a scientific education that will wipe out our semantic blockages which make impossible the sanity and cooperation that are now simply essential for remaining alive. We can no longer afford serious conflict, aggression, contempt, and hate. We can no longer tolerate studied confusion, cultivated distrust, and verbal irresponsibility. It is neither an academic nor a moral issue. It is a practical, down-to-earth question of survival. Uranium hangs heavy over our heads so long as we strive to preserve beliefs, loyalties, and institutions that disunite us—so long as we cherish the old superstitions, prides, and prejudices with which we have muddled through to the crumbling edge of blinding disintegration.

Because, through science, we have so drastically changed the conditions under which we live, we must, likewise through science, change the manner in which we live to accord with those conditions. The word *must*, as used here, merely implies acceptance of continued existence as our basic objective. It makes for a way of saying simply that if we continue to change the conditions under which we live, while maintaining attitudes, beliefs, customs, and human relationships adapted to other conditions which no longer exist, we may with reason expect increasing maladjustment and eventual catastrophe. If this seems to emphasize the prospects of gloom, that is only because of the point of view from which it is considered. The point of view intended for emphasis is that which gives due weight, not merely to the need, but also to the possibility and the exciting advantages of change. Atomic power promises abundance as readily as desolation—but only on the condition, of course, that we welcome the abundance. It provides the effective basis for a world state as readily as it provides the means for nationalistic groups to fight each other to the death—but only provided we not decline the opportunity to create a world state. It contains the germ of an economy so efficient that freedom from want and from drudgery might be realized in fact, quite as clearly as it contains the seeds of economic ruin—again provided, of course, we do not too fondly cherish want and drudgery. The exhilaration it promises is by no means less than the gnawing misery it portends—if only we are willing to endure exhilaration. The terms on which we may be permitted to remain as tenants, so to speak, are that we agree to an astonishingly marvelous job of remodeling.

We have arrived, that is, at the strange circumstance of having to accept a virtual paradise if we are not to perish: only in our more stately mansions may refuge still be found.

Semantic Exercises

*T*HE FOLLOWING ARE PRESENTED AS ILLUSTRATIVE OF CERTAIN types of assignments and exercises which can be used in classes and study groups, or by individuals. They have been selected from a considerable number that have been tried out during six years of experience in teaching general semantics at the State University of Iowa. The principle of learning by doing is to be particularly emphasized in general semantics, and therefore personal applications of the basic principles and techniques are essential. It is to be stressed, however, that any such set of assignments as the following is to be regarded as suggestive; each person must necessarily apply general semantics to his own problems and under circumstances that will be in some measure different for him from what they will be for any other individual. The following list of suggested applications will have served its purpose if it indicates possible ways of putting into practice a semantic or scientific orientation in ways that will prove most fruitful to the individual reader.

1. A SEMANTIC NOTEBOOK

One of the best ways to improve your understanding of general semantics and its implications is to cultivate the habit of observing the violations of its principles in the everyday behavior of the people about you. Quite often in snatches of conversation overheard on busses, in restaurants and elsewhere, as well as in the remarks of your friends and associates, you will hear all-out statements of antagonism or approval; pronouncements concerning Jews, capitalists, labor leaders, Congressmen, etc., expressive of allness and of generally intensional evaluation; arguments and misunderstandings revolving around unsuspected differences in the way certain words are being used; undelayed verbal reactions—and various other evidences of semantic confusion and maladjustive language behavior. By jotting down key words and phrases, with brief notes describing the circumstances in each case, an instructive collection of "semantic misfirings" will accumulate quickly.

Unconscious projection can be seen most clearly perhaps, at least so far as it colors language behavior, in situations where people tend to put up a "front," to try to impress each other. In large hotels, swanky restaurants, railway dining cars, during theater intermissions, at art exhibits, concerts,

485

formal dances and dinners, in fashionable shops, at smart-set sporting events, etc., you can observe a rich variety of remarks in which projection runs riot. Veblen's *The Theory of the Leisure Class* should be read in this connection in order to sharpen your appreciation of the "symbols of swank." People eating a dinner fit for your mother's birthday will complain of the service, the food, the floor show, referring to the more satisfactory meals they have had in New Orleans or San Francisco (where they probably complained as much at the time). Even a semanticist with amateur standing can see through such verbal behavior and sense the feelings of inferiority and insecurity which prompt the speakers to put on such a show of cultivated taste, affluence, and sophistication. To imply that anyone who might be contented at the Ritz is an oaf is to make a bid for social status that is beyond the Ritz and so beyond the reach of practically everyone within earshot. The following paragraph from *The New Yorker* (February 10, 1945, p. 15) illustrates the point:[1]

"The two ladies at the table next to ours were discussing the food shortage at lunch. The discussion lasted through the following: Whiskey sour, Yankee bean soup, mushrooms and kidneys sauté with French fried potatoes and string beans, mixed green salad, hard rolls and marmalade, chocolate éclair, coffee with cream and sugar. The ladies' conclusion was that the situation, which had formerly been serious, was now desperate."

It is relatively easy to gauge at least roughly the degree to which such statements, made as bids for social status, are projective of evaluations rather than descriptive of whatever is presumably being talked about. The jotting down of a few dozen examples, with just enough detail for essential accuracy, will heighten your awareness of the self-projective character of "language in action."

Remarks made during moments of anger, irritability, resentment, grief, or embarrassment will often be found to be richly illustrative of unconscious projection also, and of allness, flagrant identification, and delusional or nearly delusional reactions. A few of these, recorded with notes concerning the situations in which they are observed, will serve to underscore effectively many of the statements about language behavior made in this book.

Newspapers, magazines, and the radio provide a continuous source of "semanticana." Some are news bits which tell of amusing instances of communication gone wrong, such as the one about the Nebraska farmer who said, when questioned about flagging a mile-long freight train, "I wasn't tryin' to stop no train, I was just wavin'." Misunderstandings in great variety are reported in the daily press, and they range from the hilarious to the tragic. Semantic factors in such misunderstandings as seen in accidents and in the general problem of safety education have been discussed effectively

[1] Permission, *The New Yorker*. Copyright, 1945, The F-R Publishing Corporation.

by Benjamin Lee Whorf in an article entitled "The Relation of Habitual Thought and Behavior to Language" (*Etc.*, 1944, Vol. I, No. 4, pp. 197–215). A study of this article will help you to read between the lines of much that appears in the news columns of your daily paper. Misunderstandings make news, and to interpret the news they make by passing it off as due to stupidity, cussedness, selfishness, or simple misfortune—whatever you suppose such words to mean—is usually to miss the point by a wide margin, semantically speaking. A collection of news items that illustrate misunderstandings and confusions which imply semantic blockages, identifications, undue certainties, unconscious projections, and other manifestations of intensional orientation will make a valuable addition to your semantic notebook.

Editorials, commentators' columns, and advertisements especially, frequently contain plainly biased, colored, and slanted statements. Underlining these is good practice in evaluating what you read. By preserving the underlined editorials, columns, and advertisements in your notebook, making sure to date each one, you can make a revealing record of your development as a discriminating reader.

It is entertaining to collect cartoons that owe their humor to the semantic confusions which they portray. You will be impressed by the number of cartoons that fall into this general classification, once you begin to look for them. The same goes for jokes also. Such items will add spice to your notebook.

In your notebook you should also record your own semantic blunders. This is especially important. Personal application is what matters most in learning the principles and techniques of general semantics, and failures in making application of them should be observed and examined. Once you begin to make such a record you will doubtless be surprised how often you will catch yourself harboring a belief or maintaining an attitude that runs counter to a semantic or scientific orientation. And you will find yourself indulging in undelayed signal reactions, making uncritical identifications, and in other ways behaving as though you had never read this or any other book on general semantics. A record of such reactions, reviewed from time to time, will prove definitely helpful to anyone who is serious about putting the semantic principles into practice. Likewise, a record of particularly happy or effective applications will be beneficial. A sort of semantic diary is what is here suggested. It should not be too detailed or time-consuming. The items included in it should be selected with some sense of discrimination. Some of your blunders and some of your successes will be far more significant than others, and the more significant ones should be recorded.

Finally, you will profit more from your reading in general semantics if you write at least a brief comment about each book and article you read. These comments should not be mere summaries so much as reflections of your reactions in terms that are of particular importance to you personally.

If the book or article arouses a keen interest in something, or challenges a belief you have long held, or changes an attitude, or suggests an experiment, or throws light on a personal problem, or clarifies a point that had been obscure, make a brief note of it. Doing this will help you to retain and to use what you have gained from your reading.

You should have read this book carefully before starting a notebook such as is here suggested. Preferably, of course, you should also have read the source book of general semantics, Alfred Korzybski's *Science and Sanity*. And while compiling the notebook you should continue reading, either going back over material already covered so as to get a more clear understanding of it, or reading additional books such as Hayakawa's *Language in Action* or Lee's *Language Habits in Human Affairs*. Current and back issues of *Etc.: A Review of General Semantics*, published by the Society for General Semantics (Illinois Institute of Technology, Chicago, Illinois) will also prove stimulating.

The notebook entries will prove particularly interesting and enlightening a year or so after they have been made. Sharing your notebook with others and reading similar notebooks compiled by them will add considerable interest and profit to your study of general semantics.

You may, of course, use the notebook for recording your performance of any other assignments that you may do.

2. STATING A PERSONAL PROBLEM

In Chapter I a basic pattern of personal maladjustment is presented as a sequence running from idealism to frustration to demoralization, IFD. The ideals involved in this pattern are said to be high in three respects: they are vaguely defined; they are highly valued; they are, insofar as they are defined, unrealistic. Failure to recognize their achievement gives one a sense of frustration which leads to (a) a feeling of inferiority in some degree and (b) consequent reactions ranging from aggression to pronounced discouragement and loss of initiative.

Select your own most important problem and write an account of it in terms of this IFD pattern. You need not strive to be ideally exhaustive in writing this account, but be sufficiently detailed to make it reasonably comprehensible to another person who does not know you. (The implication that you could not present your personal problems in other terms is not intended. This is simply an exercise in applying the IFD formula to some problem of your own.)

It will usually prove to be the best plan to begin by stating the problem in your own words, simply writing a general answer to the question, "What's the matter?" Then discuss the problem in terms of the goals or ideals you strive for that you seem unable to attain, and the tensions, irritabilities, "aggressions," resentments, despondencies, etc., with which you react to the feelings of frustration at not being able to achieve the goals. Indicate the relative vagueness of the goals, the intensity with which you desire to achieve them, and, insofar as you can specify what the goals or ideals are, make the most realistic statement you can as to the abilities and opportunities you have which would make it likely, or improbable, that you might achieve the goals.

Finally, try to restate your goals or ideals in relatively specific terms and in such a way as to make their attainment reasonably probable for you within a tolerable time limit. Having restated the goals, write a brief statement of the most effective ways in which you might proceed to work toward them.

3. Attitude Histories

Select some attitude that you have—your attitude toward some racial group, toward some particular person or point of view, or any other attitude that is relatively important to you. Write the history of this attitude. Describe as well as you can its origins—where you got it—and the circumstances of its development. Give an account of the more important ways in which it has figured in your social relationships. Conclude this "case history of an attitude" with a semantic evaluation of it, indicating the degree to which it represents an intensional—and an extensional—orientation on your part.

You may, of course, treat as many of your attitudes in this way as you feel would be advantageous.

4. Arguments

Keep a record for a week or two of the arguments you get into, and of those you overhear. Put down a brief statement of what each argument is about, who the participants are, and the circumstances. Indicate the degree to which the participants reach agreement and what they agree on. Date each one. Classify each one in one of two general categories: (a) those due chiefly to differences in definition of one or more key terms, so that solution would require reasonable extensional agreement concerning these terms; (b) those due chiefly to differences in factual statement, so that solution would depend on observation of the disputed facts (or checking of a published factual report perhaps). Finally, compute the proportion of the arguments falling in each class that resulted in essential agreement.

5. Misunderstandings

In addition to the misunderstandings figuring in news stories, which have been discussed in the description of a semantic notebook, collect several misunderstandings in which you are personally involved. Perhaps a friend understood you were to meet him at six o'clock and you thought it was to be at seven o'clock; you order a lemon coke and get a cherry coke; you study what turns out to be the wrong assignment in one of your courses; you bring home a loaf of white bread and find that it should have been whole-wheat, etc. Within a week or so you should be able to accumulate a fairly large collection of these simple misunderstandings. Write down the essential details concerning each one, with the date. Classify them into: (a) those apparently due to the phonetic character of one or more key words (e.g., confusion of "chicken salad" with "chicken sandwich"); (b) those apparently due to unchecked assumptions (e.g., taking for granted that your wife would expect you to bring whole-wheat bread since that is the kind *you* prefer); (c) those apparently due to habit, or unconditional response (e.g., you and your roommate have been accustomed to eating lunch together at a certain restaurant, and so you go to that restaurant although, as you recall later, he had asked you to meet him elsewhere *this* time); (d) those apparently due to a failure to specify necessary details (e.g., your friend brings you three-cent stamps, which you would ordinarily want, because you forgot to specify that this time you needed two-cent stamps). If other classifications seem better, or if additional categories are needed, don't hesitate to change the classifications suggested or to add to them. Date each misunderstanding. Indicate the relative seriousness of each one in terms of its consequences. In each case indicate whether and how the misunderstanding—or its unpleasant consequences—might have been avoided by a somewhat more conscious use of language either by yourself or the other person, or both.

6. SCIENTIFIC TECHNIQUES

A. Read three or four so-called popular scientific articles in magazines or in your newspaper. Write a brief statement concerning each one. In this statement summarize what the article tells you about the *techniques* used in discovering the facts presented, and about the *reliability* of these techniques. Write out the questions you would like to ask the author if you could, after having read the article.

B. At your first opportunity, visit a scientific laboratory and, preferably through systematic observation, learn all you can about the methods used in particular research projects. Get the person in charge to tell you precisely what specific questions the research workers are trying to answer, and by what procedures, step by step, they are trying to make the observations with which to answer them. Ask about the specific uses of various pieces of apparatus. Write a brief discriminating report of what you learn.

C. If you are a member of a class or study group, or perhaps a club of some sort, try to arrange a showing of the following (or similar) films, produced by Encyclopaedia Britannica Films, Inc. (formerly Erpi Classroom Films, Inc.), 1841 Broadway, New York 23, New York:

> *Molecular Theory of Matter*
> *Electrons*
> *Colloids*

These are sound films with explanatory narrative. Your nearest university may have a visual education department from which such films can be rented.

The films will be much more interesting to you if you have read such a book as Einstein and Infeld's *The Evolution of Physics*, or Born's *The Restless Universe*, or a good physics textbook.

7. LISTENING

A. While listening to a lecture or a radio speech, take care to notice whenever you disagree with the speaker. Then quietly ask yourself whether (a) you might have given a particular word or phrase a different meaning from that intended by the speaker, (b) you might have overgeneralized—read more into a statement than the speaker put into it, (c) you might have assumed that your own knowledge was complete, or at least identical with the speaker's (after all, it could be that the speaker had information of which you were not aware).

B. Listen to a speech and record your observations in terms of the relative degree of allness expressed by the speaker. Your judgment of this will be based in part on the speaker's words—his use of *never, always, utterly*, etc.—and in part on his apparent attitude toward his own statements, particularly his degree of positiveness, as shown in gesture, tone of voice, use of qualifying phrases, etc. You may record your judgment by means of a rating scale; if so, you should describe it carefully. If you prefer, you may express your judgment in descriptive terms, citing details to support your main statements.

C. Listen to a speech and record your observations in terms of the details left out of account by the speaker. Your report will be a summary of what the speaker *did not say* in the interests of greater clarity, validity, and more adequate coverage of his subject. Don't attempt to be exhaustive and don't quibble; use a sense of discrimination, emphasizing those details that seem most important.

D. Review pages 270–282 in Chapter XII, which deal with dead-level abstracting. Then listen to a speech and write a brief report of it in terms of (a) the average level of abstraction represented by it (you can rate it only in a relative sense, of course, as unusually descriptive and factually detailed, or moderately so, or on a relatively high or very high mean level of abstraction); and (b) its variability of level of abstraction—the frequency with which the speaker varied the level and the extent to which he varied it.

8. SEEING THE TRICK

Make a careful study of a play, a movie, a political speech, a radio commercial, or a magazine article that is quite clearly presented for propaganda purposes, and write a fairly detailed analysis of the techniques used by the author to achieve his apparently desired effects. What specific identifications does he encourage? In what ways does he make use of either-or statements? By what means does he direct your attention away from the details he leaves out of account? What are the chief attitudes that he encourages, and how does he present them? In what ways does he use the technique of ethical proof, or ventriloquizing (see Chapter IV, pages 65–69)? Describe any other devices he employs in an attempt to influence your evaluations in favor of the ends which he champions.

9. OBSERVING YOUR LANGUAGE REACTIONS

If you have access to a dictaphone or better, a tape or wire recorder or any other type of speech recorder, you can make some particularly effective observations of your own language behavior. Talk into the recorder *as fast as you can* and still maintain intelligible enunciation, discussing yourself, or some other person, or any other topic that is in some way significant to you. Speak for five minutes or so, or until you have filled a record, being sure to speak as fast as possible. Now play it back while you listen to it attentively from a semantic point of view. You will get more out of this exercise if before doing it, you review especially Chapters I, XI, and XII of this book. You should listen to the record several times, taking time between playbacks to decide just what you will listen for especially each time. Record your main observations, and be sure to date the entry.

(If no speech recorder of any kind is available you can achieve the same purpose fairly well by writing as fast as you can and without revision for five or ten minutes, and then reading and rereading what you have written.)

10. SYMBOL SYSTEMS

Write an account of the system of symbols used in a club, church, sorority, fraternity, or any other organization with which you are familiar. Tell about the origins of the symbols, what they "mean," how they are used, and the responses customarily made to them. In what ways would the organization be different without them? What purposes of the organization could not be served without them? Are these purposes relatively unimportant or important as compared to the purposes to which the symbols are not essential? Evaluate the symbol system and the uses made of it with regard to the degree to which they encourage in the members an intensional or an extensional orientation.

11. USING THE EXTENSIONAL DEVICES

A. Go through a popular magazine or the editorial page of any large city newspaper, putting quotation marks around the words and phrases that strike you as being elementalistic, or unduly projective of the writer's personal and extensionally inappropriate evaluations.

Using the same material, insert *etc.* at points (particularly at the ends of sentences) where you feel important details, or alternatives, have been omitted.

Again using the same material, write dates under the words, or at the ends of the sentences, which, if undated, appear to imply undue generalization.

Still using the same material, put an index (use the number 1) under each word or phrase that seems too sweeping, inclusive, or unlimited.

Go through the material once more and see whether you can substitute suitable hyphenated terms for those you have enclosed in quotes.

B. Write a 100-word statement entitled " My Opinion of Myself," actually writing in the extensional devices at all points where you feel they appropriately qualify or increase the validity of the statement.

C. Talk to yourself, or to a cooperative friend, for five minutes about a person you dislike, or a point of view to which you are opposed, applying the extensional devices as effectively as you can.

These assignments can be repeated, of course, as many times as seems profitable.

12. NON-VERBAL ABSTRACTING

Hold an object (ash tray, pencil, or anything else that may be handy) in both hands and look at it steadily, examining it. As soon as you begin to verbalize about it to yourself, put it down. Take it up and try again. See how long you can "stay on the silent level" of abstracting. This should be practiced for a short time each day for at least a week or two, using different objects. You can also do it while watching a person, viewing a painting, listening to music, or watching a game of some sort. In such cases, of course you cannot hold in your hands what you are observing, and so you need to use a slightly different technique: before you begin to observe cross your arms, and when you begin to verbalize uncross them. This is an unusually effective exercise for demonstrating the degree to which your observations are influenced by your verbalizations about whatever you are observing.

13. APPLICATIONS TO PARTICULAR PROBLEMS

In an organized fashion state the ways in which you might apply general semantics to some such problem as one of the following: (a) teaching nature study in the first grade; (b) teaching public speaking to college freshmen; (c) teaching English to high school sophomores; (d) teaching a high-school course in American history; (e) teaching psychology to college freshmen; (f) interviewing applicants for positions in a large department store; (g) conducting a child-study group; (h) training a high school basketball team; (i) playing golf; (j) playing bridge; (k) directing a high school play; (l) doing the job of a shop foreman; (m) running a restaurant or any other business which you might own or manage; (n) studying art or music; (o) learning a new dance routine; (p) managing a household.

Before attempting this assignment you should review at least Chapters VII to X inclusive, and preferably V and VI also. This assignment may be written in outline form, but main points should be elaborated somewhat. The more important objectives, principles, and techniques should be clearly indicated. The assignment will be much more significant, of course, if the program you outline is actually carried out and a report made of the special problems encountered and the results obtained.

14. NON-ALLNESS: THE RELATIVITY OF ABSTRACTING

A. Place a teacup on the table in front of you and make a simple line drawing of its contours. Then lay the cup on its side, and make a second contour drawing of it. Continue until you have filled a blank white sheet of notebook paper with contour drawings of the cup viewed from many different angles.

Which drawing represents the cup *really?* The answer is, of course, that cup_1 is not cup_2; all the drawings are valid but partial representations of whatever *cup* names.

Now, on another sheet of paper, combine in any way you like whole lines or parts of lines from the drawings you have just made of the cup. Avoid drawing "something." That is, don't aim at making what you draw look like a horse or tree, or a familiar geometrical figure. Simply arrange the lines and parts of lines with a regard for structure as structure. Notice how powerful are the tendencies to produce a design in accordance with forms, including common object forms, that are familiar to you. Do your best to disregard these strong tendencies. If you work conscientiously you will end up with a so-called abstract drawing.

Do it again, with the aim this time of producing from the same original contour drawings a different abstraction.

Which of these two is an abstraction from the cup *really?* Again, of course, both are valid but partial abstractions.

To get the most out of this exercise, read the article by Janice V. Kent, entitled "Improving Semantic Reactions Through Art Education," (*Etc.*, 1944, Vol. I, No. 4, pp. 225–228). For a stimulating and comprehensive discussion relevant to this assignment, see *Language of Vision* by Gyorgy Kepes (with introductory essays by S. Gideon and S. I. Hayakawa), published by Paul Theobald, Chicago, 1945.

B. Stand on a street corner that is very familiar to you. Try very hard to imagine that you are standing on a street corner in a foreign country (specify which one) which you have never visited. Hold this point of view as fully as you can while you look at the buildings, the people, the events going on in front of your eyes, as though you were seeing them for the first time. Try to do this for ten or fifteen minutes. Write an account of this experience, describing as well as you can the effect of the induced point of view on your observations and interpretations.

C. Engage someone in conversation and while doing so maintain as completely as possible the assumption that the person with whom you are talking is a foreign agent, or a "mental" patient with delusional tendencies, or a professional swindler, or a federal agent secretly investigating you—or whatever else you like. Make note of all the evidence you can observe that seems to support the assumption.

After ten or fifteen minutes suddenly change the "role" you give your companion and imagine he is someone quite different (specify what you assume him to be now). Again observe the details of evidence that seem to support this new assumption.

Write a report of the effects of your assumptions on your observations.

An instructive variation of this assignment, one that may sharpen your understanding of the semantics of "racial" problems, is that of talking with, or observing, a stranger, assuming for several minutes that he is a Jew, for example, then assuming for a while that he is not. If you do this conscientiously you will be able to notice important differences in your observations of the stranger and in your reactions to him as you view him with one and then the other assumption. The extent of the differences will, in fact, serve as a rough index of the intensity of your attitude toward "Jews"—and if you do the assignment well, and several times, it should in some measure modify your attitude. It may even eliminate your tendency to attempt evaluations of individuals in terms of such a category as "Jew."

This general type of exercise, designed to demonstrate the relativity of abstracting, and so the non-all character of abstractions, can be carried out in many different ways, of course.

15. MOMENT-TO-MOMENT REACTIONS

In the other assignments fairly specific applications of general semantics are emphasized. In this one, general moment-to-moment application is stressed. Nothing in particular is specified. You are to set aside short periods, of not over five to ten minutes, and preferably two or three a day, during which you are to take special pains to behave in accordance with the principles discussed particularly in Chapters VII to X inclusive. You are to apply the principles as best you can in both your verbal and non-verbal reactions in any circumstances that may arise during these special periods. Concentrating on one principle at a time will be likely to prove advisable, especially at first. As time goes on you may extend the length of the periods somewhat, though they should ordinarily not exceed thirty minutes, so far as intensive practice purposes are concerned.

You should keep a record, which need not be detailed or time-consuming, of your more important and interesting successes and failures in applying the semantic principles during the practice periods. This assignment will be considerably more valuable if you have an instructor to whom you can show your written record from time to time, and from whom you can get suggestions and constructive criticisms.

16. ETC.

It is not intended that all who attempt these assignments will carry them out in exactly the same way, or with the same results. For any individual some of the assignments will be much more valuable than others. Above all they are meant to be suggestive, and anyone who is seriously interested can readily devise many additional ways of applying the various principles and techniques and of cultivating an extensional approach to situations and problems generally.

Further suggestions are to be found in the following references, and also in *Papers from the Second American Congress of General Semantics* and in current issues of *Etc.*:

CHISHOLM, FRANCIS P. *Introductory Lectures on General Semantics.* Chicago: Institute of General Semantics, 1944.

HAYAKAWA, S. I. *Language in Action.* New York: Harcourt, Brace & Company, Inc., 1941.

KENT, JANICE V. "Semantic Reactions in Art Education," *Etc.*, 1944, Vol. 1, No. 4, 225–228.

KEPES, GYORGY. *Language of Vision.* Chicago: Paul Theobald, 1945.

KORZYBSKI, A. *Science and Sanity.* Lancaster, Pa.: The Science Press, 1st ed., 1933, 2nd ed., 1941. (See especially Chapter XXIX.)

LEE, IRVING H. *Language Habits in Human Affairs.* New York: Harper & Brothers, 1943.

MOORE, WILBUR E. "New Patterns for Debate," *Etc.*, 1944, Vol. 1, No. 4, 258–261.

MURRAY, ELWOOD. *The Speech Personality*. Philadelphia: J. B. Lippincott Company, rev. ed., 1944.

RAPAPORT, ANATOL. "Newtonian Physics and Aviation Cadets," *Etc.*, 1944, Vol. 1, No. 3, 154–164.

RUTAN, EDWARD J., and NEUMAYER, ENGELBERT, J. "Something New in Teaching Grammar," *Etc.*, 1944, Vol. 1, No. 4, 261–263.

Appendix

RESEARCH IN LANGUAGE BEHAVIOR

---

*T*HIS APPENDIX IS DIRECTED TO THOSE READERS WHO HAVE
research interests, or who have questions concerning the experimental and
investigative possibilities suggested by general semantics. A program of
research is outlined. It is important to make clear that this particular research
program is limited in scope and does not represent by any means all of the
investigative problems, procedures, and interests of general semanticists.
It is presented simply as one example of a more or less integrated program
of scientific investigation suggested (to me) by general semantics and bearing
on some of the issues which it appears to high-light. Its value for the reader
will lie most importantly in the possibilities for further and different research
that it might indicate.

GENERAL PROBLEM

The importance of language and of symbolization generally, as a distinctly
human form of behavior and as a basic factor in personal and social problems,
is generally recognized.[1] The effective scientific investigation of such behavior,
however, depends upon the development of highly reliable and differentiating
measures, by means of which specified aspects of language behavior may be
systematically observed in relation to one another and to other variables.
With such measures, significant testable hypotheses can be formulated and
checked, and a body of dependable information can be accumulated.

---

[1] W. Johnson, *Language and Speech Hygiene*. Gen. Semantics Monogr., No. 1,
Chicago: Institute of General Semantics, 2nd ed., 1941; A. Korzybski, *Science and
Sanity, An Introduction to Non-Aristotelian Systems and General Semantics*. Lan-
caster, Pa.: The Science Press, 2nd ed., 1941; F. H. Sanford, "Speech and Person-
ality," *Psychol. Bull.*, 1942, *39*, 811–845; G. K. Zipf, *The Psychobiology of Language*.
Boston: Houghton Mifflin Company, 1935.

499

SPECIFIC OBJECTIVES

The proposed program of research is designed to:

1. Develop reliable and differentiating measures of specified aspects of language behavior.

2. Determine the degree to which the resulting measures are intercorrelated.

3. Determine the degree of correlation between these measures and such other pertinent variables as those involved in environmental influences, physiological conditions, intelligence and personality adjustment.

4. Apply the measures to a comprehensive investigation of language development.

5. Determine the degree to which language behavior, as measured, is modifiable under specified conditions.

6. Determine the degree to which modification in language behavior is associated with modifications in other aspects of behavior or adjustment.

7. Indicate the normal characteristics of language development and language behavior, and the varieties of disorder or abnormality in such behavior, in terms of the measures used.

TYPES OF LANGUAGE MEASURES TO BE INVESTIGATED

No attempt will be made here to present a review of the theoretical and experimental literature dealing with the problems with which this program is concerned. It is sufficient to say that previous work in the field has suggested many of the procedures to be employed, and that others have been suggested by preliminary research carried out by me, or under my direction. A comprehensive review of language behavior studies has been published by Sanford.[2] The following types of language measures are to be investigated:

Type-Token ratio (TTR). This is a measure of vocabulary "flexibility" or variability designed to indicate certain aspects of language adequacy. It expresses the ratio of different words (types) to total words (tokens) in a given language sample. If in speaking 100 words (tokens) an individual uses 64 different words (types), his TTR will be .64. In order to develop the most highly reliable and differentiating form of the TTR, it is to be computed for given language samples in the following various ways:

a. For all words spoken or written by a given individual, or in a given language sample, and separately for words representing the various grammatical categories; for words in different frequency categories—for example, the 500 most frequently used words, the 500 next most frequently used words, etc., as determined by the published word-counts of Thorndike,[3]

---

[2] Sanford, *op. cit.*

[3] E. L. Thorndike, *The Teacher's Word Book*. New York: Teachers College, Columbia University, 1921.

Horn,[4] and others, or by the word-counts to be derived from the present investigations, etc.

b. With varying statistical or mathematical procedures, thus:

The over-all TTR, as computed for an entire language sample. TTR's for samples of different magnitudes are not directly comparable because of the tendency for the TTR to vary inversely with size of sample. A knowledge of the precise character of this inverse relationship might make it possible to compare directly TTR's for samples differing in length, by means of a correction table. The feasibility of constructing such a table is to be investigated. The study by Chotlos[5] throws considerable light on this problem.

The Mean Segmental TTR. TTR's for samples of different magnitudes can be made comparable by dividing each sample into like-sized segments of say 100 words each, computing the TTR for each segment, and then averaging the segmental TTR's for each sample. It can be safely assumed that such segmental TTR's are directly comparable so long as they represent segments of equal size, and that means of such segmental TTR's are also directly comparable. Results obtained by using segments of different magnitudes—such as 100-word segments, 500-word segments, etc.—are to be compared in order to ascertain the size of segments that will allow for the most reliable and differentiating mean segmental TTR. The above-mentioned study by Chotlos is concerned with this problem also.

The Cumulative TTR Curve. A curve of the cumulative TTR for a given language sample can be plotted by computing successive TTR's as increments are added to the sample. For instance, the cumulative TTR for a 1000-word sample would be plotted as follows: TTR values are represented along the ordinate, and number of words along the abscissa. The abscissa values may be in units of one word, or 10 words, or 100 words, etc., as desired. If the unit is one word, 1000 TTR's will be computed in plotting the cumulative curve for the 1000-word sample; if the unit is 10 words, 100 TTR's will be computed; if the unit is 100 words, 10 TTR's will be computed, etc. Thus, if the unit is 10 words, the first value will represent the TTR for the first 10 words of the sample, the second will represent the TTR for the first 20 words, the third will represent the TTR for the first 30 words, etc. The problem of fitting an equation to the resulting curve has been dealt with in some detail by Chotlos. Basically, the problem concerns the relation between D (number of different words, or types) and N (number of words, tokens) in the given sample. This problem has been given con-

[4] E. Horn, *A Basic Writing Vocabulary: 10,000 Words Most Commonly Used in Writing.* Monogr. in Educ., No. 4, Iowa City: University of Iowa Press, 1926.

[5] J. W. Chotlos, "Studies in Language Behavior: IV. A Statistical and Comparative Analysis of Individual Written Language Samples," *Psychol. Monogr.*, 1944, *56*, 75–111. This study was carried out with the technical assistance of Dr. Don Lewis.

siderable attention by Zipf,[6] Carroll,[7] and Skinner.[8] The relevant data presented by Chotlos indicate the degree to which the relation of D to N promises a means of predicting vocabulary, in the sense that the value of D for a given N provides a basis for predicting D for a specified N of larger magnitude.

The Decremental TTR Curve. Suppose a 1000-word sample to be divided into ten 100-word segments. The TTR is computed for the first segment. Then the number of different words in the second segment that did not occur in the first segment—i.e., the number of *new* types introduced in the second segment—is found. The TTR for the second segment is then computed by dividing this number—not the number of types, but the number of *new* types—by 100, which is the number of tokens in the second segment. In the same way, the TTR's for the third, fourth, and each of the other segments may be computed by dividing the number of tokens, 100 in each case, into the number of *new* types introduced into the sample for the first time in the segments under consideration. The resulting curve of these successive segmental TTR's may be expected to show a relatively steeper slope than the cumulative TTR curve, and the measure representing the slope of this curve may be found to be of special interest. It represents, of course, the rate of decrement in the use of new types, the rate at which the individual "uses up" his vocabulary in producing a language sample. Decremental TTR's should represent in a peculiarly direct quantitative manner one aspect of language development when applied to language samples secured successively from the same children. The decremental TTR curve is, of course, the first derivative of the cumulative TTR curve, and thus it is not actually necessary to fit a curve to the decremental TTR data if the cumulative TTR curve has been computed.

Type Frequencies. A simple objective language measure is that which expresses the frequency of occurrence of each different word, or type. Such frequencies, as reported for large samples of written language by Thorndike,[9] Horn,[10] and others, have been used chiefly in the preparation of school readers, spelling books, etc. Certain other uses of such data are obvious. When type frequencies are based on the kinds of language samples to be used in the present program they may be regarded as representing language behavior norms. In previous studies of word frequencies it would seem that the primary objective has been simply to determine the relative frequency

[6] Zipf, *op. cit.*

[7] J. B. Carroll, "Diversity of Vocabulary and the Harmonic Series Law of Word-Frequency Distribution," *Psychol. Rec.*, 1938, *2*, 379–386.

[8] B. F. Skinner, "The Distribution of Associated Words," *Psychol. Rec.*, 1937, *I*, 71–76.

[9] Thorndike, *op. cit.*

[10] Horn, *op. cit.*

of occurrence of each word, and with some exceptions special interest has attached to those words which have been found to occur with especially high frequencies. The main objective of the present program in this connection is somewhat different. Chief interest lies in ascertaining individual and group differences in the relative frequency with which particular kinds of words are used. One may determine (a) type-frequency changes that characterize language development; (b) type-frequency characteristics of the language of special groups, especially those that may be found to differentiate one group from another, as schizophrenics from normal subjects, scientists from novelists, etc.; (c) the particular type frequencies that correlate significantly with such other variables as intelligence, emotional stability, educational level, etc. Attention may be given to the following types of words (and to any others that may be found to be useful):

a. Self-reference words
b. Quantifying terms (precise numerical words)
c. Pseudo-quantifying terms (words loosely indicative of amount, size, etc., such as *much, many, lots;* or *very, highly,* etc., used as qualifiers of other pseudo-quantifying terms, as in such expressions as "very much")
d. "Allness" terms (superlative or extreme words, such as *never, always, all, nobody, everyone,* etc.)
e. Words expressive of negative evaluation, such as *no, don't,* etc., and *horrid, unsatisfactory, dislike,* etc.
f. Words expressive of positive evaluation
g. Qualification terms (words that serve to qualify or limit statements, such as *except, but, however, if,* etc.)
h. Terms indicative of consciousness of projection (such words as *apparently, seems, appears, as if, to me,* etc. As indicated by the last two examples, for purposes of this type of analysis it will be necessary to treat certain phrases as single words. What we call the dogmatic or "closed mind" attitude might be expected to be characterized by language in which these terms are relatively lacking.)

Ratios of any one of the above types of words to any one of the other types may be computed for given language samples, and their significance evaluated. The ratio of the terms indicative of consciousness of abstracting to "allness" words, for example, might be expected to differentiate individuals and groups in ways that should be of theoretical and practical importance in the study of personality.

The relative frequency of use of the various grammatical types of words— nouns, adjectives, verbs, adverbs, etc.—may also be determined, as well as ratios of nouns to adjectives, adjectives to verbs, verbs to adverbs, nouns to verbs, adjectives to adverbs, etc., and the ratio of these four to all other words. With language development, the relative frequency of nouns particularly and also of verbs may be expected to decrease with reference to the relative frequency of adjectives and adverbs. The degree to which these and other possible relationships can be utilized as measures of language development and of individual and group differences should be ascertained. Busemann[11] and Boder[12] have employed the adjective-verb quotient to indicate certain kinds of personality differences and to differentiate samples of written language. Sanford [13] has reported a personality study involving this and other related measures. The present series of studies involves analyses in this general connection. Mann[14] has applied the adjective-verb quotient and also adjective-noun and adverb-verb quotients in her comparative study of the written language of schizophrenic patients and university freshmen. Fairbanks[15] has investigated the relative frequencies of occurrence of various parts of speech in comparing the spoken language of schizophrenic patients and university freshmen. Chotlos[16] has presented similar data in terms of types and tokens, respectively, and he also presents TTR values for nouns, verbs, adjectives, and adverbs, respectively, for written language samples obtained from Iowa school children.

Proportionate Vocabulary. How many different words or types make up 25, or 50, or 75 per cent of a given language sample? In the study by Fairbanks, 30,000-word samples of spoken language were obtained from schizophrenic patients and "superior" university freshmen, respectively. For the freshmen just 46 different words or types comprised 50 per cent of the 30,000-word sample, and for the schizophrenic patients this figure was 33 types. This is the more striking, perhaps, when expressed by saying that for the schizophrenic patients approximately o.1 of 1 per cent of the words made up 50 per cent of the total sample. In fact, *one* word, the one most frequently used by the schizophrenics, which was the word *I*, made up slightly over 8.3 per cent of their entire 30,000 words.

A sample of say 1000 words might be analyzed in such a way as to yield a curve as follows: Along the abscissa percentages would be represented; these percentages would correspond to numbers of tokens. For example, suppose that 100 tokens make up 10 per cent of the 1000-word sample; it is

---

[11] A. Busemann, *Die Sprache der Jugend als Ausdruck der Entwicklungsrhythmik.* Jena: Fischer, 1925.

[12] D. P. Boder, "The Adjective-Verb Quotient: A Contribution to the Psychology of Language," *Psychol. Rec.,* 1940, *3,* 310–343.

[13] F. H. Sanford, "Speech and Personality: A Comparative Case Study," *Character & Pers.,* 1942, *19,* 169–198.

[14] M. B. Mann, "Studies in Language Behavior: III. The Quantitative Differentiation of Samples of Written Language." *Psychol. Monogr.,* 1944, *56,* 41–74.

[15] H. Fairbanks, "Studies in Language Behavior: II. The Quantitative Differentiation of Samples of Spoken Language." *Psychol. Monogr.,* 1944, *56,* 19–38.

[16] Chotlos, *op. cit.*

this 10 per cent and other percentage values so computed that would be represented along the abscissa. Other percentages would lie along the ordinate; these percentages would correspond to numbers of types. Thus, suppose that 10 types comprise 1 per cent of the total 1000 tokens; this 1 per cent and other percentage values so computed would be represented along the ordinate. The curve showing the relation between these two sets of percentages would be made up of points expressing such values as the one cited above: for the schizophrenic patients 0.1 of 1 per cent of the words (this percentage representing types) made up 50 per cent of the sample (this percentage representing tokens). The relation symbolized by this curve can be expressed mathematically, of course, and it is proposed to examine its usefulness as a basis for comparing different language samples or any given sample with a norm or standard sample. The relationship discussed here can be expressed, of course, in terms of rank and frequency. That is, a curve that is fitted to word frequencies as a function of rank, the most frequent word having the lowest rank number, 1, represents in an alternative way the same phenomenon that is discussed here in terms of proportionate vocabulary.[17]

Standard Frequency Vocabulary. The word counts that have been published by earlier workers, and the one to be done in the present program, can be used separately or pooled in arriving at a standard frequency-of-use rank number for each different word included in them. Such rank numbers would represent the relative frequency with which each word had been used in the total language sample—presumably drawn from a more or less representative population of individuals—not in terms of the actual number of times each word was used, but in terms of its rank. Thus, the most frequently used word would have a rank number of 1, the next most frequently used word would have a rank number of 2, etc.

With the resulting table of rank numbers, it would be possible to score any given language sample by noting the rank number of each word (token) contained in it, and computing the mean (or median) of these rank numbers. The lower the mean of the sample the more heavily loaded it is with words that are used relatively frequently by people generally. We may say, then, that this mean rank number of a language sample represents the "standard frequency vocabulary" employed in it. It is to be reasonably expected that language development would be characterized by increase in this measure, and that the measure would serve to differentiate individuals and groups.

A less refined, and perhaps nearly as adequate, form of this measure could be worked out in terms of standard frequency rank numbers on a categorical basis. That is, the first 100 most frequently used words, for example, could all be given the same rank number, the number 1, the second 100 words could all be assigned the rank number 2, etc. Statistical analysis may indicate

17 See Zipf, *op. cit.*

advantages in classes or categories of unequal magnitudes, putting the more frequently used words in smaller groups, for instance, and the less frequently used words in larger groups, or vice versa, perhaps varying the number of words in a group in some relation to the frequency with which they are used. Comparison of results obtained from use of various forms of the measure will determine the relative merits of each.

Verbal Output. A very simple language behavior measure is that which expresses the verbal output of an individual. Individual differences and intra-individual variations with respect to verbal output are of course obvious. Their significance in relation to the various aspects of personal and social adjustment have not been thoroughly or systematically investigated. It is planned to include an attempt in this direction in the present research program.

Verbal output is not meant to be synonymous with speaking or reading rate, as that term is used to refer to verbal output under relatively optimal conditions. An individual's verbal output under various conditions may, and usually does, fall considerably under what it is when he speaks at or near his optimal steady rate. Verbal output may be expressed, of course, in terms of rate.

The measure may express number of words spoken or written per unit of time or in response to a specified stimulus under standard conditions. It may also express the proportion of a time unit during which an individual produces spoken or written language. For example, two individuals could be compared by placing them together for one hour and recording (a) the speaking time of each, (b) the total number of words spoken by each, and (c) the verbal output of each in terms of words spoken per minute. It is to be noted that these measures are different from a measure of the *rate* of verbal output *while speaking*. It would be of interest, of course, to correlate such a measure of rate with the other verbal output measures.

Word Length. Since the studies of Zipf[18] have shown word length to be highly correlated negatively with frequency of use—the shorter the word the more frequently it occurs—it is not planned at this time that measures of word length will be included to any important degree in the present program. It is mentioned here, however, because the data to be utilized will be so tabulated that word length could be studied if findings indicate that this would be advisable. It is a rigorously objective and highly reliable measure.[19]

Sentence Length. Sentence length is a measure that presents serious operational difficulties in the study of spoken language, although it may be generally satisfactory in the analysis of written language. It is planned to

18 *Ibid.*

19 O. M. Skalbeck, *A Statistical Analysis of Three Measures of Word Length.* M.A. Thesis, Iowa City: University of Iowa, 1938.

include it in the analysis of at least a selected set of the written language samples.

SPECIAL TYPES OF LANGUAGE BEHAVIOR TESTS

The Extensional Agreement Index (EAI) expresses the degree of agreement among *n* persons in defining a given term extensionally, i.e., by pointing to or exhibiting somehow the actual objects, phenomena, etc., to which the term refers.[20] Thus, the kind of behavior which the EAI is designed to measure is not observation so much as word-fact relating. The EAI may range in numerical value from 0.0 to 1.0, 0.0 representing no agreement and 1.0 representing maximum possible agreement among *n* persons in relating or applying a given word as a label to actualities. Its theoretical and practical significance lies in the fact that it makes possible not only an index of a person's conformity or idiosyncrasy in his extensional use of words, but also a measure of the degree to which any given term may be regarded as testable, or extensional, or operational—or vague. If in the statement "Stutterers are psychoneurotic" the term *psychoneurotic* has an EAI of say .18, the statement is not to be regarded as highly testable or factually meaningful, since *n* persons would disagree considerably as to just what is to be observed in order that the validity of the statement might be tested. The EAI offers, therefore, a means of quantifying to some degree such notions as are represented by the terms *verifiable, operational*, etc.

The EAI may be computed in several different ways. Tuthill[21] in a study made as part of the present program demonstrated a variety of ways of computing such a measure of extensional agreement. The basic formula is

$$EAI = \frac{x}{y}$$

in which x represents the number of obtained agreements and y the maximum possible number of agreements. The EAI, then, represents the percentage of the maximum possible number of agreements that are obtained in a given case.

For example, imagine four different pictures and 10 different persons who are each asked to apply the label *most artistic* to one of them. Suppose the label is applied to picture A by 3 persons, to picture B by none, to picture C by 5, and to picture D by 2. If there had been perfect agreement, all 10 persons would have applied the label to the same picture. Thus, the number of agreements among the 10 persons that would have occurred under these conditions is to be regarded as the maximum possible number of agreements.

---

[20] This measure was introduced and briefly discussed in Johnson, *op. cit.*

[21] C. E. Tuthill, *A Quantitative Study of Extensional Meaning with Special Reference to Stuttering*. Ph.D. Thesis, Iowa City: University of Iowa, 1939.

This number may be determined by the formula $(n-1).5n;$ and since $n=10$, the maximum possible number of agreements is $9\times 5=45$. The number of agreements actually obtained is to be computed as follows: The 3 persons who applied the label to picture A agreed three times, since when $n=3$, $(n-1).5n=3$. There were no agreements with regard to picture B in terms of the technique for computing the EAI that is here being used. Using the formula $(n-1).5n$, there were 10 agreements in the labeling of picture C, and one in the labeling of picture D. In all then, 14 agreements were obtained. Therefore, $EAI=14/45=.31$, which may be interpreted as indicating that the number of agreements obtained was 31 per cent of the maximum possible number.

This is an example of an extremely simple case, used to illustrate the application of the basic formula. Another example will serve to indicate an important modification of the basic formula. On July 9, 1939, the American Institute of Public Opinion released to newspapers the results of a survey in which each of several thousand persons was asked to apply one of the labels, *Conservative*, *Liberal*, and *Radical*, to each of ten prominent Americans.[22] The results were presented in percentages as follows:

	Conservative	Liberal	Radical
Hopkins	4	55	41
Roosevelt	1	62	37
LaGuardia	8	64	28
Farley	13	63	24
Dewey	45	47	8
Hull	51	46	3
Garner	64	32	4
Vandenberg	67	29	4
Taft	86	13	1
Hoover	92	5	3

These figures represent only the labeling reactions of persons "who knew or had some idea of the terms when later in the survey they were asked point-blank what the words . . . meant." From these data it is possible to compute an EAI for each of the three terms involved. The procedure to be used will differ in three important respects from that used in the above example of the four pictures. In the first place, in the first example there was only one label to be applied by each of 10 persons to only one of four possible referents. In the present case, there were three labels, any one of which was to be applied to each of 10 referents. In the second place, there were 10 labelers in the first example; in this one there were many thousands, and the numbers have

[22] The material upon which the present discussion is based appeared under the copyright of the American Institute of Public Opinion in the Des Moines *Register*, July 9, 1939.

been converted into percentages. These percentages will be used instead of the raw numbers in computing the EAI's. In $(n-1).5n$, n will represent 100 in computing the maximum possible number of agreements. Lastly, instead of assuming, as was done in the first example, that agreements occur only when labels are applied, and not when they are not applied, we shall assume that both the application of a label and the refusal to apply it may involve agreement. When this assumption is made, the *net* number of agreements involved in the application and non-application of a given label to a given referent can be computed as follows: Let $x =$ the number who apply the label, and $n-x$ the number who do not apply it. Then the number of agreements among those who do apply the label is found by the formula, $(x-1).5x$. Similarly, the number of agreements among those who do not apply the label equals $(n-x-1).5(n-x)$. The *net* number of agreements is found simply by subtracting the smaller of these values from the larger. And the EAI is found by dividing this *net* number of agreements by the maximum possible number of agreements. Thus,

$$\text{EAI} = \frac{\frac{(n-x-1)\ (n-x)}{2} - \frac{(x-1)x}{2}}{\frac{(n-1)n}{2}} = \left| \frac{2x-n}{n} \right|$$

In this way, the EAI of each given term is computed for each referent, and the EAI's of the term for the various referents (in the present case, 10) are averaged. For the term *Liberal* the following results were obtained:

Liberal

	% Labeling	$\left\lvert \dfrac{2x-n}{n} \right\rvert$
Hopkins	55	.10
Roosevelt	62	.24
LaGuardia	64	.28
Farley	63	.26
Dewey	47	.06
Hull	46	.08
Garner	32	.36
Vandenberg	29	.42
Taft	13	.74
Hoover	5	.90
Average EAI		.34

The obtained number of agreements was, on the average, only 34 per cent of the number representing complete agreement as to the extensional meaning of the word *Liberal*, as applied or not, to the 10 men listed, by the presumably random sample of persons surveyed by the Gallup organization in the summer of 1939. The variability is of interest. As applied to Hopkins, Dewey, and Hull, the term *Liberal* proved to be almost entirely meaningless; there was virtually no agreement as to whether these men were or were not suitable referents of the term. There was relatively high agreement, on the other hand, that Taft and Hoover were not to be labeled *Liberal*. The mean EAI was .58 for *Conservative* and .69 for *Radical*.

Dr. George Gallup, under whose name the survey report appeared in the press, did not of course report his findings in terms of these EAI's. Moreover, he stated that the survey results indicated "the way American voters— *rightly* or *wrongly*—are classifying the figures in United States political life." [The italics are mine.] The words *rightly or wrongly* seem to imply the assumption that there is a "right" way and a "wrong" way to apply such a label as *Liberal*, that such a term has somehow an intrinsic "meaning," presumably known by some means to someone somewhere, quite aside from and more valid than the extensional meanings ascribed to it by those persons who actively relate it to various referents. There would appear to be, from an extensional point of view at least, no "right" or "wrong" about it, except in the sense that in matters of this kind one might (or might not) prefer to assume that the majority is "right." Be that as it may, however, Dr. Gallup carried out in this particular survey what amounted to a very ambitious effort to determine by vote the extensional meanings of a group of words. And by using his results to compute the EAI's of these words, it becomes possible to measure fairly precisely the vagueness or factual mean- ingfulness of some of our important political terms.

The resulting EAI's afford a degree of insight into the processes of political controversy, and point to one of the fundamental problems in connection with social organization. The EAI of .34 for *Liberal* strongly suggests that such a statement as "America should (or should not) have a liberal in the White House" is to be regarded as essentially "lyrical." The remark that "So-and-so is a liberal" is not to be regarded as a statement chiefly descrip- tive of So-and-so. For the most part it merely serves to announce one of the ways in which the speaker proposes to apply the word *Liberal*, and thus it is mainly indicative of an aspect of the speaker's language behavior. To know the EAI of a word, as computed from data as adequate as those pro- vided by Dr. Gallup, is to know something quite precise and significant about the language behavior of a speaker or writer who uses it, particularly if he gives no indication of awareness of the word's descriptive limitations, as these are implied by its EAI. The descriptive limitations of a word with an EAI of .34 are probably so great as to render it practically meaningless referentially in many contexts. It is to be regarded as being in many instances, little more than noise or ink-marks, meaningful chiefly in being symptomatic of the speaker's or writer's neurosemantic state. That is, it is more revealing as behavior than as language; it symbolizes the speaker more than it symbolizes anything he may appear to be speaking about.

This rather long discussion of the EAI has been given in order to make more or less clear not only the basic operations involved in its computation, but also certain of its implications. The EAI of a term, computed from data obtained under adequate conditions, is indicative of one of the most important characteristics of word usage, the relatively precise degree to which words may be regarded as factually meaningful—or vague.

Use of the measure requires that it be computed from data obtained under known and specified conditions; moreover, the particular form of the basic formula to be used in computing it will vary somewhat with the nature and purpose of the investigation. Preliminary work done in the present program has involved construction of a test by means of which EAI's for a number of different terms were determined under a variety of conditions. The work so far completed indicates that the reliability of such a test can be expected to be quite high, that its administration and scoring offer no insurmountable problems, and that data obtained by means of it will reveal differences between words and between individuals and groups. The studies completed to date have been carried out by Gallant, Knoche, and Moore, and the data accumulated by them have been analyzed in a number of ways by Van Duzer. These studies are included in the list at the end of the appendix.

In the administration of this test the subject is given a word in a standard context, as in the statement: "Point to the pictures that show people doing *good* things." The subject then points to such pictures, among a standard set of pictures, as to him represent referents of *good* as so used. Each picture in the set is numbered and the number of each picture to which the subject points is recorded. From data so obtained from each of a group of subjects, the EAI of each word in the test is computed, as was done for the Gallup poll data presented in the preceding pages.

As part of the present program, a study has been made by J. Wilson and myself[23] in which graduate students and instructors in psychology defined extensionally, by reference to a list of statements taken from psychology texts, the terms *law, theory,* and *hypothesis.* The mean EAI's obtained were .62 for *law,* .40 for *theory,* and .28 for *hypothesis.*

Extensional Synonymity Index (ESI). Such EAI's represent the relative degree of vagueness of words as used. By treating the test data in other ways they can be made to yield two other types of information represented by an extensional synonymity index (ESI) and an extensional conformity index (ECI), respectively. By recording the percentage of all the subjects

[23] W. Johnson and J. Wilson, "The Degree of Extensional Agreement Among Twenty Psychologists in Their Use of the Labels *Hypothesis, Theory, and Law.*" *Proceed. Iowa Academy of Science,* 1945.

who point to each picture or other types of referent, in defining each word, it is possible to measure the degree of synonymity between any two words. The formula is

$$\text{ESI} = \frac{c}{\sqrt{xy}}$$

in which c represents the percentage of subjects pointing to a given picture in defining both of two given words, and x and y represent the percentages of subjects pointing to the picture in defining each of the two words, respectively. This value is computed for each picture, and the values thus obtained for all the pictures are averaged in deriving an expression of the mean degree of synonymity for any given pair of words.

Extensional Conformity Index (ECI). The percentages of subjects pointing to each picture in defining each word can also be used as word-fact relating behavior norms. Thus, the pictures may be "weighted" according to these values, and on the basis of them the pointing or labeling of a given individual can be evaluated. For example, if a given individual in defining the word *good* were to point to certain pictures, he would be showing less conformity to the group than he would be in pointing to certain other pictures. The mean of the percentage values of the pictures to which an individual points in defining a given word would represent his degree of conformity to the group in his extensional use of that word. We may call this his extensional conformity index (ECI), and individual differences expressed in terms of the ECI might be found to be a factor in personality adjustment.

The Intensional Agreement Index (IAI) expresses the degree of agreement among n persons in defining a given term intensionally, i.e., by giving its verbal equivalents. A dictionary definition is to be regarded as an intensional definition, as the term is here used. Like the EAI, the IAI may range in value from 0.0, representing no agreement, to 1.0, representing maximum possible agreement.

In a preliminary study carried out by N. Whitman and myself,[24] an attempt was made to determine IAI's for each of certain terms used in the field of psychology (*learning, perception, emotion*, and *personality*) and certain terms used in the field of biochemistry (*fats, lipids, enzymes, oxidation*, and *basal metabolism*). Textbooks in each field were examined until for each term six definitions (from six different authors) had been found. These definitions were then edited so as to exclude all words except nouns, verbs, adjectives, and adverbs (the adverbs *when* and *where*, the adjectives *that, these, those*, and *which*, and articles used as adjectives were also excluded). Then for each term the number of types (different words) used in all six definitions

---

[24] W. Johnson and N. Whitman, "Intensional Agreement Indexes of Certain Terms in Psychology and Biochemistry." Unpublished research.

was recorded, and the number of definitions in which each type was used was determined. The number of obtained agreements in the use of any given type by the six textbook authors was found by means of the formula $(n-1).5n$, in which n represents the number of definitions in which the type occurred. The values thus obtained for the various types were summed in determining the total number of obtained agreements shown by the six textbook writers in verbally defining the term in question. The maximum possible number of agreements was computed by using the formula $x(n-1)$ $.5n$, in which n represents the total number of definitions, six in each case, and x represents the total number of types used in all the definitions. The maximum possible number of agreements was then divided into the obtained number of agreements in determining the IAI of a given term. The IAI's as thus determined were:

Psychological terms		No. of Types
Learning	.024	44
Perception	.006	40
Emotion	.010	48
Personality	.007	46
Average	.012	44.5
Biochemical terms		
Fats	.080	56
Lipids	.150	59
Enzymes	.127	20
Oxidation	.067	27
Basal metabolism	.035	50
Average	.092	42.4

The difference between the mean IAI's may be regarded as indicating a measurable difference between the fields of psychology and biochemistry with regard to the degree of terminological agreement that has been achieved in them to date. One important aspect of scientific development is to be observed in the fact that among biochemists at the present time there is a tendency to abandon the term *fats* in favor of the term *lipids*—a tendency to replace one term with another that has a higher IAI. Increasing agreement as to definitions, both intensional and extensional, is a basic characteristic of the development of a science; and a means of measuring the degree of agreement that has been achieved within the various fields makes possible a peculiarly objective comparison of them in this important respect. Degree of similarity among verbal formulations generally can be measured in terms of the IAI.

The procedure followed in the above study of psychological and biochemical terms can be modified in at least three ways. First, the definitions can be obtained directly from the subjects rather than from textbooks or other published material. Second, the subjects can be irnstucted to define each word by listing synonyms of it, and the number of synonyms to be listed can be limited. Third, the words to be defined need not be presented only in isolation; they may be presented also in context, other words to be substituted by the subject for the word in question, or a definition to be written for the word as used in the particular context. The influence of differences in context on the meaning, and on agreement as to the meaning, of specific words can thus be investigated.

Intensional Synonymity Index (ISI). From data of the type just discussed it is possible to obtain measures of intensional synonymity. Degree of synonymity of given pairs of words defined extensionally can be measured by means of procedures already described. Similar procedures can be used in the present connection. For example, suppose the words *good* and *worth while* to have been defined by each of 100 subjects, each of whom defined each word by listing three synonyms for it. The degree of intensional, or verbal, synonymity between these two words can then be computed by means of the formula $\dfrac{c}{\sqrt{xy}}$, in which c represents the number of terms (types) given by the 100 subjects as synonyms for both words, and x and y represent the number of terms (types) listed as synonyms for each of the two words, respectively. The correlation between extensional and intensional synonymity indexes would be of interest.

Semantic Vocabulary Test. As has been indicated previously in this outline, vocabulary measures can be obtained from any given individual in terms of type-token ratios, type frequencies, proportionate vocabulary, and standard frequency vocabulary. Another type of vocabulary test may be attempted. A common criticism of ordinary vocabulary tests is that while they are indicative of the number of words an individual "knows" or "recognizes," they are not necessarily indicative of the range or "depth" of the individual's knowledge of or skill in using each word that he "knows." The problem raised by this criticism involves technical difficulties, but certain approaches to its solution appear to be possible.[25]

Investigation could be made of the feasibility of constructing a vocabulary test of such a nature that the individual's ability to use each word would be sampled in detail. It is possible to distinguish types of meaning, such as meaning in terms of use, variety, differentiating characteristics, sources, etc. For example, the word *orange* can be defined in terms of (a) the various uses of oranges; (b) the kinds of oranges; (c) the characteristics that differentiate oranges from other things; (d) the geographical areas where oranges are grown, the methods by which they are grown, the history of these methods, etc.; and (e) the scientific research that has been done on oranges, the

[25] R. H. Seashore and L. D. Eckerson, "The Measurement of Individual Differences in General English Vocabularies," *J. Educ. Physiol.*, 1940, *31*, 14–38.

methods used in picking, packing, processing, marketing, transporting, etc. This does not exhaust the problem of defining *orange*, but it illustrates the possibility of devising a vocabulary test of a type that should make possible a measure of vocabulary "depth" as well as "range."

Measures of Allness. Previous mention has been made of allness terms, such as *all, everyone, nobody, every, never, absolutely*, etc. Language spoken during moments of anger or despair or other relatively profound affective states appears to be particularly characterized by such terms. They give to language a character which reflects what is usually referred to as dogmatism, or stubbornness, inflexibility, etc. Orientation on the basis of dichotomies, or of the excluded middle—a two-valued, either-or orientation—appears to be basic to and to be fostered by, this sort of language. The degree to which one is prone to two-valued orientation is probably an important aspect of one's general adjustment, personality development, intelligence, etc. Insofar as it might prove possible to set up rigorous criteria of allness terms, the frequency of their use in language samples could be studied.

Another approach to the study of allness, however, is also to be proposed. From one point of view allness may be regarded as manifested in extreme responses in situations where they are not mandatory. An attempt could be made to construct a reliable test involving say 100 items, to each of which a response could be made along a graduated scale expressive of extreme and intermediate degrees of preference, attitude, behavioral tendency, etc. At least five and possibly seven or more alternative responses to each item should be provided, one expressive of neutrality or average tendency and the others distributed on either side and graduated toward the two extremes. The test would be scored not in terms of the preferences, etc., expressed, but in terms of the proportion of extreme (allness) responses. It is anticipated that two main types of evaluative tendency might be indicated by such a test, the tendency to give extreme responses, or allness, and an extreme tendency to give indecisive, indefinite, neutral responses. The latter might characterize certain schizoid conditions, for example. It is to be noted that this type of test should get away from one common weakness of pencil-and-paper tests, in that the effect of falsified responses on the score will be minimized, since the "intensity" rather than the "content" of the responses will determine the score.[26]

Tests of Verbal Differentiation. It would appear reasonable to assume that the adequacy of generalization or "abstract thinking" depends largely upon the adequacy of the analysis or differentiation upon which the generaliz-

[26] Previous work suggestive of this approach has been reported by G. B. Watson, *The Measurement of Fairmindedness*. New York: Teachers College, Columbia University, 1925. Miss Ella Yensen, graduate student at the University of Iowa, has just completed the preliminary form of a test conducted along the lines indicated here.

ing is based. This is indicated by an examination of practically any generalization process; it is especially obvious, perhaps, in medical diagnosis. The ability to observe, respond to, and relate differences would appear to limit the ability to abstract similarities effectively. In fact, abstracting (roughly, generalizing) can be defined as a process of leaving out details or differences; similarities are recognized and formulated in accordance with the way differences are disregarded, not observed, or related. Consciousness of abstracting therefore, in any given instance, is seen to depend on an awareness of the differences that are being disregarded or related in the abstracting of similarities.

It is proposed to construct a test specifically designed to measure an individual's ability to express differences, or to perform verbal differentiation. It is the intention to begin with the simple procedural plan of presenting the subject with pairs of objects, designs, etc., and requesting him to tell the differences between them. A time limit, to be determined, is to be set for each response. An attempt is to be made to score the responses in each of three ways. First, the mere length of response is to be measured; it is hardly to be expected that this will suffice, except possibly as a very gross measure. Second, the number of differences enumerated is to be noted; it will be necessary to formulate rigorous criteria of a "difference." Third, various forms of the type-token ratio are to be tried as possible expressions of the subject's level of performance.

Assuming the construction of a reliable test, scores on the test are to be related to other variables. The relation of differentiating ability to intelligence, as measured by current standard tests, and to other criteria of competence, is of particular interest.

SUPPLEMENTARY MEASURES

The entire research program here proposed involves not only the language behavior measures discussed above, but also certain other measures which are to be used in order to obtain data concerning the relation of the language measures to other aspects of behavior. Among these supplementary measures are tests of intelligence, measures of mental and chronological age, achievement and aptitude tests, measures of silent and oral reading, of speech and writing, and various indices of personality.

STUDIES COMPLETED

Twenty studies are listed below as having been completed in connection with the research program described above. With two exceptions, these studies have been done as M.A. and Ph.D. dissertations in either the Department of Speech or the Department of Psychology at the State University of Iowa. As will be noted, some of them have been published and are available, therefore, to anyone who may care to examine them; others will be published. Taken all together, they constitute an attempt to develop measures and investigative procedures for the study of language behavior viewed semantically. The program which they represent is continuing, and much of the data so far collected has not yet been analyzed. For example, approximately 1000 written language samples, each 3000 words in length, have been obtained from Iowa school children selected on the basis of sex, age, intelligence-test scores, type of school (rural, town, city), and socio-economic status. A selected set of 108 of these samples was treated in some detail in the study by Chotlos; further work on them remains to be done. Also, the spoken and written language samples obtained from schizophrenic patients by Fairbanks and Mann are still to be examined more fully. In the meantime additional measures and experimental procedures await further development.

The studies so far completed are the following:

CHOTLOS, J. W. "Studies in Language Behavior: IV. A Statistical and Comparative Analysis of Individual Written Language Samples." *Psychol. Monogr.*, 1944, *56*, 75–111.

CLEMONS, A. *A Quantitative Study of Verbal Abstracting.* M.A. Thesis. Iowa City: University of Iowa, 1939.

FAIRBANKS, H. "Studies in Language Behavior: II. The Quantitative Differentiation of Samples of Spoken Language." *Psychol. Monogr.*, 1944, *56*, 1938.

FOLSOM, A. T. *Reaction to the Dark Regarded as Language Behavior: Sixteen Cases.* M.A. Thesis. Iowa City: University of Iowa, 1937.

FRAZIER, J. *A Study of Stutterers' Theories of Their Own Stuttering.* M.A. Thesis. Iowa City: University of Iowa, 1940.

GALLANT, M. *A Statistical Evaluation of a Word-Fact Relating Test.* M.A. Thesis. Iowa City: University of Iowa, 1939.

GRINGS, W. W. "The Verbal Summator Technique and Abnormal Mental States," *J. Abn. & Soc. Psychol.*, 1942, *37*, 529–545.

JOHNSON, W., and WHITMAN, N. "Intensional Agreement Indexes of Certain Terms in Psychology and Biochemistry." Unpublished research.

JOHNSON, W., and WILSON, J. "The Degree of Extensional Agreement Among Twenty Psychologists in Their Use of the Labels *Hypothesis, Theory,* and *Law.*" *Proceedings of the Iowa Academy of Science*, 1945 (in press).

JOHNSON, W., and WOOD, C. B. "John Told Jim What Joe Told Him: A Study of the Process of Abstracting," *Etc.: A Review of General Semantics*, 1944, *2*, 10–28.

KNOCHE, R. M. *Agreement Among University Freshmen on Specified Words Defined Extensionally and Intensionally.* M.A. Thesis. Iowa City: University of Iowa, 1939.

MANN, M. B. "Studies in Language Behavior: III. The Quantitative Differentiation of Samples of Written Language." *Psychol. Monogr.*, 1944, 56, 41–74.

MOORE, R. *A Quantitative Study of the Labeling Behavior of Fifth and Sixth Grade Children from Upper and Lower Socio-economic Groups.* M.A. Thesis. Iowa City: University of Iowa, 1939.

SHAFITZ, E. *A Study of the Relation Between Word-Length and Type-Token Ratio in the Written Language of Iowa School Children.* M.A. Thesis. Iowa City: University of Iowa, 1941.

SHATTYN, G. B. *Certain Quantitative Measures of the Clinical Aspects of Language.* M.A. Thesis. Iowa City: University of Iowa, 1943.

SHERMAN, D. H. *An Objective Study of the Ability of Junior High School Pupils to Use Descriptive Language.* M.A. Thesis. Iowa City: University of Iowa, 1938.

SKALBECK, O. M. *A Statistical Analysis of Three Measures of Word Length.* M.A. Thesis. Iowa City: University of Iowa, 1938.

SPENCER, B. L. *A Study of Short Speech Samples as Personality Indicators.* M.A. Thesis. Iowa City: University of Iowa, 1943.

TUTHILL, C. E. *A Quantitative Study of Extensional Meaning With Special Reference to Stuttering.* Ph.D. Thesis. Iowa City: University of Iowa, 1939.

VAN DUZER, V. F. *A Methodological Study of Language Reaction.* M.A. Thesis. Iowa City: University of Iowa, 1944.

Bibliography

ADLER, ALFRED. *The Practice and Theory of Individual Psychology*. Tr. by P. Radin. New York: Harcourt, Brace, 1924.

ALEXANDER, JEROME. *Colloid Chemistry*. New York: Reinhold, 1944, Vol. 5.

ARNOLD, THURMAN W. *The Folklore of Capitalism*. New Haven: Yale Univ. Press, 1938.

ARNOLD, THURMAN W. *The Symbols of Government*. New Haven: Yale Univ. Press, 1935.

BEERS, CLIFFORD W. *A Mind That Found Itself*. New York: Longmans, Green, 1908.

BERGMAN, G., and SPENCE, K. W. "Operationism and Theory in Psychology," *Psychol. Rev.*, 48:1–15, 1941.

BLOOMFIELD, LEONARD. *Language*. New York: Henry Holt, rev. ed., 1933.

BODER, D. P. "The Adjective-Verb-Quotient: A Contribution to the Psychology of Language," *Psychol. Rec.*, 3:310–343, 1940.

BORING, EDWIN G. *A History of Experimental Psychology*. New York: Appleton-Century, 1929.

BORN, MAX. *The Restless Universe*. New York: Harper, 1936.

BRIDGMAN, PERCY W. *The Logic of Modern Physics*. New York: Macmillan, 1932.

BROWN, SPENCER, F. "The Loci of Stutterings in the Speech Sequence," *J. Speech Disorders*, 10:181–192, 1945.

BRYNGELSON, BRYNG. "The Interpretative Symbol," *Quart. J. Speech*, 24:569–573, 1938.

BUSEMANN, A. *Die Sprache der Jugend als Ausdruck der Entwicklungsrhythmik*. Jena: Fischer, 1925.

CAMERON, NORMAN. "Reasoning, Regression and Communication in Schizophrenics," *Psychol. Monog.*, No. 50, 1938.

CAMPBELL, DOUGLAS GORDON. "General Semantics: Implications of Linguistic Revision for Theoretical and Clinical Neuro-Psychiatry," *Amer. J. Psychiat.*, 93:769–807, 1937.

CAMPBELL, DOUGLAS GORDON. "General Semantics and Schizophrenic Reactions: Neuro-Linguistic and Neuro-Semantic Mechanisms of Pathogenesis and Their Implications for Prevention and Therapy." (A paper presented at the 1939 annual meeting of the American Psychiatric Association.) Chicago: Institute of General Semantics, 1939.

519

CAMPBELL, DOUGLAS GORDON. "General Semantics in Education, Counseling, and Theory." Reprinted from *Proceed. Nat. Educ. Assoc.*, 1939.

CAMPBELL, DOUGLAS GORDON. "Neuro-Linguistic and Neuro-Semantic Factors of Child Development." *Papers from the First American Congress for General Semantics.* Chicago: Institute of General Semantics, 1938.

CARHART, RAYMOND. "An Experimental Evaluation of Suggestion Relaxation." *Speech Monog.*, 10:29–39, 1943.

CARLSON, EARL. *Born That Way.* New York: John Day, 1941.

CARMICHAEL, R. D. *The Logic of Discovery.* Chicago: Open Court, 1930.

CARROLL, J. B. "Diversity of Vocabulary and the Harmonic Series Law of Word-Frequency Distribution," *Psychol. Rec.*, 2:379–386, 1938.

CHAKOTIN, SERGE. *The Rape of the Masses.* New York: Alliance, 1940.

CHASE, STUART. *The Tyranny of Words.* New York: Harcourt, Brace, 1938.

CHISHOLM, FRANCIS P. *Introductory Lectures on General Semantics.* Chicago: Institute of General Semantics, 1944.

CHOTLOS, J. W. "Studies in Language Behavior: IV. A Statistical and Comparative Analysis of Individual Written Language Samples," *Psychol. Monog.*, 56:75–111, 1944.

CLECKLEY, HERVEY. *The Mask of Sanity.* St. Louis: Mosby, 1941.

CLEMONS, A. "A Quantitative Study of Verbal Abstracting." Univ. of Iowa, Master's thesis, 1939.

COBB, STANLEY. *Borderlands of Psychiatry.* Cambridge: Harvard Univ. Press, 1943.

Communication Skills, the: Reading, Writing, Speaking: An Assignment Syllabus. Univ. of Iowa, 1945–46.

DAVIS, DOROTHY M. "The Relation of Repetitions in the Speech of Young Children to Certain Measures of Language Maturity and Situational Factors," *J. Speech Disorders*, 4:303–318, 5:235–241, 5:242–246, 1939–40.

DE HIRSANYA, ZSOLT. *The Star Gazer.* (A novelized biography of Galileo.) Tr. from the Hungarian by Paul Tabor. New York: Putnam, 1939.

DEVEREUX, GEORGE. "A Sociological Theory of Schizophrenia," *Psychoanal. Rev.*, 26:315–342, 1939.

DODGSON, CHARLES LUTWIDGE (LEWIS CARROLL). *Alice in Wonderland.* New York: Dutton, 1930.

DOLLARD, JOHN; MILLER, NEAL E.; DOOB, LEONARD W.; MOWRER, O. H.; and SEARS, ROBERT R. *Frustration and Aggression.* New Haven: Yale Univ. Press, 1939.

DORCUS, ROY M., and SHAFFER, G. WILSON. *Textbook of Abnormal Psychology.* Baltimore: Williams & Wilkins, 1939.

EINSTEIN, ALBERT. *Relativity: The Special and General Theory.* Tr. by Robert W. Lawson. New York: Henry Holt, 1920.

EINSTEIN, ALBERT, and INFELD, L. *The Evolution of Physics.* New York: Simon & Schuster, 1938.

Encyclopedia Americana. (Articles on molecular theory, atomic theory, Brownian movement, electronic or corpuscular theory.)

EVANS, BERGEN, in consultation with GEORGE J. MOHR. *The Psychiatry of Robert Burton,* New York: Columbia Univ. Press, 1944.

FAIRBANKS, H. "Studies in Language Behavior: II. The Quantitative Differentiation of Samples of Spoken Language," *Psychol. Monog.,* 56:19–38, 1944.

FOLSOM, A. T. "Reaction to the Dark Regarded as Language Behavior: Sixteen Cases." Univ. of Iowa, Master's thesis, 1937.

FRAZIER, J. "A Study of Stutterers' Theories of Their Own Stuttering." Univ. of Iowa. Master's thesis, 1940.

FREUD, SIGMUND. *A General Introduction to Psychoanalysis.* Tr. by Joan Riviere. New York: Liveright, 1935.

GALLANT, M. "A Statistical Evaluation of a Word-Fact Relating Test." Univ. of Iowa, Master's thesis, 1939.

GOLDSTEIN, KURT. *Aftereffects of Brain Injury in War.* New York: Grune & Stratton, 1942.

GRINGS, W. W. "The Verbal Summator Technique and Abnormal Mental States," *J. Abnor. & Soc. Psychol.,* 37:529–545, 1942.

GUTHRIE, EDWIN R. *Psychology of Human Conflict.* New York: Harper, 1938.

HAYAKAWA, S. I. "General Semantics and Propaganda," *Public Opinion Quarterly,* 3:197–208, 1939.

HAYAKAWA, S. I. *Language in Action.* New York: Harcourt, Brace, 1943.

HAYAKAWA, S. I. "The Meaning of Semantics," *New Republic,* 99:354–357, 1939.

HERRICK, CHARLES JUDSON. *An Introduction to Neurology.* Philadelphia: Saunders, 5th ed., 1931.

HERTZ, M. R. "Rorschach: Twenty Years After," *Psychol. Bull.,* 39:529–572, 1942.

HORN, E. "A Basic Writing Vocabulary: 10,000 Words Most Commonly Used in Writing," *Univ. Iowa Monog. in Educ.,* No. 4, 1926.

HORNEY, KAREN. *The Neurotic Personality of Our Time.* New York: Norton, 1937.

HULL, CLARK L. *Principles of Behavior: An Introduction to Behavior Theory.* New York: Appleton-Century, 1943.

JACOBSON, EDMUND. *Progressive Relaxation.* Chicago: Univ. Chicago Press, 1929.

JACOBSON, EDMUND. *You Must Relax.* New York: McGraw-Hill, 1934.

JOHNSON, WENDELL. "A Semantic Theory of Stuttering." In Eugene Hahn (ed.), *Stuttering: Significant Theories and Therapies.* Stanford University: Stanford Univ. Press, 1943.

JOHNSON, WENDELL. *Because I Stutter.* New York: Appleton-Century, 1930.

JOHNSON, WENDELL. "Language and Speech Hygiene," *General Semantics Monographs,* No. 1. Chicago, Institute of General Semantics, 1939.

JOHNSON, WENDELL. "The Indians Have No Word for It: I. Stuttering in Children," *Quart. J. Speech,* 30:330–337, 1944. II. "Stuttering in Adults," *ibid.,* 30:456–465, 1944. Reprinted in *Etc.,* 265–81, 1944–45.

JOHNSON, WENDELL and WHITMAN, N. "Intensional Agreement Indexes of Certain Terms in Psychology and Biochemistry." Unpublished research, Univ. of Iowa, 1938.

JOHNSON, WENDELL, and WILSON, J. "The Degrees of Extensional Agreement Among Twenty Psychologists in Their Use of the Labels *Hypothesis, Theory* and *Law,*" *Proceed. Iowa Acad. Sci.,* 1945.

JOHNSON, WENDELL, and WOOD, C. B. "John Told Jim What Joe Told Him: A Study of the Process of Abstracting," *Etc.,* 2:10–28, 1944.

JOHNSON, WENDELL, *et al.* "A Study of the Onset and Development of Stuttering," *J. Speech Disorders.* 8:251–257, 1942.

JOHNSON, WENDELL, *et al.* "Studies in the Psychology of Stuttering: I–XVIII," *J. Speech Disorders,* 1936–44.

KASANIN, J. S. (ed.) *Language and Thought in Schizophrenia.* Berkeley: Univ. California Press, 1944.

KELLER, HELEN. *The Story of My Life.* New York: Doubleday, Page, 1907.

KENDIG, M. (ed.). *Papers from the Second American Congress on General Semantics: Non-Aristotelian Methodology (Applied) for Sanity in Our Time.* Chicago: Institute of General Semantics, 1941.

KENT, JANICE V. "Semantic Reactions in Art Education," *Etc.* 1:225–228, 1944.

KEPES, GYORGY. *Language of Vision.* Chicago: Paul Theobald, 1945.

KEYSER, CASSIUS J. "Mathematics and the Science of Semantics," *Scripta Mathematica,* 2:247–260, 1934.

KNOCHE, R. M. "Agreement Among University Freshmen on Specified Words Defined Extensionally and Intensionally." Univ. of Iowa, Master's thesis, 1939.

KORZYBSKI, ALFRED. "An Outline of General Semantics: The Applications of Some Methods of Exact Sciences to the Solution of Human Problems and Educational Training for General Sanity." *Papers from the First American Congress on General Semantics.* Chicago: Institute of General Semantics, 1938.

KORZYBSKI, ALFRED. "General Semantics: Extensionalization in Mathematics, Mathematical Physics, and General Education. II. Thalamic Symbolism and Mathematics." (A paper presented before the Mathematical Section of the American Association for the Advancement of Science, 1935.) Chicago: Institute of General Semantics, 1938.

KORZYBSKI, ALFRED. "General Semantics, Psychiatry, Psychotherapy, and Prevention." (A paper presented before the 1940 annual meeting of the American Psychiatric Association.) Chicago: Institute of General Semantics, 1940.

KORZYBSKI, ALFRED. *Manhood of Humanity: The Art and Science of Human Engineering*. New York: Dutton, 1921.

KORZYBSKI, ALFRED. *Science and Sanity: An Introduction to Non-Aristotelian Systems and General Semantics*. Lancaster: Science Press, 2nd ed., 1941.

LANDIS, CARNEY, and PAGE, JAMES D. *Modern Society and Mental Disease*. New York: Farrar & Rinehart, 1938.

LANGFELD, HERBERT S. (ed.). "Symposium on Operationism." (Articles by Herbert S. Langfeld, Edward G. Boring, P. W. Bridgman, Herbert Feigl, Harold E. Israel, Carroll C. Pratt, and B. F. Skinner). *Psychol. Rev.*, 52:241–277, 1945.

LEE, IRVING J. *Language Habits in Human Affairs*. New York: Harper, 1941.

LEWIN, KURT. *A Dynamic Theory of Personality*. (Papers selected and translated by Donald K. Adams and Karl E. Zener.) New York: McGraw-Hill, 1935.

LIEBER, LILLIAN R. *The Education of T. C. Mits*. Drawings by Hugh Gray Lieber. New York: Norton, 1944.

LOUTTIT, C. M. *Clinical Psychology*. New York: Harper, 1936.

MALINOWSKI, BRONISLAW. *The Foundations of Faith and Morals*. London: Oxford Univ. Press, 1936.

MANN, M. B. "Studies in Language Behavior: III. The Quantitative Differentiation of Samples of Written Language." *Psychol. Monog.*, 56:41–74, 1944.

MASLOW, A. H., and MITTELMANN, BÉLA. *Principles of Abnormal Psychology: The Dynamics of Psychic Illness*. New York: Harper, 1941.

MILNE, A. A. *Winnie the Pooh*. New York: Dutton, 1926.

MOORE, R. "A Quantitative Study of the Labeling Behavior of Fifth and Sixth Grade Children from Upper and Lower Socio-Economic Groups." Univ. of Iowa, Master's thesis, 1939.

MOORE, WILBUR E. "New Patterns for Debate," *Etc.* 1:258–261, 1944.

MORENO, J. L. "Who Shall Survive?" *Nerv. & Ment. Dis. Monog. No. 58*, 1934.

MUMFORD, LEWIS. *The Condition of Man*. New York: Harcourt, Brace, 1944.

MURRAY, ELWOOD. *The Speech Personality*. Philadelphia: Lippincott, rev. ed., 1944.

NOCK, S. A. "The Scientist and Ethics," *Ethics*, 54:14–28, 1943–44.

NUTTALL, W. "The Memoir of a Stammerer," *Psyche*, 17: 151–184, 1937.

OGDEN, C. K. *Opposition*. London: K. Paul, Trench, Trubner, 1932.

OGDEN, C. K., and RICHARDS, I. A. *The Meaning of Meaning*. New York: Harcourt, Brace, 1923.

OTIS, ARTHUR S. *Otis Intelligence Scale: Manual of Directions for Primary Examination*. Yonkers: World Book, 1929.

PAVLOV, IVAN PETROVICH. *Conditioned reflexes: An Investigation of the*

Physiological Activity of the Cerebral Cortex. Tr. and ed. by G. V. Anrep. London: Oxford Univ. Press, 1927.

PAVLOV, IVAN PETROVICH. *Lectures on Conditioned Reflexes* (Vol. 1); *Conditioned Reflexes and Psychiatry* (Vol. 2). Tr. and ed. by W. H. Gannt. New York, International Press, 1928–41.

PIERCE, CHARLES S. *Chance, Love and Logic*. Ed. with an introduction by Morris R. Cohen. New York: Harcourt, Brace, 1923.

POLLOCK, THOMAS CLARK; SPAULDING, JOHN GORDON; and READ, ALLEN WALKER. "A Theory of Meaning Analyzed," *General Semantics Monographs No. 3*. Chicago: Institute of General Semantics, 1942.

Psychosomatic Medicine. A quarterly journal published under the sponsorship of the Committee on Problems of Neurotic Behavior, Division of Anthropology and Psychology, National Research Council, Washington, D. C.

RAPAPORT, ANATOL. "Newtonian Physics and Aviation Cadets. *Etc.*, 1:154–164, 1944.

RICHARDS, I. A. *Mencius on the Mind*. New York: Harcourt, Brace, 1932.

ROGERS, CARL R. *Counseling and Psychotherapy*. Boston: Houghton Mifflin, 1942.

ROGERS, CARL R. *The Clinical Treatment of the Problem Child*. Boston: Houghton Mifflin, 1939.

RORSCHACH, HERMANN. *Psychodiagnostics*. Translation and English edition by Paul Lemkau and Bernard Kronenberg. New York: Grune & Stratton, 1942.

ROYCE, JOSIAH. *The World and the Individual*. New York: Macmillan, 1900.

RUSSELL, BERTRAND. *An Inquiry into Meaning and Truth*. New York: Norton, 1940.

RUTAN, EDWARD J., and NEUMAYER, ENGELBERT J. "Something New in Teaching Grammar," *Etc.*, 1:261–263, 1944.

SANFORD, F. H. "Speech and Personality," *Psychol. Bull.*, 39:811–845, 1942.

SANFORD, F. H. "Speech and Personality: A Comparative Case Study," *Char. & Pers.*, 19:169–198, 1942.

SCHUCHARDT, C. *The Technique of Semantic Relaxation*. Chicago: Institute of General Semantics, 1943.

SEARS, ROBERT R. *A Survey of Objective Studies of Psycho-Analytic Concepts*. New York: Soc. Sci. Res. Council, 1943.

SEASHORE, CARL E. *The Psychology of Music*. New York: McGraw-Hill, 1938.

SEASHORE, R. H., and ECKERSON, L. D. "The Measurement of Individual Differences in General English Vocabularies," *J. Educ. Psychol.*, 31:14–38, 1940.

SHAFFER, L. R. *The Psychology of Adjustment*. Boston: Houghton Mifflin, 1936.

SIAFITZ, E. "A Study of the Relation Between Word-Length and Type-

Token Ratio in the Written Language of Iowa School Children." Univ. of Iowa, Master's thesis, 1941.

SHATTYN, G. B. "Certain Quantitative Measures of the Clinical Aspects of Language." Univ. of Iowa, Master's thesis, 1943.

SHAW, C. (ed.). *The Jack-Roller: A Delinquent Boy's Own Story.* Chicago: Univ. Chicago Press, 1930.

SHERMAN, D. H. "An Objective Study of the Ability of Junior High School Pupils to Use Descriptive Language." Univ. of Iowa, Master's thesis, 1938.

SKALBECK, O. M. "A Statistical Analysis of Three Measures of Word Length." Univ. of Iowa, Master's thesis, 1938.

SKINNER, B. F. "The Distribution of Associated Words," *Psychol. Rec.*, 1:71–76, 1937.

SMYTH, HENRY DEWOLF. *Atomic Energy for Military Purposes.* Princeton: Princeton Univ. Press, 1945.

SPENCE, KENNETH W. "The Nature of Theory Construction in Contemporary Psychology," *Psychol. Rev.*, 51:47–68, 1944.

SPENCER, B. L. "A Study of Short Speech Samples as Personality Indicators." Univ. of Iowa, Master's thesis, 1943.

STEFANSSON, VILHJALMUR. *The Standardization of Error.* New York: Norton, 1927.

STODDARD, GEORGE D. *The Meaning of Intelligence.* New York: Macmillan, 1943.

STRECKER, E. A., and EBAUGH, F. G. *Practical Clinical Psychiatry.* Philadelphia: Blakiston, 1940. Section on psychopathological problems of childhood by Leo Kanner.

SUPER, D. "The Bernreuter Personality Inventory: A Review of Research," *Psychol. Bull.*, 39:94–125, 1942.

TERMAN, LEWIS M., and MERRILL, MAUD A. *Directions for Administering Forms L and M: Revision of the Stanford-Binet Tests of Intelligence.* Boston: Houghton Mifflin, 1937.

THOMAS, WILLIAM I. *Primitive Behavior: An Introduction to the Social Sciences.* New York: McGraw-Hill, 1937.

THOMAS, WILLIAM I., and THOMAS, DOROTHY SWAINE. *The Child in America.* New York: Knopf, 1928.

THOMPSON, SILVANUS P. *Calculus Made Easy.* New York: Macmillan, 2nd ed., 1937.

THORNDIKE, EDWARD L. *Man and His Works.* Cambridge: Harvard Univ. Press., 1943.

THORNDIKE, EDWARD L. *The Teacher's Word Book.* New York: Teachers College, Columbia University, 1921.

TRAVIS, L. E., and BARUCH, D. W. *Personal Problems of Everyday Life: Practical Aspects of Mental Hygiene.* New York: Appleton-Century, 1941.

TUTHILL, C. E. "A Quantitative Study of Extensional Meaning with Special Reference to *Stuttering*." Univ. of Iowa, Doctor's thesis, 1939.

VAN DUZER, V. F. "A Methodological Study of Language Reaction." Univ. of Iowa, Master's thesis, 1944.

VAN RIPER, CHARLES. *Speech Correction: Principles and Methods*. New York: Prentice-Hall, 1942.

VEBLEN, THORSTEIN. *The Theory of the Leisure Class*. Introduction by Stuart Chase. New York: Bennett A. Cerf & Donald S. Klopfer (Modern Library), Inc., 1934.

VOLTAIRE, FRANÇOIS MARIE AROUET DE. *Candide and Other Tales*. London: Dent, Everyman Ed., 1937.

WATSON, G. B. *The Measurement of Fairmindedness*. New York: Teachers College, Columbia University, 1925.

WECHSLER, DAVID. *The Measurement of Intelligence*. Baltimore: Williams & Wilkins, 1944.

WEINBERG, ALVIN M. "General Semantics and the Teaching of Physics," *Amer. Physics Teacher*, 7:104–108, 1939.

WHITE, WILLIAM A. *Outlines of Psychiatry*. Washington: Nerv. & Ment. Dis. Publ. Co., 1935.

WHITE, WILLIAM A. "The Language of Schizophrenia," *Arch. Neurol. Psychiat.*, 16:395–413, 1926.

WILL, NELL. "The Personality Development of a Stuttering Boy," *Quart. J. Speech*, 30:88–95, 1944. Reprinted in *Etc.*, 1:165–173, 1944.

WHORF, BENJAMIN LEE. "The Relation of Habitual Thought and Behavior to Language," *Etc.*, 1:197–215, 1944.

ZIPF, G. K. *The Psychobiology of Language*. Boston: Houghton Mifflin, 1935.

INDEX